Arctic
and Antarctic

Arctic
and Antarctic

A MODERN GEOGRAPHICAL SYNTHESIS

David Sugden

Barnes & Noble Books
Totowa, New Jersey

First published in the USA 1982 by
Barnes & Noble Books
81 Adams Drive
Totowa, New Jersey, 07512

Library of Congress Cataloging in Publication Data

Sugden, David E.
  Arctic and Antarctic.

  Includes bibliographical references and index.
  1. Polar regions.   I. Title.
G587.S93 1982   919.8   82-13788
ISBN 0-389-20298-3

Printed in Great Britain

Contents

SUB-ZONAL SCALE: INTRUSIVE

Acknowledgements

A lasting memory which arises from writing this book is the immense kindness and patience of many people to whom I have turned for help and advice. Many colleagues looked at specific parts of the text and made imaginative and constructive comments. I am particularly grateful to the following for their great help: Dr. M. Baring Gould and Dr. T. A. Morehouse, University of Alaska, Mr. J. L. Courtney, Transport Canada; Mr. I. Tøpfer, Ministry for Greenland; Dr. T. Shabad, editor of *Polar Geography* and *Soviet Geography*; Dr. J. D. Ives, University of Colorado; Mr. A. Orheim, Store Norske Spitsbergen Coal Company; Dr. R. M. Laws, British Antarctic Survey; and Dr. I. B. Ralston, University of Aberdeen. They have all tried to keep me on the right track and devoted a great deal of time to correcting many mistakes. Dr. Patrick Hamilton, who suffers from having a room just across the corridor from mine, was presented with an early draft of the bulk of the book. His stimulating comments caused at least one complete re-write! My special thanks go to him.

I am indebted to many Aberdeen students who have been subjected to a course on the Arctic and Antarctic over the last 13 years. They have responded and contributed many ideas of their own. Their enthusiasm has been a powerful support during the period of writing. Others have provided stimulus through discussion, help in the field and answers to specific queries, and to all I offer my thanks. In spite of all this expert help there will still be mistakes for which I am wholly to blame.

I must make special mention of those who have helped in providing illustrations. I have been quite overwhelmed by the way that everyone I approached responded by providing splendid photographs of their own. I hope all are properly acknowledged in the captions.

This book would never have materialized but for the help of many other people. Professor J. House made the initial suggestion for the book a decade ago, while the late Professor Walton gave his enthusiastic encouragement. John Davey (perhaps ill-advisedly) resurrected the project at a critical moment. Professor Mellor has given his warm support and that of the Department of Geography in Aberdeen. Numerous secretaries have laboured on manuscripts which are reputedly the least legible in the land. Cartographers and photographers deserve special thanks for their contribution to many illustrations. I owe the University of Aberdeen great thanks for financial support to visit a number of different polar areas.

Finally I must thank my family for their support. It was the reaction of my wife, Britta, to the social inequalities she observed in a remote part of Greenland that set alight my first spark of concern. In the many years since, she has given up much to ensure periods of calm during which I could write. John, Pauline and Michael have grown up under the shadow of the Arctic and Antarctic. I just hope that their obvious interest in the areas will prove a sufficient compensation for the long absences of their father in the field or in the study.

CHAPTER ONE

Introduction

Background and aims

In September, 1962 I stood at the mouth of Hurry Inlet on the north shore of Scoresby Sund in East Greenland and watched in awe as skein upon skein of chattering geese flew out over the newly frozen fjord en route to their southern winter quarters. In 1971 in Alaska I remember the scornful look of an Inuit man (Eskimo) as he sat in front of a rusty oil-drum in the midst of the shanty town of Kotzebue and tried to sell rudimentary bone carvings to smartly attired tourists who had dropped in from a jet package tour (Figure 1.1). Later, in Scotland I remember

FIGURE 1.1   An Inuit Alaskan selling carvings to tourists in Kotzebue.

giving a talk to a Women's Rural Institute group on Antarctica; the lady in charge of the subsequent cake-baking competition gave a vote of thanks and said she was sad I had not included pictures of Eskimos or polar bears! The first occasion tells of the magnificence of the polar environment, a magnificence which makes a visitor wish to share his or her experience with those not able to experience it themselves. The Alaskan recollection symbolizes a worry and deep frustration that something has been going badly wrong in the development of the Arctic and that here is an issue which needs fuller airing. This has become all the more significant in the light of the recent political awakening of arctic peoples. The final recollection serves to illustrate the low level of understanding of the Arctic and Antarctic among people at large. These three recollections provided the main stimulus for this book. They explain the main aim, which is to describe and interpret the polar environment, to explore the problems associated with economic and social development and to provide a framework for a better under-standing of the overall geography of the polar regions.

The specific aim of the book is to analyse the regional geography of the Arctic and Antarctic. The starting point is the recognition that the natural environment and the activities of Man can be viewed as systems operating on different scales in space and time. The book examines how the various systems operate and also how they interrelate with, and act as constraints upon, one another. The fundamental natural systems considered are those associated with land, atmosphere and ocean, while the main human systems discussed are those of the original indigenous peoples and the intrusive system of commercial and industrial society. Not only is there stress on the links between the various natural systems as well as between the two human systems, but also on the link between natural and human systems.

A major problem has been the vast range of material relevant to the geography of areas as large and varied as the Arctic and Antarctic. When faced with the sheer volume and variety of material, it has been tempt-ing to give up the attempt at geographical completeness and to withdraw into the apparent security of a narrower field of study. Whereas readers may well feel that this would have been the wiser course of action, I have been influenced by a conviction that the lack of appreciation and understanding and the very nature of the problems arising in the Arctic and Antarctic result in part from precisely this type of compartment-alized approach. And so at the risk of naivety and superficiality the book attempts to be comprehensive.

The polar regions are an important area of geographical study and for several reasons:

(1) They are a large and unknown part of the world's surface and justify study in their own right. After all the Arctic and Antarctic contain about one fifth of the world's land area and about 15 per cent of its total surface area.

(2) Study of the polar regions contributes to the understanding of natural and human systems operating on a global scale. One can point to the examples of the Earth's atmosphere or plate tectonics; in both cases the evidence contained in the polar regions is crucial to the understanding of the whole pattern. A human example concerns the dispersal of races over the Earth. Study of Inuit (Eskimo) migrations sheds light on the early inhabitants of both Asia and the Americas.

(3) The polar regions possess certain attributes which contribute a unique set of broader geographical principles. An example of this from the natural environment is that they provide an example of a living Ice Age. One only has to reflect on the impact of polar studies in fields such as glaciology and glacial geomorphology where the incorporation of ideas about ice sheets has transformed both subjects. Also the modern tundra environment is a close analogue to the late Pleistocene environment of Europe where the evolution of Man took significant steps forward. Other unique contributions can be seen in terms of development. The Arctic is an area of development which lies within the political boundaries of the world's richer nations. The contrasts and similarities with development in the 'Third World' contribute potentially valuable perspectives to development processes as a whole. This is particularly true of the vexed question of the conflict between intrusive modern society and indigenous cultures. Further, the Arctic provides a unique opportunity to test the role of different political approaches to development. Given a similar natural environment and indigenous culture, the arctic approaches of the Soviets, Scandinavians and North Americans provide fascinating contrasts. Yet another unique contribution comes from Antarctica, the only continent without indigenous peoples, which is the scene of a pioneering multinational approach to resources.

(4) The polar regions are a zone marginal to the distribution of many species, including Man. It is a well-known principle in biogeography that the limit of the distribution of a particular plant or animal is an ideal location for isolating the role of relevant variables influencing its distribution. The discovery of mites and other animal life in Antarctica where air temperatures never rise as high as freezing point meant that previous ideas relating their distribution to posi-

tive air temperatures had to be revised. Instead it highlighted the importance of the micro-climate of a moss patch as an additional factor influencing their distribution. Thus observations from the periphery contributed to more general principles. This type of analogy is apparent in human geography. The roles of resource location, physical and climatic barriers and access to communications in influencing industrial development can often be more clearly demonstrated near the limits of exploitation.

(5) The fact that the Arctic and Antarctic are widely separated at opposite poles, and yet are similar, offers many advantages. In effect, principles developed in one hemisphere can be tested in the other. The importance of this is well illustrated in the field of biogeography where discussion about the role of climate on the distribution and type of arctic vegetation has long been debated. The Antarctic offered an excellent testbed for the argument in that it provided a range of similar polar climates with different species. The study of glaciers, the upper atmosphere and plate tectonics are other fields which have benefited from a bipolar approach. Understanding the distribution of indigenous peoples, resource development and exploitation, or political geography are parts of human geography which have much to gain from a bipolar approach.

It is one matter to argue that the polar regions are important to geographical study and quite another to justify a book on the subject! Nevertheless it does seem an opportune moment to try and look at the regional geography of the polar regions as a whole. Following a burst of military interest in the Arctic stimulated by the Second World War, economic exploitation of minerals and fuels is now in full swing. Massive developments have taken place in the Soviet Arctic, and Arctic America is not far behind. The surge of interest has highlighted the lack of knowledge of the environmental effects of such developments, while the demoralizing impact on the indigenous peoples has not been sufficiently appreciated. Economic development is about to strike the Antarctic and is raising environmental worries just as the sensitive Antarctic Treaty is about to come up for re-negotiation. Industrial decisions and environmental arguments about the Arctic and Antarctic are all too frequently distinguished by their quantity rather than by their quality. Myths such as the extreme fragility of the tundra emerge. Given such a background, the main hope for the future is to increase public and specialist awareness of the fuller implications of decisions concerning the Arctic and Antarctic. At the very time that more understanding is required, the plethora of polar research in a daunting number of languages in scientific, governmental and university publications makes it difficult for any single person to obtain an up-to-date synthesis. Arguably it is just this lack of synthesis that allows myths to abound and to hold up progress on a wider front.

It could justly be argued that the fact that one member of the Women's Rural Institute did not know the difference between the Arctic and Antarctic is a poor basis from which to assume a wider lack of knowledge about the polar regions! Thus it may be of interest to look at the polar knowledge of certain geography students at Aberdeen University who were attending a course on polar geography. Figure 1.2 is not a succession of maps of the Arctic and Antarctic drawn at various times in ancient history but a range of examples drawn from a class of 20 students in 1978. They were asked to add certain place-names to their sketches of the Arctic and Antarctic. I

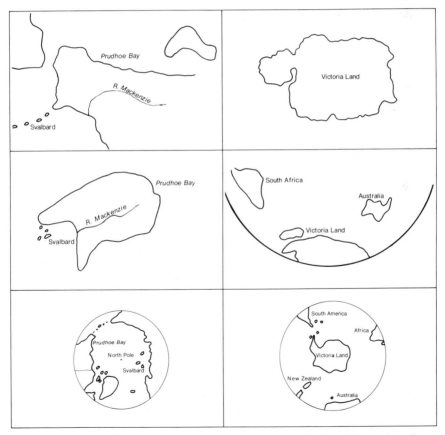

FIGURE 1.2   Examples of sketch maps of the Arctic and Antarctic drawn from a class of 20 students in 1978.

leave readers to guess whether they were drawn before or after the course! Whereas some students were exceedingly well informed, there were others of imaginative bent who created a continent in the middle of the Arctic. A surprisingly high proportion (33 per cent) found it difficult to envisage the Arctic and Antarctic from the point of view of a polar projection and relied instead on a variety of Mercator-type viewpoints. A series of questions issued in four successive years revealed that half the students got half the questions wrong (Table 1.1).

TABLE 1.1 *Polar quiz given to beginning Honours Geography students, University of Aberdeen*

---

1 Draw a sketch map of the Arctic; insert the Mackenzie River, Svalbard and Prudhoe Bay.
2 Draw a sketch map of Antarctica; insert Victoria Land and the relative positions of the southern continents.
3 Is Antarctica bigger or smaller than the U.S.A.?
4 If South Georgia was in the northern hemisphere would its latitude be closer to that of Svalbard, The Faroes or the Isle of Man?
5 Is the north–south dimension of mainland Alaska more than the length of Britain?
6 If north Greenland was superimposed on Aberdeen would the southernmost point extend as far as London, Rome or Tripoli?
7 How long is it light at the Arctic Circle in mid-winter?
8 Is the population of Greenland nearer 10000, 50000 or 100000?
9 What is a musk ox?
10 Does it rain in northern Greenland?
11 Where are the main nesting areas of penguins in the Arctic?
12 Does the U.S.A. claim part of Antarctica?

---

12 Never formally claimed an area.

9 Animal like a small bison *10 It can in summer* *11 Wrong hemisphere!*

Man *5 Yes, double* *6 Tripoli* *7 No sunshine but c. 5 hours twilight* *8 50000*

1 See Figure 1.6 *2 See Figure 1.8* *3 Antarctica is half as big again* *4 Isle of*

ANSWERS

Set against the need for more awareness of the geography of the polar regions, a book such as this can hope to play no more than a very tiny role, if any. The hope is that those interested in the Arctic and Antarctic can build on the models and hypotheses advanced if they so wish. Even better, they may be stimulated to probe deeper and replace the models and hypotheses with better ones. The book should not be viewed as a formal textbook; it is merely the view of one person. Other people would have taken a different view.

Approaches to regional geography

Most geographers accept that regional geography is concerned with the study of interrelationships between a multiplicity of phenomena in particular areas. Furthermore, many would agree that it should aim beyond description and classification of areas and attempt to understand how regional complexes have evolved and how they function today. This is the sort of problem which lends itself to a systems approach and in 1965 Haggett demonstrated how a regional complex could be viewed as a system comprising movements, hierarchies, nodes, networks and areas. The value of such an approach is that the real world consists of regional complexes where an individual element or process is influenced by numerous other elements and processes. Whereas it is often convenient to isolate a topic, such as glaciers or settlement, for systematic study, a full understanding of these topics can only be obtained when they are also viewed in a regional context with interplay with other aspects. This latter regional dimension has not thrived in recent years, but its importance can be illustrated by two examples. In the field of physical geography an outstanding advance in understanding glacier fluctuations has come from the U.S. CLIMAP programme which was designed to reconstruct the world's glacial environment at various stages in the past. The attempt to characterize the glacial mode during the maximum of the last glaciation 18000 years ago focused attention on the importance of changes in the distribution of oceanic and climatic circulation, extent of sea ice, changing sea levels and vegetation zones. It is the way these separate systems interrelate that explains the variations of glaciers and great leaps of understanding have followed study of these regional interrelationships. A second example comes from human geography. Viewed from the world's industrial cores, the exploitation of arctic resources has been seen as a threat to the polar environment. During the 1970s projects such as the trans-Alaska pipeline were seen as a battle between developers and conservationists. Devoid of its regional dimension the argument has obscured an even more important dimension, namely the effect of development on the welfare of arctic indigenous peoples. It is at least arguable that a stronger regional perspective would not have allowed the conservation arguments to dominate the issue to such an extent.

Another reason for a regional approach is that there are important tendencies which affect regions as a whole. In other words this is to argue that there are regional systems and that they are modified by regional processes. Thus the work on core/periphery development and Myrdal's (1957) concepts of differential economic growth describe processes which affect all aspects of a particular region. In such cases it is clear that full understanding is more likely to emerge if regional interrelationships are studied as a whole.

The crux of a systems approach is that it recognizes not only elements but also links between elements. Thus it affords a means of linking the two aspects of form and process; the elements tend to be forms in a spatial system and describe what's there, while the links tend to be the processes and describe what's happening. A further crucial step of a systems approach is to place a boundary around any system which is the focus of study. When this is done it is possible to separate the causes (or independent variables) affecting the system as a whole from the effects (or dependent variables) *within* the system. This deceptively simple achievement is of fundamental importance since the recognition of cause and effect represents a big step towards understanding. A further step follows from isolating a particular system. The response of a system as a whole to changes in the independent variables may take two forms: positive feedback or negative feedback. In positive feedback a series of changes take place within the system which have the effect of accentuating the initial change. In negative feedback the changes have the effect of damping-down the initial change. The balance between these two tendencies is fundamental in characterizing a system's stability or its resistance to change. Such concepts are important when studying the impact of Man on the natural environment, or intrusive society on indigenous society.

When an attempt is made to apply a systems approach to regional geography two interrelated problems immediately arise: that of identifying systems for analysis and that of coping with the problem of scale. Placing a boundary around a spatial system is largely a function of the scale of the problem being tackled. Some problems demand a global approach while others require a more localized approach. Thus the climate or the distribution of land and sea in the polar regions requires an understanding of the global systems of atmospheric circulation and plate tectonics respectively. Exploitation of polar resources by the world's cores is another example of a global-scale system. On the other hand a Distant Early Warning (D.E.W.) radar station is part of a continental-scale defence system, while an Inuit hunting group operates on a local scale.

Realization of the significance of scale has two profound implications. The first is that understanding of a particular issue depends on selecting the appropriate scale. Studies of an individual D.E.W. line station or mine will remain incomplete until they are seen in the context of their strategic or economic systems as a whole. Again, the study of an outcrop of basalt in Greenland will mean little until it is seen in the context of the geological opening of the North Atlantic ocean basin. Only when these individual elements are placed in their appropriate spatial systems is it possible to understand the influence of dependent and independent variables on their location and function. The second implication is that the status and role of any particular variable changes according to the scale of study. An example is the Alaska Highway built during the Second World War to link Alaska with the rest of the United States. This road was dependent on continental strategy and thus was one dependent variable within the system as a whole. If, however, one reduces the scale to the system represented by Yukon Territory in Canada, the Alaska Highway appears as a road striking obliquely through the Territory. In this case it is an independent variable and one which has had a major impact upon development within the Territory. To take another example, the outcrop of basalt in Greenland is a dependent element of the larger system represented by the opening of the North Atlantic. If one wishes to study the magnificently uniform cirque morphology characteristic of the basalt areas, then it becomes an important independent variable for cirque morphology.

The significance of spatial scale is duplicated in time. Some systems, usually the larger ones, operate on a long time-scale. Examples are plate tectonics, ice ages or the evolution of Man. Others, usually smaller, operate on shorter time-scales, for example an ice-cored pingo or a mining settlement. Long-term dependent variables tend to become independent variables at shorter time-scales. Thus glacio-isostasy is a dependent variable when viewed at time-scales of ice sheet build-up and decay, which is measured in tens of thousands of years. But for a beach forming today the isostatic rise of the land is an independent variable.

The structure of the book

This book is structured on a scales and systems approach. Ideally, it could be structured on a series of studies at different scales, regardless of whether or not the relevant systems are natural or human (Sugden and Hamilton, 1971). However, in practice natural systems operate on much longer time-scales than human systems of equivalent size and it is helpful to separate them initially. Thus the primary subdivision of the book is into natural and human systems. Each of these is subdivided into global and sub-zonal systems. In this case zonal is taken to mean Arctic or Antarctic and thus sub-zonal refers to subdivisions of either polar zone. The global natural systems are climate and plate tectonics (Chapters 2 and 3). These are the factors which give the polar regions their fundamental characteristics. Within each zone there are three possible environments and anyone dropped into the polar regions by parachute would have to land in one; he or she would be on a glacier, in a periglacial area or in the sea (Figure 1.3) (Chapters 4—6).

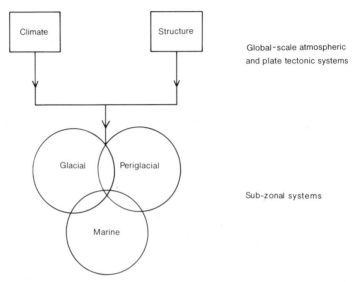

FIGURE 1.3   The global systems of the atmosphere and plate tectonics determine the location and character of the three sub-zonal systems: glacial, periglacial or marine.

Overlap between the systems occurs in that glaciers may flow into the sea or melt in a periglacial area. Also there are changes in the extent and intensity of the systems over time and this important dimension is covered in Chapter 7. The global human system is concerned with the evolution of civilization and its impact on the polar regions (Chapter 8). At the sub-zonal scale two separate systems are distinguished: the indigenous system of subsistence (Chapter 9) and the intrusive industrial/ urban system emanating from the world's industrial cores. The latter is subdivided according to political system. The advantage of a political subdivision is that it distinguishes separate peoples with different philosophies and different social and economic frameworks. These are in turn manifested on the ground by the type of development, its intensity and its location. Furthermore, the existence of statistical information by political units makes it easier to describe and understand the nature and dynamics of each system. Thus Greenland, Arctic Canada, the Soviet Arctic, Alaska and the Antarctic continent are all treated as separate sub-zonal intrusive systems (Chapters 10–14). Finally in an attempt to crystallize thoughts and ideas about polar regional geography, Chapter 15 puts forward a series of general principles. These are intended as a series of hypotheses which should be tested and challenged and replaced by more adequate hypotheses.

The problem with any structure is that it tends to separate out different components of study. This is a particularly difficult problem in regional geography where all systems are interrelated, and the book wishes to focus on precisely these interrelationships. The ideal regional geography must await the era of the electronic book where one can read about each system simultaneously and discover links between them simultaneously! Since my publishers have not offered this technology, I have attempted to tackle the problem in another less satisfactory way. In the section on physical geography the interrelationships within one particular system are indicated on flow diagrams and described in the main body of each chapter. There are many interrelationships with other natural systems of both equal and different orders as well as with human systems and these are treated in separate sections. The natural/human interrelationship is covered by considering the natural system as a resource and/or constraint for human activity, following the ideas of Chapman (1980). Thus each physical geography chapter ends with a discussion of its significance to human geography. In the human geography section of the book the device is different. First each human chapter considers those characteristics of the natural environment which are relevant to an understanding of the human patterns. There follows identification of the main elements of the human spatial system (e.g. people, nodes, networks) before the system as a whole is analysed in terms of its evolution and function today. Interrelationships between different parts of the spatial system, and between it and other spatial systems, are identified through the employment of models of regional development. These models assume a great importance in the analysis and thus their characteristics and role need further explanation.

Models of regional development

Models which are helpful in a polar context are those of network and node evolution suggested by Taaffe, Morrill and Gould (1963) and of core/periphery development put forward by Friedmann (1966) and later modified by Friedmann and Weaver (1979). Between them the models deal with the basic characteristics of spatial systems and suggest general principles applicable to the transition from a subsistence indigenous way of life to an urban and industrial state.

Taaffe, Morrill and Gould (1963) suggested that the evolution of the transport networks of Ghana and Nigeria could be represented by four main stages typical of colonial development (Figure 1.4). Stage I is characterized by a series of coastal ports with only local inland lines of communication. There is little lateral interconnection except by fishing craft and occasional trading vessels. Stage II is represented by the emergence of certain lines of inland penetration. Many of these were built to connect administrative centres on the coast with an interior area for military or political control. Others were built for economic reasons and tapped mineral deposits or agricultural resources. The line of inland penetration increases decisively the competitive advantage of the port at the coastal end and is accompanied by the establishment of a node on the interior end. Stage III is represented by the growth of lateral interconnections and feeders. Subsidiary nodes grow up at favoured locations along the line of inland penetration and feeders begin to radiate out from all nodes. The port on the coastal end of the inland link grows rapidly as a result of increased activity, as also does the original inland node. Stage IV sees the development of high-priority links running directly between the main nodes in the country. These are the routes with best rail schedules, widest roads and densest air traffic. This fourth stage was admitted to be somewhat speculative in the case of Nigeria and Ghana.

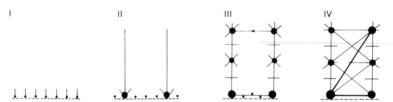

FIGURE 1.4   Model of the evolution of a network infrastructure based on Ghana and Nigeria. After Taaffe, Morrill and Gould (1963).

The importance of this model of network evolution is that it suggests that there are processes which lead to a recognizable evolution of networks and nodes in an area of progressive development. If so, then it follows that the model can be used as a means of analysing the spatial structure of an area and thus forms the basis for comparison between areas. There are obvious dangers in applying a tropical colonial model to areas of the Arctic lying within the political boundaries of developed countries. Nevertheless the comparison does seem to add some perspective and raises important issues and principles, which are discussed more fully in Chapter 15.

A powerful and representative set of ideas about economic development was put forward by Friedmann (1966), who prefaced a study of Venezuela with some general propositions. The key problem during the transition period is the tendency for economic development to occur in a burgeoning core at the expense of a stagnant or declining periphery. Friedmann followed the ideas of Myrdal (1957) in pointing to the processes of cumulative causation that lead to this tendency. The principal factors of production, labour, capital, foreign exchange and entrepreneurship are attracted to the core where opportunities are greater. The periphery remains a primary producer at the same time as it has to pay more for the goods it receives from the core. Commonly, the deprivation of those on the periphery makes itself felt through political protest. Thus a transition period is often marked by a fundamental conflict between economic goals which favour concentration at the core and social goals which favour more uniformity of progress and opportunity. The danger is that too early a concern with social inequality on the periphery may divert investment funds from the core and arrest the economic development of the area as a whole.

One of Friedmann's major contributions to this problem was the identification of five different types of region, each of which has different characteristics which require different solutions (Figure 1.5). *Core Regions* are the expanding centres of growth dependent on a flourishing urban centre or centres. *Upward Transitional Areas* are

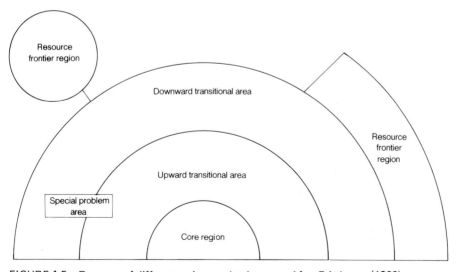

FIGURE 1.5   Response of different regions to development. After Friedmann (1966).

also expanding in response to rising commercial demands from the core. *Downward Transitional Areas* are old-established rural areas with stagnant or declining economies and out-migration. *Resource Frontier Regions*, which may or may not be contiguous to settled regions, are those in which new resources are being exploited. *Special Problem Regions* have such distinctive characteristics that they need a specialized development approach. They include military zones or tourist parks.

Two of these types of region seem especially relevant to the Arctic and the characteristics of each and the main requirements for development are summarized in Table 1.2. Resource Frontier Regions are associated with the exploitation of minerals to satisfy the needs of the Core Regions. In response to international demand the investment is often in the hands of foreign or multinational organizations. The conflict between industry and government arises from differing goals. Whereas industry may be concerned with exploiting a resource as efficiently and quickly as possible, a government may be more concerned with establishing permanent settlements and protecting indigenous people. The different goals might suggest quite different approaches to development. Towns in Resource Frontier Regions are specialized in that their main function is to export the resource, perhaps after preliminary processing. Schools, hospitals, shops and other industries may be poor or non-existent. Following exploitation of the resource, and bereft of its main function, the town might wither away to swell the ranks of ghost towns. Operational costs in Resource Frontier Regions are high. On the one hand the transport links are usually long and difficult. On the other hand labour is expensive, partly because of the highly specialized nature of modern mining jobs and partly because of incentives needed to attract workers from the comforts of the core region. Finally there are difficult social problems. Employees tend to be transient, working only a few months or years, and are thus not inclined to integrate with locals or take pride in their settlement. There is also a high proportion of single males with a noticeable lack of the civilizing influence of a mixed society.

Usually national goals are to develop Resource Frontier Regions and to aim for (1) permanent settlement, (2) integration with the national economy and (3) sustained economic growth. Friedmann recommended several ways in which the problems presented by the regions could be solved (Table 1.2). In essence these involve diversification of the economy and improvement of the infrastructure so as to reduce costs. Also educational programmes to help build community feeling are recommended. The key problem is to raise the population above the

TABLE 1.2   *The characteristics and needs of (a) Resource Frontier Regions and (b) Downward Transitional Areas (after Friedmann, 1966)*

(a) Resource Frontier Regions

Characteristics
1 Dependent on the export of one economic resource, usually a mineral
2 Investment is commonly foreign
3 Conflict between the economic goals of industry and the social goals of government
4 Centres on a town/city with specialized but very limited functions which may not achieve critical size for self-sustaining growth
5 Transport and labour costs are high due to remoteness and high level of technology.
6 Special social structure — transient, male, single

Main development needs
1 Regional development authority
2 Modern communications and settlement infrastructure
3 Quick achievement of conditions for self-sustaining growth
4 Improved communications to and from the core
5 Reduced cost of living
6 Diversified economic base
7 Creation of an integrated and stable sense of community

(b) Downward Transitional Areas

1 Old mining area or subsistence farming area; low productivity
2 Low standard of living
3 Poor or declining resources
4 High fertility, mortality and out-migration rates
5 Social demoralization
6 Inadequate services
7 All the above aggravated by ethnic or religious differences

Main development needs
1 Return flow of capital from core region
2 Rural resettlement schemes
3 Improved communications infrastructure
4 Investment in growth points (e.g. university and light processing industry)
5 Changeover from subsistence to commercial way of life

threshold necessary to create a self-sustaining urban service centre.

Downward Transitional Areas suffer as a result of the development of the core. Commonly they are old subsistence-farming or mining areas where the standard of living is low and the resource base is low or even declining. Such regions are currently remote from core regions and poorly supplied with services and communications. Too remote to benefit from investment, they are caught in a downward spiral of poverty and declining aspirations which produces a social demoralization marked by apathy, high illiteracy rates and incapacity for constructive action. Typically such areas have high fertility and mortality rates with a high level of out-migration to the core which further saps the area of its energetic inhabitants. Friedmann noted that all of the above characteristics are aggravated by ethnic or religious differences which cause one group to have low standing in face of the dominant group. 'Prevented by malice and prejudice from rising in society, the victims, crowded together in rural and urban slums, constitute a classical example of the disinherited proletariat whose only effective resource is a social revolution that will destroy the artifice by which it is held down' (Friedmann, 1966, p. 87). Some possible solutions to the problem of Downward Transitional Areas are given in Table 1.2. Investment, resettlement schemes, improved communications, development of selected growth points and a change from a subsistence to a commercial way of life were all ideas floated by Friedmann.

Friedmann's propositions are based on experience of regional development in the Americas. They pinpoint some general principles which will be seen to have considerable relevance in the Arctic. The purpose of presenting the ideas at length is to obtain a framework of ideas about the spatial aspects of development which were current in 1970, a date when many arctic development plans were instigated. Since then a flurry of protest has emerged about the application of an urban development strategy to rural peripheries and the arguments are well covered by Brookfield (1975). One response has been a new book in which Friedmann and Weaver (1979) propose a new strategy for peripheral areas (Table 1.3). In essence this calls for more autonomy and economic independence by the periphery to prevent a widening disparity between core and periphery. Such an idea adds perspective to the indigenous political protests of the Arctic in the 1970s. It is important to stress that the change of strategy concerning peripheral areas does not minimize the value of Friedmann's initial concept that there are certain characteristics diagnostic of different types of periphery (Friedmann, 1966).

In subsequent chapters both the network evolution model and Friedmann's core/periphery model will be used as yardsticks against which the present spatial systems in the Arctic and Antarctic may be compared. Their use will help identify similarities between situations which may superficially appear very different and thus help suggest some general principles to aid understanding. At all times it is important to remember that the models are used for *comparison* with reality rather than representations of reality itself.

TABLE 1.3   *New solutions to development of peripheral areas: a territorial approach at a scale appropriate to the area concerned rather than world scale economic exploitation (after Friedmann and Weaver, 1979)*

Increased political/economic/social autonomy
    selective economic closure
    community ownership of productive wealth
    equal opportunity socially

Self-reliant economic growth
    diversification
    maximum development of resources consistent with long-term view
    local rather than national markets
    self-financing to reduce external dependency
    social learning

Definitions

It remains to clarify the area covered by this book entitled rather boldly *Arctic and Antarctic*. Much effort has been expended in the past on reaching acceptable definitions of the extent of these polar regions. In an era when classification and description of regions were of prime importance then clearly definition of boundaries was a key issue. However, in this book the view is taken that the boundaries should remain flexible. Some boundaries seem appropriate for some purposes and other boundaries for others. Further, it is the characteristics of the bulk of the area rather than its boundaries that are of most importance. Having said this it is necessary, however, to give some idea of the book's areal scope.

The natural tree line is a boundary of considerable moment in the Arctic. Although there are obvious problems in deciding where trees end and give way to tundra vegetation (Larsen, 1974), on a broad scale there is a relatively sharp zone between the two (Figure 1.6). There are several advantages in accepting the tree line as the southern land boundary of the Arctic. Not only does it represent a fundamentally important vegetation boundary, but it is also important in terms of animal distributions. It coincides approximately with a mean July temperature isotherm of 10°C and thus is also of climatic significance. It causes an additional climatic contrast in that winters are more exposed north of the tree line than to the south; one result of the more sheltered conditions among the trees is that snow tends to lie more thickly in the winter. Above all, the tree line is an important human boundary, especially in North America where it separated remarkably clearly the arctic Inuit peoples from forest Indians. It also effectively represents the northern limit of outdoor agriculture. If the tree line is accepted as the land boundary of the Arctic, then this includes western and northern Alaska and a wedge of northern Canada which progressively widens towards the east; in addition the whole of Greenland is included along with a thin strip of the Soviet Union which also widens towards the east. A marine boundary is needed to supplement the land boundary at sea, and for this it is reasonable to accept the southernmost extent normally reached by arctic water (Figure 1.6). This boundary, which effectively excludes Iceland, has implications concerning the drift of sea ice and icebergs, as well as the nature of the marine fauna.

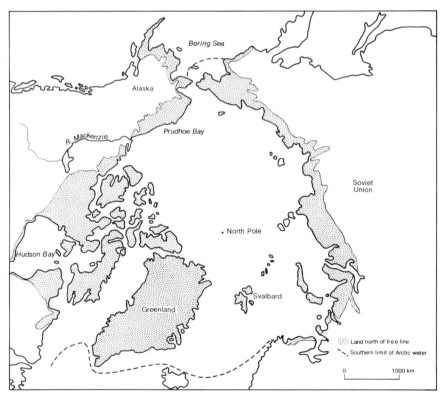

FIGURE 1.6   A natural boundary of the Arctic.

FIGURE 1.7
Dr. Clapperton photographs
the only tree in Antarctica.

Modern intrusive society in the Arctic is an extension of core areas in more temperate latitudes and understanding requires consideration of the human system as a whole. In this case the boundary is extended far to the south, although the main focus of attention is on developments north of the tree line. For convenience Alaska and Greenland

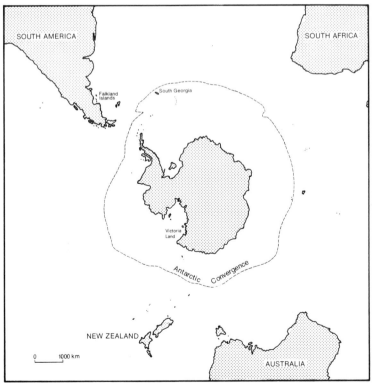

FIGURE 1.8   A distinctive boundary of the Antarctic: the Antarctic Convergence.

are treated as whole political units, while in Canada and the Soviet Union internal administrative units form convenient boundaries.

The Antarctic is devoid of trees (Figure 1.7), and as a result the boundary is chosen to coincide with the Antarctic Convergence (Figure 1.8). As will be seen in Chapter 6 this is an unbroken, well-defined circumpolar boundary roughly paralleling the February 10°C surface air isotherm. It marks the place where cold antarctic water meets warmer southern hemisphere water and is identified by an abrupt change in air and sea temperatures as well as by a sharp change in the make-up of plankton and sea birds. For ships' crews travelling to the Antarctic it is the 'anoraks and gloves' line.

Further reading

Brookfield, H. C. 1973: On one geography and a Third World, *Transactions of the Institute of British Geographers*, 58, 1—20.

Friedmann, J. 1966: *Regional development policy: a case study of Venezuela*. M.I.T. Press, Cambridge, Mass.

Polar Regions Atlas, 1978: Central Intelligence Agency, Washington.

Taaffe, E. J., Morrill, R. L. and Gould, P. R. 1963: Transport expansion in under-developed countries. *Geographical Review*, 53, 503—29.

Natural Systems
in the Arctic and Antarctic

CHAPTER TWO

Plate Tectonics

The aim of this chapter is to look at the main morphological and geological patterns in the polar regions and to view them as part of the world system of plate tectonics. By relating the patterns to the processes responsible rather than relying on description alone it is hoped that a more satisfactory explanation of the patterns will emerge. The explanation is important not only in itself but because macro-scale topography, tectonics and structure have numerous profound implications on all other earth and life systems in the polar regions.

Broad morphologic and geologic patterns

A contrast between the Arctic and Antarctic which is so fundamental and obvious that its implications can all too easily be forgotten is that the Antarctic is a continent surrounded by ocean while the Arctic is an ocean basin almost completely surrounded by continents (Figure 2.1). The Arctic Ocean is a mediterranean in the continental hemisphere of the world while the Antarctic is a remote outpost in the ocean hemisphere of the world. A measure of this contrast can be gained by the observation that it is possible to row a boat round all the continents and sub-continents in the world without crossing more than 95 km of sea except for Antarctica; the distance between Antarctica and the other southern continents ranges from 1 000 to 4 000 km.

The main physiographic features of the Arctic basin are shown in Figure 2.2. The Arctic Ocean is $9.5 \times 10^6 \, km^2$ in area, which is about four times larger than the Mediterranean Sea and represents some 3 per cent of the world's ocean area. Unusually broad continental shelves underlie 70 per cent of its area, particularly on the Eurasian side of the basin where they commonly extend more than 900 km offshore. The main relief features cut into the continental slopes are submarine canyons which link the shelf areas to the ocean basin proper (Carsola, 1954). The ocean basin itself has two main components which are separated by the Lomonosov Ridge, a submarine mountain range rising

3000m above the surrounding ocean floor within the space of a few tens of kilometres. One component is the Eurasian Basin, which is over 4000m deep and bisected by the narrow Nansen Cordillera. The other component is the Amerasian Basin, which is larger and has a uniform depth of about 3800m in the south and depths of over 4000m near the pole. It too is transected by a ridge in the north, the Alpha Cordillera, which runs parallel to the Lomonosov Ridge and 500km distant from it.

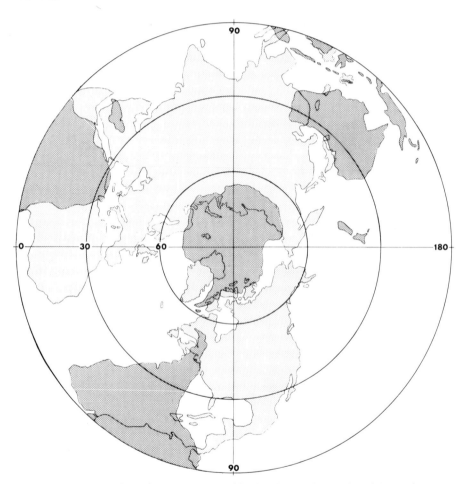

FIGURE 2.1   Comparison of the distribution of land and sea in the Arctic and Antarctic. Southern hemisphere continents are shaded heavily. The northern hemisphere appears as though viewed from below through a transparent globe.

The arctic land areas surrounding the Arctic Ocean are generally low-lying. The flattest areas in Siberia are associated with the valleys of some of the world's largest rivers such as the Ob', Yenisey and Lena and

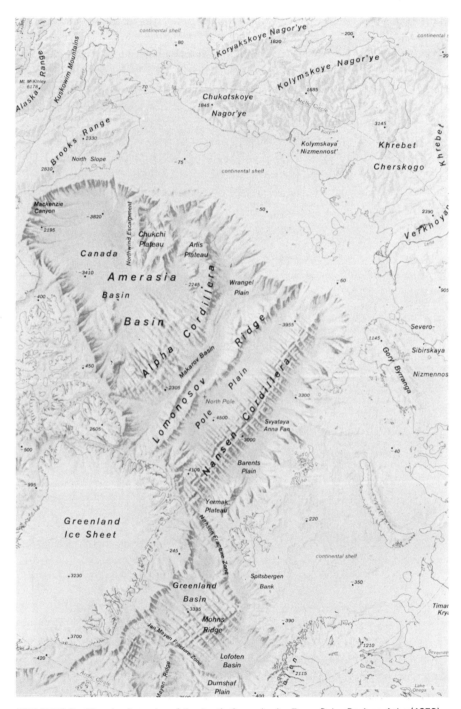

FIGURE 2.2   The physiography of the Arctic Ocean basin. From *Polar Regions Atlas* (1978).

some idea of the flatness can be judged from the fact that the estuary alone of the Yenisey is over 300 km long. There are distinctive uplands, particularly in Greenland and the eastern Canadian Arctic where mountains and plateaux exceed 2000 m in altitude over wide areas. Also the Greenland ice sheet rises above an altitude of 2500 m over much of its extent with a maximum near the centre of around 3200 m. Other less continuous uplands occur east of the Lena delta and in the peninsula of northeastern Siberia where summits commonly exceed 1800–2000 m. Narrower but higher and continuous mountains occur in Alaska which lies largely in the Western Cordillera province of North America. The Alaska Range includes summits like Mt. McKinley (6178 m) while the rugged Brooks Range includes many summits 2000–2800 m in altitude (Figure 2.3).

FIGURE 2.3   Part of the north-central Brooks Range with intensely deformed Devonian rocks. The peaks here are 2000–2500 m in altitude. Photograph by Stephen Porter.

The main tectonic features of the Arctic are shown in Figure 2.4. Three shields, formed predominantly of Precambrian granites and gneisses, are the main structural features, namely the Canadian–Greenland shield, the Baltic shield and the Angara shield. The Canadian and Greenland shields are separated by an ocean basin in Baffin Bay and the flanks of Greenland and eastern Baffin Island are overlain by Tertiary volcanic rocks (Figure 2.5). Shield rocks are commonly

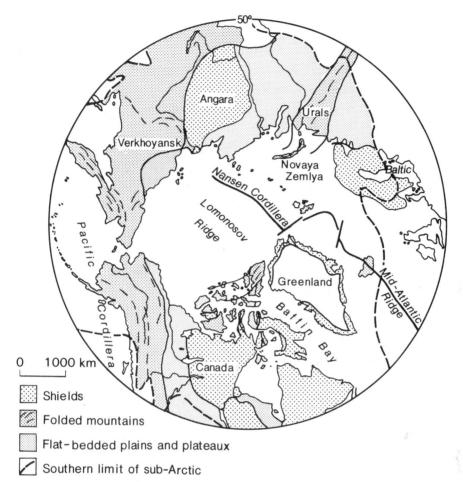

FIGURE 2.4   Major structural features of the Arctic. Various sources.

covered by flat-lying Palaeozoic sedimentary rocks nearer the peripheries, for example in the north European Plain in Russia and the Mackenzie lowlands in the western Canadian Arctic. Whereas shield rocks are extensively exposed in the Canadian Arctic and Greenland and in Scandinavia, only a small area of the Angara shield outcrops at the surface. The shield areas are fringed by orogenic belts of sedimentary rocks of Palaeozoic and younger age. A good example occurs in the Sverdrup Basin area of the northern Canadian arctic archipelago (Figure 2.6) and is continued in North Greenland and Svalbard. Other examples include the fold mountains of the Urals and Novaya Zemlya, which are Palaeozoic in age, and the Pacific Cordillera of western Canada and Alaska which vary from Palaeozoic to recent in age as one approaches the Pacific. Northeastern Siberia is tectonically chaotic and difficult to

FIGURE 2.5 Outlet glaciers cutting into horizontally bedded Tertiary lavas near Bartholins Brae, Blosseville Kyst, East Greenland. Reproduced with the permission of the Geodetic Institute, Copenhagen.

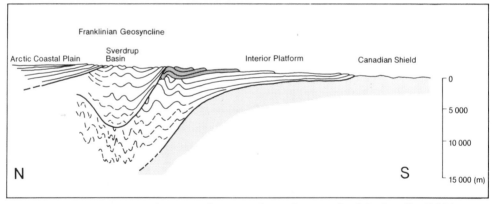

FIGURE 2.6 Diagrammatic cross-section across the northern margin of the Canadian Shield and the folded Palaeozoic sediments of the northern Arctic archipelago. After McClaren (1975).

understand at present but seems to involve fragments of shield and complex fold belts of Palaeozoic age (Hamilton, 1970). Tectonically active regions with earthquakes and associated volcanic activity include the cordillera of southern Alaska which are part of the mountain belt which rims the Pacific and the mid-ocean Nansen Cordillera and its North Atlantic continuation which includes Iceland. Apparently there

are earthquakes in the Verkhoyansk mountain area which is a continuation of the line of the Nansen Cordillera (Sykes, 1965).

The main physiographic features of Antarctica are shown in Figure
2.7. The continent measures 5500 × 4200 km and is roughly the
equivalent in size of the U.S.A. and Mexico together. It is covered by an

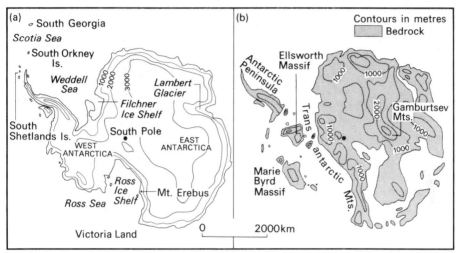

FIGURE 2.7   *(a)* Surface and *(b)* Sub-ice morphology of Antarctica.

ice sheet which rises relatively steeply near its periphery and reaches
an altitude of 4000 m in East Antarctica and several summits over
2000 m in altitude in West Antarctica.[1] The ice sheet submerges two
distinct components of the continent. In East Antarctica there is a
more or less compact continent with large areas close to sea level
but with mountains such as the Gamburtsevs rising up to 3000 m in
places. The Transantarctic Mountains traverse the continent, as their
name implies, and provide a magnificent scenic backdrop with peaks
above 4000 m high overlooking the Ross Sea (Figure 2.8). In West
Antarctica there is an archipelago with three main upland centres,
namely the Antarctic Peninsula, the Ellsworth and Marie Byrd Land
massifs. Here the subglacial relief is dramatic and rock bed depths of
−1600 m occur within 60 km of mountain summits of 5140 m in the
Ellsworth Mountains (Swithinbank, 1977). It is interesting to remember
that there were no subglacial soundings before 1951 and current
forays by radio-echo sounding are requiring constant revision of details
of the subglacial topography.

The continent as a whole is fringed by a continental shelf usually less
than 100 km wide, which attains its maximum width of over 1000 km

[1] The terms *East* and *West* Antarctica are very misleading in view of the fact that the continent is centred on the South Pole. Unfortunately, the two terms are now widely used.

FIGURE 2.8   The Transantarctic Mountains in the vicinity of the Beardmore Glacier. The
mountain range, with peaks of 4000m, is covered with local glaciers. U.S. Navy
photograph reproduced with the permission of Charles Swithinbank.

in the vicinity of the Weddell and Ross Seas. Beyond the continental
slope are ocean basins up to 4500m deep which surround the continent and are themselves traversed by an oceanic ridge running roughly
parallel to the continental edge, except in the Scotia Sea area. Here
an arcuate submarine ridge, dotted with island groups such as the
South Shetland and South Orkney Islands and South Georgia, links the
Antarctic Peninsula with South America.

Geologically there is much to learn about Antarctica. So far interpretation has depended on observations on scattered nunataks and
extrapolation by means of remote sensing techniques beneath the ice.
Although there will clearly be revisions the main structure seems clear
and indeed was recognized in 1913 by Nordenskjöld. East Antarctica
is basically a shield while West Antarctica consists of folded sediments
and associated volcanics (Figure 2.9). These two components are called
the Gondwana and Andean geological provinces respectively.

As in the Arctic the Antarctic shield is sometimes flanked by folded
sediments of Palaeozoic age, for example the rocks associated with the

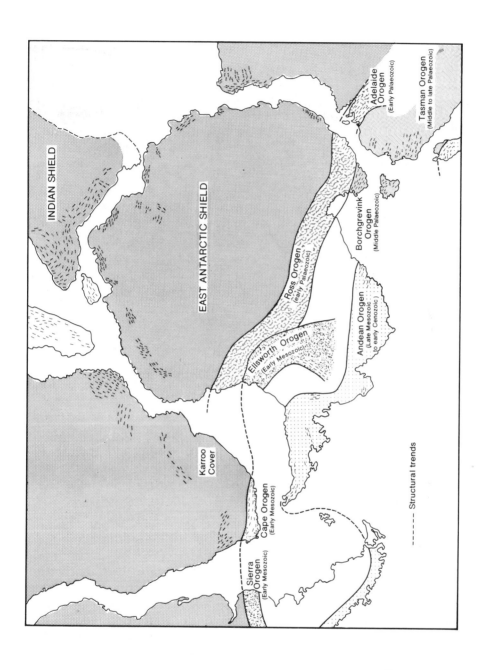

FIGURE 2.9
Geological structure
of Antarctica and
its relationship with
neighbouring
continents. After
Craddock (1970).

Ross Orogen which underlies the Transantarctic Mountains. There may be flat-lying sediments covering the shield rocks, for example the Beacon group which contains coal-bearing strata of Permian age, as in the other southern continents of Australia and Africa. The details of the geological structure in West Antarctica are far from understood. Nevertheless, there appears a tendency for the folded sediments to be successively younger towards the Pacific (Craddock, 1970). The Antarctic Peninsula and islands such as South Georgia and the South Orkneys and the area inland of the coast of Bellingshausen Sea are direct equivalents of the Andes, and range from late Mesozoic to early Cenozoic in age. Current tectonic activity is suggested by active volcanoes in the form of Mt. Erebus (3 794 m), well known through the paintings of Edward Wilson who was a member of Scott's expeditions to the Ross Sea, and Deception Island in the South Shetland Islands. LeMasurier (1972) discovered that volcanoes have erupted beneath the West Antarctic ice sheet on many occasions during the Cenozoic. The South Sandwich Islands, alone of the islands of the Scotia Sea, form an island arc with numerous active volcanoes.

The process: plate tectonics

The theory of plate tectonics does much to explain the pattern of topography and geological structure. The theory in its somewhat simpler form of continental drift has long been championed in the southern hemisphere and it is interesting to see that modern reconstructions are freely acknowledged to have improved little on Du Toit's reconstruction in 1937 (Smith and Hallam, 1970). In the Arctic however, the crucial area of the ocean is ice-covered and difficult of access and understanding of the precise plate movements is still unclear in many respects.

In a nutshell the theory of plate tectonics states that the Earth's surface is made up of a number of rigid plates consisting of either oceanic or continental material or both. These plates are moving differentially in respect to each other and as a result there is considerable activity at plate boundaries. Where plates meet, one plate disappears beneath the other in a subduction zone. If the two plates consist of oceanic crust then an island arc of volcanoes forms. When oceanic material meets continental material then the sediments flanking the continental shield cores are folded into mountains and there is considerable tectonic and explosive volcanic activity. Where plates move apart and split a continent, the continental edges are relatively undisturbed tectonically, though they may be uplifted as a whole. In time the continents are separated by an ocean basin with a tectonically active ridge forming the spreading axis.

The application of plate tectonic theory to the Arctic Ocean basin has been discussed among others by Churkin (1973), Vogt and Avery (1974) and Herron *et al.* (1974), while maps of continental positions at different times have been compiled by Smith, Briden and Drewry (1973) (Figure 2.10). A variety of evidence and absolute dating methods suggests that the Eurasian part of the Arctic basin is an extension of the North Atlantic. Spreading has taken place from the Nansen Cordillera which, though dislocated in the vicinity of Svalbard, is a continuation of the mid-Atlantic Ridge. A secondary relict spreading axis runs along the length of Baffin Bay between Greenland and Baffin Island. Spreading began about 81 million years ago along the Labrador—Baffin axis (Pitman and Herron, 1974) and then about 60 million years ago along both axes to the accompaniment of uplift and volcanic activity which spilled lavas on to the flanks of Greenland and Baffin

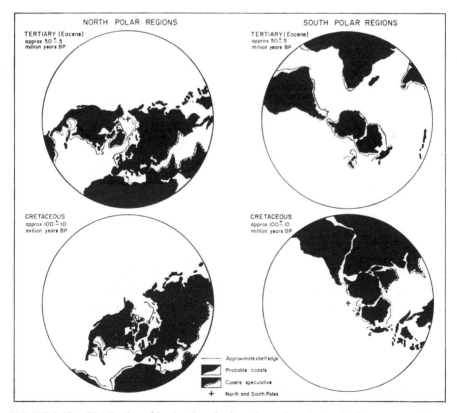

FIGURE 2.10   Distribution of land and sea in the polar regions during the Cretaceous and Tertiary. After Smith, *et al.* (1973).

Island as well as western Scotland and the Faroe Islands (Figure 2.5). The Arctic extension of the spreading centre detached a fragment of the Asian continent, the Lomonosov Ridge, and began to move it towards the pole. About 30—40 million years ago in the middle of the Tertiary, North America successfully annexed Greenland and the Baffin Bay spreading centre ceased to operate, while that in the Atlantic and Eurasian Arctic basin continued to be active. It is assumed that the tectonic activity associated with the Verkhoyansk Mountains is associated with a continuation of the Nansen Cordillera spreading axis beneath Siberia (Vogt and Avery, 1974). As would be expected in view of the above interpretation, the North Atlantic Arctic coasts are typical of plate separation and relatively unaffected by tectonic activity. In marked contrast is the situation in southern Alaska and the southern flanks of the Bering Sea where continental material meets the oceanic Pacific plate. Here, as would be expected, there is intense tectonic and volcanic activity associated with the formation of the youngest Cordillera.

A major problem in the Arctic is the mode of formation of the Amerasian Basin. At the time of writing there seem to be two main possibilities. On the one hand Ostenso and Wold (1973) suggest that the Alpha Cordillera is a relict spreading centre and that it represents an earlier phase of spreading prior to the Tertiary. On the other hand Herron *et al.* (1974) suggest that the basin formed in Jurassic times by the movement of the Kolymski plate from a position adjacent to the Canadian arctic archipelago across the basin into Siberia where it contributed to the tectonic chaos of north-east Siberia. These latter authors explain the Alpha Cordillera as an incipient island arc reflecting compression as the North Atlantic began to open in Cenozoic time. Whatever the precise origins, there seems general agreement that the Amerasian Basin is old and has been relatively stable for a long period of time (Figure 2.10).

The Palaeozoic folded sediments of the Urals and northern North America are interpreted as representing the collision of plates at an earlier phase of the Earth's history. The Urals represent the folding of marginal sediments following the collision of the European and Siberian plates in the Permian or Triassic (Hamilton, 1970), whereas the North American folded sediments may represent the original collision of the Kolymski plate with North America in the early Palaeozoic (Herron *et al.*, 1974).

In Antarctica the Gondwana geological province represents the original portion of Gondwanaland when the East Antarctic shield was part of a continent made up also of South America, South Africa,

Madagascar, India and Australia (Figure 2.9). For the fascinating story of how structural continuity, fossil and stratigraphic similarity between pre-Jurassic rocks pointed to the former existence of one continent, the reader is recommended to read an article by Adie (1965) or the imaginative geological arguments of Du Toit (1937). Now confirmed by deep sea and palaeomagnetic research it is believed that dispersal of Gondwanaland took place in the Upper Cretaceous and Tertiary times (Figure 2.10). Africa, India and Madagascar separated from Antarctica first. Australia did not separate until the Tertiary, and Kennett (1977) suggested on the basis of the dating of deep sea cores that this event began around 55 million years ago. A thin strip of continental material linked South America and the Antarctic Peninsula for much of the Tertiary (Elliot, 1972). This was breached to form Drake Strait 30–22 million years ago (Barker and Burrell, 1976; Herron and Tucholke, 1976). The sub-antarctic islands of South Georgia and the South Orkneys are fragments of this continental strip and quite different from the active subduction zone represented by the island arc of the South Sandwich Islands. The folded sediments and volcanics of West Antarctica represent subduction at the plate margins both before and after the break-up of Gondwanaland.

Interrelationships with other systems

The previous section offers an explanation of the geology and structure of the polar regions in terms of the world system of plate tectonics. Not only is this important in itself but the implications are profound in the way this macro-scale world system influences other systems operating at a world scale and all other systems operating at smaller scales. The system of plate tectonics is such a fundamental lynch-pin that it is useful to highlight its role as an independent variable for all other aspects of polar geography. Many of these relationships will be developed later.

The operation in the polar regions of other world-scale systems such as climate, ocean circulation and biogeography is fundamentally influenced by the distribution of land and sea and the main topographic barriers on land. The fact that the Arctic Ocean is in effect a gulf of the Atlantic whereas the Antarctic is isolated and surrounded by ocean favours a more meridional circulation of atmosphere and oceans in the Arctic than the Antarctic. Also the existence of a high topographic barrier such as the western American Cordillera interrupts zonal atmospheric circulation and dramatically decreases oceanic influences in the Canadian Arctic, when compared to the Eurasian Arctic which has no such barrier. It is sobering to realize just how recently in the Earth's history these patterns have formed. Ocean circulation and climate in the Arctic would have been completely different in times when the North Atlantic was non-existent or diminutive, some 60 million years ago. In the Antarctic a true zonal atmospheric and oceanic circulation can have developed only since the opening of Drake Strait 22 million years ago. Before Australia broke off 55 million years ago one can venture that zonal circulation would have been strongly interrupted as in the Arctic today (Kennett, 1978).

The basic contrasts in biogeography today between north and south owe much to the history of plate tectonic movements. Whereas the Arctic has long been in contact with most major land masses, the Antarctic has been isolated from the large northern continents for at least 22 million years. Long-continued competition between species has occurred in the Arctic (Simpson, 1947) and has favoured the evolution of a greater variety of living species adapted to a polar environment. In the Antarctic fossils demonstrate the existence of mid-Tertiary southern forests identical to those of the other southern continents during the same epoch and show that the continent was then open to wider biological competition (Holdgate, 1961). Afterwards, separate evolution of many species occurred and it is interesting to realize that there is no land vertebrate in the southern continents which is zonal in distribution. In the Antarctic there are no land vertebrates at all.

Contrasts at this world scale include the distribution of Man. Antarctica is unique in being the only continent not to support indigenous peoples. Since indigenous Man (Inuit) thrived in arctic environments much more severe than some peripheral antarctic environments, it seems reasonable to attribute the lack of an arctic type of culture at least partly to the continent's inaccessibility, or in other words to the history of plate tectonics.

The system of plate tectonics affects all smaller-scale earth and life systems in the polar regions. There is not space to deal with these in detail and the following paragraphs merely highlight some of the more important interrelationships.

Through its influence on geological structure, plate tectonics is one control on the broad distribution of landforms. The main physiographic regions in the Arctic are clearly based on plate tectonic history and yet are meaningful to someone traversing any of the regions on the ground. For example, the shield areas are characteristically rocky, rolling and dotted with numerous lakes and irregular streams. The flat-bedded plains are often overlain by glacial, fluvial and marine deposits and are poorly drained and remarkably flat, the main landscape features being small and of periglacial origin. Other large geomorphological features may be directly related to the history of plate tectonics. Three of the world's largest rivers flow into the Arctic and could reflect the great age of the Arctic basin which has provided the time and stability for large rivers to form. These rivers contribute a fresh water discharge to the Arctic which is seven times higher per unit area than any other ocean. The presence of these rivers is of the utmost significance in influencing most other physical systems and, through their usefulness as transport routes, even the location of human activities in the Arctic (see Chapter 13). The curved shape of the East Antarctic coastline is another big geomorphological feature and may be typical of a situation where a plate moves away from a relatively passive shield (Dietz, Holden and Sproll, 1972). These writers suggest that the convex coastline of West Africa is a type example of such a split and that the convex coast of East Antarctica comprises several similar components. Other little suspected relationships between plate tectonics and geomorphology may occur. It has been suggested that there may be some significance in the fact that the strandflat, often regarded as characteristic of polar coasts, is restricted in its distribution to the young uplifted coasts of the North Atlantic Arctic and the Antarctic Peninsula (John and Sugden, 1975).

Plate tectonics are a meaningful variable affecting small-scale geomorphic systems operating on short time-scales and indeed human systems. An obvious example concerns tectonically active regions. These are highly localized in the polar regions and, excluding suboceanic zones, restricted to the Pacific plate margins in southern Alaska, Siberia, the Scotia Sea and certain other areas of West Antarctica. The eruptions of Deception Island in 1967, 1969 and 1970 created a new island, melted glaciers and initiated mudflows (Clapperton, 1969). It caused the British and Chilean Antarctic bases on the island to be subsequently abandoned (Figure 2.11). The earthquake in Alaska in 1964 induced major rock avalanches on numerous mountains to flow many kilometres down adjacent valleys and glaciers, bodily lifted some coastlines by 2 m, and submerged others enough to drown many square kilometres of forest (Post, 1967; Hansen and Eckel, 1966). Fluidization of raised deltas caused violent upheaval and the ground broke up into blocks which slumped and rotated haphazardly. Not unnaturally parts of Anchorage which were on the edge of such a delta were devastated (Figure 2.12) while the port of Valdez disappeared in a tidal wave.

The system of plate tectonics has a much more profound though less spectacular effect on human systems than the localized examples

FIGURE 2.11   The U.K. base at Deception Island was devastated by a mudflow associated
with the volcanic eruption of 1969.

mentioned above. The location and distribution of mineral resources
is crucial. No assessment of the role of human activity in the Arctic and
Antarctic is possible until some perspective is gained about this constraint. Are the polar regions unusually rich or poor in minerals? Do
they have more of certain types of mineral than elsewhere? Is there
anything unique about the mineral reserves? Until these questions are
answered one can reach few meaningful conclusions about the reasons
for the contrasts in development from area to area. At the same time,
these questions are impossible to answer accurately, although an
understanding of the reasons for the geological structure does give
certain guidelines.

The shield area of East Antarctica was once part of the Gondwanaland
shield. When one looks at the rich iron and gold reserves of Western
Australia, the iron of the Deccan and the gold, uranium and copper of
South Africa, it seems reasonable to infer that comparable deposits
will exist in the large Antarctic shield area, although beneath the ice
sheet. Coal seams of Permian age occur in East Antarctica and have
counterparts in Australia and South Africa. Oil is frequently found in
folded sediments flanking shields and there is no reason to expect the
Palaeozoic sediments flanking the East Antarctic shield to be different.
At present there are hopes of large reserves on the continental shelves
underlying the Ross and Weddell Seas (Mitchell and Tinker, 1980).
The Mesozoic to Cenozoic folded sediments of West Antarctica are a

FIGURE 2.12   A street in Anchorage following the Alaskan earthquake of March, 1964.
Photograph by Vern Brickley kindly supplied by the Mayor of Anchorage.

direct continuation of the Andes. When one looks at the riches of the
Andes in the form of copper, silver, lead, zinc and tin, it seems reasonable to expect some comparable resources in West Antarctica. The
Dufek Massif has attracted a lot of interest and may prove to be a major
copper and nickel reserve.

In the Arctic the shield areas are already known to hold rich reserves of minerals such as iron, nickel, copper and zinc, and many mines are active or proposed. The Palaeozoic sediments flanking the shields hold reserves of coal and oil. One of the most interesting features of recent years is the way the oil discoveries in the folded sequences of North Alaska have been followed by exploration eastwards along the line of the folded structures into Arctic Canada, northern Greenland and, by jumping the Atlantic, into the equivalent structures of the Barents Sea and Svalbard. In addition the rich oil and gas reserves associated with the sediments in western Siberia between the two shields in Russia are now well known to be massive on a world scale. Finally, one can point to the mineral concentrations associated with the intense folding and faulting in the Alaska and the adjacent northeastern Siberian peninsulas. It is no coincidence that these areas are rich in gold and tin.

Viewing the mineral resources of the polar regions as a whole it is possible to make certain generalizations. In view of the world-wide nature of plate tectonics, it is possible to recognize certain broad structural elements which occur throughout the world. Thus there is no structural element unique to the polar regions. On the other hand one can recognize that the distribution of the continents at the moment does give a certain bias to an area within the polar regions underlain by any particular structural element. Thus one can argue that Antarctica as a whole is unlike Australia and South Africa in that it has an extensive area of folded sediments. Probably its nearest continental equivalent in terms of mineral resources is South America in the latitude of Brazil. The Arctic seems dominated to a greater extent than is normal by shield rocks and sedimentary sequences associated with shield boundaries. Probably it is fair to state that the Arctic is likely to be unusually rich in minerals of shield origin and also oil and natural gas. As generalized and tentative as these statements seem, they are fundamental to an understanding of the human geography of the polar regions.

Further reading

Adie, R. J. 1965: Antarctic geology and continental drift. *Science Journal* (August), 65—73.

Craddock. C. 1970: Geologic maps of Antarctica. *Map Folio Series*, 12, American Geographical Society.

Herman, Y. 1974: Topography of the Arctic Ocean. In Herman, Y. (editor), *Marine geology and oceanography of the Arctic Seas*, Springer, Berlin, 73—81.

Herron, E. M., Dewey, J. F. and Pitman, W. C. III 1974: Plate tectonic model for the evolution of the Arctic. *Geology*, 2, 377—80.

Smith, A. G. and Hallam, A. 1970: The fit of the southern continents. *Nature*, 225 (5228), 139–44.

CHAPTER THREE

Climate

Characteristics of polar climate

It is the climate and the changes associated with the march of the seasons that will endure longest in the memory of anyone visiting the polar regions for a year. Perhaps it is useful to imagine a year at Syd Kap, a former settlement in inner Scoresby Sund in East Greenland at latitude 71°30'N. Here winter is long, cold, still and dark. The sun will not rise above the horizon for a period of about 9 weeks beginning around 23rd November. The darkness is far from absolute, however, and twilight exists so long as the sun is not more than 6° below the horizon. Syd Kap receives twilight throughout the winter and this, combined with moonlight and the reflective snow surface, means that outdoor pursuits can be carried out throughout the winter without artificial light, albeit for a short time each day. The striking effects of the aurora borealis provide further variety (Figure 3.1). Temperatures

FIGURE 3.1
The northern lights (Aurora borealis) in northeast Greenland. Photograph by Ib Tøpfer.

in still clear weather can fall to −50°C. Not surprisingly all sounds of running water and waves are absent. Snow cover is patchy and thin; falls associated with the occasional winter storms are quickly blown into gullies leaving crests almost bare. Spring is a time when the days become increasingly light and sunny. Temperatures are still low until April with a monthly mean below −10°C, and the snow and ice cover remains intact. These are the days when sledge travel in the Arctic can be a joy (Figure 3.2). The time between spring and early summer is messy. Under bright and warm sunshine the snow first heats up and then, only when all the snowpack has reached freezing point, does it disappear. As it is uncovered, the ground surface melts and is saturated and boggy, making walking extremely trying. Most low-lying areas become snow-free in late June or the first half of July. The summer months are short but delightful. Temperatures are suitable for sunbathing for days on end, although myriads of mosquitoes thrive in the warm conditions and on exposed flesh. In the continuous sunlight air temperatures may exceed 22°C while rock surface temperatures can exceed 33°C. The air is filled with noise — the sounds of breeding birds

FIGURE 3.2   Spring sledging in northeast Greenland. Photograph by Ib Tøpfer.

up for the season, the rushing water of brooks and glacier meltwater streams, the sound of grinding pack ice in the fjord and the rumble as icebergs melt and crumble. The idyllic weather is occasionally broken by spells of rain, while in fjords strong winds can suddenly develop in the clearest weather. In late August the first night frosts occur, and in the space of a few days autumn arrives. One of the remarkable features is the change as vegetation transforms itself from summer green to vivid autumn tints of red and yellow in a matter of days. In September open water in the fjord between the larger ice floes freezes over each night, only to melt the following day, while geese gather noisily and begin to fly south in vast straggling skeins. By late September winter is fast approaching.

This description is of a moderately continental climate in an un-glacierized part of the Arctic and must be extrapolated with care. The maritime coastal areas of the Arctic and Antarctic experience warmer winters and cooler summers while the extreme continental climates of northeast Siberia experience cooler winters and longer, warmer summers. Also, the length and darkness of the winter increases towards the Pole. On ice sheets in interior Greenland and Antarctica winter is more severe and 'summer' non-existent.

The annual climatic rhythm is readily perceived by an individual and yet it results from the operation of atmospheric processes operating as part of a world-scale system. Understanding of the climate requires some perspective on the working of this world system. Thus the first aim of this chapter is to analyse polar climates as part of the world climatic system. The second aim is to identify links between climate and other environmental and human systems, mostly at smaller scales.

The overwhelming characteristic of the polar regions is their cold, both in intensity and in duration. An imaginative early attempt to quantify the degree of cold is mentioned by Cowley Abraham in 1683 when his ship was blown far south of Cape Horn into the sub-Antarctic. He noted that it was 'so extreme cold that we could bear drinking 3 quarts of Brandy in 24 hours each man, and be not at all the worse for it' (Christie, 1951). One is thankful for the sake of the safety of Cowley Abraham and his crew that he was not able to sail into latitudes with temperatures characteristic of the South Pole itself!

There are several reasons which help to explain the cold of the polar regions. The first is simply that the polar regions receive less solar radiation than the rest of the world because of the low angle of the sun in relation to the ground surface. The poles themselves receive about 40 per cent less radiation than the equator, on average. However, this is an average and conceals an interesting fact; namely that in mid-summer each pole receives more solar radiation than any other place on earth. Indeed it is a curious coincidence that the coldest spot on earth, the high East Antarctic ice sheet, receives the maximum monthly input of solar energy for any point on earth (1185 langley per day). High values of solar radiation in summer are important in providing the vast amount of energy required to melt snow and ice and to support life during the brief and intense summer. These high summer values serve to emphasize that it is the lack of sunshine in the winter months that is crucial in maintaining the relatively low annual values.

A second reason for the cold of the polar regions is that they reflect more of the solar radiation received than elsewhere in the world. The average absorption of solar radiation by the earth's surface is about 40 per cent and can rise to 90 per cent on dark soils. On fresh snow and ice it can be less than 10—20 per cent. Both polar zones have extensive areas of pack ice or snow cover, especially in early summer when solar radiation is relatively high, and this means that much of the potential for heating is lost. A third reason for the cold is the clarity of the atmosphere so characteristic of polar regions. This clarity, which is well known to Arctic visitors who are impressed when they can see details on mountains 150km away, is due to the lack of dust and water vapour. The cold air holds some ten times less moisture than in temperate latitudes and is notably clear of solid particles. This clarity means that relatively little long-wave radiation from the earth surface, which is so important in heating the atmosphere elsewhere in the world, is trapped in the atmosphere of the polar regions.

These reasons in combination ensure that the polar regions suffer a loss in net radiation for all except a few summer months. Were this loss not made up somehow then both zones would get progressively colder. The loss is compensated for by import of heat from lower latitudes in three main ways. The transfer of sensible heat (i.e. that which can be sensed or felt by a person) is one way and involves the transport of air from lower latitudes, usually in the form of cyclones. Latent heat is another way; this describes the heat produced when water vapour is converted to rain or snow. Oceanic transport is the third way and enormous amounts of heat are readily transported poleward if ocean currents flow in that direction, as for example occurs in the north-eastern Atlantic. On a world scale the polar regions are heat sinks and in order for the world atmosphere to maintain itself in equilibrium there must be a net poleward shift of heat. It is the manner in which this movement of heat takes place that determines the particular climate of any area in the polar regions.

In spite of the popular image of the uniformity of 'polar' climate consisting of perpetual blizzard, there are dramatic contrasts between north and south and between different parts of each polar zone. Many of these contrasts can be attributed to the effect of macro-scale topography of the earth's surface, and in particular the distribution of land and sea and mountains. Thus they reflect the interaction between the world atmospheric circulation and the earth-bound system of plate tectonics discussed in the previous chapter.

ATMOSPHERIC CIRCULATION

On an Earth with a uniform surface each pole would occupy a vortex surrounded by a zone of westerlies. This relates to the differential heating between poles and equator and the effect of the Earth's rotation. The temperature difference causes air over the poles to be denser

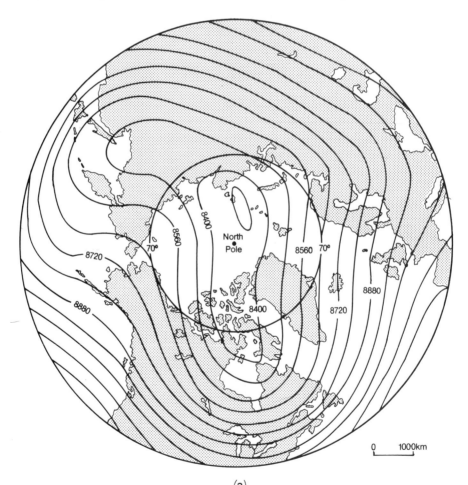

(a)

FIGURE 3.3(a)   The mean height (gpm) of the 300 mbar surface for January in the northern hemisphere. The Westerlies blow in an anticlockwise direction almost parallel to the contours at a speed proportional to the gradient. After Barry and Hare (1974).

and in effect this means that lines of equal density in the atmosphere form a bowl over the poles high at the perimeter and low at the centre. As the air flows down the gradient towards the poles it is diverted by the rotation of the Earth so that it flows roughly parallel to the contours, forming an anticlockwise vortex over the North Pole and a clockwise vortex over the South Pole. Figures 3.3a and b show the shape of the vortex at each pole. The choice of constant pressure levels of 300 and 500 mbar is simply to show the pattern at altitudes sufficiently high for the effects of friction associated with the ground surface to be negligible. In the Antarctic the vortex is fairly symmetrical and the centre is roughly coincident with the South Pole (Schwerdtfeger, 1970). However, in the Arctic the vortex is less simple in shape and less centrally situated. For example, a wave extends southwards

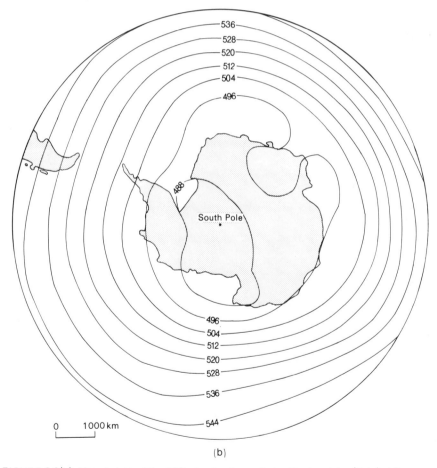

(b)

FIGURE 3.3(b) Mean height of the 500 mbar level over Antarctica in winter (July). After Schwerdtfeger (1970). The Westerlies blow in a clockwise direction.

over North America in January and probably represents the effect of the North American Cordillera (Barry and Hare, 1974).

Surface air movements closely reflect such overall wind directions but are interrupted by irregularities associated with the distribution of land and sea. In the Antarctic the basic symmetry of a polar continent surrounded by a sub-polar sea means that irregularities are at a minimum. The Westerlies of the sub-Antarctic are notoriously persistent. Cyclones associated with the southern hemisphere Polar Front in the Westerlies are frequent and tend to travel round the continent. The tendency for some cyclones to move polewards slightly, as well as eastwards, brings them into contact with the continental coastline. Few are capable of crossing the high barrier of East Antarctica, but they do manage to cross the lower barrier of West Antarctica from either the Ross or Weddell Seas.

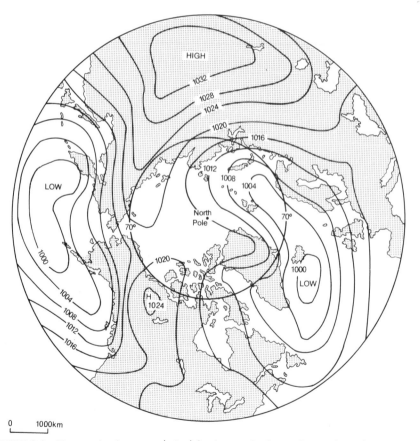

FIGURE 3.4   Mean sea level pressure (mbar) for January in the northern polar regions. After Barry and Hare (1974).

In the Arctic the alternation of continent and ocean breaks up the continuity and strength of the Westerlies and introduces a more pronounced meridional circulation. The waves associated with each continent introduce cold northwesterly winds in winter over the east of each continent, while in contrast warm air over the Atlantic is directed towards the north. Northward movement of air from the Pacific is interrupted by the Pacific Cordillera. The build-up of an intense thermal high-pressure zone over the continents and Amerasian Arctic in winter (Figure 3.4) has the effect of diverting cyclones northwards into the Atlantic–Barents Sea and accentuating the north–south exchange of air.

TEMPERATURE

Antarctic temperatures are low all the year round. Figure 3.5 shows how the mean annual temperature of the continent is everywhere below freezing, and indeed this is true of Antarctic seas to a latitude of about 60°S. On the continent the mean annual temperatures vary from *c.*−60°C on the ice sheet summit to −10°C around much of the coast. The pattern is similar throughout the year but the intensity varies. For example, in winter the mean July temperature for the centre of the ice sheet is below −70°C, while along the coast it is around −25°C. In summer (January) the temperatures in the same areas are below −40°C and −2°C. In the Arctic the pattern varies dramatically with the seasons (Figures 3.6 and 3.7). In winter (January) there are two land areas (eastern Siberia and Greenland/Arctic Canada) and an intervening zone in the Arctic Ocean where mean temperatures are below −30°C. The two land areas have the lowest temperatures, especially northeast Siberia which boasts the all-time northern hemisphere low for permanent habitation of −67.8°C at Verkhoyansk.[1] Two particular points of interest arise. First, the lowest temperatures are at the edge of the Arctic, indeed in the sub-Arctic. Second, the longitudinal contrast in January temperatures between the Lofoten Islands in northern Norway and Verkhoyansk, which are at the same latitude, is 50°C; this is similar to the difference between the pole and equator! In the summer the pattern changes to one where air temperatures over the Arctic Ocean approximate to 0°C even at the pole, while the surrounding land areas are warmer, exceeding 16°C in northeast Siberia (Figure 3.7). Siberian summers start earlier than those in the North

---

[1] Apparently the lower temperature recorded at Oymyakon is disputed (Ives, personal communication, 1980).

American Arctic (as well as being warmer) and snow has disappeared by early May in the latitude of Yakutsk and by late May at 70°N. In much of the Canadian Arctic snow melts in late June and early July.

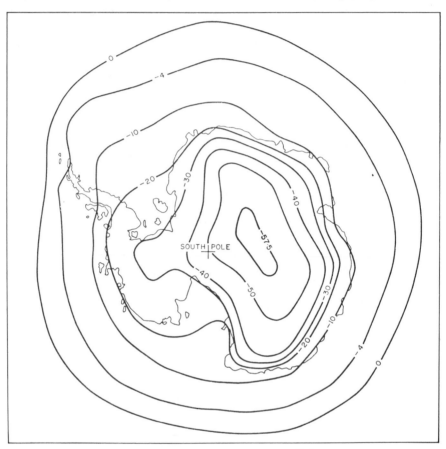

FIGURE 3.5   Mean annual surface temperatures in Antarctica (°C). After John and Sugden (1975).

One characteristic of polar climates is the presence of a temperature inversion above snow or ice surfaces which results from strong radiational cooling (Figure 3.8). The inversion may be only 10–100 m thick and yet represent a temperature difference of 30°C. Its development is commonly associated with calm anticyclonic conditions in winter and it is only disturbed by strong winds, cloud cover or precipitation associated with cyclones. The inversion is especially intense and persistent where dense cold air is trapped in valleys such as in Yukon and northeast Siberia, and this helps to account for the extremely low temperatures in these situations in winter. In the Antarctic the inversion is widespread and it is interesting to realize just how shallow the

'typical' antarctic climate is. Life 100m above the ice would be over
10°C warmer and, as will be seen later, much less windy.

Mean monthly temperatures in winter and summer do not necessarily convey much information about overall temperature conditions
throughout the year, and for this reason the freezing index and thawing
index are of great potential interest (Corte, 1969; Washburn, 1979).

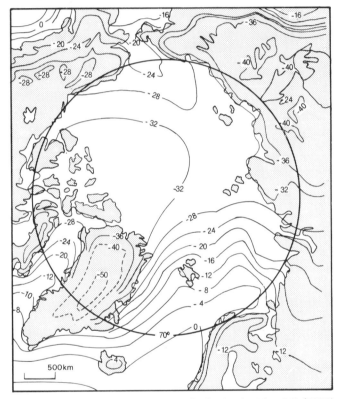

FIGURE 3.6   Mean monthly January temperatures in the Arctic. After Prik (1959).

The freezing index represents the number of degree-days of frost and
can be used to calculate the depth of winter ground freezing and the
thickness of lake or sea ice. The maps of Johnson and Hartman (1971)
show that much of the Canadian archipelago above 70°N has just over
9 000 degree-days of freeze (Figure 3.9). This compares with a figure of
12 500 in northeast Siberia and only 2 000–4 000 for the temperate
latitude of 50°N in North America. The map also brings out the great
longitudinal variation from west to east in western Siberia where values
range from 3 000 in the vicinity of Murmansk to 9 000 in the vicinity
of the Taymyr Peninsula. The thawing index is a reflection of summer
temperatures and, with the exception of the eastern Canadian Arctic,

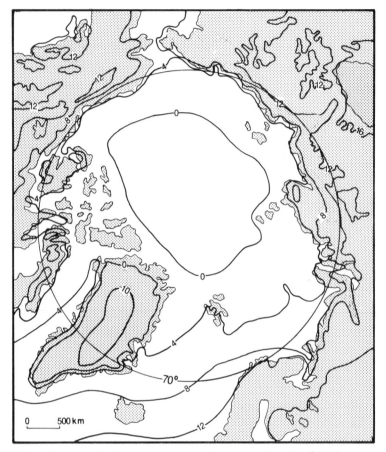

FIGURE 3.7   Mean monthly July temperatures in the Arctic. After Prik (1959).

the variations are roughly concentric round the pole (Figure 3.10). Except for some northern peninsulas most Arctic coastlines have around 1000 degree-days of thaw or slightly less.

These basic temperature patterns and contrasts in the polar regions reflect the interaction of topography and atmospheric circulation. Temperatures in Greenland and the Antarctic decline with altitude, and it is this factor above all else that accounts for the exceedingly low temperatures on the ice sheets. Over half of Antarctica is above 2000m and one-quarter is above 3000m. Using a lapse rate of 1°C per 100m altitude characteristic of ice sheets (Benson, 1962), then one can calculate that if the continent was near sea level the temperature near the South Pole would be up to 40°C warmer. This estimate, however, rough, makes one realize how much the southern hemisphere

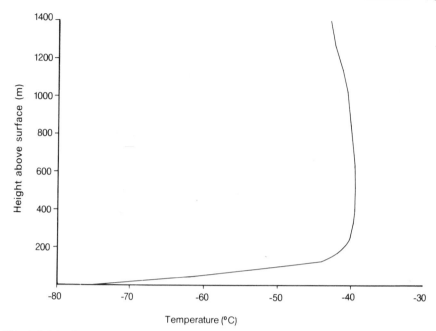

FIGURE 3.8   Temperature profile through the strong surface inversion at Plateau Station.
After Dalrymple and Frostman (1971).

climate owes to the presence of the antarctic ice sheet which is responsible for the high altitude of the continent.

The arctic patterns are largely explained in terms of the distribution
of land and sea. In winter the pole is kept anomalously warm in comparison to the surrounding land by the existence of Arctic Ocean water
below a relatively thin sea-ice cover. The ocean temperature is within a
few degrees of freezing and heat is conducted through the ice in winter.
The surrounding land areas have no such heat reservoir and temperatures plummet, particularly where cold air drainage leads to the build-
up of stable inversions. In summer the position is reversed. The melting
pack ice and ocean serve to keep temperatures close to zero over the
ocean, whereas land temperatures are free to rise.

Air circulation reinforces this basic contrast between the Arctic and
Antarctic. Whereas meridional circulation is discouraged by the symmetry of the Antarctic, arctic topography favours a northward
movement of warm air especially in winter over the Atlantic sector.
This helps to make the Antarctic colder than the Arctic. It also helps
to explain the sharp longitudinal temperature gradients in the Arctic,
a pattern which is unimportant in the Antarctic, except locally in the
vicinity of the Antarctic Peninsula.

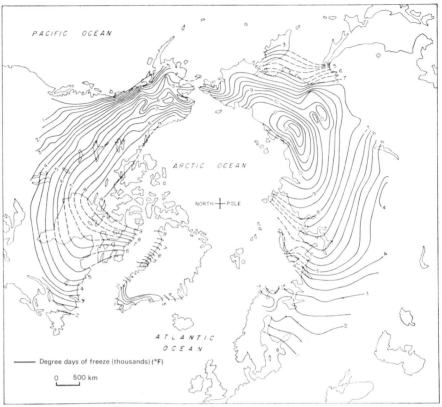

FIGURE 3.9   Freezing indices for the northern hemisphere polar zone. After Johnson and Hartman (1971).

PRECIPITATION

Precipitation in the polar regions is light and indeed most of the zone is arid. In Antarctica most of the precipitation consists of snow. Totals, measured as water equivalent, decline from a maximum near the coast, where values of 200–600 mm are common, to values of less than 50 mm over much of the central parts of East Antarctica (Bull, 1971). The interior of West Antarctica receives between 100 and 200 mm. Ice-free areas in Victoria Land receive less than 50 mm on average and in 1970 the precipitation in Wright Valley was only 7 mm, representing flurries of snow on only 11 days (Riordan, 1975). Most precipitation in Antarctica falls in the winter months. Totals in the Arctic basin are generally less than 130 mm while the arctic coasts have less than 260 mm on the whole (Vowinckel and Orvig, 1970). The lowest land values are around 140 mm and occur in eastern Siberia and northern

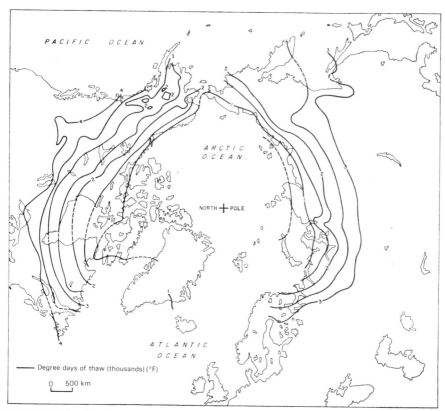

FIGURE 3.10   Thawing indices for the northern hemisphere polar zone. After Johnson and Hartman (1971).

Canada and Greenland. Totals generally rise from these areas towards the Atlantic and Pacific to above 600 mm. In contrast to coastal Antarctica winter precipitation is light. This means that snow depths are slight and by late spring thicknesses of only 350–400 mm occur on sea ice in the central Arctic and depths of 600 mm in continental areas such as the northern Canadian Arctic. Moreover, in continental areas the precipitation maximum occurs in summer which means that most is in the form of rain.

These hemispheric precipitation contrasts reflect the distribution of land, sea and high topography. In Antarctica, the decline inland reflects increasing altitude and increasing distance from the sea. Moist air is forced to rise orographically as it encroaches on the ice sheet and for this reason the maximum is reached a little way inland generally around an altitude of 1600 m (Chorlton and Lister, 1970). Beyond this the total falls off dramatically. The Greenland ice sheet resembles the

Antarctic ice sheet although there is also a latitudinal trend from a humid maritime climate in the south to continental climate in the north.

The main spatial precipitation pattern in the Arctic can be explained in terms of proximity to maritime sources of moisture. There is a decline in all directions from the northern Pacific and Atlantic Oceans, although it is attenuated in a west—east direction across the continents in the direction of movement of most cyclones. The decline in precipitation inland is more rapid in the case of the North American Arctic than in the Soviet Arctic and this reflects the blocking role of the western American Cordillera.

The seasonal contrast in precipitation maximum between north and south is also related to the distribution of land and sea. Cyclones tend to move into Antarctica and cross the lower part of the continent in winter when the westerly circulation is intensified and deep cylones form. In the Arctic in winter an enhanced westerly circulation is interrupted by strong pressure differences between land and sea. In summer the cyclones penetrate the continental interiors, bringing summer rainfall maxima.

WIND

Winds are a particularly important aspect of the polar surface environment for they can greatly aggravate any chilling effect of low temperatures. The lack of trees and the generally smooth ice surfaces over the sea and on land mean that winds are not greatly retarded by friction at ground level. The presence of the temperature inversion is of paramount importance with respect to surface winds. In Antarctica and Greenland where the slopes of the ice sheet fall towards the coast the dense cold inversion layer flows downhill under the influence of gravity to form katabatic winds (Figure 3.11). These are diverted to the left of the direct downslope direction in the southern hemisphere because of the earth's rotation. These winds only affect a layer *c.* 100 m thick. They blow fastest where the ground surface is steepest around the margins of the ice sheet, and are most persistent where a surface depression or valley favours channelling of the air drainage. They are particularly well developed in winter when the air in contact with the ice surface is chilled most effectively. Some sites are notoriously windy and it is no surprise that Douglas Mawson entitled his book *The Home of the Blizzard.* The site of his base camp on the coast of Antarctica has been subjected to as many as 340 days of gale in one year! On the other hand such regular and persistent winds have their

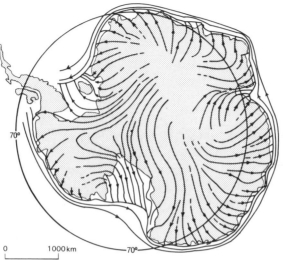

FIGURE 3.11   Mean surface wind patterns in Antarctica reflecting cold air drainage. After Mather and Miller (1967).

uses and Nansen was able to sail his sledges down the western slope of the Greenland ice sheet in 1888 (Figure 3.12). With the exception of Greenland the temperature inversion in the Arctic tends to reduce mean wind speeds, for the air is effectively isolated from faster-moving air above. Nonetheless, there are some important and dominant wind directions which can be inferred from study of maps of mean sea level pressure in winter (Figure 3.4). Most important is the veritable monsoon of cold air in winter from the high pressure of northeast Siberia

FIGURE 3.12
Nansen using katabatic winds to sail a sledge in Greenland. After Nansen (1890).

to the Pacific and the northwesterly flow across the Canadian Arctic from the high-pressure zone of the Arctic towards the low pressure of the Atlantic. Both flows are responsible for the extremely severe climatic conditions which extend far south, and in the case of Canada, persist into the early summer.

In conclusion to this section it is important to stress that polar climates result from the operation of two sets of processes. At a world scale basic geometric considerations imply a cooler climate at the poles than elsewhere and a westerly circumpolar air circulation. The interaction between these features and the distribution of land, sea and high topography introduces a second set of processes which determine the climate at any given point within the polar regions.

Interrelationship between polar climate and other systems

Climate is an important constraint and independent variable affecting the operation of many smaller-scale systems in the polar regions. The remainder of this chapter highlights a few of the more important links.

The links between climate and the various geomorphic, oceanographic and biogeographic systems are quite fundamental. The basic distinction between glaciers and ice-free ground is a function of climate. The presence, nature and distribution of pack ice is primarily a reflection of climate. The limits to vegetation productivity are determined ultimately by climate. Indeed the role of climate in influencing the operation of these systems is so fundamental that the topic must await fuller and separate treatment in the following three chapters. Instead, it is useful here to focus on the constraint climate provides to human systems. These constraints take many forms but are conveniently related to low temperature, impeded visibility, and the climatic seasonal contrast.

Low temperatures create problems for normal industrial society and their solution inevitably involves special design and extra cost. Conventional water supply, sewage and heating all would freeze and be inoperable in a polar winter and they require extensive and expensive modifications such as insulation. Diesel fuel turns viscous at low temperatures and becomes unreliable as a source of energy unless it is heated. Rubber, which is a vital component of petrol engines, loses its insulation capacity and flexibility at low temperatures. For example, it is common to find that car tyres have become stiff after a car has been parked for a while and the flat portion in contact with the road maintains its flat shape until after 1–2 km of bumpy driving heats the tyre sufficiently for it to resume its circular shape. Normal lubricants lose their lubricating qualities with low temperatures, while metal becomes brittle. Starting car engines is a major problem and it is common practice either to have electric heaters in the engine which are plugged in at each stop, or even to leave the vehicle engines running continuously throughout the arctic winter. This suggests caution when buying an apparently low-mileage car in the Arctic! All in all a simple shopping trip by car on a cold winter's day in the Arctic becomes a major expedition.

Perhaps more dangerous than absolute cold is the effective cold produced by a combination of wind and low temperature. This effect, known as windchill, has been approached in several ways. The most widely used windchill index, and one which is used in public forecasts in Canada, was calculated by Siple and Passell (1945) and gives the number of kilocalories of heat lost by 1 m² of a surface heated to 33°C, the approximate skin temperature of clothed human skin. Although other factors than wind and temperature affect cooling, the index is found to be a useful approximation to climatic severity and physiological stress. Some mean monthly windchill values for the coldest month for several locations are given by Sater *et al.* (1971):

Baker Lake, Keewatin, Canada	2030
Barrow, north Alaska	1705
Thule, northwest Greenland	1605
Verkhoyansk	1471

These serve to show how windchill values are higher in the windy Canadian Arctic, especially in Keewatin, than in Siberia where absolute temperatures are much lower but wind speeds less. The combination of wind and exceedingly low temperatures on the Greenland and Antarctic ice sheets in winter make them the physiologically coldest places on earth.

Windchill values in themselves do not convey very much at first sight. For this reason the windchill equivalent temperature is used instead. This is defined as the cooling power on exposed flesh at an arbitrary low windspeed of 2.23 m s⁻¹ (8 km/h) (Table 3.1). From this table it can be seen that a temperature of −40°C and a windspeed of 20 m s⁻¹ (72 km/h) has a windchill equivalent temperature of −78°C. Recently some other indices of physiological cold have been calculated. Steadman (1971), for example, calculated the windchill from the clothed body.

TABLE 3.1   *Windchill equivalent temperatures* (°)

Air temperature (°C)	Wind speed (m s⁻¹)				
	Calm	2.5	5	10	20
0	19	0	−7	−12	−18
−5	16	−6	−13	−19	−26
−10	13.5	−11	−19	−26	−33
−20	9	−21	−31	−40	−48
−30	4.5	−31	−43	−54	−63
−40	0	−41	−55	−68	−78

All in all one can summarize the many effects of cold on human life as one of increasing the friction of distance in human systems. This in turn means that successful systems are those which are compactly organized from a spatial point of view.

Visibility in the polar regions is generally clear. However, there are characteristic conditions common near the ground which limit visibility dramatically. One feature unique to the polar regions is ice-fog, which forms when a continuous supply of water vapour is supplied into air with a temperature of −30°C or below and condenses into tiny ice crystals. Such conditions are common in arctic towns in valleys where an inversion causes low temperatures and restricts mixing of air, and where combustion associated with vehicles and heating plants contributes more water into the atmosphere than can be absorbed without condensing. Fairbanks is a notorious example, and when temperatures remain below −40°C for a week, visibility at ground level is reduced to less than 10 m, although the fog may only be 10 m thick (Benson, 1969, 1970). More serious than the ice crystals themselves is the pollution associated with the fog. Lead and carbon dioxide concentrations exceed those found in any other urban centres on Earth. Ice fogs may occur in Fairbanks any time from late November to the end of March. They are a growing problem in smaller Canadian Arctic towns such as Whitehorse, Inuvik and Frobisher Bay, and are well known in eastern Siberian towns.

Persistent fog and low cloud is characteristic of areas of melting sea ice in summer. Arctic Ocean sea ice stations frequently experience more than 100 days of such fog a year (Sater *et al.*, 1971). The fog is caused by the movement of warm air across the cold melting ice surface. These fogs plague coastal settlements, for example those along the east coast of northern Baffin Island, and visitors yearning for the sun should move inland and/or uphill.

Blizzards are another surface phenomenon which restrict surface visibility. When surface winds reach about $10\,\mathrm{m\,s^{-1}}$ snow is picked up from the ground and saltates along the surface generally within a metre of the ground surface (Loewe, 1970). When wind speeds rise to $15\,\mathrm{m\,s^{-1}}$ the blowing snow is sufficiently dense and the layer sufficiently thick to reduce surface visibility to near zero. Snow does not need to be falling from the sky for blizzards to occur, and indeed it is common to be able to see the clear blue sky even when surface visibility is very restricted. However, particularly in the Arctic, blizzards are also associated with the passage of cyclones. In Keewatin blizzards are common and visibility is less than 1 mile for one-third of the time in winter. At Byrd Station on the flanks of the West Antarctic ice sheet wind speeds of over $10\,\mathrm{m\,s^{-1}}$ (sufficient for drifting snow) occurred for two-thirds of the time whereas wind speeds in excess of $15\,\mathrm{m\,s^{-1}}$ (heavy blizzard) occurred for about one-third of the time (Morris and Peters, 1960).

A white-out is commonly mistaken in the popular mind for a blizzard. However, white-out refers to a situation when a person's vision loses perception of depth. The situation occurs commonly when the surface is uniformly snow-covered and when the light is diffuse as when the sky is filled with stratus, two common conditions in the polar regions. Under these circumstances it may be impossible to judge surface relief or distance and it is quite possible for a person to walk over a cliff, and easier still for a car to leave a road or an aircraft to miss its landing. Most people are sceptical about the effects of white-out until they experience it and find it dramatically disconcerting, especially when they realize that loss of a sense of orientation can cause acute nausea.

Visibility problems concern surface transport and air flights which depend on airstrips. Such visibility difficulties increase costs and introduce delays, sometimes quite prolonged if the sea fog does not lift for a week. Balanced against this is the generally superior visibility and weather for higher-altitude flying which is characteristic of cold dust-free air of the polar regions.

Seasonal contrasts in the polar regions are dramatic and conditions associated with summer and winter are strikingly different. After 9 months of snow, ice, cold and relative darkness, there are a few weeks of thaw when the ground is awash and boggy and then a summer period of heat and insects. Overland travel is easy when ground surfaces are firmly frozen, but difficult when they are not, in summer. At sea techniques of travel appropriate to land are necessary in winter but to water in summer. This marked seasonal climatic contrast provides two dramatically different environments and these provide a constraint and challenge to human systems, whether of a hunting type, like the traditional Inuit, or of a modern industrialized type.

Further reading

Barry, R. G. and Hare, F. K. 1974: Arctic climate. In Ives, J. D. and Barry, R. G. (editors) *Arctic and alpine environments.* Methuen, London, 17--54.

Benson, C. S. 1969: The role of air pollution in arctic planning and development. *Polar Record*, 14 (93), 783–90.

Hare, F. K. and Thomas, M. K. 1974: *Climate Canada.* Wiley, Toronto.

Mather, K. B. and Miller, G. S. 1967: The problem of the katabatic winds on the coast of Terre Adélie. *Polar Record*, 13 (85), 425–2.

Orvig, S. (editor) 1970: *Climates of the Polar Regions.* World survey of climatology, vol. 14, Elsevier, Amsterdam.

Weller, G. and Bowling, S. A. (editors) 1975: *Climate of the Arctic.* Proceedings of the 24th Alaska Science Conference, August 1973. University of Alaska. (Many good papers.)

CHAPTER FOUR

The Glacier System

Glacier-covered areas comprise one of the three sub-zonal environmental systems within the polar regions (Figure 1.3). The presence or absence of glaciers in any area reflects the interaction of the world-scale systems of plate tectonics and climate. It is important to understand the basic distribution, character and behaviour of glaciers if one is to appreciate the nature of this particular environment. Furthermore it is important to understand the way in which glaciers impinge upon and constrain other systems, in particular the marine and tundra environments and human activities. This chapter aims to discuss both the glacier system *per se* and the ways in which it interacts with other systems. The structure of the chapter is outlined graphically in the flow diagram in Figure 4.1.

Glaciers in the polar regions

Glaciers cover some 99 per cent of the land area in Antarctica, and this represents by far the greatest amount of glacier-covered land area in the world (Table 4.1). The main exceptions are high mountain peaks which project as nunataks above the ice surface and isolated 'oases' of ice-free ground such as that of the McMurdo dry valley area. In the Arctic glaciers are much more limited in their distribution (Figure 4.2). Apart from the overwhelmingly important Greenland ice sheet, Arctic glaciers are mainly restricted to the eastern uplands of the Canadian Arctic, and the maritime islands and peninsulas off northwestern Eurasia, for example, Svalbard, Franz Josef Land, northern Novaya Zemlya and Severna Zemlya. Outside these areas glaciers occur in isolated uplands such as the Romanzof Mountains of the Brooks Range in northeastern Alaska and some mountains in eastern Siberia, but they are very limited in areal extent. Glaciers in the Arctic are restricted today when compared to their maximum extent which is thought to have been approached on several occasions in the last few million years (Figure 4.2).

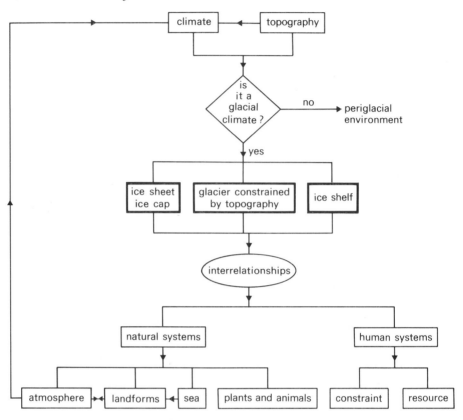

FIGURE 4.1   The glacier system (heavy boxes) and some interrelationships with other natural and human systems.

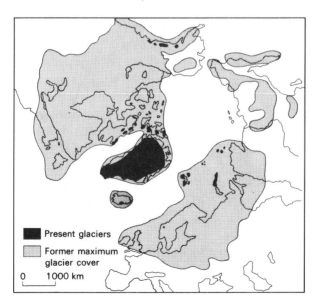

FIGURE 4.2
The current distribution of glaciers in the Arctic and areas formerly covered by glaciers in the Cenozoic.

TABLE 4.1   *Present-day glacier extent in the polar regions (after Flint, 1971)*

Region	Area (km^2)	Totals
South polar region		
Antarctic ice sheet (excluding shelves)	12535000	
Other antarctic glaciers	50000	
Sub-antarctic glaciers	3000	
		12588000
North polar region		
Greenland ice sheet	1726400	
Other Greenland glaciers	76200	
Canadian archipelago	153169	
Svalbard	58016	
Other arctic islands	55658	
		2069443
POLAR TOTAL		14657443
WORLD TOTAL		14898320

Perspective on the reasons for the distribution of present-day glaciers comes from consideration of the nature of glaciers. In mid and high latitudes a glacier builds up when summer temperature conditions are incapable of removing the previous winter's snowfall. If the snow collects year by year it will accumulate and undergo a change to glacier ice. The term 'firn' is used to describe any snow which has begun this transformation and survived one summer season. Generally it consists of loosely packed ice crystals with interconnecting air passages. When consolidation has proceeded sufficiently to isolate the contained air into separate bubbles the firn becomes *glacier ice*. In cold conditions such as at Plateau Station in Antarctica this transformation does not take place until a depth of 160 m is reached and this represents a period of time of around 3500 years (Gow, 1971). In areas of warmer summers where melting occurs the transformation takes place in a matter of years. In continental arctic climates the winter snowfall may be completely melted but the meltwater freezes on to the under-lying cold glacier surface to form what is termed superimposed ice; in these cases the transformation may be completed within a year.

The relationship between winter precipitation and the amount of summer melting suggests reasons for the distribution of glaciers in the polar regions. Conditions favourable for glacier survival are low summer temperatures and/or high winter snowfalls (Figure 4.3).

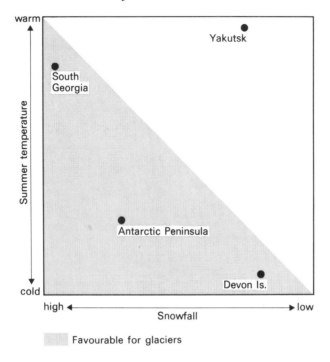

FIGURE 4.3
Diagram to illustrate
the suitability of
different environments
for glaciers in terms of
the two main variables:
high winter snowfall
and low summer
temperatures.

Summer temperatures reflect a latitudinal decline in solar radiation towards the poles as well as a decline from continental interiors towards maritime coasts. Superimposed on this any increase in elevation will lead to a lower than normal summer temperature. Thus from a temperature standpoint glaciers are most favoured at high latitudes and in the coastal areas of polar continents, particularly where there are upland areas. High winter snowfalls reflect proximity to both oceans and the storm tracks of mid-latitudes. Thus once again continental margins in cool temperate latitudes are favourable for glacier build-up, especially if they are elevated, while continental interiors which are remote from winter storm tracks are unfavourable. The distribution of glaciers in the Arctic neatly illustrates these generalizations. Most glaciers are on uplands and close to ice-free oceans and winter storm tracks (Hattersley-Smith, 1974). This is most clear in the case of the Atlantic borders and the decline in glacier activity with increasing distance from the open oceans is relatively gradual. This is particularly true of the northern coast of Eurasia which is a favoured track for winter storms. In the case of the Pacific the change is more abrupt. Whereas the cordillera of southern Alaska support many glaciers, little precipitation penetrates over the mountains into northern Alaska and thus the high Brooks Range is largely free of glaciers. The least favourable place for glaciers is the Yakutsk area of Siberia where winter snowfall is light (because of low temperatures and distance from storm tracks) and summer temperatures are high. In the Antarctic, glacier cover reflects extremely low summer temperatures which are incapable of melting the winter snowfall, however scanty it may be, as well as proximity to an ocean and storm tracks. In this context it is interesting to consider that extensive glaciation of the Antarctic is thought to have occurred only when the split of Australia from Antarctica, and later the breaching of Drake Strait, favoured an intense westerly circulation and associated storm activity (Chapter 7).

Glaciers are dynamic features of the Earth's surface which flow, and it is this characteristic above all else that accounts for their importance as an environmental system. Glaciers flow because ice is a relatively weak solid which deforms under its own weight. If the rock slope is sufficiently steep the glacier will flow down the rock surface by internal deformation and/or sliding. If the rock bed is flattish, then the glacier builds up until its surface slope is sufficiently steep to cause internal deformation and/or basal sliding.

It is useful to conceptualize a glacier as a system. Above a certain altitude, generally conceived of as the equilibrium line altitude, is the glacier accumulation area. Here more snow and ice is accumulated each year than is melted away. Below the equilibrium line is the ablation area where more snow and ice is lost by ablation each year than is received at the surface. If the glacier is to remain in equilibrium and not grow or diminish in size, then the difference must be made up by the transfer of ice from the accumulation area to the ablation area and as a result the glacier flows. Glaciers viewed as systems have been discussed in much more detail elsewhere (Andrews, 1975; Sugden and John, 1976) and interested readers are referred to these sources. However, even the simplified statement given above helps explain several characteristics of glaciers with fundamental implications. The conceptualization emphasizes the link between input and output on a glacier. If the winter precipitation is high, so also must be ablation and the rate of flow if the glacier is to remain in equilibrium. This is the reason why glacier velocities are higher in maritime areas of high precipitation than in continental areas. One can compare, for example, the rate of flow of 3—4 m per year for Meserve glacier in the dry desert environment of Victoria Land, Antarctica (Holdsworth and Bull, 1970) with rates of several hundred metres per year characteristic of glaciers in maritime South Georgia (Figure 4.4) or the extremely high rates of 7—12 km per year in parts of West Greenland (Fristrup, 1966 and Figure 4.5). The need for input to balance output also explains why glaciers with a high accumulation flow into lower, warmer climes in order for ablation to match input; in southern Alaska where snow accumulation rates are very high glaciers may terminate in lush forests. Conversely glaciers with little snow accumulation can end in severe continental climates; in Victoria Land, for example, where there is little melting, there is little snow to melt. If the equilibrium line is at a low altitude or near sea level, there may be insufficient ablation area for the glacier to terminate on land. In these cases the glaciers extend into the sea and the balance of ablation is by calving. This situation occurs round much of the Antarctic continent.

These abstract generalizations become more meaningful if they are linked to specific types of glaciers. Table 4.2 shows a simple morphological classification of glaciers and the functioning of the main types is represented diagramatically in Figure 4.6.

FIGURE 4.4   The snout of Harker Glacier, a fast-moving glacier in South Georgia, Antarctica. Photograph by Gordon Thom.

FIGURE 4.5   The snout of the fast-flowing Rinks Isbrae in West Greenland, calving icebergs and brash ice into the fjord. Reproduced with the permission of the Geodetic Institute, Copenhagen.

TABLE 4.2   *A morphological classification of glaciers (Sugden and John, 1976)*

Ice sheet and ice cap (unconstrained by topography)	ice dome
	outlet glacier
Ice shelf	ice shelf
Glacier constrained by topography	icefield
	valley glacier
	cirque glacier
	other small glaciers

ICE SHEETS AND ICE CAPS

Ice sheets and ice caps build up on a flattish land area and superimpose a roughly radial outflow of ice over the area. The difference between an ice sheet and ice cap is usually accepted as being one of scale. Ice caps are smaller, generally less than $50000 km^2$ in area (Armstrong

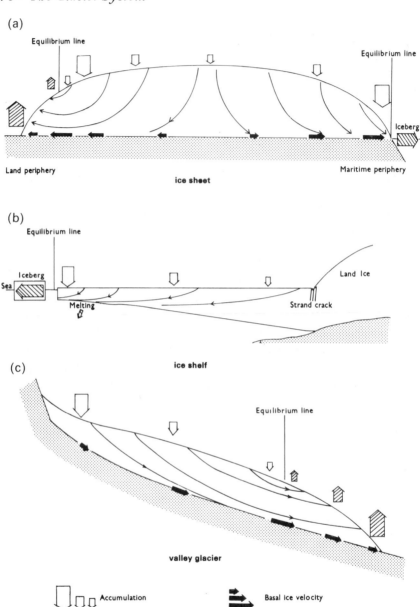

FIGURE 4.6   Models of *(a)* ice sheet *(b)* ice shelf and *(c)* valley glacier, showing the distribution of accumulation and ablation and related flow characteristics. Basal slipping is assumed to occur in models *(a)* and *(c)* and is at a maximum in the vicinity of the equilibrium line. From Sugden and John (1976).

et al., 1973). The main component is an ice dome (Figure 4.7). In East Antarctica the dome reaches an altitude of 4200m (Figure 2.7) while in Greenland it is around 3200m. The domes build up over the underlying relief and may completely submerge mountain ranges and basins with little sign of the achievement on the ice surface. Parts of the Antarctic ice dome are as much as 4300m thick. The overwhelming characteristic of ice domes is the convex-upwards profile with the slope gentlest near the centre and progressively steepening towards the edge. These slopes reflect the underlying flow properties of ice and are consistent from dome to dome at least when the ice is flowing on a rigid rock bed. To give some idea of the slopes involved it is helpful to imagine a continental-sized ice dome beginning at your feet. Ten kilometres distant it would be 450m higher; 50km distant about 960m higher; 100km distant 1400m higher; 500km distant 2700 m higher and 1000km distant 3300m higher. These slopes are characteristic of land-based ice domes (Sugden, 1977). In situations such as West Antarctica where the ice is grounded well below sea level the convex profile is less marked and the ice dome surface is lower.

Figure 4.6a shows the patterns of ablation and accumulation, the trajectory of particles in the ice dome and ice velocities (represented in these models by basal sliding). On domes of continental size precipitation falls off inland with increasing distance from the sea and thus most activity and glacier movement is restricted to the peripheral areas. On smaller ice caps this tendency may not arise. The right-hand side of the ice dome has an equilibrium line at sea level and represents the Antarctic situation. In such a case ice velocities increase towards the coast and calving is the rule. The left-hand side includes an ablation zone which ends on land, as in middle West Greenland. Ice velocities decrease near the margin and the ablation is by melting and creates massive meltwater streams.

Outlet glaciers are a component of the peripheral parts of ice domes and may drain the bulk of ice from the dome. They consists of glaciers constrained by rock walls which may push many kilometres beyond the ice dome margin (Figure 4.8 and also Figure 2.5). Gradients are more gentle than the ice dome (Buckley, 1969) and thus within the dome they form depressions. The best example of this is the 700km long and 50km wide Lambert Glacier which creates a significant depression in East Antarctica (Figure 2.7). An impressive series of outlet glaciers cuts through the Transantarctic Mountains. The Beardmore Glacier, well known from the epic polar journeys of Robert Scott, is one of these and is some 200km long and 23km wide and flows at a velocity of around 1m per day (Swithinbank, 1964). Outlet glaciers from the Greenland ice sheet are similar, only they seem to flow at considerably higher velocities. Rinks Isbrae is one of several fast-moving outlet glaciers in West Greenland contributing icebergs to the sea (Figure 4.5).

FIGURE 4.7   Nordøstrundingen, an ice dome in North Greenland. Reproduced with the permission of the Geodetic Institute, Copenhagen.

ICE SHELVES

An ice shelf is a floating sheet of ice derived from snow falling on its surface or from land-based glaciers discharging into the shelf. In Antarctica ice shelves comprise some 7 per cent of the total ice-covered area but make up as much as 30 per cent of the length of the coastline. They occur in embayments in the coastline and the two largest are the Ronne/Filchner Ice Shelf in the Weddell Sea embayment and the Ross Ice Shelf in the Ross Sea embayment. The latter extends some 900 km inland and is some 800 km across. In the Arctic small ice shelves occur along the northern coast of Ellesmere Island (Lyons, Savin and Tamburi, 1971) and in northern Greenland (Figure 4.9).

FIGURE 4.8 Outlet glaciers draining a small ice dome in the Blosseville Kyst area, East Greenland. Note the medial moraines and surface meltwater streams. Reproduced with the permission of the Geodetic Institute, Copenhagen.

The main characteristics of ice shelves have been clearly described by Swithinbank and Zumberge (1965). The seaward margin forms a sheer cliff which rises some 30 m above sea level. This is the feature that gave the Ross Ice Shelf the name of the Great Barrier. The ice thickness near the cliff is commonly 200 m but may thicken inland to as much as 1 000 m. The surface of an ice shelf is virtually flat. The main irregularities are areas of crevassing associated with the hinge line between grounded and floating ice, known as the strandcrack. As tides move the floating ice shelf up and down in relation to the grounded ice there is a great deal of cracking and groaning as ice takes up the stresses.

Some dynamic features of ice shelves are illustrated in Figure 4.6b. Freed of basal friction ice velocities are high and velocities of 0.8—2.8 km per year are common (Swithinbank and Zumberge, 1965). Generally snowfall increases nearer the sea and as a result there is a downward component of movement which is usually accentuated by bottom melting at the ice/sea-water interface (Drewry and Cooper, 1981).

FIGURE 4.9   A floating ice shelf in Osborne Fjord, northern Greenland. The ice shelf ends where the fjord widens and large icebergs have calved off and are surrounded by sea ice. Reproduced with the permission of the Geodetic Institute, Copenhagen.

Periodically, calving removes huge tabular icebergs from the front of the ice shelf (Figure 4.10). The ice islands used as bases by the U.S.A. in the Arctic are derived from the ice shelves of northern Ellesmere Island and Greenland (Figure 4.9), while icebergs up to 144 km long have been observed to break away from ice shelves in Antarctica.

GLACIERS CONSTRAINED BY TOPOGRAPHY

These glaciers are small in comparison to the previous categories and are closely influenced in their shape and direction of flow by the form

FIGURE 4.10   A tabular iceberg derived from an ice shelf being moved from the approaches to McMurdo Station, Antarctica, by three U.S. ice breakers in 1966. U.S. Navy photograph.

of the underlying ground. They are characteristic of glaciated mountains in the Arctic and those few parts of the Antarctic rising above the ice sheet. In view of their relatively limited extent they do not merit much space here, and readers interested in their more detailed characteristics are recommended to read the illustrated glossary of Armstrong *et al.* (1973), or the detailed inventory of Ommanney (1969).

An icefield is an approximately level area of ice which is distinguished from an ice cap because its surface does not achieve the characteristic domelike shape, and because flow is strongly influenced by the underlying topography. Thin icefields are common on uplands in northern Canada. A valley glacier is characteristic of areas of upland topography where the glacier is overlooked by valley walls. Although such glaciers may approach 100 km in length, 10–30 km is more common. They extend over a high altitudinal range for their size (Figure 4.6c). This implies a steeply sloping rock bed and a sharp increase in net accumulation with altitude which may be supplemented even further by valley-side snow avalanches. These characteristics, and the fact that flow is confined to a narrow valley, tend to encourage relatively high ice velocities, when compared to the glacier size (Figure 4.4).

Cirque glaciers occupying armchair-shaped hollows are characteristic of marginally glaciated mountains; for example, northeastern Siberia and the Brooks Range. Cirque glaciers are the best known of an amazingly diverse collection of small glaciers which are restricted to characteristic topographic positions. Any importance is due to their scenic impact on a visitor. They may cling to hollows on steep valley sides, form sheets of ice on rock slopes, nestle in irregular depressions, fringe a coastline or occupy a summit only a few square metres in extent. As a generalization such diverse glaciers are more common in maritime polar environments such as that of the northern Antarctic Peninsula where a combination of low sunshine hours, rime ice (super-cooled water which freezes to a surface on impact), and high snowfall favour glacier growth in a wide variety of topographic situations (Figure 4.11). In continental climates, small glaciers are restricted to exceptionally favourable topographic situations such as shady cirques.

FIGURE 4.11   A variety of glacier forms on the east coast of Adelaide Island, Antarctica.
The U.K. Rothera base is on the point adjacent to the open water in the
background. Photograph copyright of the Directorate of Overseas Surveys.

Interrelationships between glaciers and other systems

From Figure 4.1 it can be seen that there are numerous ways in which glaciers affect or otherwise constrain other physical and human systems. The links between glaciers and the higher-order systems of climate and plate tectonics are complex. Whereas the obvious role of climate is in providing conditions suitable for glacier growth, there are important feedback mechanisms by which glaciers may influence climate. Most of these operate to accentuate the conditions suitable for glacier growth, and reflect the role of increased albedo and altitude of the earth surface in further diminishing temperatures. This is most dramatically illustrated in the large-scale case of the Antarctic ice sheet, for it seems that the world cooling associated with its growth was a vital factor in allowing the subsequent glaciation and cooling of the Arctic where trees had been growing in northern Baffin Island (Andrews *et al.*, 1972). Furthermore, it is likely that the Greenland ice sheet is self-maintaining. In other words if it was removed overnight it probably would not reform under present climatic conditions (Weidick, 1975). Glaciers may affect climate in the accentuation of the surface temperature inversion and associated low temperatures and katabatic winds.

Recently it has become accepted that glaciers can change climate in other ways. In its more extreme theory the view is that glaciers can self-destruct by crossing some threshold and surging. Extremely high velocities associated with surging over the whole ice sheet would soon lower the ice sheet surface. The view of ice sheet surging first suggested by Wilson (1964) and Hollin (1965) for the whole Antarctic ice sheet, now seems very pertinent to ice sheets which are based on bedrock floors below sea level. Ice sheets like that in West Antarctica are examples, and there are theoretical grounds for believing they are potentially unstable (Weertman, 1974; Hughes, 1975). In a nutshell the ice sheet is analogous to an iceberg which is sufficiently thick to be grounded below sea level. Any rise in sea level or thinning of the ice sheet (for dynamic or climatic reasons) could cause more of the ice to float. This process would accelerate and the whole ice sheet disappear into the ocean in a matter of centuries (Hughes, 1975). The effects on world climate are difficult to predict. Hughes has argued for an overall cooling caused by the greater expanse of ice in the southern ocean. On the other hand the lower altitude and oceanic circulation over what is now West Antarctica could raise world temperatures overall. Such a scenario might seem in the realms of science fiction. However, a comparable event took place only 8 000 years ago when the North American ice sheet over Hudson Bay collapsed within a matter of a few centuries

(Andrews and Peltier, 1976). Such an event must have had major climatic implications. There are fears that the high-latitude warming which may result from the increasing amount of carbon dioxide in the atmosphere produced by burning fossil fuels could be sufficient to cause the West Antarctic ice sheet to collapse in the near future (Mercer, 1978a).

The interrelationships between glaciers and other systems is mainly one in which the glaciers provide a constraint on the operation of the other system. This constraint can be viewed as an independent variable and it can play anything from a fundamental to minor role.

The effect of a glacier on plant growth is overwhelming in that nothing but a red alga grows on ice or permanent snow. A very limited exception is forest growing on ice-cored moraine, for example in southern Alaska. On the other hand a supply of meltwater from a glacier during the summer months in drier parts of the tundra is vital in encouraging a rich flora both in density and the number of species represented (Porsild, 1951). Large tracts of glacier form a barrier to plant diffusion and there is a major field of research among botanists into the problems of plant survival in ice-free refuges throughout the Ice Age in the Arctic (Ives, 1974). However, there is a danger in assuming that glaciers are an absolute barrier to plant movement, for several species of plants are found on nunataks in East Greenland surrounded by ice sheet.

Animals are less restricted than plants and Hattersley-Smith (1974) noted, for example, that arctic fox tracks are common on all ice caps and glaciers in northern Ellesmere Island. However, the Greenland ice sheet is a different matter and caribou and musk-oxen on either side of the Greenland ice sheet are independent groups subject to different histories. Caribou and musk-oxen existed side by side in East Greenland in the early years of this century, but caribou were wiped out by a combination of climatic change and hunting. There is no sign of the West Greenland herds replacing the East Greenland herds. As unbelievable as it may seem, arctic foxes have been seen high on the Greenland ice sheet and, indeed, Vibe (1967) has even suggested that they migrate between northeast and northwest Greenland via the ice sheet.

Where glaciers calve into the sea they provide icebergs and smaller ice fragments known as brash ice. The effects of icebergs on the marine system are examined in a subsequent chapter. Here it is sufficient to note that the input is in restricted places. In the Arctic the majority of icebergs are discharged into the seas of western and northwestern Greenland (Figure 4.12). Subsidiary iceberg sources are in the East Greenland fjords. All these icebergs are relatively small in that their size

FIGURE 4.12 Icebergs at the entrance of Umanak harbour, West Greenland. Photograph by
Valerie Haynes.

is limited by characteristic crevasse patterns on outlet glaciers. Much ice
is provided as small fragments. Occasionally an iceberg may measure
1 km across. Ice shelves provide big tabular icebergs. The only sources
in the Arctic are in northern Ellesmere Island and Greenland and these
have calved the ice islands which may be 32 km long and used by the
U.S.A. as Arctic research stations (Koenig *et al.*, 1952). The largest
tabular icebergs and the largest supply is in the Antarctic where ice
shelves are common (Swithinbank, 1969).

The glacier system has an important effect on several earthbound
systems. Where glaciers have extended beyond their present limits in
peripheral Antarctica and in much of the Arctic the landscape of
today bears many signs of glacial modification. Much of my research
in recent years has been devoted to an examination of the characteristics of landscapes of glacial erosion in the Arctic and fuller details can
be found elsewhere, for example in Greenland (Sugden, 1974), in
Arctic Canada (Sugden, 1977, 1978a) and in Antarctica (Sugden and
John, 1976). The crux of this work is that the main landscape features
of the formerly glaciated areas of the polar regions can be interpreted

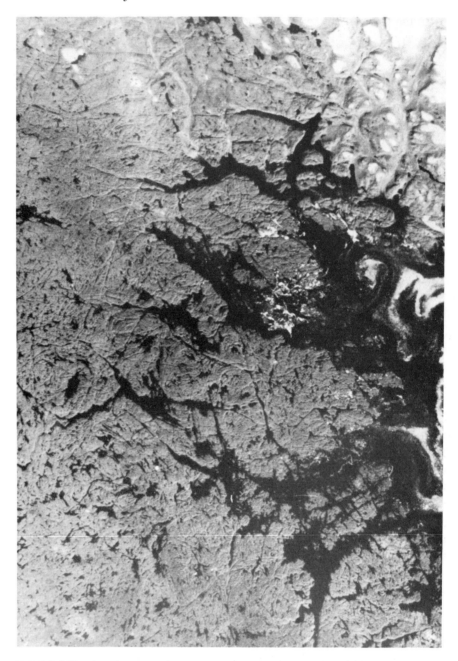

FIGURE 4.13   Satellite image of ice-scoured shield at the head of Cumberland Sound, Baffin Island, which is typical of a landscape of areal scouring. The lake pattern picks out the structural etching by ice. The area measures 165 km from north (top) to south (bottom). LANDSAT-1, N.A.S.A.

in terms of whether there has been modification by glaciers and, if so, what type of modification.

The landscapes may be classified into several types on morphological grounds. Although there is bound to be overlap between the various categories, their recognition does allow some progress to be made in understanding the main processes involved. *Landscapes with little or no sign of glacial erosion* include those areas known to have been covered by ice but which bear no obvious sign of the event; gentle, regolith-covered slopes, river valleys and features such as hill-top tors are characteristic. *Landscapes of areal scouring* everywhere bear signs of glacial erosion (Figure 4.13). Joints, faults and dykes are the master features which are generally eroded to form depressions. In between are upstanding bosses of rocks which are often shaped like roches moutonnées with blocky, craggy, downstream facets and smoothly convex, polished upstream slopes. *Landscapes of selective linear erosion* describe situations where glacial erosion has been confined to the excavation of troughs and where intervening uplands are undisturbed and may support thick regolith and tors (Figure 4.14). Finally, *Alpine landscapes* consist of jagged mountain peaks separated by a network of glacial troughs (Figure 4.15).

The various landscape types may be related to the processes operating at the base of the ice. Landscapes with little or no erosion represent areas where the ice is colder than its melting point and frozen to the bed. Under these circumstances, and provided the ice is free of debris, there is no erosion and the glacier moves solely by internal deformation. Areal scouring is thought to represent glacier sliding, a process which occurs when the basal ice is at the melting point and a film of water may be present. Selective linear erosion represents an intermediate situation where the basal ice over the troughs is at the melting point but where the ice over the intervening uplands is frozen to the bed. Alpine scenery occurs when a mountain massif protrudes above the ice sheet surface and is sculpted by valley glaciers, the common situation in current nunatak areas such as the Ellsworth Mountains in West Antarctica.

Although the above explanation of particular landscape types is merely a hypothesis it does seem to help explain the distribution of the various landscape types, for example in Arctic Canada and coastal Greenland (Figure 4.16). Although there are many variables affecting basal ice temperatures, there are certain generalizations which can be made. Cold-based ice sheets tend to be found in continental climates, especially where the ice is less than around 2500m thick. Thus northern Greenland and the northern Canadian archipelago appear to have escaped pronounced modification by ice and pre-glacial fluvial land-scapes prevail. Warm-based ice occurs beneath the centre of thick ice sheets and on the maritime peripheries of ice sheets. This accounts for the areal scouring around Hudson Bay and in maritime Labrador as well as for the tendency for areal scouring to be dominant in maritime western Greenland rather than in eastern Greenland. Basal ice temperatures tend to be lower over uplands where ice diverges and higher over depressions where ice converges. This helps to explain the landscapes of selective linear erosion associated with all except the most maritime uplands of Greenland and Arctic Canada. In these areas the ice was cold-based except where it was channelled into fjords. Good Alpine relief in Greenland and Arctic Canada is restricted to uplands which are calculated to have been sufficiently high and sufficiently close to

FIGURE 4.14   Well-preserved plateau remnants immediately adjacent to Nordvest Fjord, East Greenland, which are typical of a landscape of selective linear erosion. An outlet glacier from the Greenland ice sheet calves into the fjord. Reproduced with the permission of the Geodetic Institute, Copenhagen.

FIGURE 4.15   An alpine landscape being sculpted by glaciers, Sorte Brae, Blosseville Kyst
area, East Greenland. Reproduced with the permission of the Geodetic
Institute, Copenhagen.

the ice sheet margin to have risen above the ice sheet profile at its
maximum.

In the absence of analysis of the landscapes of glacial erosion in
Eurasia, little can be said about their distribution. Superficially one
notes the areal scouring characteristic of the shield areas around the
Baltic Sea lie beneath the former Scandinavian ice sheet centre. Selective linear landscapes occur in the Sarek uplands of northern Sweden.
Areal scouring occurs in the maritime west. One could predict that
landscape modification by the ice sheets of continental eastern Siberia
would have modified the landscape to a relatively small extent and
large areas of little glacial erosion might exist. In Antarctica the coastal
margins where ice free are characteristic of areal scouring. This would
be expected along a maritime periphery. Selective linear erosion is
characteristic of uplands such as the Prince Charles Mountains. Alpine
relief occurs on most existing nunataks that rise high above the ice
sheet surface.

Landforms of glacial deposition also characterize the Arctic and
Antarctic. As one might expect, moraines, zones of drumlin formation, spreads of till and eskers can be common. However, one major
characteristic of the Arctic is the sparseness of drift when compared

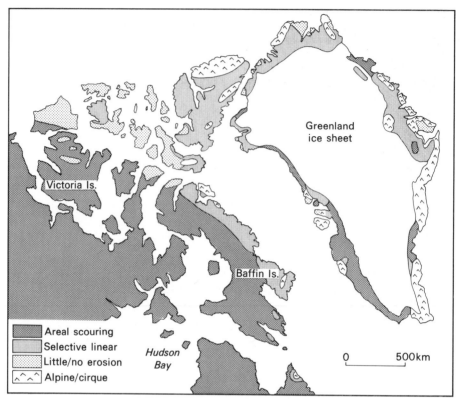

FIGURE 4.16   Distribution of main types of landscape of glacial erosion in Greenland and Arctic Canada.

to mid-latitude landscapes of glacial deposition. In the Arctic and Antarctic a thin veneer of erratic boulders is characteristic. Depositional landforms are relatively rare, although this is not to deny their often outstanding importance for their size; for example eskers as a source of fill.

Finally, it is worth mentioning the relationship between glaciers and adjacent geomorphological systems. Where glaciers end on land most ablation is by melting and the meltwater is discharged by means of streams. Meltwater streams are highly seasonal. They reach their peak discharge in middle to late summer when meltwater is free to flow off the glacier rather than freeze when it comes into contact with snow or ice below 0°C (as is common in spring and early summer until the glacier surface warms to 0°C). Superimposed on this overall seasonal rhythm there are flood periods with durations of several days, diurnal variations and those lasting only a matter of hours or minutes (Paterson, 1981; Østrem *et al.*, 1967; Ziegler, 1972). There are important regional variations in meltwater activity in the polar regions. Meltwater streams are unimportant in the Antarctic, even in Victoria Land, but important in the Arctic where most glaciers end on land. The world's biggest meltwater streams flow from the western edge of the Greenland ice sheet to the sea and are capable of prodigious feats of sediment transport.

The relationship between glaciers and human systems is apparently so obvious that it hardly bears further consideration. Yet it is helpful to examine how glaciers provide both a constraint and a resource. The dynamic nature of glaciers as surface landforms has a curious two-fold effect. Whereas the existence of uniform surfaces provides one of the easiest land surfaces for travel in the world, it is at the same time one of the most difficult in which to maintain more permanent features such as settlements and physical communications. Given an aeroplane with skis, most of the Antarctic and Greenland ice sheets become accessible for landings. On the other hand a building soon becomes buried by accumulating snow and sinks to uneconomic depths and pressures. The higher the accumulation, the quicker the tendency to sink. Thus a base like Halley near the Antarctic periphery has a potentially shorter life than one near the ice sheet centre, for example the Amundsen-Scott base at the South Pole. Also any permanent base is subjected to horizontal movement as the ice deforms. On ice shelves where annual movement can be of the order of a kilometre or so each year, the lack of a fixed site can become important for various scientific experiments which depend on comparable data from year to year. Furthermore, future projects to drill for oil through ice sheets will find this horizontal displacement a major problem.

Ice surface conditions present special problems for ground travel. Crevasses form when the ice accelerates too quickly for the tension to be taken up by deformation within the ice. Zones of differential flow in steep topography or near ice sheet margins present problems well documented in many expedition accounts. A particularly common problem is the crevassing associated with the acceleration of ice as a glacier floats, for example the strandcrack at the landward edge of an ice shelf. Crevasses in this zone of the Filchner Ice Shelf provided a major obstacle for the Commonwealth Trans-Antarctic Expedition 1956—58 (Figure 4.17), whereas tractor trains passing from the Ross Ice Shelf to Byrd Station relied on a specially prepared, bulldozed track across the strandcrack zone. The morphology and strength of the surface snow is an important constraint on surface movement. Sastrugi, or snow dunes, are hard-packed and play havoc with tractor tracks. Such dunes are most common in windy, peripheral areas of ice sheets

FIGURE 4.17   A sno-cat experiencing crevasse trouble during the course of the
Commonwealth Trans-Antarctic Expedition, 1956–58. Reproduced by
permission of the British Antarctic Survey.

where katabatic winds prevail. On the other hand, the absence of wind,
for example in central East Antarctica, means that the snow pack is
soft. Problems of travel in soft snow is one of the reasons why it took
the Russians longer than expected to establish Vostok base in central
East Antarctica in 1956/57. Other areas to avoid where possible are
zones of melting snowpacks such as are common on arctic glaciers in
summer. It is a common experience for an expedition to walk up a
glacier in summer, starting on bare ice near the snout, and to wade
through thigh-deep slush before reaching firmer, unmelted snow in the
upper reaches of the glacier.

Ice edges are dynamic environments with their own particular problems. In Antarctica several bases are sited on ice shelves. Periodic
collapse of the ice front may present problems for offloading ships'
stores, whereas more serious is the problem of the base finding itself
on a detached iceberg. One such abandoned base from the Ross Ice
Shelf, Camp Michigan, was seen in the side of an iceberg in 1972
(Zumberge, 1974). On land, ice edges present problems if disturbed.
One potentially interesting example is the Isua iron ore deposit in
southwest Greenland which lies partially beneath the ice edge (Colbeck,
1974). A plan for open-cast mining by removing the ice overburden has
been proposed and will involve the removal of around $172 \times 10^6 \, \text{m}^3$ of

ice in order to expose the ore. The resultant steepening of the ice edge will accelerate ice flow and a further $7.9 \times 10^6 \, \text{m}^3$ of ice will need to be removed each year to keep the ice from advancing into the pit. Even if undisturbed an ice edge may advance over the years. Thus an ice-free environment close to a glacier snout is a potentially unreliable site for occupation, although mass balance studies will give some fore-warning of a re-advance.

Glaciers in the Arctic and Antarctic provide one very real world resource — fresh water. Nearly 75 per cent of the world's fresh water resources are contained in glacier form in the polar regions (Nace, 1969). The resource is potentially important in two situations. In the Arctic an adequate supply of untainted water is difficult to obtain in liquid form — at least for large centres. Glaciers are compact reser-voirs of fresh water conveniently stored in solid form which have yet to be utilized (Hattersley-Smith, 1974). In the Antarctic icebergs derived from ice shelves provide mobile, stable sources of water. The feasibility of transporting these icebergs to desert areas of the southern hemisphere has been the subject of several symposia (Weeks, 1980), and it seems likely that trials may take place in the future.

Glaciers may yet prove to be important resources in other ways other than for their intrinsic scientific interest. The idea of using glaciers for long-term cold storage for food has been mooted (Potter, 1969). Also, and less welcome, was the proposal in the mid-1970s to use the Antarctic ice sheet as a dump for nuclear waste (Zeller, Saunders and Angino, 1973, 1976). The idea is elegant at first sight. The waste is deposited in the middle on the ice surface. By the time it reaches the periphery, *c.* 100000 years later, the waste is no longer radioactive. However, problems could arise if the container is fractured against the rocky bed, because radioactivity could then contaminate basal meltwater which has a much more rapid transit time and could reach the ice sheet edge in a matter of decades.

Further reading

Armstrong, T. E., Roberts, B. and Swithinbank, C. W. M. 1973: *Illus-trated glossary of snow and ice.* 2nd edn. Scott Polar Research Institute, Cambridge.

Hattersley-Smith, G. 1974: Present arctic ice cover. In Ives, J. D. and Barry, R. G. (editors), *Arctic and alpine environments.* Methuen, London, 195–223.

Mercer, J. H. 1978: West Antarctic ice sheet and CO_2 greenhouse effect: a threat of disaster. *Nature*, 271, 321–5.

Sugden, D. E. 1978: Glacial erosion by the Laurentide ice sheet. *Journal of Glaciology*, 20 (83), 367—91.

Swithinbank, C. W. M. and Zumberge, J. H. 1965: The ice shelves. In Hatherton, T. (editor), *Antarctica*. Methuen, London, 199—220.

Weeks, W. F. 1980: Iceberg water: an assessment. *Annals of Glaciology*, 1, 5—10.

The epic exploration literature gives a vivid impression of life on an ice sheet, for example:

Nansen, F. 1890: *The first crossing of Greenland*. Longman Green, London.

Shackleton, E. H. 1909: *The heart of the Antarctic*. 2 vols. Heinemann, London.

CHAPTER FIVE

The Periglacial System

The second sub-zonal polar environment is 'periglacial'. Although strictly speaking the word means areas 'surrounding glaciers', it has now become accepted as a general description of those non-glacierized areas subjected to cold climates. The distinction between glacial and periglacial environments depends ultimately on a single threshold — whether or not snowfall which accumulates in winter melts in the following summer. If it does melt, then glaciers cannot form and the ground emerges from its winter shroud of snow every summer, albeit briefly. This summer exposure to sunlight is usually sufficient to support plant and animal life. It is the nature of this periglacial environment, its interrelationships with other terrestrial systems and the constraints that it lays upon human activities that form the focus of this chapter.

The periglacial environment is extensive in the Arctic and is virtually uninterrupted by glaciers except in Greenland and the higher parts of the northern Canadian arctic archipelago (Figure 4.2). In Antarctica, however, the reverse is true; the periglacial environment is patchy and restricted to nunataks or occasional 'oases' of ice-free ground around the peripheries of the continent, for example the McMurdo dry valleys of Victoria Land or Bunger 'oasis'. There are several excellent treatises on the periglacial environment and the interested reader wishing to follow up particular aspects will find the books by Washburn (1979) and French (1976) an invaluable guide.

Nature of the periglacial system

Experience of the summer pastures of continental Yakutsk, the wind-swept raw peninsulas of the maritime South Shetland Islands and a remote nunatak in interior Antarctica would be sufficient to convince any traveller of the great range of climatic environments spanned by the periglacial environment. Indeed it might be difficult to see any justification for discussing such varied environments together. And yet there are important characteristics in common — namely the prolonged winter and short summer, the absence of trees and, most important of all, the presence of permafrost.

Permafrost is fundamental in affecting periglacial geomorphology and polar biogeography, and forms the key to understanding the dynamics of the environment. This central role is recognized in Figure 5.1 which portrays the most important links in the system. The flow diagram forms the basic structure of this chapter which tries to explain the characteristics of each 'box' as well as the ways in which the boxes are linked together.

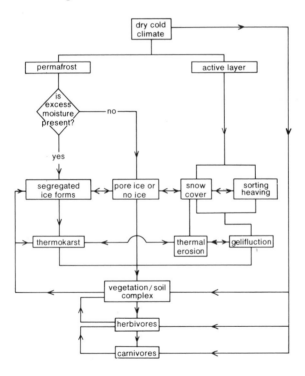

FIGURE 5.1
Flow diagram showing the main links in the periglacial system. The diagram illustrates the structure of this chapter.

Permafrost may be defined as ground where the temperature is continuously below 0°C in both winter and summer. At one extreme this includes any ground which freezes in the winter and survives through the following summer into the next winter; at the other extreme it includes ground which has been frozen for millions of years (Brown, 1970). This definition on the basis of temperature means that permafrost includes ground which contains unfrozen water at temperatures below 0°C, for example ground water with impurities, sea water or water under pressure in small pores. It also includes cold glaciers with ice temperatures below the pressure melting point, although they are not considered in this chapter.

It is helpful to subdivide permafrost into those areas where it is continuous under land areas and those where it is patchy and discontinuous (Figure 5.2). In North America most of the arctic area north

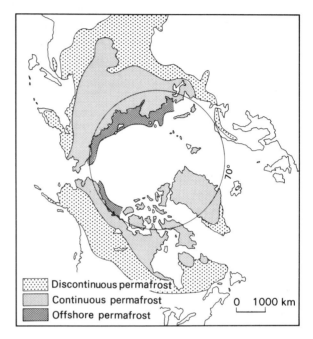

FIGURE 5.2
Permafrost distribution in the northern hemisphere. After Péwé reproduced in Washburn (1979).

▨ Discontinuous permafrost
▨ Continuous permafrost
▨ Offshore permafrost

0   1000 km

of the tree line lies in the zone of continuous permafrost and it is absent only under water bodies which are sufficiently deep to escape freezing each year (Figure 5.3). In the Soviet Arctic permafrost is continuous north of the tree line east of the Ural Mountains. West of the mountains the permafrost is discontinuous. There is a broad

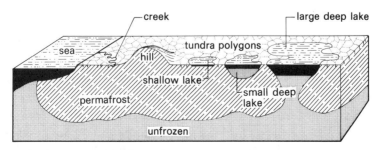

FIGURE 5.3   The distribution of permafrost in the continuous zone, assuming it is in equilibrium with the existing climate. After Lachenbruch (1968).

correlation between these zones and temperature. The southern limit of continuous permafrost coincides with the general position of the −6° to −8°C mean annual air temperature isotherm.

Near the northern coasts of each continent permafrost extends to depths of the order of 500–600 m and it tends to thin southwards until it is about 60–100 m thick at the southern boundary of the continuous permafrost boundary. The significance of such figures was vividly brought home to a merchant in Yakutsk in the early nineteenth century who reputedly was the first to try and sink a well right through the permafrost in search of water. He dug to a depth of 116 m before he abandoned the well (Baer, 1838a)!

Any understanding of permafrost demands an appreciation of the temperature regime (Figure 5.4). The upper layers are subjected to an annual

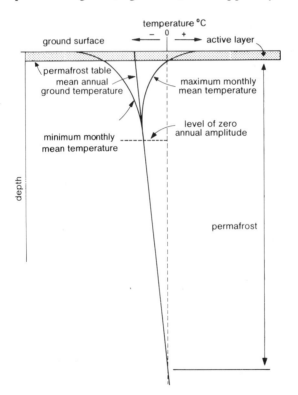

FIGURE 5.4
Typical temperature regime in permafrost. After Brown (1970).

fluctuation in temperatures. The amplitude of the fluctuation is greatest near the surface where it approximates to the contrast between summer and winter temperatures but falls off exponentially with depth until it is negligible at a depth of 6–25 m. The surface layer which thaws each summer is known as the active layer and it is important to distinguish it from the underlying permafrost from which it is separated by the permafrost table. The active layer varies in thickness, but ranges from a depth of 5 m where unprotected by vegetation to typical values of 30–100 cm beneath a coherent vegetation cover and 15 cm within peat (Mackay, 1970). Below the permafrost table the temperature then rises with depth in response to geothermal heat flow. The depth of the permafrost depends on both the absolute temperature and the gradient of this warming with depth which is of the order of $1°C$ per 50 m. If the mean annual air temperature is $-10°C$ then one would expect permafrost to extend to a depth of around 500 m. This rough rule of thumb is of limited use, however, because many other important factors play a role for example, the differing conductivity of the ground from place to place and the contrasts in climatic history. The processes and landforms associated with the active layer are so different from those below the permafrost table that this distinction forms the basis of the periglacial model in Figure 5.1.

Following this diagram further, permafrost is of two fundamental kinds, depending on whether or not there is excess water in the ground. The notion of excess water refers to the volume of water/ice present in the material in comparison to mineral particles. The amount can be calculated by melting a column of frozen sediment and comparing the volume of supersaturated sediment with that of standing water. If, for example, the relative volumes of supersaturated sediment and standing water were 300 and 250 cm^3 respectively, then the excess ice value would be $250/(300 + 250) \times 100 = 45.5$ per cent. This index is important because it is a measure of the amount of settlement that might be expected to occur if the permafrost thaws.

Excess ice forms when ground ice builds up as discrete lenses which physically separate soil particles (Figure 5.5). Thus in Figure 5.1 the features are described as segregated ice forms. Common values of excess ice in unconsolidated sediments lie between 15 and 50 per cent, but in some areas percentages can rise to as high as 80 per cent. This later figure means that four-fifths of the permafrost volume consists of ice. Segregated ice is extremely common in the unconsolidated sediments of the arctic coastal plain of Alaska and northwest Canada and in the lower reaches of the big Russian rivers like the Ob' and Yenisey. Where ice forms in the pore spaces between soil particles it is known as pore ice (Mackay, 1972). In these situations thawing would lead to no settlement of the ground. The amount of pore ice can vary from saturation to nil depending on the environment. Thus much of the arid Brooks Range and the polar deserts have little ice in the ground.

The threshold determining whether or not excess ice exists depends on several factors such as water supply, freezing rate, etc. (Pavlik, 1980). However, one critical factor is the grain size of the sediment

FIGURE 5.5   An ice lens in Sarfartoq, West Greenland.

and it has long been recognized by engineers that fine-grained soils are 'frost-susceptible'. One reason for this is explained by Mackay (1972). In a nutshell, if a saturated sediment such as a sand or gravel is subjected to freezing from the surface, the volume increase as the water changes to ice is compensated for by the expulsion of unfrozen water away from the surface through the large pore spaces. In such a case the freezing plane moves down into the sediment with ice freezing in the pores. In a saturated fine-grained sediment, however, the water is unable to move freely through the pore spaces and escape. Instead a number of imperfectly understood processes cause water to migrate towards the freezing plane and build up a lens of ice.

PERMAFROST LANDFORMS

Segregated ice in permafrost is responsible for several types of landform, most of which are regarded as characteristic of the periglacial environment. Perusal of the fine photographs in Washburn's *Geocryology* (1979) is worth more than a thousand words of description here, and so I will confine this discussion to the three basic forms — mounds, wedges and sheets.

Mounds are characteristic of areas of fine-grained soils where there is sufficient moisture. They come in many sizes and forms with a host of bewildering names in English, Russian and Scandinavian. Fundamentally, the mounds are due to the growth of ice lenses (or hydrolaccoliths) which force the ground above into a boil or mound as they grow. They may be small like frost mounds and typically measure 2 m across and 30 cm high, medium-sized like the palsas which are 10–50 m in diameter and 1–7 m high or big like pingos which can be as much as 300 m in diameter and 60 m in height (Figure 5.6). Further subdivision

FIGURE 5.6   A pingo in northeast Greenland situated near the base of an alluvial fan. Photograph by Svend Wørm.

of these features depends on their source of moisture supply and manner of freezing, both of which are the subject of much debate. Figure 5.7 is an attempt to show the origin of two main forms of pingo, and serves to illustrate the main principles involved. The mounds generally have limited lives. Small ones may last a few years; large ones several thousand years. Eventually, the uplifted ground surface is eroded away or the mound cracks to expose the ice lens, which then melts.

Anyone who is acquainted with the periglacial literature but not periglacial areas might be forgiven for thinking that the scenery is marked by myriads of ice mounds, so great has been the attention

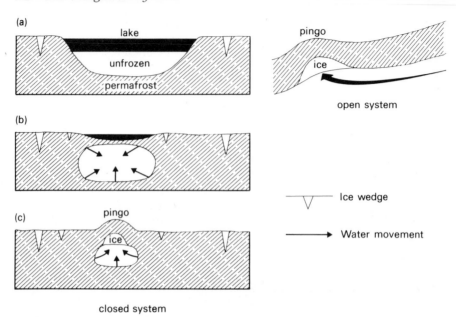

FIGURE 5.7   The origin of pingos. Closed system pingos result when a lake is drained or
infilled and the unfrozen ground (talik) beneath the lake is progressively frozen
from all sides. The resultant volume increase is taken up by the growth of an ice
lens which forces the ground up to form a pingo (Mackay, 1972). Open system
pingos occur when the ice lens is nourished by extraneous water, as for example
in the case of the river fan in Figure 5.6. These basic processes account for most
ice-cored mounds.

devoted to them. However, the sight of a pingo is still a cause for
excitement. They occur frequently enough in the coastal places of
the Soviet Arctic and Alaska and in the Mackenzie areas where Walker
(1973), for example, noted that on a clear day he could see 38 pingos
when standing on the roof of a building at the head of the Colville
River delta, Alaska. Pingos are rarer in more severe arctic environments,
although locally dense clusters may be found, for example on Prince
Patrick Island (Pissart, 1967).

Far more important in terms of areal coverage are ice-wedge polygons (Figures 5.8 and 5.9). Goldthwait (1976) estimated that 20–40
per cent of polar land areas are marked by ice-wedge polygons. The
polygons normally measure 15–40m across. They may have three to
seven sides. Their borders are marked by an uplifted rim separated by
a narrow ditch. In summer their centres may be marshy or even covered
by a pool of water. The rims are underlain by ice wedges. The mode
of formation is indicated in Figure 5.10. In winter when temperatures
are already below freezing and there is a further rapid fall in temperature the ground contracts. As a result it cracks, often audibly. The next

FIGURE 5.8   An ice wedge exposed by thermal undercutting in Alaska. Photograph by
H. J. Walker.

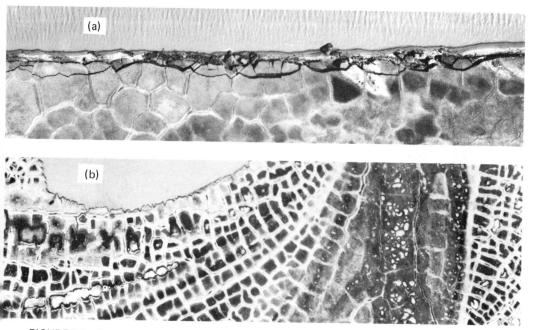

FIGURE 5.9   Ice wedge polygons from the air in Alaska: *(a)* a random pattern experiencing
undercutting by a river and *(b)* a non-random pattern reflecting changes in
former river courses. Photographs by H. J. Walker.

summer the crack fills with water and a vein of ice forms in the perma-frost part of the crack. In following years (not necessarily every year) the ground cracks again along the same line of weakness and the vein grows. Eventually it forms a wedge which can be 8 m wide (Walker, 1973) but which is normally 1–1.5 m wide. Sediment displaced by the

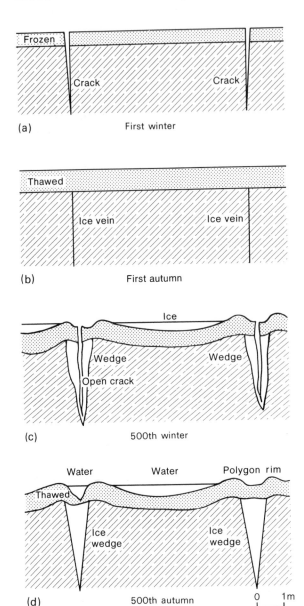

FIGURE 5.10
The origin of ice wedge polygons. After Lachenbruch (1962).

wedge growth is forced up to form the polygon rims on either side. Water is often trapped in depressions between the rims and in the polygon centre. Ice wedges can build up to such a degree that 50 per cent of the upper 3 m of the ground may consist of excess ice (Brown, 1966). The contraction-crack pattern determines the nature of the polygon net. This in turn depends on the sedimentary characteristics of the ground and any lateral temperature gradients. In uniform sediments the pattern can often be demonstrated to be random. Where there is a thermal constraint — for example, the existence of a relatively warm river channel — the polygons are four-sided and two sides are parallel to the river bank.

Although the term ice-wedge polygon is widely accepted, they are part of a family of contraction-crack polygons. As such the cracks need not necessarily be filled with water, but with sand or other debris. Such a situation is common in drier areas, such as in northern Arctic Canada (Pissart, 1968) and in the arid dry valley area of Victoria Land in Antarctica (Péwé, 1959). As a general rule it appears that contraction-crack polygons are actively forming only in areas of continuous permafrost (Péwé, 1969).

In parts of the Arctic the whole land surface is so dependent for its existence on thick sheets of ground ice that if the ice thawed, the land would lie below sea level. Mackay (1971) has drawn attention to these massive icy beds which seem particularly common along the western Canadian Arctic coast but also are common in the extensive alluvial plains of the Yana-Indigirka lowland in the Soviet Arctic (Popov, 1969). The beds include every conceivable gradation between icy muds and pure ice. In Canada some beds consist of ice and are 38 m thick. Others slightly less thick may be traced for many hundreds of kilometres along coastal bluffs. (Mackay 1971) noted that 75 per cent of a 10–15 m high bluff on Hooper Island consists of ice. The origin of these great sheets of ice is not fully clear. In Russia they are held to be due to the growth of ice wedges in an aggrading alluvial environment. However, Mackay believes that they grew in a manner similar to smaller ice lenses, only they had an exceptional supply of water. Perhaps they built up during a period of permafrost aggradation during a fall in sea level during a glacial period. Whatever their origin, these massive icy beds appear to require special environmental conditions and are relatively uncommon elsewhere in the Arctic, at least on a significant scale.

When the ground contains excess ice, thawing leads to subsidence which results in thermokarst (Figure 5.1). Many of the most distinctive forms of the periglacial environment are of thermokarst origin. Perhaps the most common form is the thaw lake. These may be circular or oval in shape. Characteristically they are less than 300 m across although some have diameters of 1–2 km. They are shallow and depths of less than 1 m are characteristic. Maximum depths do not exceed 3–4 m (French, 1976). Thaw lakes originate when an underlying ice mass is exposed and melts. Sometimes they may be caused by an ice lens growing till it becomes exposed at the surface. More commonly it is some chance factor which exposes segregated ice to melting. The lake quickly assumes a circular form as it melts and undercuts the adjacent ice-rich permafrost. Vagaries of wind, vegetation recolonization and ice content of the permafrost cause thaw lakes frequently to migrate and constantly change shape. Eventually the permafrost underlying the lake shore is insulated from the lake water by vegetation or other sediment and the lake is revegetated and filled in. The density of thaw lake depressions and evidence of their evolution is dramatically brought out in Figures 5.11 and 5.12 from the Point Barrow area,

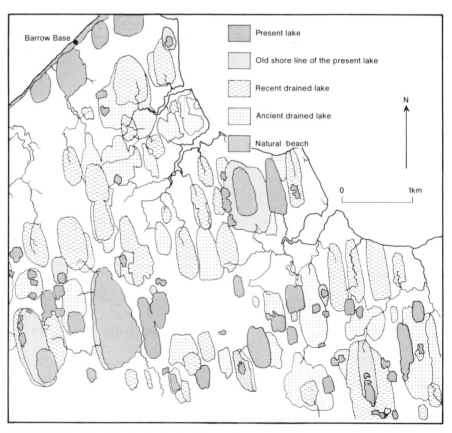

FIGURE 5.11   Thaw lakes and associated depressions near Point Barrow, Alaska. After Carson and Hussey (1962).

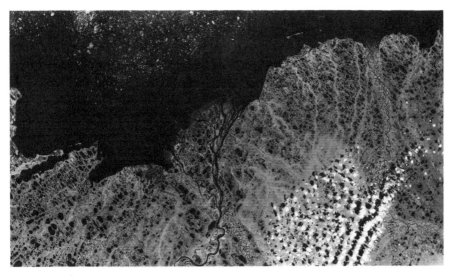

FIGURE 5.12   Satellite image of part of the Alaskan North Slope near Point Barrow, showing
the density of thaw lakes and the Colville River delta. (E—1740—21194—7.)

Alaska. Similar morphology occurs throughout the periglacial zone
whenever there is a flat alluvial plain with excess ground ice. The coastal plain of the northeastern Soviet Arctic is an extensive example of
such a situation.

Other thermokarst features may reflect the shape of the initiating
ground ice. One such example includes polygons with high centres
and low rims. In this case the ice wedges are melting out. In places in
eastern Banks Island all that is left are curious upstanding mounds
(French, 1976).

ACTIVE LAYER PROCESSES AND LANDFORMS

The key to understanding landforms associated with the active layer is
appreciation of the dramatic annual cycle (Figure 5.13). In winter the
ground is frozen solid and insulated beneath snow. In early summer the
surface snow and ice in the upper few metres or centimetres of the
ground melts. Drainage is usually impeded by the underlying permafrost table and the regolith may be saturated. These are the conditions
that make walking indescribably hard work. With each step the ground
vibrates like jelly before giving way beneath your weight and deteriorating into a quagmire. In autumn the ground freezes again from the
surface and to a lesser extent from below. Under these conditions a
number of imperfectly understood processes operate. Their net effect

is to displace unfrozen material (by cryostatic pressure), heave material upwards, and to sort coarse material from fine material.

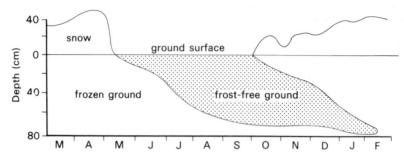

FIGURE 5.13   The annual cycle of snow accumulation and the freezing and thawing of the active layer in Stordalen, Abisko, Scandinavia. After Rydén (1981).

The winter snow cover is intimately associated with active layer processes. In winter the snow forms an irregular blanket whose main effect is to smooth out irregularities in the relief. In the Barrow area it accumulates to a depth of 30 cm on flat ground but varies from a few metres thick in depressions to nothing over crests of mounds (Sellman, 1972). In polar desert areas the cover is much more patchy and many windswept crests are clear of snow. Snow is an excellent insulator (Figure 5.14) and its variable thickness means that the intensity of frost experienced by the underlying ground varies dramatically from

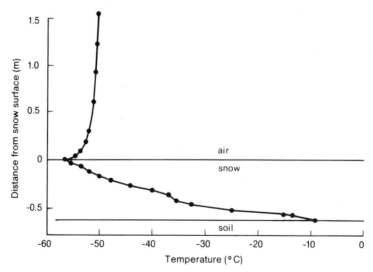

FIGURE 5.14   Temperature gradient through the snow pack in central Alaska showing the effective insulation provided by snow. After Johnson (1953).

place to place. In summer the snow is important as a source of moisture; variations in snow thickness from place to place have important implications on soil moisture.

One of the most common active-layer landforms in the Arctic is a hummock of vegetation with a core of ice or mineral soil which may or may not be exposed at the surface. Hummocks vary from a few centimetres to several metres in height with all gradations in between (Bird, 1967). Perhaps a typical form is a hummock which is 30 cm across, 20 cm high and spaced within 1 m of its neighbours (Figure 5.15). It does not take much imagination to see that such ground is appalling walking country! In spite of their ubiquity the origin of hummocks is far from clear. Some may form from the growth of ice lenses, some from differential frost heaving and some from the expulsion of underlying unfrozen material to the surface during the autumn freeze-up.

FIGURE 5.15   Tundra hummocks, Mesters Vig, northeast Greenland. Photograph by
A. L. Washburn.

Another distinctive active-layer landform is sorted patterned ground. After a lifetime working in polar regions Goldthwait (1976) concluded that perhaps 10–20 per cent of polar land areas are covered with frost-sorted patterns. Although the mechanisms are still unclear it seems that the general process is for coarse stones to move to the surface and outwards from freezing centres. If the centres are dispersed then stone circles form (Figure 5.16). If they impinge on one another then poly-

FIGURE 5.16
Sorted stone circles, South
Shetland Islands, Antarctica.
Photograph by Brian John.

FIGURE 5.17   Detail of sorted polygon net, Thule, Greenland. Ruler is 15 cm long.
Photograph by A. L. Washburn.

gon nets of coarse stones form between the centres (Figure 5.17). In polar regions the sorted polygons are often 2–20 m in diameter, the larger sizes being associated with larger stones. If the sorting takes place on a slope then the polygons are elongated downslope until on slopes steeper than 4–11° they form stone stripes (Figure 5.18).

Frost-sorted ground is best developed in wet sites and common occurrences are on gently sloping valley floors or in depressions on plateau uplands, especially where snowpatches linger through the summer and provide an abundant moisture source. A typical example of such a site and the variety of forms present is given in Figure 5.19. Goldthwait (1976) noted that the soil must be frost-susceptible (with at least 10 per cent silt and clay), as well as containing a fair percentage of large stones. These conditions are most common in areas underlain by glacial till and it may be that the former extent of glaciation is one factor in explaining their broad distribution. However, there are exceptions and sorted patterned ground occurs in beach deposits in the South Shetland Islands, Antarctica (Thom, 1981).

FIGURE 5.18   Sorted stripes, South Georgia, Antarctica. Photograph by Gordon Thom.

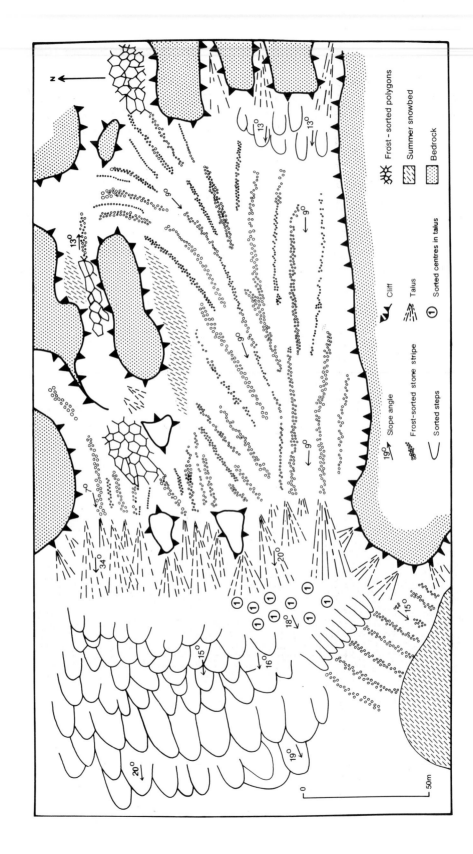

N

Frost - sorted polygons		
Summer snowbed		
Bedrock		

Cliff	Slope angle	19°
Talus	Frost-sorted stone stripe	
① Sorted centres in talus	Sorted steps	

0 ____ 50m

In Figure 5.1 gelifluction is described as a process associated with summer thaw. As such it is used to describe the slow flow downslope of regolith, which has been saturated by melting snow and ice within the active layer. However the term gelifluction also includes the process of frost creep whereby the displacement of regolith on a slope by repeated freezing and thawing will cause particles to migrate down-slope. Washburn (1979) has shown how the critical variable affecting gelifluction is soil moisture content rather than vegetation or gradient. It occurs on slopes as gentle as 1°. Generally gelifluction occurs at rates of 1–5 cm per year, though most of this may occur in a few days. Surprisingly, rates do not increase regularly with increasing slope angle, as is common with most other forms of mass wasting. This may be because steeper slopes tend to be better drained than gentler slopes.

The most common features associated with gelifluction are sheets. Sheets are uniform monotonous expanses of regolith often with angles as low as 1–3° which may be continuous over several square kilometres. They are characteristic of high arctic regions in Canada, where there is low-lying topography covered with water-retentive unconsolidated sediments (French, 1976). Sometimes they may be bounded on the downslope side by a small vegetated riser some 10–50 cm high, but commonly they merge into the valley floor. Other gelifluction features which are more common in steeper terrain are steps (Figure 5.20).

FIGURE 5.20   Sorted steps, South Georgia, Antarctica. Photograph by Gordon Thom.

FIGURE 5.19   (Opposite) An example of the relationship between sorted patterned ground and local topography on Byers Peninsula, Livingston Island, South Shetland Islands, Antarctica. Mapped by Gordon Thom.

Measuring tens of metres across, these may be bounded on their down-slope side by large stones or vegetation. Commonly they occur where snow patches linger into the summer and provide moisture.

LANDFORMS CAUSED BY THE INTERPLAY BETWEEN THE ACTIVE LAYER AND PERMAFROST: THERMAL EROSION

Thermal erosion is a summer process which produces characteristic landforms through the interplay between the active layer processes and permafrost. It involves the melting of permafrost by running water or wind-driven waves or lakes. It is thus distinct from processes which involve subsidence (Mackay, 1970). It may occur if small rivulets expose underlying permafrost. This produces, for example, characteristic beaded streams, where pools open out over the site of ice wedges. It is also a process which contributes to the erosion of river banks in permafrost. A thermo-erosional niche may undercut a river bank at the water-line until the bank collapses (Walker and Arnborg, 1966). Thermal erosion may occur in association with thermokarst subsidence where the slope conditions are suitable for stream development, and rapid gullying may then occur.

VEGETATION AND SOIL COMPLEX

As in other parts of the world the vegetation and soil complex of the periglacial environment is a fundamental part of the land surface system. Its structure reflects both climatic conditions and ground conditions, especially the presence of permafrost and frost-churned soil. In turn it influences the nature of permafrost and frost action in the soil.

Figure 5.21 shows the distribution of three broadly concentric vegetation and soil zones in the Arctic. Low arctic tundra vegetation occurs in the most favourable part of the Arctic and includes northern Alaska, southern Baffin Island, the southern coastal areas of Greenland and a strip in the Soviet Arctic which broadens out in the mountainous northeastern Siberia. Unless bare rock outcrops at the surface, tundra vegetation may completely cover the ground and consists of dwarf shrubs, mosses, sedges, grass and lichen. The appearance of the vegetation at any one place depends on microclimatic and soil moisture variations. Thus on well-drained sites the vegetation consists mainly of dwarf shrubs like willow and birch, berry-bearing members of the *Vaccinium* family, arctic heather (*Cassiope*) and a carpet of moss. This is the attractive and much-photographed tundra community which is

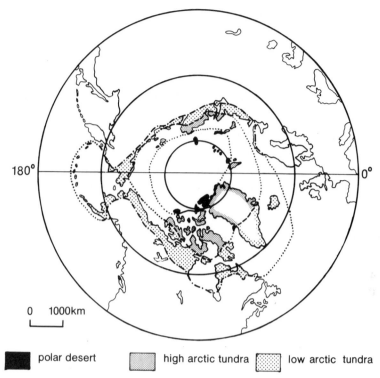

0   1000km

polar desert   high arctic tundra   low arctic tundra

FIGURE 5.21   The distribution of the three major types of arctic vegetation. After Webber (1974).

full of colourful flowers in summer and which dramatically changes to vivid autumn tints of red and yellow in a few days upon the arrival of autumn. In damper areas grasses and sedges dominate and one of the characteristic summer sights is the fluffy cotton balls of *Eriophorum* often giving the landscape the appearance of being dusted with snow (Figure 5.22). In Antarctica a special tundra vegetation exists in the form of thigh-high tussock grass communities (*Poa*) on sub-antarctic islands like South Georgia and the Kerguelen Islands (Figure 5.23). Tedrow (1977) showed that a characteristic weakly podsolic *arctic brown* soil is associated with well-drained sites of the tundra vegetation zone in the Arctic, whereas widespread wet-site soils are represented by a *tundra* soil profile (Figure 5.24).

Towards the pole is the *high arctic tundra* which consists of a more or less continuous cover of herbs and moss with occasional prostrate species. Sedge-moss bogs occur on poorly drained sites. Plant cover is frequently less than 80 per cent and bare rock is frequently exposed at the surface. Tedrow (1977) suggested that much of this zone is characteristically underlain by *sub-polar* soils.

Polar desert vegetation is sparse and consists mainly of scattered cushion plants covering less than 10 per cent of the ground surface. With moss and lichens the plant cover may rise locally as high as 80 per cent, but considerably lower percentages are typical. The intervening rock areas have many characteristics of deserts such as a surface stone layer or desert pavement, and efflorescence of salts at the surface. A comparable vegetation type is found at high altitudes in milder sub-antarctic islands like South Georgia, and is widespread in more southerly

FIGURE 5.22
Eriophorum (cotton grass)
near Søndre Strømfjord,
West Greenland.

FIGURE 5.23   Tussock grass on Harcourt Peninsula, South Georgia. The piece of wood is a a relic from Neumayer's expedition in 1876. The Ross Glacier is in the background. Photograph by Gordon Thom.

islands like the South Shetlands (Greene, 1964). Here only two flowering plants — *Deschampsia antarctica* and *Colobanthus* — exist in sheltered sites. Elsewhere lichens such as *Usnea* add a greenish tinge to the
landscape. Distinctive *polar desert* soils with desert pavements of surface stones occur in the area (Tedrow, 1977).

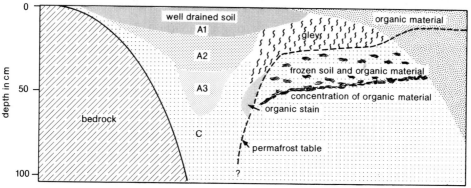

dry tundra profiles with free internal drainage					wet tundra profiles with impeded internal drainage			
desert soils		arctic brown			tundra		bog	
rock land	shallow soils (and regosols)	shallow phase	normal phase	mod.well -drained phase	upland tundra	meadow tundra	half - bog	(full) bog

FIGURE 5.24   Schematic diagram of the major soil characteristics in the Arctic and their
relationship to differing climatic and site conditions. After Tedrow *et al.*
(1958). In effect the dry—wet continuum represents a north—south transect
through the Arctic with site variations superimposed on this general trend.

A variant of polar desert vegetation which is sufficiently distinctive
to merit a special category occurs in continental Antarctica. Here no
flowering plants occur. Instead an extremely sparse cover of lichens
exists and resembles crumbs of dirt on the rocks. A few mosses may
survive in crevices (Greene, 1964). Bare soil surfaces are affected by
weathering crusts, desert varnish, tafoni, salt efflorescences and saline
conditions. Lake Vanda, in Wright Valley, is a highly saline lake of
internal drainage. Soils are characterized by soil-forming processes
lacking an organic component (Tedrow and Ugolini, 1966).

The vegetation and soil complexes of the periglacial system described above are clearly influenced by climatic and geomorphological
conditions. The distribution of vegetation shown in Figure 5.21 is
zonal and reflects the progressive changes as the climate becomes drier,
cooler and the summer shorter towards the pole. Plant cover becomes
less complete and plant height decreases towards the pole. In general

this is a reflection of the decreasing number of species which can survive in severe polar climates. As an example a transect from the mainland Arctic in northwest Canada to northern Canadian arctic archipelago reveals 600 species of flowering plant in the Mackenzie Delta area, 169 species on Banks Island, 100–111 in Melville Island and 49–81 species on the high arctic Prince Patrick and Ellef Ringnes Islands (Bliss and Peterson, 1975). Although factors such as land accessibility and historical development in relation to glacier fluctuations play a role, the trend is primarily climatic in origin. In Antarctica, inaccessibility probably plays a larger role in limiting the number of flowering plants. In the relatively mild South Georgia environment, for example, there are only 50 species of flowering plant and 24 of these are found only on the island (Greene, 1964). The zonal trend in soil formation reflects the gradation of several climatically controlled processes. Podsolization and the amount of organic material decrease towards the pole, while calcification and alkalization/salinization increase towards the pole (Tedrow, 1977).

The vegetation that does persist in the Arctic has some general characteristics which are well adapted to the climatic environment, a link shown on Figure 5.1. Many physiological adaptations are discussed by Billings (1974) and some are contained in Table 5.1. From this it can be seen that the main characteristics such as low growth forms, rarity of annuals and predominance of perennials are features well adapted to a highly seasonal climate with a cold winter and short summer.

The vegetation patterns in the polar regions are also strongly influenced by landforms and landforming processes. In high latitudes slope angle and orientation can make a difference to local climate equivalent to several degrees of latitude. Thus plants typical of the low arctic may thrive in isolated sun traps in the far north. The two species of flowering plant in the South Shetland Islands, Antarctica, are invariably restricted to slopes orientated towards the maximum insolation. The availability of moisture is a key control on plant distribution and verdant patches are frequently associated with wet areas downslope of snow patches or alongside stream channels. Alluvial landforms are frequently underlain by ground ice and this can cause moss-sedge tundra to occur in otherwise arid areas. For example, Babb and Bliss (1974) record moss-sedge tundra in the polar desert of the Queen Elizabeth Islands. On a small scale, mounds and polygons influence vegetation patterns. In East Greenland dwarf birch is often associated with hummocks while the intervening hollows are covered with sedge plants. On the arctic slope of Alaska the upraised rims of polygons may

TABLE 5.1   *Some adaptations of arctic vegetation to polar climates (after Billings, 1974)*

1	Prostrate shrub	insulation beneath snow, warmer micro-climate
2	Cushion plants	warm micro-climate (cushion up to $25°C$ warmer than air)
3	Annuals rare	growing season too short for full cycle
4	Herbaceous perennials common	large underground root structure, store food over winter
5	Reproduction often by rhizomes, bulbs or layering	avoids reliance on completing flower–seed production cycle
6	Pre-formed flower buds	maximizes time for seed production
7	Growth at low positive temperatures	
8	Optimum photosynthesis rate at lower temperatures than most plants	maximizes length of 'growing season'
9	Frost resistance	true of flowers, fruit and seeds
10	Longevity	suitable for 'opportunist' life style; lichens may live for several thousand years
11	Drought resistance	suitable for rock surfaces or arid climates

play the same role as the hummocks and are picked out by dwarf shrubs, unlike the boggy vegetation of the polygon centres. Frost-churned soils are difficult for root establishment and areas of active soil movement are colonized by species able to tolerate the disturbance.

Since all animal life is dependent upon green plants, it is useful to compare the primary productivity of arctic vegetation with that elsewhere in the world. Any comparison gives a maximum 'yield' for arctic areas. The problem has been discussed by Webber (1974). From Table 5.2 it can be seen that the productivity of the three vegetation types is low by world standards. The richer areas of the tundra are comparable with temperate grasslands while poorer tundra areas are similar to hot desert scrubs. Values are far below those of the world's forested areas. Nevertheless primary productivity on a single day during the peak growing season may equal that of more southerly climes.

TABLE 5.2   *Net primary productivity of the Arctic compared with other world vegetation zones (after Lieth, 1975) in g m^{-2} per year*

Polar desert	0—1
Arctic tundra	100—400
Temperate grassland	100—1500
Desert scrub	10—250
Tropical rain forest	1000—3500
Warm temperate mixed forest	600—2500
Boreal forest	200—1500

HERBIVORES AND CARNIVORES

Animal life is an integral part of the periglacial system and is influenced by vegetation characteristics as well as directly by climate. To portray these links on Figure 5.1 is not to suggest that these two factors are the only controls on the animal part of the ecosystem. Indeed the most fundamental feature of land animal distribution in the polar regions, the lack of land vertebrates in the Antarctic, is probably due to inaccessibility. Once introduced to South Georgia by whalers, reindeer and brown rats found the environment satisfactory and their thriving population of today has the dubious honour of comprising the only 'wild' Antarctic land vertebrates (Stonehouse, 1965).

Figure 5.25 is a simple representation of the vertebrate food web in

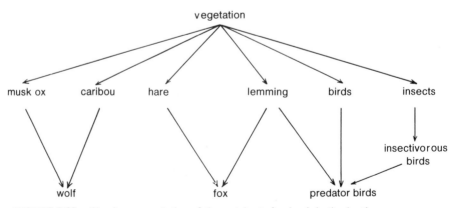

FIGURE 5.25   Simple representation of the vertebrate food web in the Arctic.

the Arctic. With few exceptions the distribution of vertebrates is circumpolar. The caribou occurs wild in North America and in its domesticated form as reindeer in Asia. It is known for its migration in huge numbers. The musk-ox usually roams the tundra in groups of around 12, although lone bulls may often be encountered. The shaggy beasts have long hair but also a shorter woollen coat (Figure 5.26). This wool is shed in summer and makes excellent socks. When approached, a herd will draw up into a phalanx with the animals facing outwards and shielding their young behind them. If approached too closely the bull may charge and is now notorious for its speed over the first 10 m! Among other herbivores the magnificent chatter of the vast number of geese, for example in East Greenland, is worthy of special mention.

FIGURE 5.26   Musk-oxen in northeast Greenland. Photograph by Svend Wørm.

Carnivores include the snowy owl, the oft-maligned Arctic wolf and the Arctic fox. The latter, historically much in demand for its white winter coat, is a dull colour in summer. It is a camp-follower par excellence and may often be heard around a camp supplementing its diet of lemmings and small birds with soap and leather bootlaces (Figure 5.27). No description of carnivores is complete without mention of the infuriating man-eating beast, the mosquito (Figure 5.28). Many an Arctic visitor has regretted nature's apparent forgetfulness in not supplying a greater number of insectivorous birds!

The main characteristics of arctic land life have been discussed by

FIGURE 5.27   Arctic fox scavenging, northeast Greenland. Photograph by Svend Wørm.

FIGURE 5.28
Mosquitoes in West Green-
land encountered by
members of an Oxford
University Expedition in
the late 1930s.

Hoffman (1974). The first characteristic is its simplicity. Very few species are involved and, for example, at Point Barrow in Alaska there are only brown and collared lemmings, caribou (until recently), and 18 species of birds and insects. In a wider perspective, Dunbar (1968) notes that of 8600 bird species in the world only 70 breed in the Arctic, while of 3200 mammals in the world only 23 occur north of the tree line. Also there are no reptiles.

There are often large numbers of individuals of particular species, and it is the sight of immense herds of caribou migrating, or of lemming explosions well known to Walt Disney fans, that give the impression of a rich fauna. However, Hoffman (1974) argued that more rigorous census techniques reveal relatively low densities. For example, caribou densities in Arctic Canada average 0.07/ha (Thomas, 1969). There is good evidence that population numbers of individual species vary cyclically. The 3—7-year lemming cycle is well known and is a dramatic case of violent fluctuations which has repercussions for their predators. Fur traders dealing with Arctic fox furs have long known of a similar cycle in foxes. The cause of such population fluctuations is not fully understood but it seems to be an inherent characteristic of simple ecosystems (Dunbar, 1968).

The influence of polar climate on arctic fauna has been a source of much debate in the literature. Table 5.3 lists some of the main features. In a nutshell one can point to the low number of species able to thrive in the polar environment, low mean densities, the tendency for birds to migrate, the well-insulated coats of large animals and active winter life beneath snow for smaller rodents. Hibernation is not common, probably because ground temperatures are too low.

TABLE 5.3 *Some faunal adaptations to polar climate*

1. Severe climate	low number of species low mean densities
2. Low temperature	high quality fur insulation increased metabolic rates
3. Snow	life below snow patch for smaller animals large herbivores favour soft/thin snow
4. Short summer	birds migrate Breeding cycle compressed large clutch/litter size

Vegetation and geomorphological conditions affect the fauna in many ways. The low productivity of arctic vegetation provides a relatively low upper limit to the food supply. The distribution of vegetation has effects at many scales. The zonal decrease in vegetation northwards is mirrored by a decrease in faunal densities and also by a decrease in the number of species. On a regional scale the extent and distribution of lush vegetation is important. In the polar desert areas of the northern Canadian archipelago Babb and Bliss (1974) note that musk-oxen depend on just a few oases of rich vegetation associated with sedge-moss tundra. At the scale of a few metres, lemmings in the arctic plain of Alaska live and burrow in the rims of ice-wedge polygons where soil and vegetation conditions are suitable. Also the very abundance of lakes in areas underlain by ground ice is mirrored by the fact that over half the migrant birds to the Arctic are aquatic.

FEEDBACK

So far Figure 5.1 has been followed in one direction as a one-way system. However, in reality the system is characterized by powerful feedback loops. This means that change in some relatively minor aspect of the system can have profound repercussions in other more fundamental parts of the system. This is not peculiar to the periglacial system. However, one feature that is unique is permafrost and a slight temperature variation can cause it to thaw. The fact that water changes phase at the threshold of $0°C$ means that a small change can have dramatic implications.

The key variable is vegetation. It insulates the permafrost from winter cold and summer thaw and thus influences the thickness of the active layer. If the vegetation is removed or disturbed the usual effect is for the ground to lose its insulation properties and for the summer thaw to extend deeper than usual. This deepening of the active layer becomes important when the permafrost holds excess ice, for the ground surface slumps in response (Figure 5.29). This then aggravates the initial disturbance. Vegetation disturbance is the norm in the natural periglacial system. It can be destroyed by fire, by erosion, by the spread of thaw lakes or by over-grazing. This latter aspect has not often been discussed in terms of permafrost degradation but it is likely to play a role when populations of certain herbivores peak in a boom year (Hoffman, 1974). Vegetation also recolonizes newly exposed ground, for example around the shores of old thaw lakes. Here the active layer will thin and the permafrost table will rise. Such situations of aggrading permafrost are stable, and seem to apply whenever vegetation is re-establishing itself. It is important to emphasize that this change in the thickness of the active layer has a minimal effect on ground which contains no excess ice.

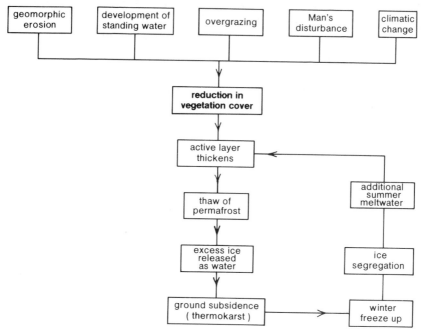

FIGURE 5.29   The effect of reduced vegetation cover in causing ground subsidence in ice-rich ground. Some factors leading to a reduction in vegetation are indicated.

Interrelationships with other systems

GEOMORPHOLOGICAL SYSTEMS

So far there has been little mention of fluvial, coastal, aeolian or mass wasting processes (other than gelifluction). This is not to imply that these processes are not important in the polar regions. Rather, because they are ubiquitous, there seems no point in describing their polar occurrences. However, there are ways in which these processes interact with the polar environment to produce unique landforms and processes. It is the purpose of this section to highlight these unique relationships.

Rivers whose basins lie wholly within the Arctic hold hardly any water in winter. One hundred and forty years ago Professor Baer told the Royal Geographical Society in London how Admiral Wrangel made this discovery in Russia:

He was riding [to the north of Yakutsk, in about 65°N] over the ice of a pretty considerable river, when the ice suddenly gave way, and his horse sank; he was himself saved by being thrown on the ice, at the moment his horse fell. He was lamenting the loss of his horse to the Yakutzkers who accompanied him, as he knew not how to get another when they laughed, and assured him they would soon get his horse back, and with a dry skin too. They got some poles, and broke away the ice, under which the bed of the river was perfectly dry, as well as the horse and his pack. (Baer, 1838b).

Such a situation applies to a river like the Colville in Alaska where in winter sea water flows 50 km *up* the river from the delta (Arnborg *et al.*, 1966). Longer rivers such as the Ob' and Mackenzie, whose headwaters lie in lower latitudes, maintain flow throughout the year, though it is much diminished.

During the freeze-up, while water is still flowing down the channel or through the ground, it is common for *icings* to form. These are extensive sheets of ice which build up as water is forced up to the surface where it freezes. Icings may measure several kilometres across and completely cover the surface vegetation.

The dominant feature of arctic rivers is their intense seasonality of flow as the snow, ice and surface of the active layer thaws (Figure 5.30). In the Colville River the break-up period lasts 3 weeks and accounts for 42 per cent of the annual discharge. On smaller arctic rivers the break-up flood may account for 90 per cent of the discharge (McCann *et al.*, 1972). Discharge is generally low during the summer but very sensitive to rainstorms, because the permafrost and relatively scanty vegetation means that there is little interception of rainwater. Since break-up floods begin when ice occupies much of the river channel and covers its bottom there is a complicated relationship between sediment load and discharge. In effect sediment peaks later than discharge since bedload cannot be picked up until ice is removed from the river bed. A curious and unique relationship occurs at the delta since much of the flood debris is deposited onto the surface of sea ice which has not yet broken away from the coast (Reimnitz and Bruder, 1972). Thermal erosion of river banks is of little importance during break-up since water temperatures are close to 0°C. Later in the summer, however, the water temperatures may rise as high as 19°C (Gill, 1972), and then thermal erosion becomes important and causes bank collapse (Figure 5.9a).

The coastal geomorphology of polar regions is marked by the presence

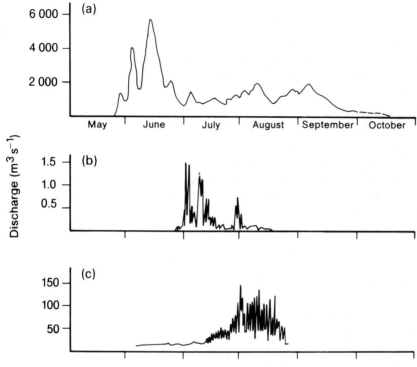

FIGURE 5.30   The seasonal run-off regimes of periglacial rivers: *(a)* Colville River, Alaska (1962) and *(b)* the small Jason's Creek, Devon Island (1970) compared with the glacial meltwater stream from Lewis Glacier (1963). After Church (1974).

of ice — ice on the sea, ice in the ground and under the beach and ice on the beach. Although normal coastal processes control the basic coastal forms one can point to several characteristic features (John and Sugden, 1975). Sea ice can have a direct effect by forming ice-pushed ridges as it is driven on to the beach and an indirect effect by reducing wave energy on the beach. Ground ice onshore has the effect of cementing unconsolidated deposits until it thaws when exposed to wave action and summer air temperatures. This thermal degradation is rapid and retreat of 5 m high ice-rich cliffs in Alaska may exceed 10 m per year (Lewellen, 1970). In the Soviet Arctic Zenkovich (1967) mentions rates of shore retreat in excess of 50 m and even 100 m per year. Characteristic slump forms are associated with such shores. Ice on the beach itself has various effects. Ice blocks incorporated within the beach may melt out or form karstic beach forms. Permafrost under the beach may inhibit permeability and locally intensify backwash down the beach. In winter in inter-tidal areas an ice-foot freezes firmly to the beach and effectively protects it from all wave action.

HUMAN ACTIVITIES: RESOURCE VERSUS FRAGILITY

The periglacial system is a resource and a constraint for human activities. Its main resource is as an area of pastureland comparable to mid-latitude grasslands. This resource was utilized in the Eurasian Arctic by cultures based on herding of reindeer. In the North American context herding did not take place and exploitation of the caribou and musk-oxen was by hunting. Even so, only one Inuit group in the Barren Lands of Keewatin depended wholly on the caribou. For all its inconspicuous size the Arctic fox became an important resource for fur trappers. With regard to modern industrial society the periglacial system is a resource in that it provides good land access to minerals beneath the ground. In many areas the abundance of lakes makes summer travel by float plane possible, whereas the absence of trees allows winter travel over frozen tundra. The presence and alignment of long rivers like the Mackenzie, Ob', Yenisey and Lena is an important resource. In summer they can be used by barge traffic; in winter their frozen surfaces can be used as roads for tracked traffic — so long as one avoids the thin ice discovered by Wrangel!

In the popular mind the resources mentioned above have been obscured by the view that the arctic tundra is fragile and extremely difficult to exploit without leading to catastrophe. So widespread is this view that it must be regarded as a major constraint to human activity. One only has to think of the prolonged 7-year hassle over the trans-Alaska oil pipeline completed in 1977 to recognize the reality of the constraint. The origin of the 'fragile tundra' view is difficult to pin down but it seems to involve two components — firstly, that the ecosystem is highly susceptible to interference, and secondly, that permafrost is easily disturbed, with catastrophic and long-lasting results.

Argument that the ecosystem is fragile rests on the common-sense view that where few species are involved, the decline of one species would have a greater than normal effect. Dunbar (1968) makes the point that many arctic lakes have only one species of herbivore and one carnivore. In such a case pollution which killed the herbivore would kill off all life. Also it has been seen that lemming cycles have a direct effect on the number of their predators such as owls and foxes. When lemmings are in short supply there is no adequate alternative food supply for the predators. An additional factor is the low density of animal life. This is probably why it has been so easy for indigenous people armed with rifles to exterminate caribou over relatively large areas. A further factor is the longevity of plants and some animals which implies that they will take a long time to recover from disturbance.

Whereas little evidence contradicts any of the above, one must distinguish between fragility and oscillation. The arctic ecosystem is one that is characterized by quite violent natural oscillations such as the lemming cycle. The fact that it recovers from such fluctuations demonstrates its *resilience*, not its fragility (Dunbar, 1973). These fluctuations are far more violent than are likely to follow even extravagantly thoughtless exploitation. All factors mentioned in the previous paragraph contribute towards an ecosystem which oscillates around some equilibrium. Whereas Man's interference may easily cause an oscillation, it is far from certain that his activities will cause lasting damage. Having said this, one important proviso is that the ecosystem depends on great spatial range for its ability to recover from disturbance (Dunbar, 1973). It becomes important therefore not to parcel up the tundra into small units.

The disturbance to permafrost is a much more real problem and difficulties are superbly illustrated by Ferrians *et al.* (1969). The main problem is the destruction of ice-rich permafrost by heat from buildings, pipelines, etc., and from changes to the surface vegetation by bulldozing, driving across frozen tundra with wheeled vehicles, etc.

If the ground contains excess ice then the heat of a building on the surface will gradually melt the permafrost and after a few years the building will buckle or sink. If the ice content of the ground varies from place to place, as it commonly does in the case of ice-wedge terrain, then the settlement will occur differentially. Similarly a hot pipeline, whether filled with oil, hot water or sewage, will thaw a cylinder in permafrost around it (Lachenbruch, 1970). Again differential thawing and settlement in ice-rich sediments could lead to fracture. Roads and railways laid on the ground do not provide the insulation qualities of vegetation and as a result of the thickening of the active layer the underlying ice might melt, causing irregularities. Such problems may be averted by adopting certain building techniques. The simplest is to place warm buildings on pads of gravel which are sufficiently thick to insulate the underlying permafrost from the heat. Gravel is commonly used for air strips and roads, railways and light or temporary buildings. At Prudhoe Bay oilfield the road gravel is over 1.25 m thick (Sharpe, 1975). A more permanent solution is to build on stilts or piles which are frozen into the permafrost (Figure 5.31). The air circulates beneath the building and insulates the ground from the heat of the building. Occasionally the air beneath the building may be refrigerated. Often piles are combined with gravel, as at Prudhoe

Bay. The gravel pads provide a working surface for erecting and maintaining the buildings. The hot-oil pipelines (60°C) are likewise mounted on 0.6m high piles in ice-rich permafrost (Figure 5.32).

FIGURE 5.31   Building oil installations on piles embedded in permafrost, Prudhoe Bay, Alaska. For scale, the tank is being carried on two trailers side by side.

Unwitting or witting disturbance of vegetation by Man's activities can upset the thermal regime of the permafrost and cause slumping along the lines indicated in Figure 5.29. Figure 5.33 is a diagrammatic section to show the main effects of vegetation disturbance by a bulldozer. Such tracks were common during exploration for oil in the Arctic and many are visible from the air some 20 years later. They are undoubted blemishes when seen from the air, but one feels that too much has been made of it. Often from the ground the 'scars' are invisible and a new equilibrium with new vegetation cover has formed in only 5 years (Mackay, 1970). Exceptions to this are when running water has gone down the line of disturbance and contributed to rapid thermal erosion (Kerfoot, 1973). It is clear that the landscape can be changed visually by disturbance in ice-rich areas. In such a case it is

FIGURE 5.32   Pipes leading from producing wells to gathering centres where gas and water are separated from crude oil. They are mounted on piles above a gravel pad. Sohio photograph.

advisable to try and avoid the most susceptible areas. A great deal of interest has been shown in this in Canada recently and a significant achievement in 1972 was the production of a series of 'Terrain classification and sensitivity' maps at a scale of 1:250 000 for the proposed Mackenzie Valley pipeline. Criteria used for mapping include soil grain size, excess ice content and active layer conditions. These maps, as well as others, suggest that the Mackenzie Delta area is particularly sensitive. Elsewhere in the Canadian Arctic and particularly in the northern islands susceptible areas are highly localized and most areas are not underlain by ice-rich ground. Extensive areas in the Canadian north are not regarded as being particularly sensitive (Ives, 1970; Babb and Bliss, 1974). Other sensitive areas in the Arctic include northern Alaska and the lowlands bordering the Laptev Sea in the Soviet Arctic.

Another constraint provided by permafrost on northern development concerns frost heaving in the active layer, which can lift piles out of the ground. Areas particularly vulnerable to this occur beside large rivers where there may be abundant water for ice lenses to build up. Bridge piers are particularly susceptible. Modern building practice is to ensure that the pile is embedded sufficiently deeply in permafrost to resist upfreezing within the active layer. As an example at Prudhoe Bay the piles are sunk to a depth of *c.* 11m (Sharpe, 1975). These piles are expensive and in the early 1970s cost around $3 000 each to install.

Services are difficult to provide in permafrost. Water pipes and

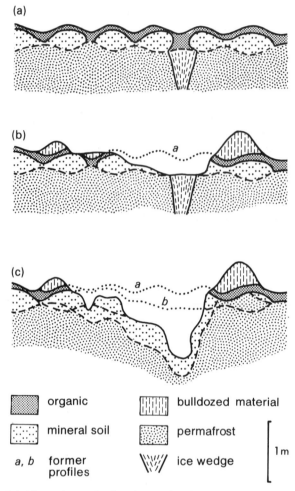

(a)

(b)

(c)

	organic		bulldozed material
	mineral soil		permafrost
a, b	former profiles		ice wedge

1 m

FIGURE 5.33　Subsidence due to the disturbance of surface vegetation by a bulldozer. After Kerfoot (1973).

sewers cannot be laid underground without special protection and insulation. One solution has been to build pipes in utilidors above ground and to insulate them all. A central heating pipe is often used as a source of heat. The problem with surface utilidors is that they are subjected to extremely low air temperatures and are expensive to run and maintain. There is now a tendency to adopt a practice more common in Russia, which is to insulate the pipes and bury them. If ice-rich soil can be avoided and there is no subsidence, then there is the advantage that the pipes are subjected to less severe temperatures than at the surface. Also the towns or villages are more attractive visually.

Water supply presents certain difficulties — as our merchant digging a well in Yakutsk discovered! Lakes deep enough to escape freezing are a source of year-round water, but these are not always available. A number of settlements still rely on the melting of ice in winter. Waste disposal is a problem because rubbish does not decompose in permafrost. The same problem applies to corpses! It is as common to unearth perfectly preserved human corpses in permafrost as it is to find mammoth corpses several thousand years old.

This brief survey of constraints on human activities presented by the periglacial system isolates ice-rich ground as presenting the most difficult environmental problem. Yet these problems are surmountable at the cost of preventative measures. Some of the wilder fears about the fragility of the environment seem unfounded. Thus in terms of human activities the environment can be seen as representing a higher-than-average cost surface, with highs most pronounced in areas of ice-rich sediments.

Further reading

Bliss, L. C., Cragg, J. B., Heal, D. W. and Moore, J. J. (editors) 1981: *Tundra ecosystems: a comparative analysis.* Cambridge University Press, Cambridge.

Dunbar, M. J. 1973: Stability and fragility in Arctic ecosystems. *Arctic*, 26, 179–85.

Ferrians, O. J., Kachadoorian, R. and Greene, G. W. 1969: *Permafrost and related engineering problems in Alaska.* United States Geological Survey Professional Paper 678.

French, H. M. 1976: *The periglacial environment.* Longman, London.

Greene, S. W. 1964: Plants of the land. In Priestley, R., Adie, R. J., and Robin, G. de Q. (editors), *Antarctic Research.* Butterworth, London, 240–53.

Mackay, J. R. 1972: The world of underground ice. *Annals of the Association of American Geographers*, 62 (1), 1–23.

Sharpe, T. A. 1975: Problems of ice and the effect of low temperatures on production installations on land. In Malaurie, J. (editor), *Arctic oil and gas: problems and possibilities.* Mouton, Paris, 268–86.

Washburn, A. L. 1979: *Geocryology: a survey of periglacial processes and environments.* Edward Arnold, London.

CHAPTER SIX

The Polar Marine System

Introduction

The aim of this chapter is to describe and explain the polar marine environment, the third major system encountered in the polar regions. Compared to other oceanic environments the distinguishing feature of the polar marine system is the presence of a thin lid of cold surface water and floating sea ice for at least part of the year. Both characteristics are an expression of the cold climate and they present a unique set of problems and interrelationships, some of them obvious and some less so. In the Antarctic the Antarctic Convergence marks the northern limit of cold polar water. Using this as the northern boundary, the Antarctic extends into latitudes 62–47°S some 1500–2250km from the continental shore and its areal extent is very approximately four times the size of the continent itself (Figure 1.8). In the Arctic the polar marine environment is centred on the ocean surrounding the pole. The exact position of the boundary with the Atlantic and Pacific oceans varies with the criteria selected. One of the most convenient and meaningful boundaries is provided by the mean maximum extent of sea ice. As such the system includes the Bering Sea and the Sea of Okhotsk where sea ice extends into latitudes as far south as that of France. In the Atlantic sector, however, the boundary is pushed some 3750km further north into the vicinity of Svalbard. The arctic marine system is approximately one-third the size of the antarctic equivalent.

Figure 6.1 shows the main components of the polar marine system and their interrelationships. Oceanic circulation, sea ice and the ecosystem are the main subsystems, whereas polar climate and the distribution of land and sea are the major independent variables affecting the total system. In addition to the direct effect of climate and topography on each of the subsystems, there is also an indirect effect in that they influence the oceanic circulation which in turn influences the sea-ice system and ecosystem. There are complex inter-linkages; for example the relationship between marine life and the unique

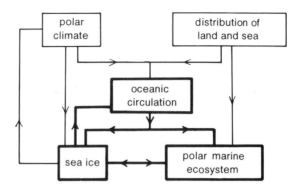

FIGURE 6.1
The polar marine system (heavy lines) and its relationship to the external variables of climate and the distribution of land and sea.

environment provided by sea ice. Also there are important feedback effects with the oceanic circulation and sea-ice extent influencing climate and the existence of sea-ice cover affecting oceanic circulation. It is the purpose of this chapter to focus in turn on each of the three main components of the polar marine system and to explore their interrelationships. Finally, it is proposed to look at the relationships between the polar marine system and both natural terrestrial systems and human systems for which it can be viewed both as a constraint and a resource.

Oceanic circulation

ARCTIC

The Arctic Ocean consists of Atlantic Ocean water covered with a 200 m thick cap of less saline, colder water (Figure 6.2). These characteristics are markedly similar from place to place in the Arctic and point to a stable situation with little vertical exchange.

The salinity of the surface water is lowest (27 parts per thousand) in the vicinity of the large Siberian rivers and generally increases to values

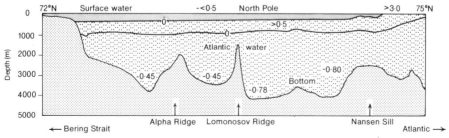

FIGURE 6.2   The water masses of the Arctic Ocean. After Coachman and Aagaard (1974). The numbers refer to temperatures in °C.

of 33 to 34.5 parts per thousand towards the Atlantic Ocean. Its temperature is generally close to the freezing point of saline water and varies from −5°C to −1.9°C as the salinity varies. In ice-free seas in summer the temperature may rise to several degrees above freezing. The characteristics of the surface layer vary with depth and from place to place according to its origin. Thus in the Amerasian Basin, Bering Sea water forms the surface water below a depth of 30–50m, and indeed may be differentiated according to whether it traversed the Bering Straits in summer or winter (Treshnikov and Baranov, 1973). In the Eurasian sector the water consists mainly of river water which mixes with Atlantic water upwelling from the submarine canyons incised into the Asian continental shelf (Coachman and Aagaard, 1974).

Atlantic water underlies the surface water and comprises 90 per cent of the water in the Arctic Ocean. It is uniformly more saline (34.8–35 parts per thousand) and is usually subdivided into two categories on the basis of temperature. The upper layer is above 0°C and extends from depths of *c*. 200m to around 1 000m. Temperatures here may be as high as 3.0°C near Svalbard but generally the highest temperatures are 0.5 to 1.5°C. The lowest layer, referred to as Atlantic bottom water, accounts for 60 per cent of the ocean and fills the Arctic Ocean basin below 1000m, the approximate depth of the threshold leading into the Atlantic. Temperatures are everywhere below 0°C and generally −0.4 to −0.5°C in the Amerasian Basin and −0.8°C on the Eurasian side.

The surface circulation in the Arctic comprises two main components which are represented by the direction of sea ice drift. One was appreciated last century by Nansen who deduced correctly that tree stumps incorporated in the pack ice off East Greenland must have originated in Siberia. On the strength of this (and other evidence!) in 1893 he allowed the *Fram* to become frozen into the ice off Asia and its three-year drift across the pole towards East Greenland verified the existence of one major oceanic current in the Arctic (Figure 6.3). The other main component is a clockwise circulation in the Amerasian Basin. On the strength of the drift patterns of Soviet and American drifting ice stations such as T3, which are documented by Treshnikov *et al.* (1977) and Sater *et al.* (1971), it has been discovered that it takes 9–11 years to complete a circuit on the outer edge of the gyral and *c*. 3 years nearer the centre. The cell is not completely closed, however, and ice escapes through the straits of the Canadian arctic archipelago into the eastern Atlantic. Also ice from the gyral may join the East Greenland current on completing a circuit. Although the sea ice drift does not reflect the velocity of the underlying ocean current exactly,

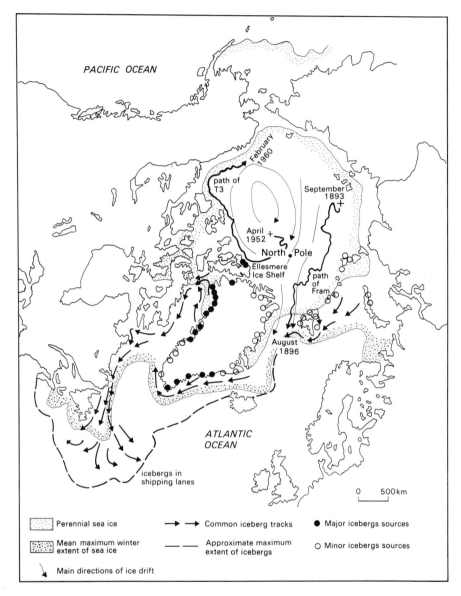

FIGURE 6.3 Surface circulation and seasonal distribution of sea ice in the Arctic. After John and Sugden (1975).

it is a reasonable approximation of the movement of arctic surface water.

The circulation of atlantic water compensates for the surface movements. The water sweeps into the Arctic between Svalbard and Greenland, especially on the Svalbard side, flows parallel to the edge of the continental shelf of western Eurasia and then turns to flow round the Amerasian Basin in an anti-clockwise direction. The relative importance of the various currents can be appreciated by perusal of the water balance of the Arctic (Table 6.1). From this it can be seen that water from the Atlantic is the dominant inflow into the Arctic and that the main outflow is via the East Greenland current. The Bering Straits are the site of a modest inflow and the Canadian straits of a modest outflow. Although the 2 per cent inflow from rivers is very small, it is some seven times higher per unit area than for any other ocean (Treshnikov *et al.*, 1977).

TABLE 6.1   *Water balance of the Arctic Ocean (after Timofeyev, 1963)*

	Sverdrup units (10^6 m^3 s^{-1})	Percentage
Inflow		
Atlantic water	4.2	79
Bering Strait	1.0	19
River runoff	0.1	2
Outflow		
East Greenland	4.0	75
Canadian archipelago	1.3	25

The Arctic oceanic circulation reflects both climatic and topographic factors (Figure 6.1). Sea ice tends to drift at velocities which are between 40 and 120 times slower than wind speeds (Sater *et al.*, 1971). The Amerasian clockwise gyral reflects in part the dominant anti-clockwise weather patterns of this part of the Arctic and the low velocities reflect the weakness of the atmospheric pressure patterns (Dunbar and Wittman, 1963). The easterly current from Eurasia to East Greenland reflects the easterly winds which result from the persistence of low pressure in the North Atlantic. However, pressure patterns in the Arctic are variable and insufficient on their own to account for these surface movements. The topographic fact that the Arctic Ocean is a gulf of the Atlantic Ocean while only a shallow threshold 45 m deep links it with the Pacific is reflected by the dominance of atlantic water and the anomalously warm temperatures of the North Atlantic Arctic. The importance of topography on water circulation can be demonstrated by the observation that Baffin Bay between Greenland and Canada is a miniature replica of the Arctic Ocean basin. Here, as in the Arctic Ocean proper, atlantic water enters along the eastern flanks off the

Greenland coast while arctic water egresses along the western Baffin shore.

ANTARCTIC

Oceanic circulation around the Antarctic is zonal and relatively consistent from place to place. There are three main water masses (Figure 6.4). Antarctic surface water consists of a layer 100–150 m thick which has a fairly low salinity and a temperature close to the freezing point. At its northern extent near the Antarctic Convergence, it is about 1–2°C in winter and 3–5°C in summer, while in the south temperatures of −1.0 to −1.9°C are common. The Antarctic Convergence itself is a shallow frontal feature where antarctic surface water meets and sinks below warmer waters of the southern oceans. It is marked by a temperature change at the sea surface amounting to some 3°C in 30 km, a difference which is sufficiently marked for crews on Antarctic-bound ships to suddenly unearth their anoraks. Beneath this thin cap of antarctic surface water is a zone of warm deep water at 0.5 to 2.0°C which is a continuation of the deep ocean water of the Atlantic, Pacific and Indian oceans respectively. Beneath this is a layer of cold antarctic bottom water which flows down the antarctic continental shelf.

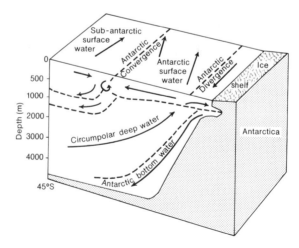

FIGURE 6.4
Ocean currents and water masses around Antarctica. After Deacon (1937, 1964) and Gordon and Goldberg (1970).

The circulation pattern closely reflects average wind directions (Figure 6.5). North of about 63°S the water is driven by the dominant westerly winds and is called the west wind drift. With a coriolis component which deflects winds and currents to the left in the southern hemisphere, the dominant direction is out from the continent in a northeasterly direction. Close to the continent itself the dominant

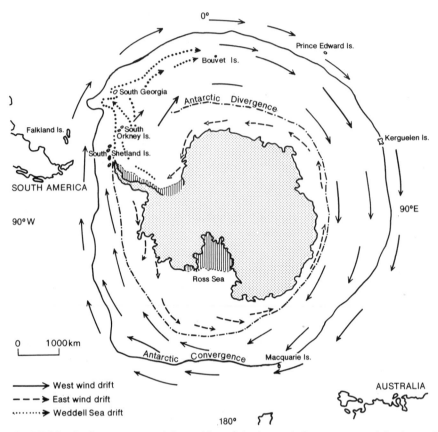

FIGURE 6.5   Surface currents and the position of the Antarctic Convergence and the Antarctic Divergence. Various sources.

wind direction reflecting outflow of katabatic winds from the ice sheet is from the east. This encourages an east wind drift. There is a zone of divergence between the two currents which is associated with upwelling from underlying deep water. Antarctic bottom water probably forms where water comes into contact with ice shelves and is cooled sufficiently for its density to increase and for it to flow down the continental slope. The outflow of surface and bottom currents away from the continent is made up by an inflow of deep ocean water, a point of considerable biogeographical significance, as will be seen later.

Although the main features of the antarctic water circulation are readily explained in terms of atmospheric circulation, there are several important features imparted by the topography of the continent and the sea floor. The Antarctic Peninsula juts out into the southern ocean and causes the east wind drift to circle round the Weddell Sea and to join the west wind drift in the lee of the tip of the peninsula. This circuit, called the Weddell Sea drift, is the one discovered by Ernest Shackleton when H.M.S. *Endurance* was frozen into the ice in the Weddell Sea in 1915. The expedition drifted into the vicinity of Elephant Island, one of the South Shetland Island group, where it made its first landfall some months later. Bottom topography is also important in affecting the main currents, especially in the constricted Scotia Sea between the Antarctic Peninsula and South America. Here it is believed that localized zones of upwelling and the position of such features as the Antarctic Convergence itself are influenced by the bathymetry of the sea floor.

Sea ice

NATURE AND GROWTH

Sea ice is a thin layer of ice floating on the sea surface and forms when the temperature of the sea falls below its freezing point. The salinity of sea water depresses the freezing point and thus freezing usually takes place at a temperature of $-1.91°C$. Sea ice has been a constant concern of seamen and explorers for many centuries and now is the focus of a large body of scientific interest (Glaciological Data, 1978). Table 6.2 gives a list of some commonly used terms and follows the usage recommended by Armstrong *et al.* (1973) in their *Illustrated Glossary of Snow and Ice.*

Sea ice has several characteristics which distinguish it from freshwater ice. Fresh water reaches its maximum density at $4°C$ and its density is decreased if it is cooled further. This means that as the surface layers are cooled below this critical temperature their density decreases and they form a stable cap to the water column. Thus it is necessary to cool only a thin surface layer for ice to form. The density of sea water, on the other hand, increases with falling temperature down to the onset of freezing. Thus, as the surface layer is cooled towards the freezing point, its density increases and it sinks. As a result a whole column of sea water of uniform salinity must be cooled to the freezing point before sea ice can form. The depth of this uniform layer may extend to the sea floor but more usually it is truncated by a salinity discontinuity at a depth of 10–40 m. Sea ice includes patches of brine and the amount depends on the rate of freezing. If freezing is slow the brine content is low, but if freezing is quick more salts are trapped. Normally fresh sea ice has a salinity of 4–6 per cent which means that 80–90 per cent of the salts have been refined out during freezing.

TABLE 6.2   *Some terms for floating ice (after Armstrong et al., 1973)*

Sea ice	any ice found at sea originating from the freezing of sea water
fast/landfast ice	ice which remains attached to the shore
pack ice	freely floating ice
ice floe	piece of floating ice (10 m to over 10 km across)
ice cake	piece of floating ice less than 10 m across
frazil ice	spicules or plates of ice in suspension in water
grease ice	coagulated layer of ice crystals floating on sea surface
ice rind	brittle layer of floating ice less than 5 cm thick
ice keel/bummock	from the point of view of a submariner, a downward projection of ice
pressure ridge	ridge of broken floating ice caused by pressure, usually with corresponding ice keel below the water
anchor ice	submerged ice attached to the bottom
ice foot	narrow fringe of ice firmly attached to the coast
polyna	area of open water in sea ice other than a lead
lead	navigable passage through floating ice
ice blink	white glare on the underside of clouds, indicating the presence of ice
Icebergs	large mass of floating ice which has broken away from a glacier
ice island	tabular berg found in the Arctic Ocean derived from an ice shelf
bergy bit	piece of floating ice about the size of a small cottage, usually glacier ice
growler	piece of ice almost awash; smaller than bergy bit
brash ice	accumulations of floating ice made up of fragments less than 2 m across of both glacier and sea ice

The first stage in freezing is for *frazil ice* to form as individual crystals in the water. These are platelets often 2–15 cm across and 2 mm thick. Next these crystals float to the surface where they collect to form a soupy layer which gives the sea a matt appearance and is known as *grease ice.* The ice layer is flexible and it is uncanny to see the bow-wave of a boat passing through the ice cover with little impediment. Subsequently these crystals freeze together to form a brittle ice skin known as *ice rind.* At this stage the ice will crack and shear when disturbed. Even so it is only half the strength of fresh water ice of equivalent thickness and may sink disconcertingly beneath a person's weight. Only when the ice thicknesses approach 1 m is it sufficiently strong to park an aircraft with confidence! One winter season in the high Arctic is sufficient to build up ice to a thickness of about 3 m (Figure 6.6).

A coherent layer of frozen sea ice is called *congelation ice.* Once

FIGURE 6.6   An arctic ice floe stranded by the falling tide near Broughton Island, Baffin Island. Person on right gives the scale.

formed two other types of ice can contribute to further thickening. The *sub-ice platelet* layer consists mainly of an aggregation of individual crystals of ice which form in the water column beneath the ice and float upwards (Lewis and Weeks, 1971). In the McMurdo area of the Antarctic the plates may form in the upper 33 m of the sea and they accumulate to a thickness of 2–4 m beneath congelation ice (Dayton *et al.*, 1969). Some ice grows on the sea bottom where it is shallower than 33 m to form *anchor ice.* Periodically it breaks off and may carry sponges and bottom sediment up into the sub-ice platelet layer. *Infiltration ice* forms above the congelation ice when the snow pack on the ice depresses it below sea level and the seawater saturates the snow before freezing. In the Antarctic this generally occurs when the snow thickness is over one-quarter that of the underlying ice thickness. In addition to these various ice types, sea ice may also bear an unmodified snow cover.

The exact mechanisms of ice melting depend on the nature of the ice involved as well as environmental factors. Nevertheless, there are some points of general importance. Generally the ice will increase in thickness until spring. In early summer the high albedo of the snow surface (*c.* 90 per cent) reflects much short-wave radiation. Some heat, however, is absorbed and gradually warms the snow. Eventually after several weeks temperatures reach the melting point and the snow begins to melt. The albedo drops from 90 to 40 per cent and, with long hours of sunshine at this time of year, the snow may disappear in a matter of days and meltwater saturate the ice surface. Surface travel at such a time varies from extremely unpleasant to impossible! The ice itself, which is always at its melting point at the contact with sea water, is soon raised to the melting point throughout. Flaws in the ice, algae patches, etc., melt out selectively and surface water drains through the ice leaving hummocks of white ice separated by pools. At this stage the ice resembles a rotten Gruyère cheese.

In warmer polar environments the ice may disappear completely in 1 year. If not, then refreezing commences again before the ice melts away. In such a case the ice has lost most of its salt content and indeed ice of over 1 year old is perfectly drinkable. Also the melting and refreezing modifies the crystal structure so that the ice is much tougher than previously. Usually ice which is over 1 year old is classified as multi-year ice. It is distinguishable from 1-year ice by its hummocky surface with a relief of around 1 m. Also surface meltwater pools on multi-year ice are blue-green in colour, unlike the grey pools of 1-year-old ice. In the high Arctic multi-year ice maintains an equilibrium thickness of around 3 m. About 1 m thickness is added to the bottom and 1 m lost from the top each year (Sater *et al.*, 1971).

One of the most helpful ways of classifying sea ice is in terms of its environment of formation (Figure 6.7). *Landfast ice* (or *fast ice*) occurs

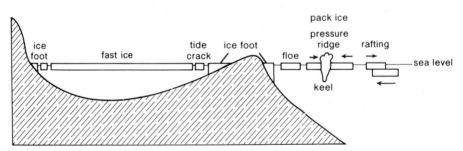

FIGURE 6.7   A morphological and environmental classification of sea ice. The shaded area is land.

in embayments or shallow areas protected by shoals and as a result horizontal movement is negligible. It is common in fjords and also off shallow coasts. In the Laptev Sea it may extend up to 20—400 km from the shore. Landfast ice is usually flat and smooth over wide areas. It moves up and down with the tide and this causes areas of broken floes between it and the shore. In North Greenland and Ellesmere Island the landfast ice may persist from year to year and form an ice shelf.

In warmer latitudes, however, it breaks away in the summer. Tidal fluctuations cause an *ice foot* to form at the shore. The ice foot is firmly attached to the shore and forms by the gradual accretion of ice in the intertidal zone after each tidal cycle. Its upper surface may consist of various additional components of snow, infiltration ice and spray, and indeed there is a considerable literature describing various types of ice foot (John and Sugden, 1975). Generally the ice foot is widest where the inter-tidal shore slopes gently and is narrow or non-existent when the shore is steep (McCann and Carlisle, 1972). Its upper surface is generally flat. It usually persists until after the adjacent ice in the sea has disappeared (Figure 6.8).

FIGURE 6.8 A dramatic sketch of an ice foot in Bear Sound, Baffin Island, following the disappearance of floating ice. From Hall (1865).

Pack ice describes sea ice which is floating free and subject to the influence of winds and currents. Generally it consists of individual ice floes which may measure from a few tens of metres to several

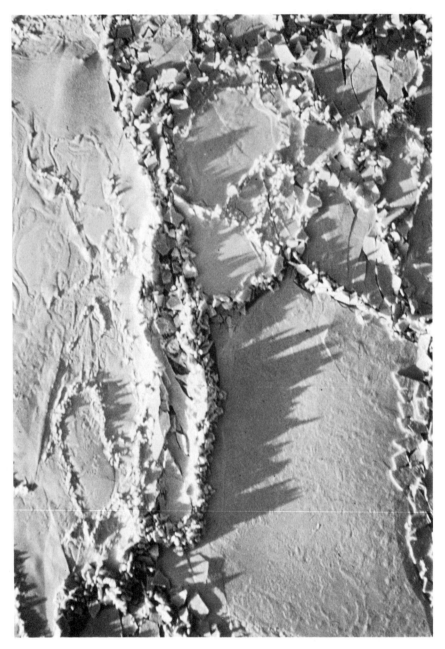

FIGURE 6.9   A vertical air photograph of ice floes and pressure ridges in arctic pack ice. Photograph by W. Weeks.

kilometres in diameter. In an area of a mixture of multi-year and 1-year ice the floes tend to be centres on more resistant multi-year ice. Subjected to varying atmospheric and oceanic stresses and to the presence of immovable coastlines, there is differential movement within pack ice. One way this is taken up is by the formation of *pressure ridges* (Figure 6.9). On the surface they are represented by ridges up to 10 m high, while below they may form *keels* or the more expressive submariner's term *bummocks* up to 30 m deep. Figure 6.10 is a replica

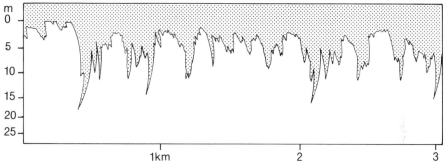

FIGURE 6.10   The underside of sea ice at 83°N, 06°E as recorded by H.M.S. *Dreadnought* in March, 1971. The curvature of the keels is introduced by the stylus of the recorder. After Swithinbank (1972).

of the irregular underside of a stretch of Arctic pack ice as recorded by H.M.S. *Dreadnought* in 1971 (Swithinbank, 1972). Normally the material in the ridge consists of 1-year ice which is compressed between more resistant multi-year floes. Pressure ridges are vividly described in the classic polar literature where ships repeatedly were crushed by pressure ridges (Figure 6.11). The main problem is that in the open pack the ship is trapped in a lead which then freezes over. Under stress it is this young thin ice of the lead which gives way to form a pressure ridge. Under some circumstances pressure may force whole floes to raft over one another or even to be upended so that they stand on their edges.

The one over-riding feature of pack ice is its variability. All the time it is changing its morphology as new leads open up, freeze over and then become squeezed into pressure ridges. In summer there tends to be open water between the individual floes since leads do not freeze up. However, even under cold winter conditions there is always some open water in existence.

It is apparent that there may be important spatial variations in the morphology and nature of pack ice. As a generalization one can high-light three important situations which tend to cause pack ice to be irregular and tough:

FIGURE 6.11   Nansen's ship *Fram* caught in a pressure ridge, 10th January, 1895. From a photograph by Nansen (1897).

(1) When the ice is old. This is because multi-year ice is intrinsically tougher than 1-year ice because of recrystallization but also because rafting and ridge formation over time has the overall effect of thickening the ice.
(2) Where the environment is stormy. This is because strong winds can lead to high stresses within the ice and cause ridging.
(3) Where the ice abuts the coast. This is simply the result of ice being piled up against the coast. Photographs of peninsulas jutting out into the Arctic sometimes show the build-up of a series of parallel and adjacent pressure ridges over a distance of several kilometres.

SEA ICE DISTRIBUTION

Armed with these general principles concerning sea ice it is useful to look at its distribution and character in the Arctic and Antarctic.

Most maps show the mean position of pack ice in the winter and summer. These means average out the real margin at any one time and perhaps it is more meaningful to look at the actual sea ice distribution for particular days in summer and winter. Figure 6.12a shows the actual ice distribution as mapped from passive microwave images obtained on 15th January, 1973. This date is a little earlier than the maximum extent but one can see clearly how all the Arctic and Bering Sea areas are ice-bound. Also the bight of ice-free area in the Barents

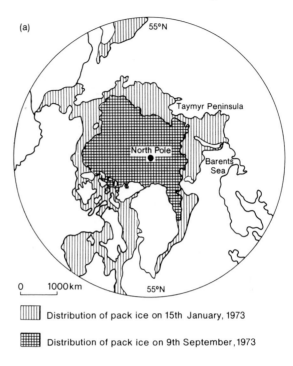

(a)

55°N

Taymyr Peninsula

North Pole

Barents Sea

55°N

0   1000 km

⬛ Distribution of pack ice on 15th January, 1973

⬛ Distribution of pack ice on 9th September, 1973

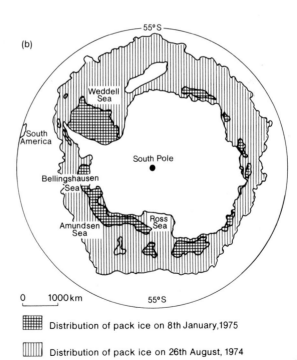

(b)

55°S

Weddell Sea

South America

South Pole

Bellingshausen Sea

Amundsen Sea

Ross Sea

0   1000 km   55°S

⬛ Distribution of pack ice on 8th January, 1975

⬛ Distribution of pack ice on 26th August, 1974

FIGURE 6.12
(a) Sea ice distribution in the Arctic on 15th January and 9th September, 1973, mapped from passive microwave images. *(b)* Sea ice distribution in the Antarctic on 26th August, 1974 and 8th January, 1975 as mapped from passive microwave images. After Zwally and Gloersen (1977). The area of each map is identical.

Sea is striking. As expected the actual boundary is more irregular than that indicated by the means shown, for example, on Figure 6.3. The figure also shows the pack ice boundary on September 9th in the same year. Open water exists off the Alaska/Canadian shores west of the Mackenzie and off most of the Siberian coast, where the only ice clusters remain in the vicinity of the Taymyr Peninsula and the East Siberian Sea. The detailed form of the Asian ice edge probably reflects upwelling of warm atlantic water along submarine canyons. North Greenland and the northern exits of the straits of the Canadian archipelago are ice-bound. West Greenland, southeast Greenland and Hudson Bay are clear of ice.

The two components of ice movement, the Amerasian gyral and the flow from Siberia across the Pole to East Greenland, have been mentioned in terms of ocean currents. The overwhelmingly important implication is that ice in the Amerasian cell is old and often exceeds 10 years in age, while that off the coast of Siberia is generally less than 1 year old. The East Greenland ice may contain ice from both sources and consists mainly of multi-year ice. While most Siberian ice tends to move offshore, Canadian ice has an onshore component, a factor which induces ice pressure along the flanks of the Beaufort Sea in northern Canada.

Figure 6.12b shows the distribution of Antarctic sea ice in midwinter on 26th August, 1974. It shows the effective ice-covered area of the continent has been doubled. The margin of the sea ice agrees fairly well with the mean position established by ships over the year, but in detail it is much more irregular. Salients apparently are related to submarine topography and its effect in deflecting the west wind drift (Zwally and Gloersen, 1977). Minor fluctuations may reflect winds. A striking feature is the open water polyna east of the Weddell Sea. This is thought to reflect the role of the Antarctic Divergence and is an area of particularly important upwelling (Zwally *et al.*, 1976). The summer image from 8th January, 1975 shows ice cover to be reduced to only 15 per cent of its winter extent. The major areas of year-round ice are in the Weddell, Bellingshausen and Amundsen seas. There is clear open water in the Ross and eastern Weddell seas.

These images are clear reflections of the dynamics of sea ice movement around Antarctica. The outward flow of air and antarctic surface water carries 85 per cent of the winter ice out to warmer climes where it melts. The remaining 15 per cent is affected by the east wind drift. In the Weddell Sea this imparts a clockwise rotation. In the lee of the Antarctic Peninsula the east wind drift is less pronounced and again ice lingers onshore. Katabatic winds drain down the depression occupied by the Ross Ice Shelf and blow the Ross Sea clear of ice. In terms of regional variability, the ice-infested areas persisting in summer are the only areas where multi-year ice survives in the Antarctic. Generally this is less than 2–5 years old (Heap, 1965).

CONTRASTS BETWEEN ARCTIC AND ANTARCTIC

Sea ice in the Arctic and Antarctic is similar in many respects but there are some important differences which result from the differing interrelationships with other environmental variables in each region.

Snow plays a more important role in Antarctic sea ice than in the Arctic. Arctic winter snowfall is light and rarely exceeds 30 cm. Winter in the Antarctic is a stormy season and snow thicknesses of 1 m are common in a zone fringing the coastline. This difference in snow cover has several effects. A thinner snow cover is a less effective insulator and thus on average Arctic ice contains a higher proportion of congelation ice. Also surface infiltration tends to be uncommon in the Arctic but common in the Antarctic where the snow accumulation is sufficient to drown the ice. The snow cover also affects the rate of freezing and Lewis and Weeks (1971) suggested that the development of a sub-ice platelet layer is favoured by the slower cooling associated with a thick insulating snow layer. This layer is uncommon or much thinner in the Arctic. Overall these contrasts mean that antarctic ice has a higher component of relatively weak ice structures, when compared to arctic ice.

There is also a significant difference in the age of ice in the Arctic and Antarctic. Whereas only 15 per cent of antarctic ice is more than a year old, most arctic ice other than near Siberia is over 1 year old and some is over 10 years old. Thus pressure ridging, rafting and the process of age-hardening of ice are more important in the Arctic than in the Antarctic. This tendency is accentuated because, with the exception of the Weddell Sea gyral, most antarctic ice tends to move offshore and thus avoids the disturbance associated with onshore movements.

Overall it can be concluded that, although the fundamental processes of sea ice formation are the same in the Arctic and Antarctic, differing environmental conditions make antarctic ice significantly weaker and less persistent in the summer months than arctic ice.

The marine ecosystem

Anyone brought up on a diet of Walt Disney films of Alaskan beaches crowded with fur seals and walruses would be forgiven for concluding that the arctic seas are a zone of plenty. The Antarctic too, with its history of Man's plundering fur seals and whales and film commentaries on the millions of penguins frequenting isolated and sub-antarctic islands, again seems a world of plenty (Figure 6.13). Although there are elements of truth in these views there are important qualifications which need to be made. As with land animals, the marine fauna and flora is characterized by large numbers of individuals from only a limited number of species. Also, when the number of penguins is averaged out over the antarctic seas, the density is distinctly modest (Holdgate, 1967). Also the breeding colonies are present for only a brief period of the year and, indeed, may involve individuals who live most of their lives outside polar waters.

FIGURE 6.13
An audience of Adélie penguins learning about the geomorphology of their local area from Brian John, Fildes Peninsula, King George Island, South Shetland Islands.

In order to get a realistic view of the absolute and relative wealth of the biological marine resources in the Arctic and Antarctic it is necessary to analyse the ecosystem in more detail. An understanding of how it functions involves a study of the role of variables such as climate, distribution of land and sea, oceanic circulation and variations in the type and distribution of sea ice.

MAIN COMPONENTS AND STRUCTURE

The basis of all marine ecosystems is phytoplantation or freely floating microscopic plants (Figure 6.14). The productivity of phytoplankton or primary productivity of the sea is the fundamental control on the size or biomass of the ecosystem. In polar latitudes the dominant members of the phytoplankton are diatoms, which are unicellular organisms with delicate silica skeletons. Since phytoplankton densities vary from place to place and from season to season it is extremely difficult to obtain reliable quantitative information about primary productivity. However, it is possible to reach certain general conclusions:

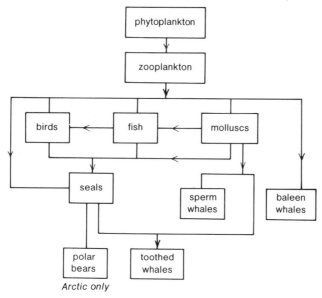

FIGURE 6.14   The main structure of the polar marine ecosystem.

(1) The Arctic Ocean itself is something of a desert and numbers and productivity of phytoplankton are low in relation to the world's oceans. This is thought to reflect low levels of light beneath sea ice and the lack of nutrients in the stable water layers which characterize the ocean (Allen, 1971).

(2) The areas of ocean current mixing in sub-arctic waters such as the Bering Sea and North Atlantic are about 100 times more productive than the high Arctic, especially in the summer when daylight hours are long (Allen, 1971).

(3) Coastal and inshore waters of Antarctica are highly productive and are among the richest sea areas in the world (Fogg, 1977). This is particularly true of the seas around the islands of the Scotia Sea.

(4) Elsewhere in the Antarctic Ocean rates of primary production are lower and at the moment it is not possible to say whether the primary production of the southern ocean as a whole is greater or less than other sea areas (Fogg, 1977; El-Sayed, 1970).

(5) A special under-ice community of algae, called the epontic community, grows in the lower ice layers and contributes to a short phytoplankton 'bloom' immediately after ice break-up (El-Sayed, 1971).

(6) There is an intense seasonality to primary production. In summer a combination of long daylight, rich nutrient supply and ice-free water promotes high rates of growth.

The next link in the marine ecosystem involves zooplankton, a group of drifting animals some of which consume phytoplankton directly and others of which consume other members of the group. In the north the most important species is the crustacean *Calanus*, which is a copepod some 6 mm in length, while in the Antarctic the most important is krill, *Euphausia superba*, which is a shrimp-like creature up to 8 cm in length (Figure 6.15). When compared to warmer oceans polar

0   1cm

FIGURE 6.15
Euphausia superba,
Antarctic krill.

zooplankton tend to have larger populations but fewer species. Also the individuals tend to be larger than elsewhere. Since zooplankton depend ultimately on phytoplankton both distributions are similar. Thus the Arctic Ocean is poor in zooplankton while sub-arctic waters are rich. Antarctic waters in general seem to be rich, and Foxton (1956) estimated the standing crop to be at least four times that of tropical waters. But such average figures disguise strong spatial variations (Figure 6.16). Particularly high standing crops are found associated with islands of the Scotia Sea. Southeast of South Georgia, for example, one can often see pink patches in the water a few metres across where there are swarms of krill. Sampling of such swarms has yielded incredible hauls of 15 kg m^{-3} (Makarov *et al.*, 1970). When such swarms drift into the hot shallow water near the shore of the active volcano, Deception Island, the resulting odour of cooking needs to be experienced to be believed!

Much is known about Antarctic krill, largely because of the impetus of the results of the *Discovery* expeditions in the 1930s (Hardy and Gunther, 1935; Marr, 1964; Mackintosh, 1972). The life history of krill is intimately bound up with ocean currents. The young hatch in the east wind drift and the growing animals then tend to drift northwards with the west wind drift. Eggs laid by adults sink and find their way back to the east wind drift by movement of deep ocean water and upwelling. The dense concentrations of krill on Figure 6.16 are related to zones of mixing between the waters of the east wind drift and the west wind drift. This is particularly important in the Drake Strait and Scotia Sea areas.

The zooplankton is the staple food both directly and indirectly for marine mammals, fish, birds and molluscs. Little is known about the latter other than that the squid is the staple food of the sperm whale

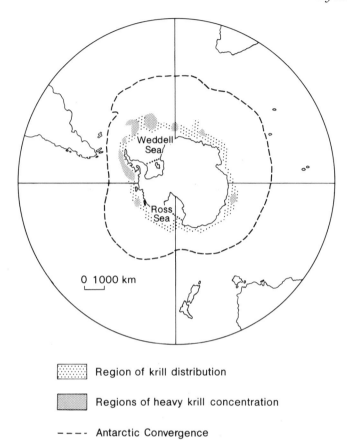

Region of krill distribution

Regions of heavy krill concentration

– – – – Antarctic Convergence

FIGURE 6.16   Spatial variations in the distribution of krill. After El-Sayed (1976).

in both hemispheres and the elephant seal in the Antarctic. Several species of fish depend on krill in the Antarctic and apparently fish densities are high (Permitim, 1970). This is confirmed by my fishing experience at Deception Island when I tied three shiny screws to a piece of string and dropped the device over the side of the ship. Pulled up immediately, there was one *Nototheniid* on each screw! There are numerous species of fish in the sub-Arctic. Indeed in Alaska alone 50 species are fished by Man (Burns and Morrow, 1975). Generally the fish are small and overall densities low. Nonetheless, some insight on locally high sub-arctic densities is given by the calculation that the bird colony of the Cape Thomson cliffs in Alaska consumes 190 000 arctic cod per day (Swartz, 1966)! Towards the pole, the variety of species falls away abruptly and the polar cod is the only fish that has been caught in the high Arctic (Sater *et al.*, 1971).

It is worth noting that all bird life in the Antarctic is dependent on the sea. There are 43 species involved south of the Antarctic Convergence, but only 12 species actually breed on the continent proper (Stonehouse, 1965). Penguins are essentially aquatic and feed on krill over a foraging range more than 300km. Petrels and albatrosses feed on plankton as well as carrion.

The large mammals are the most conspicuous element of the polar marine environment. The sub-order *Pinnipedia* involves three groups of seals, namely the fur seal, walrus and hair seal. Laws (1977) estimated that 56 per cent of total seal numbers and 79 per cent of their biomass is in the Antarctic; the discrepancy represents the larger size of antarctic seals (Figure 6.17). Fur seals occur in the sub-Arctic and sub-Antarctic.

Species		Population (thousands)
Crabeater		14 858
Weddell		730
Leopard		220
Ross		220
Elephant		600
Fur		200

FIGURE 6.17
Populations of antarctic seals. From Laws (1977).

They spend most of the time at sea but haul out onto selected sites for breeding in the summer (Figure 6.18). The southern fur seal used to breed in its millions in the South Shetland Islands and South Georgia as well as in other sub-antarctic islands such as Marion Island, Macquarie Island and Kerguelen. Hunted almost to extinction it is now rapidly regaining its former densities, at least in South Georgia (Bonner, 1976; Payne, 1977). The northern fur seal breeds in the Pribilof and Komandorski Islands of the Bering Sea. The walrus occurs only in the Arctic and consists of an Atlantic and Pacific species. It feeds on marine molluscs and other bottom fauna and has always been highly prized for its tusks. Figure 6.17 shows some of the fur and hair seal species in the Antarctic along with some estimates of the huge numbers involved. The elephant seal is the largest, and full-grown males can weigh up to 5 tons (Figure 6.19). It is a seasonal migrant and spends summer hauled up on convenient raised beaches in packed herds. It is unwise to camp near or downwind of such a congregation unless one has no power of

FIGURE 6.18
A fur seal in South Georgia.
Photograph by Gordon Thom.

FIGURE 6.19
Elephant seal in South
Georgia. Photograph by
Gordon Thom.

smell! The remaining antarctic hair seals are permanent residents. Crabeater seals are krill eaters and huge numbers are dispersed throughout the pack ice. According to Erickson *et al.* (1971) there may be many more than indicated in Figure 6.17 and they suggest a total of 50–75 million for the Antarctic. Although little is known about the habits of dispersed antarctic seals it seems that there are clear environmental controls in their distribution. For example, crabeater seals tend to favour small ice floes with approximately 50 per cent of the sea open water (Erickson *et al.*, 1971). Weddell seals prefer landfast ice. In the Arctic the harbour, ring and bearded seals are year-round residents. The latter, like the walrus, is a bottom feeder. Like their antarctic equivalent, the Weddell seal, they survive in winter by keeping open breathing holes in the ice. The harp and hooded seals are arctic immigrants and congregate annually in the summer. The breeding grounds of the harp seal are on the sea ice off eastern Canada and are notorious for the annual cull, which attracts worldwide protest.

Whales are highly mobile and extend over most oceans of the world. They are common in antarctic and arctic waters in summer when they fatten up on the ample food supplies, but in winter most migrate to warmer climes and apparently eat little or nothing. The baleen whales feed directly on krill and a large blue whale, the world's largest creature, can consume 4 tons in a day. The main antarctic and arctic species are shown in Figure 6.20, the numbers referring to estimates of the population before whaling commenced in the twentieth century. Mackintosh (1965) considered that before exploitation the southern stocks of

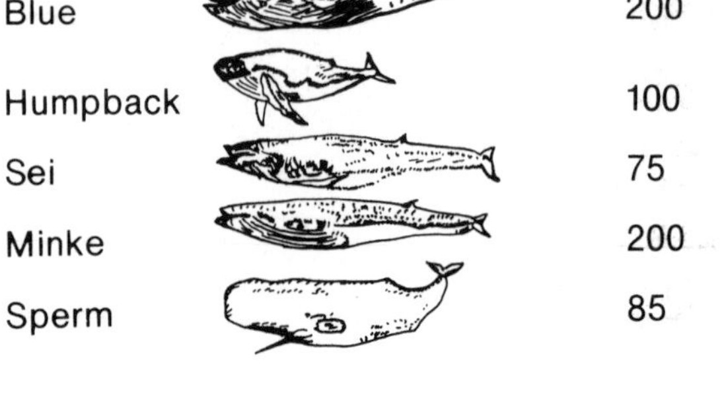

Species		Initial population (thousands)
Fin		400
Blue		200
Humpback		100
Sei		75
Minke		200
Sperm		85

FIGURE 6.20
Estimated populations of antarctic whales before whaling. From Laws (1977).

baleen whales were four times as abundant as those in the north. Southern whales are estimated to have consumed some 150 million tons of krill per year, which is more than twice the weight of the world's annual fish catch in the 1970s. There are several complex ecological relationships. The whales arrive in the south as a series of waves, depending on the species. They congregate where krill concentrations are high. They tend to follow the pack ice edge south as it melts in the summer, probably following the planktonic bloom which accompanies break-up. The whales keep out of the pack ice where possible and indeed their distribution was used by navigators searching for open water. An interesting example is mentioned by Kemp and Bennett (1932). They tell of a veteran South Shetland whaler who met pack ice north of the islands in 1914. He looked for an opening through the ice but could find none and instead caught blue whales at the ice edge. Suddenly the whales disappeared. He realized at once that a passage to the south must have opened and next day he found an opening to the south.

In the Arctic, baleen whales have long been reduced to small numbers. In summer they move into ice-free water bordering the central Arctic pack ice, utilizing the temporary planktonic bloom. An example of a seasonal migrant is the white whale which breeds annually in the waters off the Mackenzie Delta. Apparently whales once moved freely through the straits of the Canadian archipelago, at least to judge from the frequency with which whalebones are found in old Inuit ruins.

Toothed whales form a separate sub-order of whales. They include the squid-eating 'Moby Dick' sperm whale which penetrates into the Bering Sea and the Scotia Sea in summer, and the killer whale which likewise occurs in both hemispheres. The latter eats penguins and seals and is credited with the scars which are frequently seen on crabeater seals. It has an evil reputation among sailors which seems completely unmerited. As Fraser (1964) noted, there is no single instance in the polar literature of a human being suffering damage from attack by this animal. Several species of toothed whales occur only in the Arctic; for example the grey whale, one-tusked narwhal and white whale.

Finally, in polar marine ecosystems there is the polar bear which is an option restricted to the Arctic. With its diet of ring seal and fish the bear is adapted to life on ice floes and is wholly dependent on the sea for its food. In recent years it has broadened its diet and scavenges garbage dumps near settlements. Rather than illustrating the pleasures of garbage dumps, this perhaps shows just how difficult it is to catch a seal or a fish if you are a bear!

RELATIONSHIP TO OTHER VARIABLES

The climatic environment of the polar regions exerts certain constraints which are common to both north and south oceans, namely water temperatures close to freezing and intense seasonality of food supplies, ice cover and daylight. These severe constraints are reflected in the generally low numbers of species which, however, tend to include large numbers of individuals. This is similar to terrestrial polar eco-systems. Although it is sometimes argued that this makes the system highly unstable, it is probably true to argue that it has a tendency to a greater oscillation than more temperate marine ecosystems. This can be illustrated by the way the population of fur seals, which were virtually hunted to extinction in South Georgia, are now recovering rapidly. In 1933 the fur seal population of Bird Island in northwest South Georgia amounted to 38 (Bonner, 1968). In 1975, 90000 pups were produced in one breeding season (Payne, 1977) and growth con-tinues at around 16.8 per cent signalling a most remarkable recovery. Similar arguments seem to apply to those whales which are now pro-tected and which are now recovering rapidly (Gulland, 1976).

The cool climatic environment makes itself felt in other direct ways. There are a number of ways in which warm-blooded mammals are adapted to cold conditions (Stonehouse, 1965; Dunbar, 1968). Large size of individuals is efficient from the point of view of minimum heat loss. A thick layer of blubber is characteristic and its significance illustrated by such facts that a blue whale 27 m long and weighing 120 tons has 25 tons of blubber (Robertson, 1956). Perhaps there is a tendency to over-rate such cold adaptation in marine mammals for, after all, the water temperature never stays far below freezing and is far less inclement than winter temperatures in the air above.

The distribution of land and sea is of profound importance and accounts for many contrasts between the Arctic and Antarctic. In terms of deep-sea marine life the Antarctic has a rich and varied eco-system in contrast to the monotonous arctic equivalent (Knox, 1970; Hedgpeth, 1970; Andriashev, 1965). This may well reflect the fact that the Antarctic Ocean is open to all the world's major oceans, whereas the Arctic is virtually landlocked. Conversely the Antarctic's isolation from other continents seems to be reflected in the lack of variety of shallow-water marine fauna and birds (Dell, 1965), as well as the absence of predators like the polar bear, arctic fox or wolf. One can suggest that penguins owe their existence to this geological inheri-tance. It is very difficult to believe that a flightless bird which must nest on land could evolve side by side with foxes and wolves. The adage 'polar bears in the north, penguins in the south' is a fair summary of much that is significant in polar biogeography! The segmented Arctic seas may account for the way a greater variety of species of sea mammals, both seals and whales, has evolved in the Arctic (Laws, 1977). The antarctic environment is too similar in a circumpolar direction to favour such speciation as a pacific or atlantic walrus — or even the walrus at all! Nonetheless, there is a significantly more varied shallow-water marine fauna in the Antarctic Peninsula area than elsewhere in the Antarctic, presumably because of the proximity of South America and the stepping stones of the islands of the Scotia Sea (Dell, 1965). Laws (1977) also noted that there are no bottom-eating seals in the Antarctic, unlike the Arctic, and suggested that this may reflect the greater depth and restricted extent of continental shelf in the Antarctic when compared to the Arctic.

Oceanic circulation is probably responsible for the major contrast between arctic and antarctic marine ecosystems — their productivity and their biomass. The upwelling of nutrient-rich water in the Antarctic and the fact that most of it is clear of sea ice in the summer is fundamental in producing rich seas comparable to or exceeding other oceans. The lack of upwelling in the Arctic and the presence of sea ice over most of the ocean depresses overall productivity well below that of other oceans.

Sea ice has other complex relationships with the ecosystem. Not only are there algae peculiar to the underside of the ice, but there is a burst of phytoplankton activity associated with break-up. The reasons are far from understood but they may be related to salinity changes due to ice build-up and decay, changes in light reaching the sea, release of the ice flora and other factors. Variations in ice types influence the distribution of overwintering seals and migrants like whales. The formation of anchor ice on the bottom can build up on seaweed and wrench it to the surface by flotation. In the McMurdo Sound area Dayton *et al.* (1969) noted that sponges only occurred below a critical depth of 33 m beneath the upper layer of chilled water. The scouring of ice against steep shores or the build-up of the ice-foot in winter are other factors which limit shoreline faunas. These interrelationships between the ecosystem and sea ice are imperfectly understood, and it is difficult to draw meaningful comparisons between the Arctic and Antarctic. One can suggest that the denser perennial sea ice of the central Arctic is more of a constraint to the ecosystem than antarctic pack ice. Also, anchor ice effects are more likely to be common in the Antarctic.

Interrelationships between the polar marine system and other systems

NATURAL SYSTEMS

There are powerful feedback links between the marine system and polar climate. Pack ice increases albedo and its extent at any one time influences temperatures and air mass characteristics. There are many instances of pack ice extending relatively far south into the Atlantic Ocean and depressing European temperatures, either seasonally or over a period of years (Lamb, 1977). In the Arctic, pack ice fluctuations from year to year can have similar climatic repercussions and cause dramatic seasonal contrasts from year to year, for example in areas like Svalbard or West Greenland. Ocean currents may have a similar effect. The warmth and high precipitation of the Atlantic Arctic depend on the influx of warm Atlantic water. Variations in the current can have important effects. One interesting inverse effect is that an increase of flow of Atlantic water into the Arctic is compensated for by an increased outflow of cold water off the coast of Labrador and Newfoundland. Thus amelioration in the eastern Atlantic could be associated in the short term with deterioration in eastern Canadian waters (Dunbar, 1976).

The main zone of interplay between marine and terrestrial systems must obviously be along the coast. Some special interrelationships relevant to coastal geomorphology which make polar coasts unique have already been mentioned and concern the role of sea ice in damping down wave energy and also in protecting the inter-tidal zone beneath a fixed ice-foot (p. 121). Terrestrial conditions also affect sea ice in several ways. Rivers draining into the ocean reduce salinities and raise summer temperatures. Also fresh water ice in the estuaries often remains frozen for longer than the sea ice, especially in the case of longer Russian rivers (Sater *et al.*, 1971). On the other hand in Alaska smaller rivers may discharge their spring floods partially on to sea ice depositing debris and fresh water up to 10 km offshore (Reimnitz and Bruder, 1972).

A final point concerning the relationship of terrestrial and marine systems concerns the major contrast between the Arctic and Antarctic. The antarctic terrestrial ecosystem is very poor while the marine ecosystem is rich. In the Arctic the terrestrial ecosystem is rich while the marine system is poor.

RESOURCE AND CONSTRAINT FOR HUMAN SYSTEMS

The animal life in polar seas provides a major resource for human activities in the polar regions. The ease with which it may be utilized depends on many factors.

The way of life of individual species affects their potential resource value. Animals which migrate into polar seas seasonally are in effect concentrating the resources of wide ocean areas so that they may be harvested within a small area. This is true of the seasonal migration of whales to the Antarctic which concentrates animals in a few localities. Especially suitable for harvesting are those migrant species which breed in localized areas, such as fur seals, elephant seals, whales and some fish. The history of these species at the hand of Man shows just how vulnerable to hunters such a lifestyle is. In the South Shetland Islands, for example, 250000 fur seals were killed with nothing more sophisticated than clubs in only one season in 1820—21 (Bonner and Laws, 1964). Whereas such lifestyles lend themselves to hunting for commercial purposes, another fundamentally more important characteristic for any indigenous human activity is the presence of seals living all the year round in polar areas, for example the ring seal in the Arctic.

The total amounts of marine life in the polar regions provide a world resource. In the north the rich sub-arctic areas of the North Atlantic and the Bering Sea are already fished to near capacity, and it seems that there is little obvious potential in the high Arctic. However, a vast untapped resource exists in the Antarctic. The history of antarctic whaling has a fortunate side-effect in that it allows some perspective to be gained on the potential size of the resource. The number of baleen whales feeding in the Antarctic has fallen by 85—90 per cent in the years from 1930 to 1970 (Mackintosh, 1970). Making allowance for average body size, one can estimate the amount of krill that the original population of whales consumed annually. The shortfall between the original total and the present-day consumption represents a potential surplus of krill. Various estimates have been made and indicate that the potential surplus is in the order of 100—150 million tons (Laws, 1977; Zenkovich, 1970). It is probable that at least part of the surplus has been taken up by an explosion in the growth of populations of other krill eaters, such as penguins, fur seals, and crabeater seals (Bonner, 1976; Laws, 1977). Nonetheless, it seems reasonable to assume that a harvest of 100 million tons of krill per year or its equivalent is sustainable in the Antarctic. For perspective this is almost *twice* the total world marine fisheries in the early 1970s.

Consuming krill directly is potentially the most efficient way of utilizing the antarctic marine resource since there is a sharp energy loss as one moves up the food chain. Also krill consists of 16 per cent protein, a valuable commodity in a protein-short world. Notwithstanding Russian experiments on krill processing, and the fact that South Georgia krill appears in Moscow supermarkets as 'ocean paste' (Laws, 1977), it may prove more attractive and easier to harvest the resource at a higher trophic level. One obvious possibility is by harvesting whales at their maximum sustainable yield. The food chain is short and relatively efficient. Already there are signs that blue whales and humpback whales which have been protected for 10 years are recovering, while other species could withstand a reasonable level of hunting (Gulland, 1976). Probably a sustainable whale catch of 1–1.5 million tons per year is possible (Gulland, 1970). Other possibilities include fishing and also harvesting antarctic seals, surely one of the world's largest untapped mammal resources.

The above paragraph carries the implication that antarctic whales and seals could be harvested, and will be received with outrage by many people. The purpose of blandly stating some figures is to separate arguments about quantities and sustainable yield from value judgements about the pros and cons of killing animals like the whale and the ethics of interfering further with the antarctic ecosystem. There is little doubt that whales and seals could be harvested without endangering the species, and this conclusion has to be weighed against other arguments.

The main constraint to human activities posed by the polar marine system is the presence of sea ice which impedes shipping (Figure 6.21). The main effect is to increase costs by demanding ice-strengthened ships and/or ice-breaker support, higher insurance rates and usually a marked seasonality to operations. In 1969 the S.S. *Manhattan*, a 120 000-ton ice-strengthened tanker, made an experimental journey through the Northwest Passage between eastern U.S.A. and Alaska (Figure 6.22). The success of the voyage showed that sufficiently powerful vessels can penetrate pack ice at all times of the year. Nonetheless, no decision to build special tankers has yet been made and one can conclude that at present alternative land pipelines are cheaper and/or more desirable on other grounds.

A key problem presented by sea ice is in the coastal zone. Structures need to be exceedingly strong and specially designed to withstand ice pressures. Certain drilling rigs in Cook Inlet in Alaska are built on one central leg in order to minimize resistance, and designs would need to be strengthened further to withstand the tougher Arctic Ocean sea ice (Cochard, 1975). Harbours too need to withstand ice pressures. A special problem concerns the shallow coast of Alaska and parts of the Soviet Arctic where offshore terminals or artificial islands are needed

FIGURE 6.21   R.R.S. *Shackleton* in pack ice off the South Orkney Islands, 1965.

in deeper water (Figure 6.23). One needs to guard against ice removing the terminal or sweeping over it! Also the problem of linking the terminal to land is difficult. A pipeline would be exposed to scouring as ice keels scrape the bottom, sometimes leaving scars 3 m deep (Shearer and Blasco, 1975). In the coastal waters off Labrador there are worries about the effects of icebergs striking offshore rigs and scouring the continental shelf to depths of up to 180 m (Barrie, 1980). Figure 6.24 illustrates some iceberg drift tracks, and the irregularities induced by tides and winds make prediction of drift difficult.

It is impossible to give meaningful estimates of present or potential costs introduced by the existence of pack ice. However, it is possible to draw attention to *relative* differences reflecting spatial variations in the thickness and toughness. In general, in the Antarctic, sea ice is easier to penetrate than in the Arctic. Also, within each polar zone there are important contrasts. The sea passage north of the Soviet Arctic (the Northeast Passage) tends to involve thinner, younger and more regular ice than the Northwest Passage off North America. The Northwest Passage suffers from difficult ice conditions even in summer in the western Canadian straits and north of the Arctic islands. Thus problems and costs of maintaining a regular sea route in the Soviet Arctic are less than in North America. There are numerous other

FIGURE 6.22   S.S. *Manhattan* in pack ice off North America. Photograph by Charles Swithinbank.

FIGURE 6.23   Sohio exploration site on a man-made island in the Beaufort Sea, 1980—81. Sohio photograph.

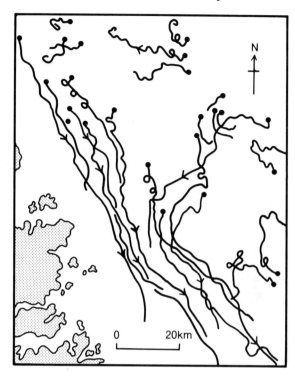

FIGURE 6.24
Iceberg drift tracks off
Saglek, Labrador in August,
1972. Irregularities in the
drift pattern reflect the
influence of tides and winds.
After Dempster and
Bruneau (1975).

smaller-scale variations, for example between the dense, tough ice off East Greenland and the sparse, younger ice off northwest Greenland. Also there are notable ice clusters near promontories jutting out into the Arctic Ocean which form bottlenecks. Point Barrow in Alaska is an example. In the Antarctic one can point to the Bellingshausen coast as being difficult of access, whereas elsewhere access is relatively easy.

Pack ice variations shed an interesting light on the history of polar exploration (see Chapter 8). For example, in retrospect, one appreciates the elegance of Nansen's *Fram* expedition utilizing the pack ice drift, while sympathizing with those who attempted to walk against the ice drift towards the North Pole from Svalbard, such as Edward Parry in 1827. Also one sympathizes with lack of success associated with onslaught on the difficult Northwest Passage by British seaborne expeditions in the early nineteenth century. In the Antarctic one appreciates Scott's good fortune that the most southerly seaborne access point to the continent at McMurdo Sound was also free of severe sea ice problems. Also one wishes that Shackleton's Transantarctic Expedition of 1914 had by chance approached a few degrees of longitude to the east and thereby missed being trapped in the Weddell Sea ice gyral. If Bellingshausen had approached the continent in less ice-infested waters than those of the sea named after him, then the continent might now have been Russian. If ...

Further reading

Coachman, L. K. and Aagaard, K. 1974: Physical oceanography of Arctic and sub-Arctic seas. In Herman, Y. (editor), *Marine geology and oceanography of the Arctic Seas.* Springer-Verlag, New York, 1–72.

Gulland, J. A. 1976: Antarctic baleen whales: history and prospects. *Polar Record*, 18 (112), 5–13.

Heap, J. A. 1965: Antarctic pack ice. In Hatherton, T. (editor) *Antarctica*, pp. 187–96. Methuen, London.

Holdgate, M. W. 1967: The Antarctic ecosystem. *Philosophical Transactions of the Royal Society* (London), B, 252, 363–83.

Holdgate, M. W. (editor) 1970: *Antarctic ecology*. vols. 1 and 2. Scientific Committee for Antarctic Research, Academic Press, London and New York. (Many good papers.)

Laws, R. M. 1977: Seals and whales of the southern ocean. *Philosophical Transactions of the Royal Society* (London), B, 279, 81–96.

Lewis, E. L. and Weeks, W. F. 1971: Sea ice: some polar contrasts. In Deacon, G. (editor), *Symposium on Antarctic ice and water masses, Tokyo, September, 1970.* Scientific Committee for Antarctic Research, Cambridge, 23–34.

For a vivid impression of the nature of sea ice try the exploration classics:

Nansen, F. 1897: *Farthest North*, 2 vols. Constable, London.

Shackleton, E. H. 1919: *South.* Heinemann, London.

CHAPTER SEVEN

Environmental Change

Each of the environmental systems discussed in the preceding chapters is constantly changing in response to internal and external stimuli. Some changes, as for example those associated with plate tectonics, are obvious only over millions of years while others, such as climate, have dramatic cyclical changes on time-scales as short as 24 hours. There is a multitude of other changes which occur at time-scales between these two extremes. The complexity of the interaction between these changes on different time-scales means that the physical environment is constantly changing over time. Study of this change is important for two main reasons. Firstly, because there is a lag in response to change, much of the present environment may be explicable only in terms of the past. Thus the emerging coastline of Hudson Bay is rising isostatically as a direct result of the decay of the Laurentide ice sheet some thousands of years earlier. Secondly, it is necessary to gain some insight into the stability of environmental systems over time if their role in influencing Man's history is to be assessed or if they are to be viewed as a resource for Man today. It is no use investing in a fishing industry only to discover the fish are no longer there. The fact that precisely this situation has arisen in Greenland serves to emphasize the current relevance of such a study of fluctuations over time.

Since changes over the last 40 million years or so affect the present physical environment it is relevant to look at change over this period. Clearly it is difficult to compress 40 million years into a few pages, and thus, for simplicity, it is helpful to focus on change on different time-scales. Table 7.1 attempts to show how the different physical systems respond to change on different time-scales. The impact on human affairs is also indicated.

Change over millions of years

Had this book been written 40 million years ago, the chapter headings would have been very different! At such a time temperate forests

TABLE 7.1   *Environmental change in the polar regions on different time-scales and some effects on human activities*

System	Millions of years	100 000–10 000 years	1 000–100 years	Decades
	← ——————————————— *T i m e - s p a n* ——————————————— →			
	long		*short*	
World scale				
Plate tectonics	Isolation of Antarctica Opening of Atlantic/ Arctic			
Climate	Creation of cold polar climate	Major cyclic fluctuations	Medium-term changes in temperature and precipitation	Short-term changes in temperature and precipitation
Sub-zonal scale				
Glacial	Initiation of glaciation	Glacial/interglacials Major landform changes Isostatic response	Changes in glacier snout positions, and snow fields	Minor glacier snout and meltwater changes
Periglacial	Initiation of tundra	Variation in intensity, and spatial extent Major landform, vegetation and fauna variations	Change in distribution, and depth of permafrost Medium landform, vegetation and fauna variations	Slight change in temperature of permafrost Change in depth and extent of snow cover Changes in growth rates and productivity of tundra
Oceanic	Initiation of polar water masses and sea ice	Major changes in circulation, temperature and sea ice distribution Marked sea level fluctuations	Changes in specific ocean currents, water temperatures and sea ice distribution	Locally significant ocean current changes Change in iceberg frequency and seasonal pack ice distribution
Human	–	Restricted land area in glacials Variation in continental accessibility via Bering 'land bridge'	Effect on diffusion of early Inuit culture Effect on history of polar exploration	Changing difficulty of ice navigation Variation in distribution of marine resources Varying productivity of tundra for herding or hunting

thrived around the shores of the Arctic and in most of Antarctica. Glaciers and sea ice were unknown, glacial geomorphologists unemployable. It was not until about 3.2 million years ago that the polar regions resembled their present situation with extensive ice sheets or pack ice at both poles. The change came about in the intervening millions of years and involved a number of important thresholds. The story begins in Antarctica.

The most detailed evidence of the onset of glaciation has come from analysis of deep-sea cores in the 1970s. Although there are many ambiguous pieces of evidence whose future interpretation will inevitably lead to modifications of the chronology, the main features are emerging. The first possible signs of ice-rafted quartz grains derived from melting icebergs and the presence of sea ice is picked up in antarctic deep-sea cores about 38 million years ago (Margolis and Kennett, 1971; Kennett, 1977). It may be that the next few million years saw the progressive development of sea-calving glaciers in maritime mountains in Antarctica such as the Transantarctic Mountains and Queen Maud Land (Figure 7.1). Although Mercer (1973) and Drewry (1975) are sceptical about the date of the onset of this glaciation because of the difficulty of identifying ice-rafted quartz grains unambiguously, there is general agreement that the evidence for iceberg rafting of erratics by 20–26 million years ago is conclusive. Plant remains indicate the presence of cool temperate forests in Antarctica during this period and it is probably fair to regard the sea-calving glaciers of southern Chile as an apt analogy for this early phase of glaciation in Antarctica. The main East Antarctic ice sheet built up for the first time 14–11 million years ago. This event was marked by a general cooling of the oceans, a sharp northward expansion of sea ice and icebergs as well as a related change in the isotopic composition of the ocean water as light oxygen isotopes were abstracted from the sea and stored in the ice sheet (Kennett, 1977). At this stage West Antarctica was an island archipelago which probably resembled glacierized islands like South Georgia today (Figure 4.4). There is evidence of glaciation over 7

FIGURE 7.1   A glacial cirque cut into the Transantarctic Mountains overlooking Mill Glacier. Such features of mountain glaciation may have been initiated before the development of the East Antarctic ice sheet. Photograph by David Drewry.

million years ago, since striated rock surfaces in the Jones Mountains underlie lavas of that age (Rutford *et al.*, 1972).

A further cooling and expansion of the polar ocean water around Antarctica, as well as a further marked change in the isotopic composition of the oceans 4–5 million years ago, probably marked the first build-up of the West Antarctic ice sheet (Drewry, 1978). Mercer (1973) argued that such a build-up over a submarine bedrock floor could only take place when mean sea level temperatures were below 0°C and thus allowed the formation, then coalescence and grounding of ice shelves. Soon afterwards the overall Antarctic ice sheet expanded for the first time to its maximum extent as far as the edge of the continental shelf. This expansion, which is inferred from study of deep-sea cores, was probably also the expansion(s) responsible for the cutting by East Antarctic outlet glaciers of the dry valleys of Victoria Land. Here, dates of lavas erupted into the bottoms of the former glacial troughs are 4.2 million years old, implying that the troughs were cut earlier (Calkin, 1973).

In the Arctic the overall pattern of the initiation of glaciation is far from clear. Glacio-marine deposits suggest that mountain glaciers were active in the mountains facing the Gulf of Alaska 10–13 million years ago (Péwé, 1975) and in the Wrangell Mountains 10 million years ago (Denton and Armstrong, 1969). Probably conditions were warmer than today and the glaciers invaded a forest of beech trees. For example, 5.7 million years ago the northern Seward Peninsula supported a British Columbia type of forest in a zone which is now tundra (Hopkins *et al.*, 1971).

Glaciers probably existed in mountains bordering the Arctic 4–6 million years ago, as is suggested by ice-rafted pebbles in the sediments of the Arctic Ocean floor (Herman, 1970). On the basis of deep sea cores in the North Atlantic, Shackleton and Opdyke (1977) argued that the first major ice sheet glaciation in the northern hemisphere did not begin until about 3.2 million years ago. The sea ice cover of the Arctic ocean seems to have developed 1.5 to 0.7 million years ago (Herman, 1970).

The timing and pattern of the build-up of polar glaciation points to the importance of plate tectonics in producing conditions favourable to glaciation. Polar latitude on its own is not enough, since the Antarctic continent lay in a polar position during the early Tertiary and yet supported no glaciers. A crucial role seems to have been played by the development of a westerly circumpolar, oceanic and atmospheric circulation around Antarctica. This was not possible until an effective ocean opened up between Antarctica and adjacent continents.

This occurred between Antarctica and Australia some time after 50 million years ago and between Antarctica and South America after Drake Strait was breached 22–30 million years ago. The westerly circulation that resulted reduced meridional flows and thus lowered polar temperatures, while continental break-up allowed moisture to encroach onto coastal mountains. This fortuitous combination of decreasing temperature and increasing moisture was ideal for glacier build-up.

The stepped progress of glaciation points to the effect of certain thresholds. Cooling to less than 0°C at sea level was necessary before the West Antarctic ice sheet could build up. The delayed onset of ice sheet glaciation in the Arctic is a puzzle, but perhaps it relates to another tectonic threshold, such as the closing of Panama Strait between the Americas.

The implications of the build-up of polar glaciation are profound. A new set of glacial processes was unleashed on a formerly unglaciated area and began to modify the land surface by erosion and deposition. The overall topography of the polar regions was changed as continents were smothered in a new sedimentary rock – ice. Antarctica became the highest of the world's continents. For the first time in the recent geological history of the Earth a polar climate recognizably like that of today was established. On land this created the periglacial environment, permafrost and tundra. At sea the cooling created sea ice and produced new ecological niches for marine life.

Changes of 100 000–10 000 years duration

The main environmental changes on this time-scale have been concerned with interglacial/glacial fluctuations of ice sheets throughout the Cenozoic. In the 1960s the classical view was that there had been four main glaciations in Pleistocene time. This can now be seen to be a mid-latitude view and mistaken at that (Kukla, 1977). Worldwide there is now evidence from deep-sea cores that ice sheet fluctuations have occurred regularly over the last 3.2 million years or so (Hays *et al.*, 1976). Kukla has recognized 17 glaciations in the loess stratigraphy of central Europe while the deep-sea core evidence implies that there may have been more.

As a general rule glaciations have lasted longer than interglacials. Glaciations appear to have been of the order of 50 000–100 000 years in duration while interglacials have commonly been 10 000–20 000 years long. Hays *et al.* (1976) have shown convincingly that the cyclical fluctuations are related to irregularities in the Earth's orbit which affect the amount of solar radiation received.

Given this background world picture, there is little actual evidence in the polar regions that can be used to trace even a fraction of the full Cenozoic record. Nonetheless it is useful to recognize a maximum *glacial mode* and an *interglacial mode* before discussing further implications.

Figures 7.2 and 7.3 are tentative attempts to portray the Antarctic and Arctic during glacial maxima. In Antarctica the ice sheet extended as far as the edge of the continental shelf as is evidenced by submarine glacial troughs. Comparison with Figure 2.7 shows that the ice of East Antarctica extended over the presently ice-free coast and submerged the now dry valleys of Victoria Land. The main change was in West Antarctica where ice built up over the floors of the Ross and Weddell Seas. Little ice-free land will have existed other than several high mountain chains. Altogether the volume of ice may have been 80 per cent greater than now. Analysis of deep-sea cores suggests that the Antarctic Convergence and the pack ice limits extended further north.

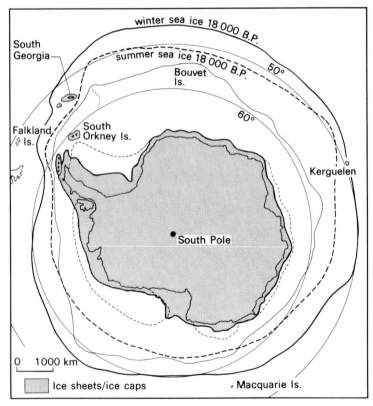

FIGURE 7.2   The Antarctic during glacial maxima, based on Denton and Hughes (1981), Hays (1978) and Sugden and Clapperton (1977). The thinner lines represent the modern equivalents.

The ocean waters were a few degrees cooler than now. Maximum conditions in the maritime Antarctic islands were represented by local ice caps extending over offshore platforms.

In the Arctic major ice sheets covered eastern North America, Greenland and western Eurasia with ice fields in mountains. With a sea level some 100 m lower than that of today, extensive ice-free tundra existed in Alaska, northeastern Siberia, the Bering Straits and the offshore platform of the Beaufort Sea. Following the CLIMAP reconstruction, the ice sheets on Figure 7.3 are shown flowing to join an extensive floating ice shelf covering the Arctic Ocean and North Atlantic (Hughes *et al.*, 1977). An alternative scenario in the Arctic is that the ocean remained covered by sea ice rather than an ice shelf. If this was so, then it is possible that the atmospheric circulation displaced by the Laurentide ice sheet would have introduced an oceanic circulation opposite to that of today (Lamb, 1977).

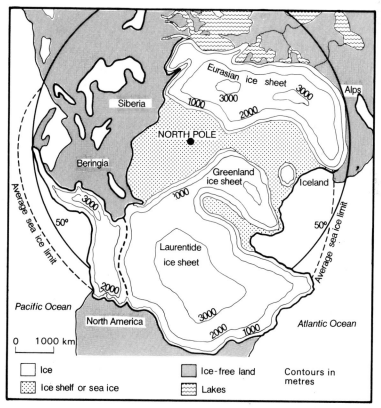

FIGURE 7.3   The Arctic during glacial maxima, based mainly on a reconstruction by Hughes *et al.* (1977). Ice sheet contours on the Laurentide ice sheet are from Sugden (1977) and a similar method has been applied to other ice sheets. Sea ice limits are based on Lamb (1977).

The maps of the poles during glacial maxima are not intended to represent conditions at each of the 17 or more glacial maxima during the Cenozoic, but rather idealized models of maximum conditions. After all there are known to be considerable variations between the recent glaciation for which there is evidence and the picture portrayed in Figures 7.2 and 7.3. In general glaciers of the last glaciation were less extensive than during earlier maxima in Arctic Alaska and Asia (Andrews, 1974). For example, around 18000 years ago large areas of East and northern Greenland were ice-free (Funder and Hjort, 1973; Weidick, 1976) as also was the coast of Labrador and Baffin Island (Ives, 1957; Andrews, 1974). The same conclusion also applies to Antarctica (Sugden, 1978b). Nevertheless such modifications do little to affect the broad pattern and thus the maps serve to emphasize the main characteristics of glacial maximum conditions in the polar world.

Interglacial conditions are represented by conditions today and need little elaboration. The North American and Eurasian ice sheets appear to have disappeared regularly, perhaps because they were in warmer latitudes and because they were centred on basins or gulfs of the sea, which favoured rapid calving and collapse during deglaciation. Little is known of the Greenland ice sheet's interglacial history but the consensus is that its present restricted size withdrawn from the coast is typical. Perhaps its stability is related to the fact that in its smaller withdrawn mode it is essentially land-bound and thus its centre is shielded from sapping by the sea.

The current situation in Antarctica may be typical of most 'inter-glacials'. In the case of East Antarctica the ice sheet has withdrawn to its present grounded position, some 50—100km in from the edge of the continental shelf and exposing several coastal 'oases' and valleys. The continuity of glacio-marine deposition in the deep-sea cores implies that it has survived intact since its inception and thus it seems reasonable to regard the existing minor withdrawal as typical of 'interglacials'. The situation in West Antarctica is quite different. The ice sheet is marine-based and unstable and may well have disappeared during inter-glacials either warmer or longer than that of the present. For example, Mercer (1968) and John (1972) describe glacial and marine deposits which could imply that the West Antarctic ice sheet had disappeared during the last interglacial some 120000 years ago. In such a situation the seas around West Antarctica can be expected to have been much warmer than at present, a conclusion supported by the discovery in glacial till of shells requiring warmer water than at present (Sugden and Clapperton, 1980).

The length of time involved in a change from one mode to another is obviously important, but at present there is much uncertainty about the subject. The shape of curves showing variations in the isotopic ratios in deep-sea cores is assymmetric, with a gentle but fluctuating build-up towards a glacial maximum lasting around 100 000 years, and a sharp return to interglacial conditions in 10 000 years or less. Examples may be seen in the work of Emiliani (1978). This pattern seems to have applied during the last glaciation where evidence of former world sea levels points to a progressive but irregular lowering as the ice built up irregularly (Broecker and Van Donk, 1970). The build-up began around 120 000 years ago and culminated around 18 000 years ago. By 6 000 years ago normal 'interglacial' conditions were re-established in the Arctic following the dramatic collapse of the North American and Eurasian ice sheets and the stabilization of the Greenland ice sheet. In the millenium between 8 000 and 7 000 years B.P. the main heart of the Laurentide ice sheet which was nearly 3 000 km in diameter disappeared.

The ice sheet fluctuations of the Cenozoic, and especially the pattern and timing of ice withdrawal since the last maximum, have many profound implications on the present environmental systems in the polar regions. Isostatic recovery of the land in response to the removal of the weight of the last ice sheets is still progressing. The effect is most significant in Arctic Canada where the ice sheet was large and disappeared most recently. In general the amount of isostatic deformation is related to the weight of overlying ice. Since ice sheets tend to be thicker near their centres, this is the region of greatest and most rapid uplift. In Arctic Canada the highest trace of former shorelines extends up to altitudes of 250 m in the centre, falling towards the periphery (Figure 7.4). These figures imply that a large part of low-lying Arctic Canada has emerged from the sea only in the space of the last few thousand years and is frequently highlighted by suites of raised beaches. Immediately after deglaciation rates of uplift were as high as 10 m per century. Rates then dropped and the highest present-day rate of uplift is 1.3 m per century in southern Hudson Bay (Figure 7.5). Such shoreline changes are of obvious significance to the coast where changing configuration, fetch and material supply imply constant long-term change. As an illustration Figure 7.6 looks forward to the bleak future of Hudson Bay and portrays its sadly depleted shape once isostatic recovery is complete several thousand years hence!

There are important regional variations in the effect of isostasy in the polar regions which can be resolved into three models. The Arctic Canada model with large amounts of uplift continuing to the present

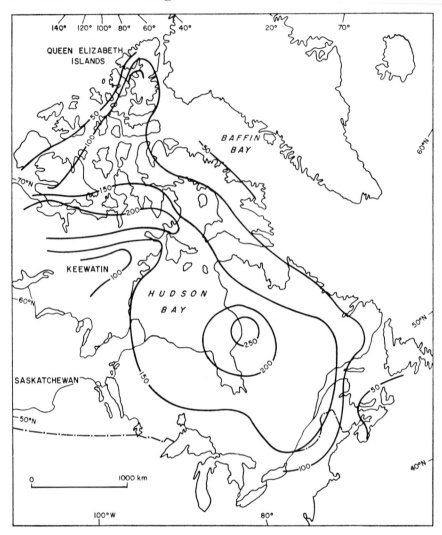

FIGURE 7.4   The altitude (in metres) of the highest marine traces in Arctic Canada. After
Andrews (1970a).

day applies also to the western Soviet Arctic which is responding similarly to the loss of the Eurasian ice sheet. A second model applies
to Greenland and probably much of coastal Antarctica. In these cases
the stabilization and continued existence of the ice sheet has suppressed isostatic recovery. In the case of Greenland there has been little
movement in the last 5000 years. Since world sea level has also remained close to the present level for a similar period the coasts of
Greenland have experienced little vertical movement and even a little
subsidence in the last 5000 years (Weidick, 1972). Immediately above

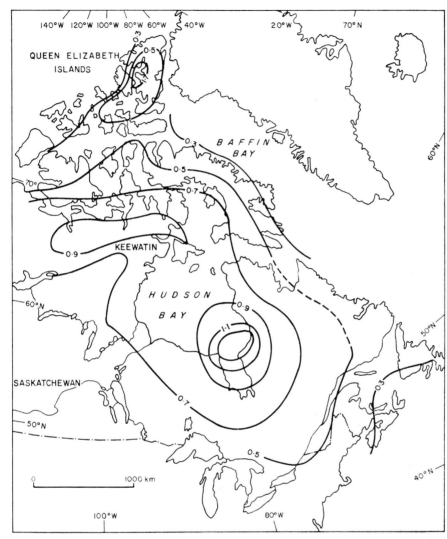

FIGURE 7.5   Rates of modern isostatic uplift in Arctic Canada in metres per century. After Andrews (1970b).

the present shoreline are raised beaches older than 5 000 years which relate to the earlier retreat of the maximum ice sheet. It is likely that a similar model applies around the coastal margins of the Antarctic continent where there are scattered raised beaches (Figure 7.7). The third model concerns those unglaciated areas beyond the limits of the ice sheet glaciation. In general these are coasts which experienced a period of submergence as world sea level rose during global deglaciation, followed by a period of relative stability over the last 5 000 years. The above models are generalizations and do not take into account

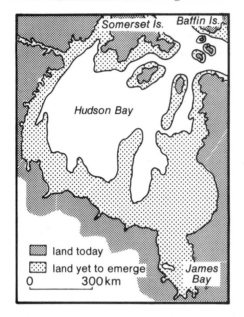

FIGURE 7.6
The sad future shape of
Hudson Bay once isostatic
uplift is complete. After
Barr (1972).

FIGURE 7.7　View from helicopter door of a series of raised shingle beaches emerging from
snow on Spark Point, Greenwich Island, South Shetland Islands, Antarctica.
The beaches extend to an altitude of 54 m.

vertical movements caused by non-glacial factors such as tectonics and isostatic depression of deltas. They also ignore the more localized effects of glacio-isostasy beyond the limits of ice sheets (Walcott, 1970) and irregularities in the geoid representing world sea level (Clark, 1977).

The main effect of the Cenozoic ice sheet fluctuations on the modern periglacial system has been to divide it into two types. On the one hand there are the unglaciated areas which have been subjected to an unbroken periglacial climate for millions of years. Permafrost is deep, regolith is thick and ice-cored periglacial landforms are well developed and abundant. On the other hand the formerly glaciated areas may have been exposed to periglacial conditions for only 7000—10000 years. Not only is the landscape often ice-moulded and regolith non-existent (see Chapter 4), but there has been less time for permafrost to penetrate the ground deeply; also ice-cored periglacial landforms are rarer and younger.

Another major effect is that the periglacial environment changed location on many occasions with serious repercussions on plant and animal life. During glacial maxima the periglacial zone was obliterated from the Atlantic Arctic and migrated south into Europe into areas with a more marked diurnal climatic variation rather than seasonal variation. This is in marked contrast to North America where the tundra zone south of the ice sheet was pinched out and forests thrived close to the ice edge (Wright, 1971). In the Bering Strait area, on the other hand, the exposure of the sea floor as sea level fell introduced a broad land link between Asia and North America and allowed a major area of polar periglacial environment to persist. Given low-lying, gentle plains, an abundant supply of meltwater, periodic sprinklings of loess and a climate only slightly cooler than that of today (Péwé, 1975), the 'Beringia' area was an extensive area of lush tundra.

The effects of these changing periglacial environments on plants have been discussed by Löve and Löve (1974). Approximately one-third of the original 1500 circumpolar plant species became extinct. This was particularly true of Eurasia and eastern North America where they could not adapt to the new sunshine regimes of mid-latitudes. The flora of Arctic islands was decimated. Several species lost their circumpolar distribution and now form isolated sub-species, for example *Papaver relictum* (Lundstr.). Still others, such as *Salix herbacea* (L.) are characteristic of only the Atlantic Arctic. At a smaller scale there are curious local distributions of particular species, implying that they have survived glaciation in isolated plant refuges (Ives, 1974). An example is the curiously rich and varied flora of mosses on Ellesmere Island (Brassard, 1971), which contrasts with the poverty of adjacent islands in the Canadian Arctic archipelago.

It used to be implied that the impressive Ice Age fauna of mammoths, bison and numerous other animals now extinct were killed off by the severity of climatic conditions. Whereas it is true that many species did become extinct during the ice ages, the severity of the climate may not have been critical. Animals are more mobile than plants and better able to adjust to the migrating environment and, after all, Beringia was lush tundra ideal for grazers (Péwé, 1975). Furthermore, dates of remains of mammoths in permafrost show that many died as recently as 10 000 years ago, which is several thousand years after the peak of the last glaciation. Since mammoths survived many earlier interglacials successfully, Martin (1974) argued that hunting by man was probably the critical factor in their extinction. It is ironic that it was the very existence of land between Asia and America from 25 000 to 12 000 years ago which allowed man to colonize America and accomplish this sad feat.

The oceanic environment fluctuated in response to ice sheet variations. In the Antarctic the circumpolar ocean zones pushed outwards in sympathy with glacial maxima (Kennett, 1977; Hays, 1978). The main effect was an increase in polar water area as the Antarctic Convergence moved north and an increase in pack ice extent, especially in summer. Changes in the Arctic were much more dramatic. With Bering Straits closed, the continental shelves occupied by ice sheets and the sea covered by an ice shelf, the circulation and marine life must have been greatly disturbed. It seems probable that all arctic marine life had to survive in mid-latitudes in the Atlantic and along the southern shore of Beringia. Perhaps this dramatic environmental change in the Arctic and its recent date is partially responsible for the relative poverty of arctic marine life, at least when compared to the Antarctic.

Changes of 1000–100 years duration

The only good evidence for fluctuations on this time-scale comes from the Holocene period following the disappearance of the last ice sheets. Study of this period gives some idea of the constant changes which have probably affected the polar environment throughout the Cenozoic as well as an indication of its recent history. Broadly speaking the climate was warmer than at present in the years immediately after deglaciation and remained so until 3 000–4 000 years ago, since when temperatures have approximated to those of the present (Lamb, 1977). A number of fluctuations of a few centuries in duration are superimposed on this trend. Warmer periods are thought to reflect increased vigour in atmospheric conditions.

An example of reconstructed summer temperatures is given in Figure 7.8 which is based on interpretation of pollen stratigraphy in dated peats at six sites in Arctic Canada. Here temperatures did not reach their highest values until after 7 000 B.P. because of the effect of the lingering remnants of the Laurentide ice sheet. The warmest period of the optimum was interrupted by a sharp temporary deterioration soon after 5 000 years ago. A more fundamental drop in summer temperature took place between 4 000 and 3 000 years B.P. Since then two temporary cold fluctuations took place 2 500 years ago and during the Little Ice Age of *c*. A.D.1600–1840 when temperatures were lower than at present. In the intervening period in the years A.D.850–1200 temperatures were higher than today.

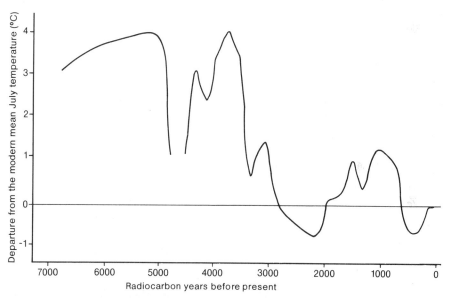

FIGURE 7.8   Reconstructed summer temperatures for Keewatin and Mackenzie areas of Arctic Canada. After Nichols (1975).

The palaeoclimate reconstruction by Nichols in Figure 7.8 is a useful model for general temperature trends in the Arctic, although modifications are necessary from place to place. For example the warm optimum seems to have been established 10 000 years ago in Alaska when trees were already growing north of their existing limit (McCulloch and Hopkins, 1966). In West Greenland temperatures were warmer than today 8 000 years ago (Kelly and Funder, 1974). In Axel Heibeg Island and northern Greenland, where deglaciation was accomplished later, the optimum was reached between 4000 and 3300 years ago (Nichols, 1974). Similar regional variations occurred in the Soviet Arctic but the main trends seem to have been comparable (Kind, 1967).

In the Antarctic there is relatively little information. However the position of dated shells in raised beaches in the South Shetland Islands implies that glaciers had retreated as far as their present position by 9000 years ago (Sugden and John, 1973). This implies an early start to deglaciation and agrees with the conclusion of Mercer (1978b) and Shackleton (1978) that present levels of warmth were achieved some 2000–3000 years earlier than in the northern hemisphere.

The climatic fluctuations of postglacial time have affected each of the main environmental systems. In the Arctic many local glaciers have advanced to moraines some kilometres in front of their present positions (Figure 7.9). In many cases these advanced positions relate to the Little Ice Age of recent centuries and are marked by clear limits of poorly vegetated moraine. Numerous arctic climbing expeditions will remember the often harrowing approach to a glacier through a chaotic and confusing wilderness of loose debris. Sometimes dating reveals that moraines may be related to other maxima achieved earlier during

FIGURE 7.9   Little Ice Age moraines representing the greater ice extent of the last few centuries, Vimmelskaftet, Sukkertoppen ice cap, West Greenland. Reproduced with permission of the Geodetic Institute, Copenhagen.

the Holocene, for example in Baffin Island (Miller, 1973). Although there are signs that these earlier advances may relate to widespread glacier resurgences 2500 and 5000 years ago (Denton and Karlén, 1973), the response of individual glaciers to climatic change is so variable that there are many exceptions.

Glacier responses in the Antarctic seem to have been relatively unaffected by the Little Ice Age. In the South Shetland Islands the maximum glacier advance in the last 10000 years or so was apparently achieved between A.D.1200 and 1450 (radiocarbon years), somewhat earlier than most northern hemisphere advances. In South Georgia, the maximum Holocene advance took place after the end of the eighteenth century, somewhat later than in the north (Clapperton *et al.*, 1978). The climatic significance of these dates is not yet clear although they do imply that, unlike long-term changes, short-term responses in the northern and southern hemispheres may reflect regional environmental changes.

The periglacial environment was affected by Holocene climatic fluctuations in several ways. During the warm optimum Frenzel (1959) showed the southern limit of sporadic permafrost in the Soviet Arctic was up to 600km north of its present position. Presumably elsewhere permafrost was less intense and shallower than at present. The vegetation zones and especially the forest/tundra boundary fluctuated by several hundred kilometres in North America in sympathy with even the short-term fluctuations. During the optimum trees were growing on the northern coast of the Soviet Arctic west of the longitude of Novaya Zemlya and were within a few hundred kilometres of most of the rest of the northern coast, a marked northward advance into the tundra of today (Lamb, 1977). In North America a similar northward advance of up to several hundred kilometres was noted by Nichols (1975). During periods cooler than at present the tundra expanded and the tree line was south of its present position. These periods coincided with the extensive growth of permanent snow fields on upland areas such as Baffin Island, where snow and ice killed the lichen vegetation (Ives, 1962; Andrews *et al.*, 1976).

Oceanic fluctuations in the Holocene involved changing currents and sea ice distribution. During the Little Ice Age (and presumably other cold fluctuations also) mean Atlantic ocean temperatures in mid-latitudes were about 1°C cooler than today. However, in the sub-Arctic near the convergence with polar waters, conditions were much more seriously affected. Lamb (1977) argued that in the Little Ice Age the water between the Faroes and Iceland was 4–5°C cooler than today, reflecting the increased dominance of polar water. Similar or greater changes probably affected Greenland, the eastern Canadian Arctic and the Barents Sea. Sea ice probably extended further south than normal as is indicated by the long records of ice incidence off the coast of Iceland (Koch, 1945; Bergthorsson, 1969). Sea ice was unknown off Iceland in A.D.1100 but was present for 2 months a year around A.D.1300 and then for 2–3 months a year from A.D.1600 to 1840, the culmination of the Little Ice Age. A fascinating byproduct of this greater extent of ice in the North Atlantic was the appearance of Greenlanders in kayaks off Scotland. One such kayak from East Greenland is preserved in Aberdeen University and was found together with its occupant on a nearby beach in 1700.

During warmer periods such as that preceding the Little Ice Age, and the longer one which terminated some 3500 years ago, ocean currents were probably displaced northwards with warmer temperatures in the North Atlantic Arctic. Blake (1972) reported that in the northern Canadian arctic islands extensive driftwood is associated with raised beaches 6000–2500 years old, implying that the straits were less impeded by sea ice during this period than they are at present. In the more recent warm period of A.D.950–1200 the Viking colonizers of southern Greenland rarely encountered pack ice near the shore of Greenland, something which changed in the fourteenth century and which is very different today.'

These fluctuations over hundreds or thousands of years have profound implications for the marine fauna. An interesting documented example is mentioned by Dunbar and Thomson (1979). They noted that salmon were common off West Greenland around 1600, 1810 and and the 1950s, probably because of the strengthening of the East Greenland and Irminger currents following warm periods. One can predict that cod, which do not survive in water cooler than 2°C, will have changed their habitat continuously over the last 10000 years, moving south in cold periods and north in warm periods. Whales are influenced by pack ice concentrations. Apparently they were abundant in the Canadian arctic straits during the main optimum, a point of no small significance for the spread of an Inuit whaling culture at the time (McGhee, 1974).

Oceanic fluctuations in the Antarctic may not have been in phase with those of the northern hemisphere, although the longer-term trends were probably similar (Lamb, 1977). For example, the Little Ice Age cold period was apparently of minor significance, if it occurred at all. During a period of bad arctic pack ice conditions, in the Antarctic both Cook in 1773 and Biscoe in 1831 were able to sail 1–2° further south than would be possible today.

Changes over decades

The last few decades coincide with instrumental observations of climate, and data are much more precise. Nevertheless there is a paucity of observations in the Arctic and Antarctic and it is sometimes difficult to appreciate the overall pattern. Perhaps the key problem concerns that of lags and the lack of understanding of the effects a particular change in one area has on another. Nevertheless some broad trends seem recognizable and important.

The broad background to world temperature variations since the 1880s is shown in Figure 7.10. There has been a rise in overall temperature probably beginning in the 1700s and culminating in the 1940s.

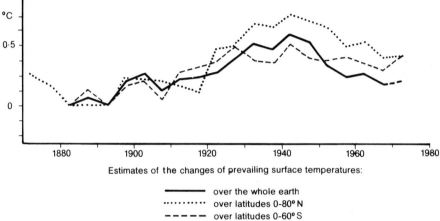

Estimates of the changes of prevailing surface temperatures:

————— over the whole earth

············· over latitudes 0–80° N

– – – – over latitudes 0–60° S

FIGURE 7.10   Changes in the average temperatures over the whole Earth since the 1880s. Successive 5-year means are expressed as departures from the mean for 1880–84. After Lamb (1977).

A subsequent phase of cooling occurred until the late 1960s, since when the decline has been arrested. In the Arctic the amplitude of this trend is some four times higher than the world trend and ten times higher than that in tropical environments (Lamb, 1977). The greatest change occurs in the zone of the Arctic most open to the North Atlantic, from Greenland through the Barents Sea to Franz Josef Land, and also in the northern continental interiors (Figure 7.11). The dramatic 5°C fall in mean annual temperature in Franz Josef Land from the mid-1950s to mid-1960s is shown in Figure 7.12a. Changes elsewhere are less dramatic and illustrated by the 2.5°C rise of temperature in West Greenland between 1920 and 1960 (Figure 7.12b).

In the Antarctic the best long-term record comes from Laurie Island in the South Orkney Islands where there appears to be a partial anti-phase relationship with the overall arctic trend. The mean annual

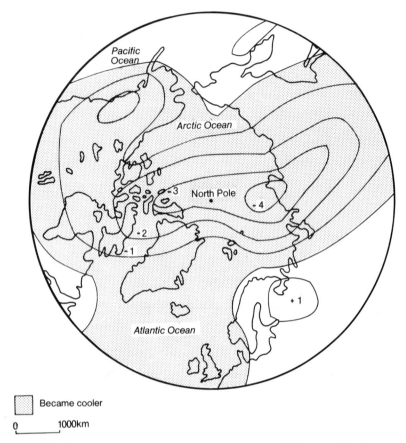

Became cooler

0   1000km

FIGURE 7.11   Temperature changes in the Arctic between the 1940s and 1950s (degrees
              centigrade). After Mitchell (1963).

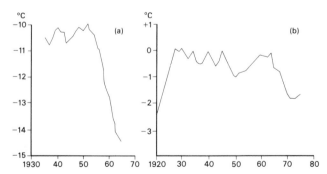

FIGURE 7.12   Recent changes in mean annual temperature in the Arctic *(a)* Franz Josef Land
              (Rodewald, 1972) and *(b)* Godthåb (Gordon, 1980).

temperature fell from −4°C in the 1900s to −6°C in 1930 at a time of general rise elsewhere. It then rose to −2.5°C in 1955 before falling to −4.5°C in the 1960s (Limbert, 1974). This record is apparently typical of the Weddell Sea/Antarctic Peninsula areas but it is not known how typical it is of the rest of Antarctica.

Precipitation changes in the polar regions generally show a maximum which was attained early in the twentieth century followed by a decline until the 1960s, since when there has been an increase (Lamb, 1977). The amplitude of the change has been greatest in continental interiors and, for example, precipitation since 1970 in Siberia has been 50–100 per cent higher than the 1930–60 average. Studies of ice cores in Greenland and Antarctica show a maximum of snow accumulation around 1924, implying that both poles were involved in the trend (Lamb, 1977).

The amplitude of change in recent decades in the polar regions is sufficiently great to have had significant effects on the three main environmental systems. Small glaciers and snow beds in many parts of the Arctic have been expanding, for example in Ellesmere Island (Hattersley-Smith and Serson, 1973), Baffin Island (Andrews *et al.*, 1972) and Greenland (Gordon, 1980). This trend is favoured both by recent precipitation and temperature changes. There is little documented evidence of change in the periglacial environment. However, tree-ring widths have been used in the sub-Arctic to show that summers were cooler than normal in the early nineteenth century and also in the early 1970s (Figure 7.13). If the same trends applied in the adjacent

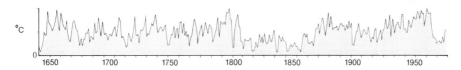

FIGURE 7.13   The variation of summer temperatures (April–November) as indicated by tree-ring widths at Fort Chimo near the tree line in northeastern Canada. From H. C. Fritts (personal communication).

tundra in Arctic Canada, then it is likely that, following a period of rapid growth from the 1930s to the 1960s, the rates of growth and tundra productivity are now in decline. Plants which moved into marginally suitable sites in the first half of this century may now be unable to survive in these locations. A check or reduction in plant cover will affect permafrost depths and accentuate the effects of mass wasting.

The fluctuations in the oceanic environment are better documented. A peak in ocean temperatures in the North Atlantic arena probably lagged some years behind the atmospheric peak and was achieved in

1950 (Lamb, 1977). Since then there has been an overall cooling. This is well illustrated by pack ice variations. In August 1938 arctic pack ice was withdrawn to its smallest known extent and most of Svalbard and the Siberian coast were ice-free (Figure 7.14). In the 1960s the

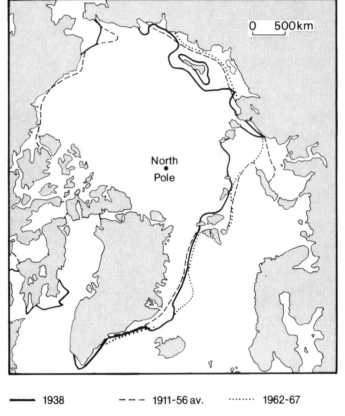

———— 1938   — — — 1911-56 av.   ········· 1962-67

FIGURE 7.14   Summer sea ice variations in the Arctic, showing the more southerly limits of recent decades when compared to 1938. After Lamb (1972).

average position was much further south and approached the position of the last years of the previous century, and impinged on much of the Siberian coast (Bulatov and Zakharov, 1978). The 1975 season off Siberia was the worst for 20 years. Off southwest Greenland ocean temperatures rose 1.5°C between 1920 and 1930 and remained high until 1961, since when there has been a sharp drop. Sea ice frequency has mirrored these trends. Off Labrador it is only in the 1970s that cooling has occurred. In response the number of icebergs drifting across latitude 48°N has increased from about 140 per year in the 1960s to 1590 in 1972 (an all-time record) and 800 in 1973 (Schell *et al.*, 1975).

These changes are sufficiently dramatic to influence marine life. For example, cod which had been spreading up the west coast of Greenland during the warming in the first half of the century (Jensen, 1939), had their progress checked in the 1960s and are now being restricted further and further to the south. An inverse trend has occurred with the ice-loving seals. After withdrawing northwards in the first half of the century they are now expanding southwards (Dunbar, 1976).

There are few observations of sufficient length to give much indication of recent trends in the Antarctic. Heap (1964) drew attention to the correlation between the duration of fast ice persistence and temperature in the vicinity of Laurie Island in the South Orkneys, which suggests a severe spell of ice condition between 1923 and 1933. This spell was reflected in a small glacier resurgence in South Georgia in the 1930s (Smith, 1960) and an increase in iceberg frequency. Sea ice fluctuations around Antarctica are now attracting a lot of interest. Although there are differences from sector to sector, sea ice extent in the 1970s seemed greater than in the late 1950s, with 1972 being a particularly bad ice year (Kukla *et al.*, 1977).

The environmental trends of the last few decades are of fundamental importance to human affairs. As will be seen in subsequent chapters, many decisions concerning the current development of fisheries, sea routes, ports and even offshore oil drilling were made in the light of data obtained for the unusually warm conditions of the early years of this century. The plans are now encountering severe problems because they are being put into practice against a background of a changing and generally deteriorating environment.

Further reading

Denton, G. H. and Hughes, T. J. 1981: *The last great ice sheets.* Wiley, New York.

Dunbar, M. J. 1976: Climatic change and northern development. *Arctic*, 29 (4), 183–93.

Imbrie, J. and Imbrie, K. P. 1979: *Ice ages.* Macmillan, London.

Jensen, A. S. 1939: Concerning a change of climate during recent decades in the Arctic and Subarctic regions, from Greenland in the West to Eurasia in the East, and contemporary biological and geographical changes. *Det Konlige Danske Videnskabernes Selskab, Biologiske Meddelelser*, 14 (8), 1–75. (A Classic.)

Lamb, H. H. 1977: *Climate present, past and future.* vol. 2: *Climatic history and the future.* Methuen, London.

Sugden, D. E. 1978: Ice age earth: extremes of a glacial planet. *Geographical Magazine*, 51 (2), 119–28.

Human Systems
in the Arctic and Antarctic

CHAPTER EIGHT

Evolution,Population and Settlement

Introduction

If our planet is viewed as a whole the polar zones, along with deserts, stand out because of their sparse population and exceedingly slim infrastructure of settlements and transport links. It is still common to fly overland for many hours without encountering a sign of human activity. It is the aim of this chapter to try and probe the reasons for this low population density. To do so it is useful to take an appropriate world perspective and evaluate the role of the polar zones during the evolution of Man on Earth. Such an approach is important. In the first place it tackles one of the fundamental features of the polar zones. In the second place it gives historical perspective on the operation of, and our understanding of, national and sub-national human systems of today. Sometimes these constraints are not recognized clearly and their role is easily misunderstood or even unsuspected.

A long-held and helpful subdivision of Man's evolution on Earth distinguishes the fundamentally different economies of (a) hunting and gathering, (b) farming/herding and (c) urban life (Childe, 1960; G. Clark, 1952; 1977). These can be viewed as a series of evolutionary stages at least in the world's core areas. Hunting and gathering are related to Man's span on Earth until after the waning of the last ice sheets and in Europe reached its height in the late-glacial Advanced Palaeolithic cultures; typically, at such a stage society centred on small dispersed groups of nomadic hunters. Following a transitional Mesolithic stage during which progress was made in domesticating animals and developing crops, the mixed farming stage is equated with Neolithic society. The main features were the increase in population and growth of permanent villages. In northwest Europe the transition to a Neolithic mixed farming society was achieved between approximately 7000 and 3500 years ago (G. Clark, 1967). The urban economy depends on improved communications, and taps the resources of a far wider area, allowing surplus food production to be used to support specialist artisans in the towns. Established at an early date in southwest Asia, the urban economy affected much of Europe in Roman times. Commercially and industrially based urban colonialism spread to the world in the last few centuries, though as recently as 1930 only one-fifth of mankind lived in urban centres (Sorre, 1952). It is this wave which Brookfield (1973) aptly names *intrusive*. This chapter takes these three stages of economic development in turn and examines how the polar regions fared in relation to each.

Hunting and gathering and the polar regions

From origins earlier than *c.* 40 000 years ago until late glacial times Man was everywhere a hunter and gatherer. In certain desert and polar environments he remained a hunter and gatherer (though with increasing sophistication) until the time of contact with 'urban' Europeans. The sequence of events over much of the Arctic is far from certain (Dumond, 1977; Giddings, 1968; McGhee, 1974), but the main outlines are shown in Figure 8.1.

The oldest recognizable culture is Palaeo-Arctic and is presumed to have existed until around 7 000 years B.P. It involved the hunting of land animals on tundra areas exposed at the height of the last Weichselian/Wisconsin glaciation. The heartland was the unglaciated lowland of northeast Siberia and its ice-free peninsula of Beringia, exposed by a lowered sea level and girt on all sides by ice (Figure 7.3). Woolly mammoth, horse, bison and caribou were the main quarry sought by groups of people armed with stone-tipped spears. In winter the people lived in semi-subterranean houses roofed with sods while in summer they used tents. Their clothes were sewn furs and skins. Presumably these were the hunters who were sufficiently successful to wipe out the woolly mammoth. This arctic culture was similar to the contemporary Advanced Paleolithic culture of Europe which depended on the caribou of the tundra around the southern and eastern margins of the European ice sheet.

Subsequently the Arctic was the scene of two rapidly spreading waves of hunting and gathering cultures, each of which was followed by a period of consolidation and regional differentiation. The first took place *c.* 4000 years ago and was based on the hunting of land animals, especially caribou and musk-oxen, together with seasonal fishing. Known as the Arctic Small Tool Tradition (after their distinctive

FIGURE 8.1   (Opposite) The evolution of hunting and gathering cultures in various parts of the American Arctic. The relationships over time are shown in the columns and over space in the rows (various sources).

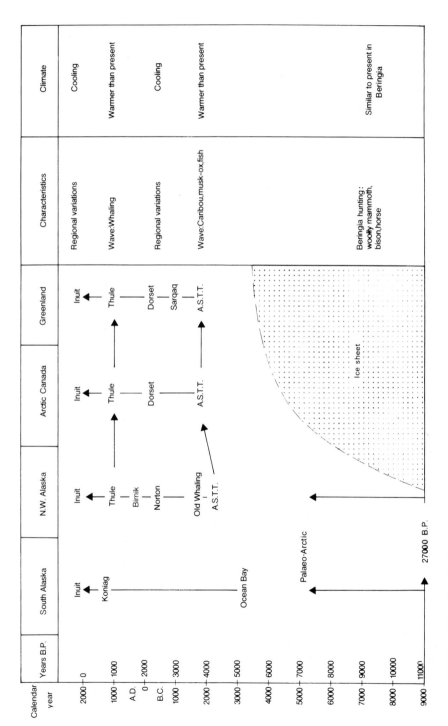

A.S.T.T. Arctic Small Tool Tradition

miniaturized artifacts), it originated in Siberia and swept across Arctic Canada to northern Greenland. This was the first immigration into Arctic Canada in the wake of the disappearance of the Laurentide Ice Sheet. At its peak the culture extended from northeast Greenland across the American and Siberian Arctic at least as far as the Lena River. The migration wave was followed by a period of several thousand years when separate cultures evolved to suit local circumstances. For example, the Sarqaq culture in Greenland supplemented its dependence on caribou with fishing, while in Alaska there was the progressive development of whaling cultures. In the eastern Canadian Arctic the Dorset modification saw the increasing importance of ice hunting for seal and the invention of the snow igloo.

A second wave occurred in the tenth century A.D., called the Thule culture. It originated in the Bering Straits area and was based on coastal villages dependent on whaling from umiaks and kayaks. Within 100 years it swept along the Canadian Straits as far as Greenland, successfully replacing the pre-existing Dorset culture but incorporating such highlights as the igloo and ice hunting techniques. The speed of the wave implies that there was migration of people as well as of a culture. The uniformity of this 'eastern' Thule culture throughout a vast area was remarkable (Figure 8.2) and even today Inuit in East Greenland can converse with those in Alaska; the language difference may be compared to that between Norwegian and Swedish. The 'western' Inuit in the southern Bering Straits area were not affected by the Thule culture and maintained a distinctive culture and language. The difference between the 'eastern' and 'western' languages is like that between English and German. In the years up to European contact regional variations within the 'eastern' Inuit again began to develop, with caribou hunting assuming a relatively greater importance in Arctic Canada and ice hunting for seal in Greenland and Eastern Canada. Whaling remained important in Alaska.

The reasons for sudden waves of migration are not easy to infer from a patchy archaeological record. Nevertheless one can point to environmental change as one relevant factor (McGhee, 1974). The first wave exploited tundra resources during the climatic optimum at a time when conditions were warmer than today and much new land had been exposed by retreating ice conditions. The Thule whaling culture coincided with a warm interval when the Canadian Straits were sufficiently free of ice in summer to permit the passage of bowhead whales, a state unlike that of today (Chapter 7). The periods of regional differentiation coincided with climate cooling. It is tempting to suggest that the Dorset invention of ice hunting for seal and the snow igloo were responses to an environmental cooling which severely reduced the abundance of land animals and whales. Likewise the other regional variants seem well suited to their respective environments. In pointing to environmental correlations there is a danger of overlooking social factors. After all it is difficult to escape the conclusion that the timing of each migration wave, the extreme rapidity of their diffusion and their place of origin must relate to social conditions which are as yet unknown.

Set against the success of early Man in sweeping into arctic tundra and coastal areas is the stark contrast of Antarctica which escaped such colonization. Advanced Palaeolithic hunters and gatherers had reached Tierra del Fuego in late glacial times and their Yahgan descendants persisted there and were described effectively by Charles Darwin. When one views the ease with which early Man coped with a range of arctic environments it is difficult to regard the relatively mild and richly endowed coastline of the Antarctic Peninsula as anything but favourable for occupation. Indeed the very lushness of life in the sub-Antarctic serves to emphasize the role of inaccessibility in preventing colonization. The width of Drake Strait and the spacing of the sub-antarctic island stepping stones proved an impassable barrier to hunting Man.

There are several important implications to be drawn from this brief review of hunting cultures in the polar regions. Seen in the context of pre-history the traditional Inuit hunting economy is a direct descendant of ancient Ice Age cultures. Advanced Palaeolithic Man in Europe had evolved barbed harpoons, houses and clothing suitable for arctic conditions, and similar basic principles were still applied in immediate pre-contact Inuit society. In addition other important inventions were derived from the interchange of ideas with Mesolithic cultures which were undergoing a transition to animal husbandry. The use of dog sledges, skin boats, more sophisticated hooks and stoneware were all Mesolithic inventions probably derived from Eurasia (G. Clark, 1967)

Seen from the point of view of hunters and gatherers, the Arctic was attractive; the large migrating herds of land mammals and rich seasonal migrations of marine mammals were a major resource. This view may be justified in two ways. If one takes immediate pre-contact Inuit populations as representative of hunters and gatherers, then the densities are comparable with hunters and gatherers in other environments and indeed are often high. Lee and Devore (1968) believed densities of 1–10 persons per $100 km^2$ to be typical of hunters and gatherers. Inuit densities spanned this range and were typically 6 per $100 km^2$ while densities as high as 30 per $100 km^2$ occurred on favoured island sites (Oswalt, 1967). Only in very poor inland areas did densities drop to the lower end of the range and approach 1 per 100km². Another justification can be taken from the veritable florescence of cave art associated with the specialized Magdalenian reindeer hunters of south-west France in late glacial times. The abundance and the quality of carved artifacts far outclassed the succeeding Mesolithic forest cultures which had to adapt to seasonally less abundant game (Clark and Piggott, 1965). Although implications of affluence and cultural progress can easily be overplayed, one can at least suggest that tundra conditions are suitable for such developments. It is reasonable to conclude that availability of game rather than cold is the most significant factor to a hunter, and that at this level of culture the tundra was attractive and well populated, at least when seen from a world viewpoint.

Farming/herding and the polar regions

The domestication of animals for food and haulage and the cultivation of crops increased food supplies and led to a hundredfold increase in population density when compared with the pre-existing hunting and gathering culture. For example, over much of Neolithic Europe clusters of 10–50 houses formed villages dispersed at distances commonly of 1–2km, a far cry from the former small, nomadic hunting groups (Childe, 1954). By 3500 years ago farming had successfully displaced hunting and gathering economies over most of northwest Europe as far as the northern limit of the deciduous forest (G. Clark, 1952). Hunting and gathering continued in the coniferous forest zone but profited from interchange of ideas and artifacts (such as pottery) with peoples to the south. In North America the transition was less complete in that hunting and gathering economies survived in the Great Plains and among some Palaeo-Indian groups of the deciduous forest, perhaps because the lack of a domesticated draught animal made large-scale cultivation difficult (Clark and Piggott, 1965). At this stage the arctic tundra of both continents was unaffected by the Neolithic farming system, while the circumpolar forest belt was inhabited by hunters and gatherers who were in effective contact with Neolithic farmers only in Europe.

A later development which affected Eurasia in the two millenia A.D. was the development of reindeer herding. Introduced by the Lapps or their immediate forebears, it was taken up by other peoples who moved from the south into the tundra areas (Figure 8.2). It involved a nomadic existence following the reindeer into the tundra in summer and retreat-ing to the forest in winter. Arctic reindeer herding involved several waves of both Uralic and Altaic peoples. The last significant wave was the northward migration of the Yakut people around A.D.1300 who moved north from the Asian steppe at the time of the Mongol expansion. Reindeer herding squeezed out or replaced the pre-existing hunting and gathering economies in Asia except among the Yukaghir, the coastal Inuit and certain Chukchi groups. Reindeer herding did not reach Arctic America where Inuit hunting and gathering remained unmolested until modern times.

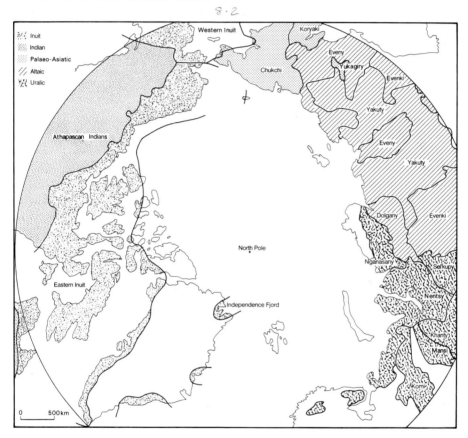

FIGURE 8.2   The distribution of indigenous peoples in the Arctic. Various sources.

The reasons for this contrast between Arctic America and Arctic Asia is undoubtedly complex, but it is worth mentioning two factors. First in environmental terms, the Eurasian Arctic is better suited to reindeer herding than much of the eastern American Arctic. Whereas the Eurasian tundra is a thin strip of land with relatively easy access from the forest edge, the eastern American Arctic tundra is much wider from north to south and is also broken up by straits impassable in summer. A nomadic existence, exploiting the northern tundra in summer and forest in winter, is impossible in much of the eastern Canadian Arctic and Greenland. Second, the Eurasian Arctic, unlike the American Arctic, was adjacent to the most developed Neolithic farming and herding cultures. Herding on a large scale was unknown in North America and there was thus less chance of introducing the technique to the north.

The worldwide adoption of farming and herding signals a major landmark in the evolution of arctic peoples, for it is this development which first marks the relative decline in population density compared with other parts of the world. Whereas temperate-latitude peoples were able to increase densities by a hundredfold, cultivation was effectively ruled out on climatic grounds in the Arctic and the population density remained stable. An added contrast within the Arctic was introduced by the later introduction of reindeer herding in the Eurasian Arctic; employing a more efficient form of food production and by spilling over into the adjacent forests during the difficult winter period, a somewhat denser population could be supported. The restriction of reindeer herding to Eurasia introduced for the first time a fundamental contrast between the arctic areas of both continents. In the Eurasian Arctic the population was denser and involved peoples who looked south in terms of both tradition and new ideas. In Arctic America the population remained sparse and was cut off from southern influences. Indeed, the southern boundary between Inuit and Indian was one of continual friction.

Urban systems and the polar regions

The development of towns in mid-latitudes resulted from the ability to tap resources over a wider area than had been possible under a Neolithic farming system. It went hand in hand with improvements in transport and the greater efficiency of production that allowed population densities to increase yet again. In a polar context it is the growth of towns, first in Europe, then North America and finally Japan that has affected the history of exploration and development. First influenced by the European trading empires of the Vikings, Dutch, British and other European nations, the polar regions have now become relevant to the prosperity of the world's industrial nations.

The history of the polar regions since the tenth century is the story of how the burgeoning urban core areas gradually came to extend their influence into the cold sector of the world 'periphery'. In the more accessible land areas of the Arctic and the seasonally ice-free coasts of both north and south, the first wave was commercial in nature and based on the trade of polar products with the core, for example, furs and whales. In the central polar regions, however, the task was different. It was necessary first to discover what was there, and in order to do so it was necessary to evolve an efficient means of travel over ice sheets and sea ice. The quest for this mastery is the story of polar exploration and it is an important geographical topic because it is part of the spread of the intrusive system into the least accessible polar areas and has implications which persist today. Success on a scale commensurate with economic development only came with the development of the aircraft in the first half of the twentieth century.

When viewing the complex history of ten centuries of exploration and exploitation, it is helpful to hang the discussion round a simple core–periphery model (Figure 8.3). Here the core area and its effective area of control is represented by a *plus*, while the area outside the boundary beyond the control of the core is represented by a *minus*.

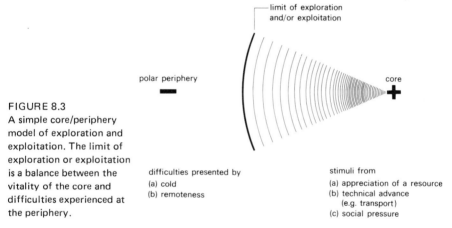

FIGURE 8.3
A simple core/periphery model of exploration and exploitation. The limit of exploration or exploitation is a balance between the vitality of the core and difficulties experienced at the periphery.

difficulties presented by
(a) cold
(b) remoteness

stimuli from
(a) appreciation of a resource
(b) technical advance
(e.g. transport)
(c) social pressure

The boundary can be envisaged as the limit of exploration or exploitation at any one stage and is a balance between the vitality and expertise of the core and the difficulties presented by the periphery. Throughout polar history the factors which affect the vitality of the core are seen to be threefold:

(1) appreciation of a resource for trade, raw materials or strategy;
(2) expertise in techniques of travel;
(3) social pressure, for example, overpopulation, personal prestige etc.

Factors influencing the difficulties presented by the periphery are mainly:

(1) the rigorous environment, especially the absence of local food and population;
(2) distance from the core.

Figure 8.4 shows the fluctuation of the boundary delimiting the core over time. It can be seen that its progress into the polar regions is far from regular and indeed is marked by sudden thrusts or even reverses. These trends and fluctuations form the focus of the rest of this chapter.

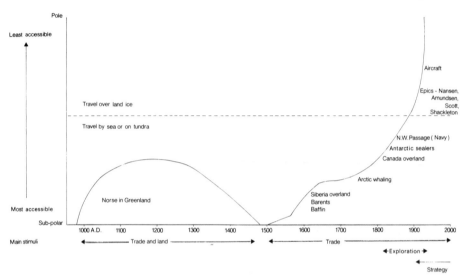

FIGURE 8.4   The spread of the world's intrusive system into the polar regions over time. The vertical axis reflects relative accessibility while the horizontal axis represents time. The shading represents the area in the effective control of the core.

THE NORSE IN GREENLAND

The Norse colonization of Greenland offers a rare chance to examine an expansion of the core into the polar periphery including both its initiation and its decline. Thus it provides an opportunity of studying the complete cycle and gives perspective on some of the main principles affecting successful exploitation of the periphery by the core. Lest anyone doubt the success of the Greenland colony it is worth remembering that it lasted 500 years. It remains to be seen whether subsequent European colonization of North America survives as long!

The story of the colonization is magnificently told in Icelandic sagas and matched to archaeological finds by Jones (1964), Mowat (1965), Magnusson and Pálsson (1965) and Krogh (1967), while a recent summary is given by Garner (1978). In the year A.D. 981 Eirik the Red started a 3-year exile from Iceland exploring land to the west. Well versed in the principles of perception geography, he named the land 'Greenland' since, as the saga relates, 'men would be all the more drawn to go there if the land had an attractive name' ('Eirik the Red's Saga'; Jones, 1964). Although confusing generations of schoolchildren ever since, the ruse worked and in A.D.986 one of the biggest polar expeditions of all time set sail from Iceland in 25 ships. Fourteen ships arrived safely with around 400 people who established farms on the inner reaches of fjords around the present sites of Julianehåb (eastern settlement) and Godthåb (western settlement) (Figures 8.5 and 8.6).

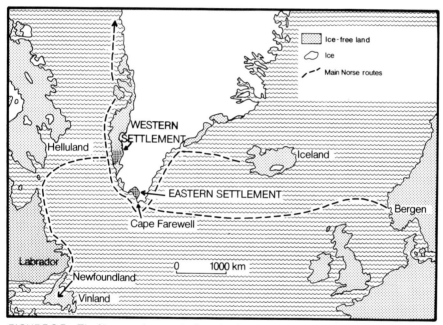

FIGURE 8.5   The Norse settlements in Greenland and sea routes. After Garner, 1978.

At its peak in A.D.1100 the colony may have totalled 6000 people. The larger eastern settlement had *c.* 190 farms and a cathedral, where as the western settlement had 90 farms and four churches. The western settlement was reported to have been abandoned by 1342 while the eastern settlement apparently lasted until the late fifteenth century. No colonists remained when Davis reached the coast in 1586.

Life centred on farms mostly situated in sunny situations overlooking pockets of tillable land and with access to the sea and gently sloping outpastures (Figure 8.7; Pollitt, 1976). 12–28 cows were common, while Eirik the Red, who had annexed the best site had 40. Sheep utilized the outpastures while pigs and horses were also kept. A few

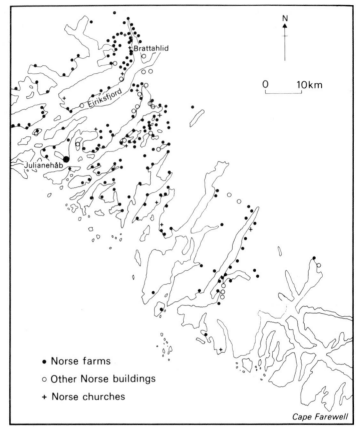

FIGURE 8.6   Location of buildings in the eastern settlement. After Gad, 1970.

people grew hay and corn. Meat was obtained mainly by hunting seal and caribou. Communication between farms within each settlement was by small boat or horse. The culture remained firmly Scandinavian and this is reflected by the nature of church weddings, funerals and even details of clothing discovered in graves. Though largely self-sufficient, the Greenland Norse were dependent on trade for goods which were vital to maintain their Scandinavian way of life. Iron, weapons, corn, wood, clothing and honey were all items which came predominantly from Norway. Some trade also took place with Iceland which was an outpost of the Viking core and probably some wood was obtained from Vinland in North America (Figure 8.5). In return, the Greenland colonizers provided Europe with some rare and high-quality goods such as furs, walrus-hide rope, ivory, wool, polar bears and Greenland falcons. It is difficult to appreciate the significance of such goods but they were not as frivolous as they might appear to a twentieth-century reader. Walrus-hide rope was a technical breakthrough in terms of strength and its resistance to rotting, while the wool was noteworthy for its quality. In the days before the invention of the gun, falcons were greatly prized and an insight into their importance comes from the story that in 1396 'the Duke of Burgundy sent to Bayezid as a ransom for his son twelve Greenland falcons' (quoted by Jones, 1964). The strength of the trade links with Norway is illustrated by the fact that in 1261 Greenland accepted the sovereignty of Norway in an agreement which gave Norway the monopoly of trade and shipping to and from Greenland.

FIGURE 8.7   September activity on Sandnes farm in the western settlement about A.D. 1120–1130. Watercolour by Jens Rosing, photograph by Lennart Larsen.

The fundamental reasons for the rise and fall of the Greenland colony may never emerge but analysis of factors operating at the core and periphery offers some insights. There was strong pressure at the core at the time of colonization. Firstly, there was a land shortage in Iceland. The island supported a rural population of 80000 people, a total far in excess of the rural population of today, and overpopulation is suggested by the severe famine in 976. Secondly, personal pressures applied to Eirik the Red. Setting aside the feeling obtained from the sagas that he had the charisma and ambitions of an Amundsen, he had other sound reasons for leaving Iceland. Having added applied geomorphology to his geographical skills by successfully killing his neighbours in a landslide, he was eventually banished from Iceland. Already banished from Norway there was little option but to go west! Finally, the Viking trading empire was vibrant and outward-looking and enthusiastically embraced new opportunities such as presented by trade with the new land of Greenland.

The periphery was also more attractive to tenth-century settlers than might first appear. The fjords formed sheltered harbours, and being close to the ice sheet they enjoy a sunny climate quite different from either the coast or indeed maritime Iceland. Again, unlike Iceland, there was caribou to be hunted on land. More important, the time of colonization coincided with a period when the climate was several degrees warmer than today (Chapter 7). In south Greenland this had important effects. There was apparently no pack ice to impede navigation; the longer summer growing season made crops possible and allowed livestock to live part of the year outside while fish abounded in inshore waters.

The decline of the colony in the fourteenth and fifteenth centuries is likely to have resulted from a combination of factors. On the one hand the vitality of the core decreased. Norway's prestige declined and indeed in the late fourteenth century the country was annexed by Denmark which had little interest in the North Atlantic. Furthermore, the port responsible for Greenland trade, Bergen, was sacked on more than one occasion. At the same time Greenland's products lost their attractiveness to Europe. Activity in the White Sea area of Eurasia had discovered a closer and cheaper source of arctic products such as fur, hides, walrus-rope and bears; high-quality African elephant ivory displaced the lower-quality arctic ivory and the burgeoning textile industries of England and Holland had closer supplies of wool. Given this background it is not surprising that the frequency of ships to Greenland declined; the last recorded voyage from Norway took place in 1367. With no ships of their own, the settlements had their trade routes severed and with it their cultural and economic links with the core.

On the other hand the climate on the periphery too was becoming more difficult, reaching its nadir in the seventeenth and eighteenth centuries. Pack ice was impeding the sea routes, thus increasing the effective distance of the colony in cost and time. Sailing directions in 1360 described how 'nowadays ice has come down from the northeast...that without risk to life no one can sail the old course and be heard of again' (Bardarson, *Landnámabók*, quoted in Jones, 1964). The shortening of the growing season would have prevented crops from ripening and increased the hazard of livestock-rearing. Forced to rely more on hunting, the Norse came increasingly into contact and competition with Inuit peoples of the Thule culture who at that time were moving southwards in pursuit of seal. There are records of several battles during which at least some Norse were killed (Figure 8.8). The cumulative effect of all these factors, and perhaps others, took their toll and both settlements were abandoned. Whether the colonists died in Greenland, mixed with the Inuit, or migrated to America or back to Iceland is still a msytery.

FIGURE 8.8
An illustration by the Greenlander Aron of Kangeq of an Inuit tale of conflict with the Norse (Rink, 1875).

The lessons to be drawn from this first venture of the European core into the Arctic are instructive. When the core was buoyant and the periphery more favourable than normal, Greenland was a viable outpost. When the balance tipped the other way, Greenland proved too marginal, a fully self-sufficient way of life based on agriculture and hunting proving unsupportable even in this least severe of Arctic environments. These conclusions seem all the more convincing when one views the case of Iceland which was one step closer to the core of Norway and boasted more agricultural assets. Iceland survived, but only after experiencing great problems and a much reduced population. In A.D. 1800, towards the end of the Little Ice Age, Iceland's population was only 47 000; little more than half of the 80 000 achieved soon after the initial Norse immigration. While Iceland was just able to survive as an outpost of Europe, Greenland was not.

EXPLORING THE POLAR PERIPHERIES
(SIXTEENTH TO LATE NINETEENTH CENTURIES)

A second wave of interest in the polar regions burst out from Europe in the late sixteenth and early seventeenth centuries (Kirwan, 1962). Stimulated by the wish to tap the riches of Cathay, English and Dutch shipping interests sought to exploit a direct route to the Far East via the Arctic, thus avoiding clashes at sea with the then dominant Spanish and Portuguese. With supreme confidence, including special hulls for use in tropical waters and instructions for dealing with tropical islanders, an assault was mounted on the Northeast Passage north of Eurasia. By 1630 a variety of expeditions had explored the western entrances to what is now known as the Northern Sea Route and had discovered the limitations presented by pack ice. In 1596 these limitations forced Barents to spend an unplanned winter in a makeshift hut on Novaya Zemlya, an event which had the distinction of being the first arctic wintering, albeit unintentional. The Northwest Passage north of America was also under siege by a series of seamen whose names tell of the sites of their discoveries, for example Hudson, Baffin and Davis (Figure 8.9). Notable perhaps is the early exploitation of minerals by Frobisher. A voyage to Frobisher Bay in 1576 unearthed ore thought to contain gold. A second two-ship expedition mined 200 tons of the ore and a third fifteen-ship expedition was mounted and aimed to establish the Arctic's first mining camp. It is sad to relate the failure of this first attempt by the core to exploit arctic resources. The fleet was forced to retreat by bad weather and the ore turned out to be 'fools' gold', namely iron pyrites! But other marine discoveries were not mistaken. The records of abundant whales and seals in the approaches to both Northeast and Northwest Passages gave rise to the vast arctic whaling and sealing industries of the next few centuries.

The land peripheries of the Arctic were concurrently being opened up in Eurasia. Following the collapse of the Tartar Kingdom of Sibir in 1584, Russians swept across the Siberian sub-Arctic and into the Arctic proper, mainly in search of furs. Before this date fur trapping had been confined to the area west of the Urals (Armstrong, 1965). It is remarkable that as early as 1648 Dezhnev sailed from the mouth of the Kolyma round the tip of Asia through what was to become known as Bering Straits, thus establishing the existence of a segment of the Northern Sea Route which was not to be utilized economically for another 300 years. A network of trading posts and water routes grew up to further the import of grain and luxuries from the European

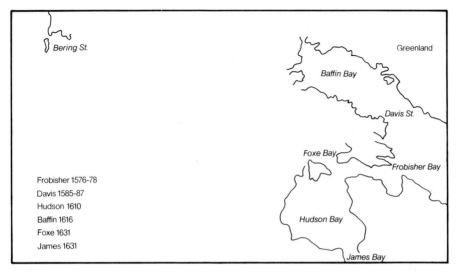

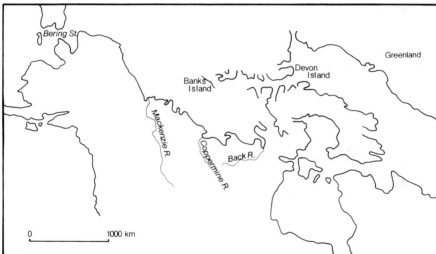

FIGURE 8.9 (Top) The Northwest Passage in 1731. (Below) The Northwest Passage
in 1840 (just before the Franklin disaster).

core in return for the fur pelts (Figure 8.10). Consolidated by official
expeditions associated with the name of Vitus Bering, the Russian wave
of exploitation soaked up the riches of the Bering Sea area before
sweeping down to California by the late eighteenth century.

With the polar peripheries involved in commerce and the European
core busy fighting at home, further arctic exploration had to wait until
the nineteenth century. By this time interest was reawakening in the
Northwest Passage. Worried by Russian expansion into North America

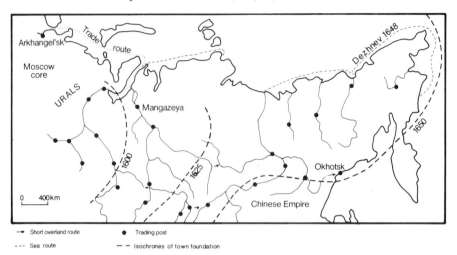

FIGURE 8.10　The late sixteenth- and early seventeenth-century wave of fur exploitation
into Siberia, showing navigable waterways and main trading points.
Isochrones give the dates of the foundation of the main towns. The wave
did not spread into China where there was competition. Various sources.

and possessing an under-employed Navy after the Napoleonic wars,
Sir John Barrow initiated a series of strategically motivated British
expeditions to the area. Organized in the best naval traditions of the
time, complete with naval uniforms and gifts for the natives, John
Ross made first contact with the polar Inuit in 1818 (Figure 8.11).
The next year Edward Parry explored much of the route that was to
become the Northwest Passage (Figure 8.9). Meanwhile the Hudson

FIGURE 8.11　John Ross in official dress meets the polar Inuit for the first time in 1818.
Reproduced in Victor, 1964.

Bay Company, which had been rather conservative since its foundation in 1670, was forced in the late eighteenth century to explore its land hinterland because of competition with rival traders. Mackenzie reached the mouth of the river of the same name in 1789 and in the next 30 years much of the mainland coast and major rivers were explored. Figure 8.9 shows the state of play just before the great naval extravaganza of the Franklin Expedition and the following 30 years. Sir John Franklin set sail in *Erebus* and *Terror* in 1845 to traverse the last unknown stretch of the Northwest Passage and disappeared together with the ships' companies of 134 men. Forty relief expeditions were sent out in the next 10 years and, with a few exceptions such as that of Leopold McClintock, the whole venture was marked by 'ineptitude extraordinary' (Wright, 1959). Eventually these expeditions found traces of the pathetic trail of corpses leading southwards from Franklin's ice-beset ships. Also a series of land-sledge journeys established the outline of the southern coastline of the arctic archipelago. The effort of centuries to traverse the Northeast and Northwest Passages in a single ship had to await two single-minded Scandinavians. The Northeast Passage was completed by Nordenskiöld in 1879 while the Northwest Passage was first traversed by the young Amundsen in the years 1903—06.

The antarctic peripheries emerged for the first time in the nineteenth century (Dater, 1975). Prior to that in the years 1772—76 James Cook had established the probable nature of any southern continent. He had explored the 'savage and horrible' island of South Georgia, doomed 'never to yield to the warmth of the sun' and concluded that if anyone discovered the fabled southern continent, 'I shall not envy him the fame of his discoveries, but I make bold to declare that the world will derive no benefit from it' (Kirwan, 1962, p. 86). Nevertheless Cook's description of marine riches attracted sealers and by the second decade of the nineteenth century some 200 American and British sealers were at work in the sub-Antarctic exploiting fur seals. The exploitation was devastating and within a few years the fur seals were virtually exterminated from sub-antarctic islands such as the South Shetlands, South Orkneys and South Georgia. Nevertheless within a few years sealers had discovered islands and small patches of mainland in much of Antarctica and these exploits are commemorated by their names, such as Biscoe, Weddell, Kemp and Balleny (Figure 8.12a).

Stimulated by the need to consolidate or expand commercial activities and by a striking growth in interest in science, a number of national expeditions were deployed to Antarctica and charted stretches of coastline. The first expedition was Russian and led by Bellingshausen.

In his two ships *Vostok* and *Mirny* he was the first to sight the continent in part of Queen Maud Land coast in 1820 (although he did not realize it) and later Alexander Island. Subsequently expeditions from America, France and Britain (Wilkes, 1840; d'Urville, 1840; Ross, 1841 respectively) made impressive discoveries in what are now the Australian, French and New Zealand sectors of Antarctica in search of the magnetic pole. Ross established a farthest south, and discovered that the sea route was blocked by the ice shelf barrier now named after him (Figure 8.12a). He noted that he might 'with equal chance of success try to sail through the cliffs of Dover' (Kirwan, 1962, p. 171). But,

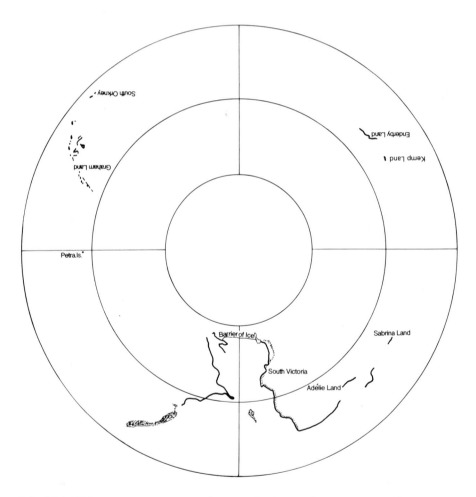

FIGURE 8.12(a)   Antarctica as mapped by James Clark Ross after his voyage in 1841, incorporating the discoveries of sealers. The original of the map may be found in Ross (1847).

while commercial exploitation of sub-antarctic seal and whale continued (Figure 8.13), explorers were diverted to the Franklin search
in the Northwest Passage and inland antarctic exploration had to wait
another 50 years.

Full analysis of the reasons for the sporadic and uneven spread of
the cores into the polar regions until the late nineteenth century is
beyond the scope of this chapter and interested readers might consult
Kirwan (1962) and Victor (1964). Nevertheless it is possible to point
to certain factors operating in both the core and the periphery. Appreciation of a resource stimulated many waves of interest. The initial

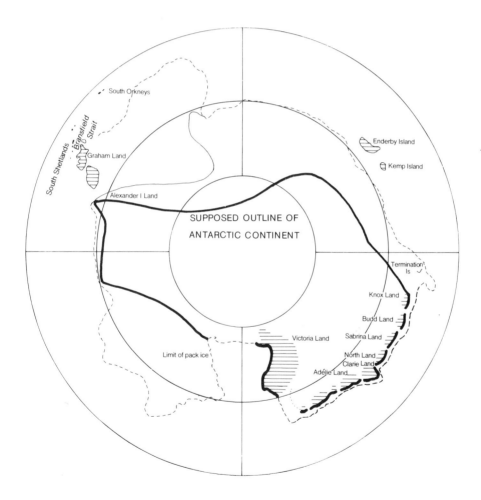

FIGURE 8.12(b)   Antarctica mapped in 1886, incorporating the results of the *Challenger*
Expedition which demonstrated the existence of sea-bed glacial erratics
derived from a continent. The original is in Murray (1886).

FIGURE 8.13
Wreck of a sealing or
whaling vessel on Fildes
Peninsula, King George
Island, South Shetland
Islands. Photographed in
1966.

Elizabethan search for the Northeast and Northwest Passages was
stimulated by the wish to exploit a direct northern route to the Spice
Islands of Cathay. The wave lost impetus when the Spanish and Portuguese grip in more conventional sea routes lessened. Interest in furs
fuelled the land-borne waves across Arctic Russia and Canada, while
Cook's accounts of fur seals attracted swarms of sealers to the Antarctic.
The high prices paid for furs at the core does much to explain the
intensity of the search. As an example a fur seal pelt could command a
price of 5 dollars at the beginning of the nineteenth century (Bonner
and Laws, 1964). Such prices help to explain the willingness of crews
to sail into inhospitable climates in such puny ships. After all, one small
vessel could catch 50000 pelts in a season. Strategic considerations by
the nations at the core also played their role in stimulating interest in
the Arctic. Sir John Barrow was able to play on fears of Russian expansion into America in order to justify his nineteenth-century blitz on
the Northwest Passage, while one of Bellinghausen's duties was to
search for suitable strategic harbours. One might add that the core areas
were only interested in the polar regions when they were not preoccu-
pied at home. For example, the Napoleonic wars at the beginning of
the nineteenth century gave little time for exploration.

Conditions at the periphery are likely to have varied as the world
endured the peak of the Little Ice Age in the eighteenth century
(Chapter 7). One can point to certain broad correlations between
environmental change and progress of exploration. The relatively good
ice conditions of the Elizabethan era in the late sixteenth century
favoured the successful voyages of the first wave. The difficult period
of the eighteenth century coincided with relatively little exploration
by sea. Perhaps in this case reports of bad ice conditions by sealers

and whalers discouraged explorers. Whatever the role of this factor, it is certain that the timing of Sir John Barrow's Northwest Passage thrust was influenced by the whaling captain, William Scoresby, who noted that ice conditions in 1817 were better than normal; favourable pack ice certainly helped Parry in his 1819 expedition.

Thus, towards the end of the nineteenth century, European- and American-based crews had explored and were successfully exploiting the peripheries of the polar regions. Sailing ships were able to cope with seasonal pack ice, and seals and whales were taken seasonally by fleets of ships based at ports in the core, for example Stonington in the U.S.A. and Dundee in Scotland. On ice-free land in the Arctic a network of routes and trading posts had fanned out from the cores in order to exploit furs. Interestingly, exploration and exploitation of the North American Arctic lagged behind that of the Russian Arctic by some 200 years. The importance of this phase of exploration of the polar regions can be summarized as follows:

(1) it unveiled large areas of formerly unknown land and sea to the world's core areas;
(2) as will be seen, it provided the basis for some modern territorial claims;
(3) it provided a springboard for subsequent attacks on the still unknown central polar areas and determined the location of subsequent activity;
(4) it established many techniques of polar travel; the development of the naval tradition of man-hauling sledges on Northwest Passage Expeditions was to have a tragic sequel in the race to the South Pole, while the use of the navy in polar exploration has been maintained to modern times, for example in the case of the U.S. Antarctic programme.

EXPLORING CENTRAL POLAR AREAS (1889 TO MODERN TIMES)

Effective incorporation of the central polar areas into the world intrusive system had to await the development of techniques of travel over large expanses of ice — sea ice in the Arctic and ice-sheet in the Antarctic. Whereas competent indigenous means of travel had been known for hundreds of years, the story is one of explorers from the core areas belatedly rediscovering the value of such techniques and then finding that they too could travel freely in formerly unexplored areas. As soon as this lesson was learnt, the arrival of the aircraft, with its ability to move freely across ice, suddenly transformed the significance of the polar regions into one of a strategic and resource frontier for the world's industrial cores. Today it is difficult to appreciate the contemporary ignorance of the central polar regions. Nothing was known of interior Antarctica, other than the implication of the *Challenger* Expedition that it was a true continent (Figure 8.12b). In the Arctic even this was uncertain. For example, upon hearing of Nansen's plan to freeze the ship *Fram* into arctic pack ice, in 1892 the eminent Sir Allen Young stated 'Dr. Nansen assumes the blank space around the axis of the earth to be a pool of water or ice; I think the great danger to contend with will be the land in nearly every direction near the Pole' (Nansen, 1897, p. 44).

The search for effective means of travel over ice is bound up with a 'heroic' age of exploration marked by the emergence of individuals. Rather than recount the achievements of the main expeditions it is perhaps more interesting to focus on two episodes — Nansen's exploration in the Arctic and the attempt to reach the South Pole over the antarctic ice sheet. Both illustrate the superiority of indigenous (mainly Inuit) techniques and how their use opened up formerly undiscovered areas. Both represent the extreme vanguard of the intrusive system.

Fridtjof Nansen was a zoologist by training who showed early signs of adventure by carrying out his undergraduate thesis on sealing in Svalbard. In 1888 he was the first to cross the Greenland ice sheet and discover its true nature (Nansen, 1890). Wishing to use Inuit equipment such as dog sledges he could obtain none, and made do instead with Lapp techniques such as skis and reindeer-skin clothing (and two Lapp companions!). Coupled with his own inventions of the Nansen sledge and Nansen cooker, the expedition crossed 650 km from east to west and wintered with the West Greenland Inuit (Figure 3.12). In 1893—96 Nansen embarked on an even more audacious exploration of the Arctic. The specially built *Fram* and its crew of 13 was frozen into the sea ice in September, 1893, in the Kara Sea (Figure 6.11). In the spring of 1895 Nansen and H. Johansen left the ship to strike out across the sea ice to the Pole equipped with dog sledges, kayaks and Inuit clothing. They turned before reaching the Pole and, many incident-packed months later, they wintered in a rough stone hut in northern Franz Josef Land before being picked up in the summer of 1896. The *Fram* broke free of ice in the same year and the expedition was a triumphant success (Nansen, 1897). The true oceanic nature of the polar basin was discovered while the climatic, oceanographic and pack ice observations remain important to this day. The idea of using the drifting ice as a base has also persisted to modern times, though now in a military context. Moreover, Nansen had demonstrated the value of Inuit techniques for travel over sea ice. He closes his account of the expedition by noting that 'Even if explorers have to live in Eskimo fashion...they may...make good headway and cover considerable distances in regions which have hitherto been regarded as almost inaccessible' (Nansen, 1898, p. 438).

The lesson took longer to learn in the Antarctic. Here the intense competition to reach the South Pole affords a unique possibility of examining the relative success of different approaches to travel over an ice sheet. In this case other variables can be held constant; the goal was the same while the participants pushed themselves and their technology to the very limits. The saga is well covered in the original accounts and elsewhere (Kirwan, 1962; Victor, 1964; Huntford, 1979), but certain highlights are instructive. The British Expeditions comprised Robert Scott's *Discovery* Expedition (1902–04); Ernest Shackleton's *Nimrod* Expedition (1907–09) and Scott's last *Terra Nova* Expedition (1911–13), while Roald Amundsen's Norwegian Expedition was in 1911–12. The expeditions took the nearest known coast to the Pole in the Ross Sea (Figure 8.12a) and pushed south over the Ross Ice Shelf (Figure 8.14). Scott's first expedition, using dogs, penetrated some 550 km southwards before being forced to retreat. Shackleton, who suffered from scurvy on this first expedition, was sent home, but returned in 1908 with his own expedition. Using Siberian ponies and then man-hauling, Shackleton turned only 155 km from the Pole and just got back with everyone intact, but with margins so tight that they had to return to pick up one member. Scott's last expedition, also relying on ponies initially, is perhaps the most famous polar tragedy of all time as a scurvy-wracked, starved and exhausted manhauling party finally died on their return from the Pole. The tragedy was all the more piquant when compared with Amundsen's classic journey of the same season. Covering similar territory, Amundsen's party, equipped with Inuit clothing and using skis and dogs, skied for pleasure in the Transantarctic Mountains and had sufficient margin to stay at the Pole for 3 days and even leave behind a tent (Figure 8.15).

In retrospect it is easy to see the errors in Scott's plans, the most serious of which was the failure to appreciate the value of Inuit (and Lapp) techniques. This had been appreciated by the time of the second expedition, for Scott himself wrote 'one continues to wonder as to the possibilities of fur clothing as made by the Esquimaux, with a sneaking feeling that it may outclass our more civilised garb' (Scott, 1913, p. 368). The failure to use dogs was not unthinking. They proved disastrous on the *Discovery* Expedition and the experience of shooting laggards was unpleasant. Whereas it is easy to see now that the dogs

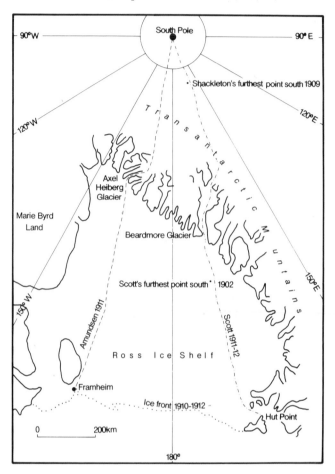

FIGURE 8.14
The assault on the
South Pole, 1902—12.

FIGURE 8.15
Amundsen (left) and his
companions at the South
Pole, December 14th, 1911.

were too few, ill-matched and inexpertly driven, Scott concluded not unreasonably that the failure was caused by the special difficulties presented by the antarctic environment; unlike the successful arctic sea ice journeys with dogs, in Antarctica they were being used away from the sea and sources of food (seals), in colder temperatures and in blizzards. Also Scott showed his naval ancestry and the attitude of the times when he wrote: 'In my mind no journey ever made with dogs can approach the height of that fine conception which is realised when a party of men go forth to face hardships, dangers, and difficulties with their own unaided efforts' (Scott, 1905, p. 467). The problems encountered with scurvy can also be attributed to the contemporary habit of equating it with hygiene rather than vitamin C deficiency. When it appeared, one response was to cook meat still longer and thus aggravate the deficiency all the more. A more discerning look at Inuit practices would have been salutary. The blame for not appreciating the value of Inuit techniques is not Scott's alone. Rather it comes from the attitudes of an intrusive society extending its domination over the world. It can be recognized in the choice of soap as an appropriate gift for the Inuit carried by the first explorers, and is apparent today in the attitude of the unsympathetic 'white' worker who disparages Inuit competence to do a 'skilled and hard day's work'. Whatever the causes, the result was that it took 300 years to learn from the millennia of experience encompassed by Inuit culture. Amundsen triumphantly demonstrated the sophistication of these Inuit techniques. By employing them the people from the core areas could move freely throughout the polar regions. However, the techniques were quite inappropriate for any economic exploitation.

Focus on the race to the South Pole is misleading in the sense that many notable expeditions were simultaneously exploring the unknown parts of coastal Antarctica (Dater, 1975), for example, those headed by Drygalski (1901–03), Nordenskjöld (1901–03), Bruce (1902–03) and Charcot (1903–05). These and the scientists of the British South Pole expeditions made many important scientific discoveries. They also improved techniques. In this context, and to balance the record, it is worth noting the use of the first car in Antarctica (Shackleton) and the first motor sledge (Scott).

The final phase of polar exploration and exploitation occurred this century when the world's cores realized that technological progress had made the polar regions accessible, both to military and economic exploitation. It was this appreciation of a resource by the core which led to this political and economic wave. One can recognize: (1) a phase of pioneering flights and the use of base camps which led to the realization that even the poles were accessible; (2) a phase whereby political claims were made on a sometimes imaginative and contradictory basis; and (3) a phase of effective administrative control. It is this latter phase which leads directly to the present-day political sub-systems which form the bases of Chapters 10—14.

The air age opened in 1897 when Salomon Andrée successfully showed that balloons were *not* the answer to air travel in the Arctic (Andrée *et al.*, 1931); after an erratic flight of some 500 km the balloon grounded and its three occupants died soon afterwards (Figure 8.16).

FIGURE 8.16   Andrée's balloon immediately after coming down on the ice, 14th July, 1897. Andrée's photograph was developed in Sweden 33 years later (Andrée's Museum).

Efforts to reach the North Pole in the 1920s culminated in 1926 when, within a space of 2 days, both Richard Byrd in a fixed-wing aircraft and Umberto Nobile in an airship with the ever-adventurous Amundsen flew over it. In the Antarctic, if one excludes Scott's early use of a tethered observation balloon, the air age commenced in 1928 with the first use of aircraft on the continent. The next year, 1929, saw Byrd fly over the pole while in 1935 Lincoln Ellsworth successfully flew across the continent. By 1934 modern ground transport was well established and Byrd's second Antarctic expedition of 1933—35 saw tractor trains covering 20 000 km.

Political claims were quickly associated with such progress. In the Arctic the 1920s saw official confirmation of the present political geography, although some tentative claims had been made earlier (Table 8.1). For the most part contiguity was the dominant principle behind the claims and each circumpolar nation claimed a sector adjoining its northlands (Svarlien, 1960). In many cases the claims were rather slimly justified on the basis of the history of exploration. The Russians claimed the Franz Josef archipelago although no Russian party had explored there. Canada claimed islands discovered by Sverdrup and later actually paid over $100000 to the heirs of Sverdrup's estate as recognition of his discoveries. Greenland was different in that there was no contiguous land mass to the south. The Danes had been administering the west coast since 1721, but it was only in 1921 that Danish sovereignty was claimed over the whole island. The United States waived claims in the north based on American exploration, but the Norwegians claimed sovereignty in East Greenland through hunting rights, and did not finally accept Danish sovereignty until the International Court at the Hague ruled in Denmark's favour in 1933. Svalbard, another island with no immediately adjacent land to the south, was again the scene of confusion and its coal resources were exploited by companies from various countries. It was assigned to Norway in 1920 by the League of Nations but only on the grounds of free access by other nations and so long as it was never used for military purposes.

TABLE 8.1   *Political claims in the Arctic*

1920	Svalbard awarded to Norway by League of Nations. (Sovereignty assumed in 1925)
1921	Greenland claimed by Denmark
1924	U.S.A. claimed any land north of Alaska (purchased Alaska from Russia in 1867)
1925	Canada claimed all land between 60° and 141°W (preliminary claim by Britain in 1907)
1926	U.S.S.R. claimed all land, ice and air in sector north of Bering Straits to Franz Josef Land

Following these claims the arctic lands had to be effectively administered and controlled. The importance of this had been well illustrated by Denmark's success in holding on to the claim for Greenland. In the 1920s Canada established police posts specifically to prove occupation and as a demonstration of sovereignty. In 1924 Denmark established the new settlement of Scoresbysund in East Greenland. The United States and Russia operated on a much larger scale, stimulated by the needs of strategy. It suddenly became clear during the Second World War that the Arctic was a short and direct route between the superpowers. Bases were established on arctic sea ice in the 1940s and 1950s, the Russians using temporary camps on ice floes (Armstrong, 1958) and the Americans more permanent bases on ice islands or icebergs derived from arctic ice shelves (e.g. T1, T2 and T3). In the American sector of the Arctic large bases were established, for example at Thule in northern Greenland. Between 1952 and 1957 a line of almost 40 Distant Early Warning radar stations (D.E.W. Line) was built along the 70th parallel to give warning of any manned bomber attack (Figure 8.17). Though partly obsolete today in an age of intercontinental missiles, they are still manned. Also there are new stations forming a Ballistic Missile Early Warning System (B.M.E.W.S.) defence screen. Presumably comparable systems exist in the Soviet Arctic, especially in the Kola Peninsula area, home of the Russian nuclear submarine fleet. These massive strategic developments demonstrate only too clearly how the Arctic is involved in the defence of the core.

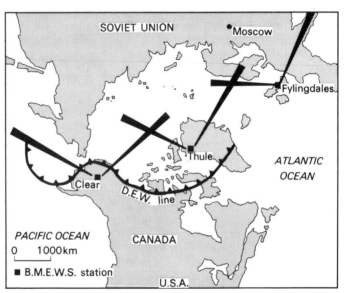

FIGURE 8.17   The distribution of Ballistic Missile Early Warning System and Distant Early Warning line stations in the Arctic (from Kemp, 1977).

The Antarctic claims followed a similar pattern to those of the Arctic (Figure 8.18). The situation is somewhat more complex, however, in that they overlap in the Antarctic Peninsula area while another part of West Antarctica is unclaimed (Hanessian, 1964; Christie, 1951). These claims were put into deep freeze until 1991 by the Antarctic Treaty of 1959. The main reasons for the original claims were strategic and economic. Strategic considerations concerning the importance of Drake Strait were factors influencing Britain's early claim, while the

Australian and New Zealand claims were made by Britain in order to secure the nearest antarctic coastline to these two countries for strategic reasons. Chile and Argentina also claimed that part of Antarctica closest to their coastlines. Economic factors, especially the whaling industry of the twentieth century, influenced both Britain and Norway in their claims. So, as in the Arctic, there was little regard for priority due to discovery, with the main exception of the French claim which spans d'Urville's discovery in 1840. Sometimes historical precedence is used to justify the claims. Such claims are highly selective, however, and ignore such events as Wilke's discovery of much of the coast of the Australian sector or Amundsen's claim of the south polar plateau for Norway.

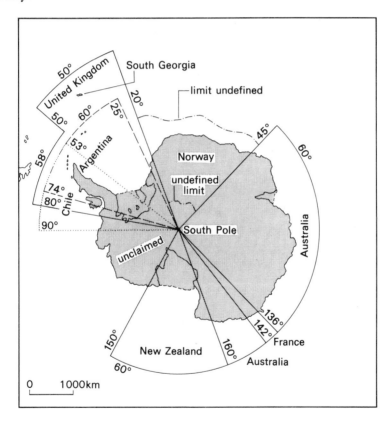

FIGURE 8.18   Political claims in Antarctica.

The phase of effective administration and control continues to this day in Antarctica. An early enlightened example is the way whaling revenues accruing to the British Government in the early twentieth century were ploughed back into the *Discovery* Expeditions which laid the foundations of whale research in Antarctica. Many other ploys have been employed. The creation of semi-permanent bases is the most important. However, others involve the visits of heads of state, the birth and registration of children, the establishment of magistrates, post offices and mail services (Figure 8.19). Competition may produce excellent service. When Britain, Chile and Argentina had bases in Deception Island (before the volcanic eruption of 1967) it was possible to send letters from the same location stamped by either or all of the three national 'post offices'.

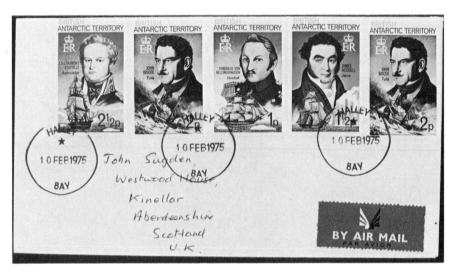

FIGURE 8.19   A letter stamped by the post office at the U.K. base of Halley.

For a variety of reasons the interest of the world core in Antarctica has caused a further unique and promising development to take place, that of freezing national claims and pointing the continent towards international control. The segmentation of Antarctica into national sectors excluded two countries with great interest in the continent. In spite of a long history of antarctic exploration, the United States has made no claim; while the Soviet Union, with unequalled arctic experience, has refused to recognize any claim and has suggested instead that the whole continent is Russian, since it was first sighted by Bellingshausen. Setting aside the embarrassing contradiction that such a claim presents if applied to parts of Russia's own Arctic(!), the two superpowers were keen to reach a solution (Hanessian, 1964). An international solution had attractions in that it would allow access to all the continent as well as sidestepping embarrassing competitive wrangles. The International Geophysical Year of 1957 provided the catalyst. Supporting the demands of scientists for a year during which observations of the sun could be made on a worldwide basis, including Antarctica, governments of 12 nations built 50 bases throughout Antarctica. The international scientific experiment proved so successful that 2 years later the Antarctic Treaty was agreed. Briefly the Treaty envisaged the use of the continent for peaceful purposes only, the free exchange of scientific information and personnel, the banning of military activity, nuclear explosions and dumping of nuclear waste, and open access by observers to the whole of Antarctica.

Political annexation of the polar regions has opened the way for long-term economic and social development by the world's industrial cores. The exploitation of minerals and fuels first occurred in the Soviet Arctic in the 1930s and the American Arctic in the 1960s. It has yet to affect the Antarctic. The effects of this current phase of mineral exploitation are influenced by environmental factors and the politics of the different countries involved, and form the focus of much of the rest of the book.

Conclusions

The story of the impact of the world urban system on the polar regions allows three conclusions to be drawn. Firstly in terms of general principles we can see how success depends upon factors at work in the world's core areas as well as at the peripheries. Appreciation of a resource has been a powerful stimulus, whether it was possibilities for trade in Elizabethan times, strategic defence in the Arctic or the availability of raw materials. Technical innovations have played their part (Victor, 1964). The most important of these has been the impact of the aeroplane, which is so well suited to polar travel, but there is the earlier example of the Viking ship which provided the basis for a prolonged attack on the polar regions. Social considerations too are important. One can look to overpopulation in Norse Iceland or to the sort of personal ambition which drove men like Eirik the Red, Amundsen and Shackleton. Conditions at the periphery have also played their role and it is difficult to avoid the conclusion that some long-term trends are closely paralleled by environmental trends.

Secondly, in terms of population and settlement, one can highlight the arrival of small urban outposts in the Arctic and Antarctic. These have had the effect of increasing local population totals above indigenous levels. Mostly this was due to the setting up of trading posts or, more recently, specialized bases in barren areas. Nevertheless, the increase associated with the development of urban systems over the world as a whole has worked to the *relative* disadvantage of the polar regions. From a position of approximate equality during hunting and gathering times, the adoption of agriculture on a world scale first accentuated the relative poverty of the polar regions. The subsequent urban system has only served to accentuate the difference between the urban core areas and their polar periphery.

Thirdly, one can re-emphasize the importance of taking a world perspective on the history of the polar regions. In the chapters that follow it will be seen that this world perspective offers many insights into modern practices of development.

Further reading

Garner, F. 1978: The vanished Norseman: mystery of Greenlanders' disappearance. *Geographical Magazine*, 50 (7), 446–51.

Hanessian, J. 1964: National interests in Antarctica. In Hatherton, T. (editor), *Antarctica*. Methuen, London, 3–53.

Jones, G. 1964: *The Norse Atlantic saga.* Oxford University Press, London.

Kemp, T. 1977: The new strategic map. *Survival* (International Institute for Strategic Studies), 19 (2), 50–9.

Kirwan, L. P. 1962: *A history of polar exploration.* Penguin, Harmondsworth.

McGhee, R. 1974: The peopling of arctic North America. In Ives, J. D. and Barry, R. G. (editors) *Arctic and alpine environments.* Methuen, London, 831–55.

CHAPTER NINE

The Inuit Indigenous System

Introduction

This chapter examines the geography of Inuit society before contact with intrusive, technological society of the last few centuries. The aim is twofold. Firstly, it is hoped to derive an understanding of the geography of indigenous people in an arctic environment. Secondly, such a study helps one to understand the impact of intrusive society on indigenous people in the Arctic. As such, Inuit beliefs and practices may be viewed as an independent variable relevant to the geography of intrusive society.

The word Inuit is used because it is the word used by the people to describe themselves (Figure 9.1). It seems preferable to avoid the popular word Eskimo, however widely used, which is derived from the North American Indians and in somewhat derogative terms means 'eaters of raw meat'. The Inuit are one of many indigenous peoples in the Arctic and their traditional hunting way of life was restricted to the seasonally ice-bound coasts of North America, Greenland and part of northeast Siberia (Figure 8.2). They owed their existence wholly to the exploitation of resources in the arctic environment and were generally successful only north of the tree line. In contrast most Asian indigenous peoples depended on the boreal forest during the critical winter period and followed their migrating herds of reindeer into the Arctic proper only in summer. This contrast between the two continents makes the Inuit the most obvious people to investigate in detail as an example of a true arctic indigenous group.

As mentioned in Chapter 8 the Inuit Thule culture based on whaling evolved in the Bering Strait area and around A.D. 1000 spread across North America to Greenland in 50 years or so (Figure 8.1). The classic image of the Inuit as a hunter battling against his environment and living in a snow igloo comes from somewhat romanticized study of the eastern Inuit in Greenland and Baffin Island. As such it describes a relatively recent cultural adaptation which occurred during the climatic deterioration of the Little Ice Age (p. 177). In particular it seems to

FIGURE 9.1   Inuit seal hunters at Thule, North Greenland, in 1909. Photograph by Th. Krabbe, reproduced with the permission of the National Museum of Denmark, Department of Ethnography.

have required greater mobility than the Thule culture as well as the exploitation of other animals to replace the whales which could no longer navigate the ice-bound straits. At the time of early contacts with Europeans the culture may have been no more than a few centuries old and was probably evolving rapidly. It is this pre-contact culture that is the prime concern of this chapter. At such time there were probably around 48000 Inuit in all, the eastern Inuit numbering around 28000 and the western Inuit around 20000 (Oswalt, 1967).

Following brief discussion of the constraints and resources of the physical environment, the spatial structure of the human system is analysed following Haggett (1965) under the main topics: movements, nodes, networks and surfaces. This is followed by some consideration of the functional aspects of the system as a whole.

Physical constraints and resources

A low-latitude dweller stranded in the Arctic and confronted with the problem of survival would soon discover the main constraints of the physical environment. Ruling out inhospitable glaciers and life on an ice floe the choice narrows down to the periglacial environment and inshore waters. On land our intrepid visitor would notice the shortage of fruit and edible plants (except for a few berries), the lack of wood and the presence of fleet-footed animals. A seasonal bonus would be the run of arctic char up non-glacial rivers. Offshore he or she would see relative riches, even if a little elusive. Not only would seals be found throughout the year, but in summer a veritable glut of sea mammals migrate into ice-free waters. A problem would be presented by the dramatic seasonal change in sea surface from solid to liquid with the change from winter to summer, requiring in effect two sets of technology to exploit the marine resource. Above all our visitor from warmer climes would notice the length of the winter and the shortness of the respite which passes for summer.

If our visitor survived for more than a year he or she would have probably evolved a lifestyle similar to that of the Inuit. The focus of life would be the coast, an interface providing access to both land and sea resources. The food supply would be obtained by hunting and fishing. The hunting technology would evolve to exploit the contrasts afforded by land and sea environments in both winter and summer.

The human spatial pattern

MOVEMENTS

The dominant movements of the Inuit were in response to the annual rhythm and were concerned with the search for food and clothing. Also, however, there were wider trading journeys lasting a few years and longer-term migrations of whole peoples. All were fundamental to the spatial organization of Inuit groups, and illustrate the adjustment necessary for a hunting system to succeed in an Arctic environment.

Annual and shorter movements
The primary need was for food and materials for clothing and shelter at all times of the year. Since the availability of different game varied from place to place and from season to season there was need to evolve efficient forms of travel. The method of travel and hunting depended on the season and the type of quarry. The nature of these movements is clearly illustrated by the traditional Inuit life in the Melville Bay area of northern West Greenland and is well described by Birket-Smith (1936).

The relationship between seasonal environment, transport and game is illustrated in Table 9.1. In winter inshore waters are covered with

TABLE 9.1   *The relationship between seasonal environment, transport and hunting in northwest Greenland*

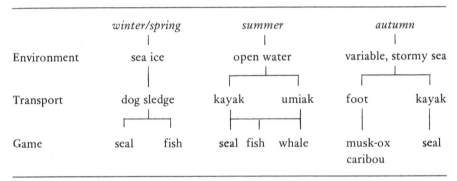

	winter/spring	*summer*	*autumn*
Environment	sea ice	open water	variable, stormy sea
Transport	dog sledge	kayak umiak	foot kayak
Game	seal fish	seal fish whale	musk-ox seal caribou

landfast ice and the basis of life was hunting seals which overwinter by keeping open breathing holes in the ice (Figure 9.2). The key to travel over such a surface was the dog sledge, and basically the more important the winter hunting of seals the better the quality of the dog-driving and the more sophisticated the sledge. The West Greenland sledge was one of the most sophisticated and was built of pieces of wood lashed together and with handlebars at the rear. The dogs pulled on independent lines arranged in a fan trace (Figure 9.3). The dog sledge was an immensely successful solution to the problem of winter travel and could be pulled 80 km in a day, thus offering a considerable daily hunting range. The quarry consisted of seals and involved different techniques of pursuit depending on the season and ice surface. On clear ice, for example in early winter, the hunter crept up to the breathing hole muffling his steps with polar-bear shoes and waited for the seal

FIGURE 9.2   Ice hunting techniques in Greenland in the eighteenth century as recorded by Hans Egede and reproduced by Gad (1970).

before harpooning it. When the ice was snow-covered and the holes obscured by snow, the hunter used dogs to sniff out the hole. Then, inserting a stick into the hole to act as an indicator when the seal surfaced, he would wait before harpooning. Both these forms of hunting usually involved cooperation between several hunters; since a seal utilizes several holes it was more efficient to monitor several adjacent holes at the same time. In spring when seals tend to bask on the ice beside their holes they commonly snooze for 30 seconds, look around and snooze again. Under these circumstances the hunter would creep up during each snooze period, and lie down and imitate a seal while under observation, even to the extent of scraping the ice with a seal flipper. Gradually approaching the seal, he then harpooned before it had time to gain the safety of its hole. Also carried out in winter was fishing through artificial or natural holes in the ice.

The rich inshore waters in summer were an obvious food source and it is perhaps not surprising that the Inuit evolved sophisticated means of sea travel (Figure 9.4). The sealskin kayak is too well known to need detailed description. It was built snugly to fit a particular person. It was a swift means of travel and I have seen a Greenlander from Scoresbysund easily keep up with a modern 20 m fishing boat for 2 hours at a stretch. Convincing evidence of their seaworthiness is provided here in Aberdeen where the university museum contains the East Greenland kayak which was found on the local beach with its occupant after a trans-Atlantic journey about A.D. 1700. Kayaks were capable of considerable load-carrying feats. In 1962 I remember seeing a hunter paddling his kayak with his son sitting on the foredeck. They landed and the hunter and son slipped ashore. The hunter was followed by his wife and another son who had been below-decks! The kayak was used for seal hunting for which its other main virtue of silence made it ideal (Figure 9.5). Typically the kayaker would fit a white screen onto the deck for camouflage amongst floating ice and glide up to the seal before harpooning it.

Though less well known, the open skin boat, the umiak, was an equally sophisticated vessel. Built with a wooden frame, it was 10 m long with gracefully pointed bow and stern. Though fitted with a mast and sail, it was also propelled with single-bladed paddles or oars. Capable of carrying around 25–30 people, it was used in pursuit of whales.

FIGURE 9.3   Polar Inuit dog sledges crossing a pass near Thule in the early twentieth century. Photograph reproduced with the permission of the National Museum of Denmark, Department of Ethnography.

FIGURE 9.4 Umiak and kayaks at Angmagssalik, East Greenland, in 1904. Photograph by Th. Krabbe reproduced with the permission of the National Museum of Denmark, Department of Ethnography.

Floats were secured to the gunwhale to prevent it capsizing and the harpooner stood in the bow as they joined in the hunt. One doesn't need to read *Moby Dick* to realize the dangers of such a pursuit! The umiak was also used as a transport for whole families as well as by traders.

The autumn is a troublesome season in that the open sea is stormy and the ice cover is intermittent. Since this is also the time of year when land animals are well-fattened and have glossy coats it was common to find land-hunting assuming a greater importance than at other times of the year. Although travel was by foot, an umiak was used to travel to the hunting area.

The spatial location of particular game at particular seasons imparted a strong annual cyclic movement on a particular Inuit group. A good example comes from Lake Harbour, a settlement in southern Baffin Island (Figure 9.6) (Kemp, 1971). In summer the main quarry was white whale and seal and hunting took place over an area with a radius of approximately 70 km from the main settlement. As the sea ice built up

FIGURE 9.5   Sea hunting techniques in Greenland in the eighteenth century as recorded by Hans Egede and reproduced in Gad (1970).

in winter the edge of the fast ice extended progressively outwards and sealing took place at the floe edge or through holes in the fast ice. Also, this was a time when caribou were hunted inland. By spring, floe edge hunting was 40 km from the main settlement and was supplemented by egg-collecting in two areas of rocky coast. Traditionally, the spatial variations in the game supply at different times of the year meant that the Inuit community frequently moved their settlement so as to be close to the main game supply.

It is difficult for outsiders to appreciate the importance of these annual movements in search of game. But to the traditional Inuit game provided virtually all their needs with the main exception of wood, stone and iron. All food came from hunting and egg-collecting.

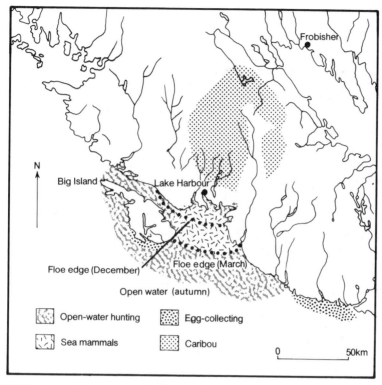

FIGURE 9.6   The spatial and seasonal variations in game supply, Lake Harbour, Baffin Island. After Kemp (1971).

All clothing depended on successful hunting (Figure 9.7). Birdskin was used for underclothes while sealskin was used as a waterproof necessary for travel in kayaks and umiaks. Caribou skin found its use as an all-purpose light, warm coat. Musk-ox skin was used when warmer clothes were needed, but was heavy and dirty. Bear skin was necessary when exceedingly warm clothing was needed, as for example when waiting motionless for hours beside a seal hole in winter. The majority of traditional Inuit implements such as harpoon heads, knives, toggles and fish-hooks were wholly or partially fashioned from ivory or bone from the hunted animals as also were line, thread, sealskin floats, tents and blubber oil used for fuel.

Movements of goods

A few key items such as flint, jade, iron and soapstone occur sporadically in the Arctic and were the objects of exchange (Guemple, 1972). For example, a meteorite near Cape York in West Greenland provided a source of iron utilized by the local Inuit and was exchanged as far

FIGURE 9.7
Inuit woman making clothes,
Scoresbysund, East
Greenland. Photograph by
Ib Tøpfer.

afield as Baffin Island and East Greenland. A special type of green jade found only in Alaska was bartered as far east as Hudson Bay. Stefansson (1914) suggested that so well established were these routes that an article in Siberia might travel the 4000 km to the eastern Canadian Arctic in a little more than 5 years. Crossing the Bering Straits the article would pass from group to group and move around the northern Alaskan coast and through Banks and Victoria Islands either to Lancaster Sound or western Hudson Bay. Slate and soapstone were more abundant and tended to involve trade on a more limited basis.

An appreciation of what these movements involved comes from Holm's account of the Angmagssalik Inuit in East Greenland when they were first discovered in 1884 (Holm, 1914). He described how exchange of soapstone involved a summer umiak journey southwards and a return trip the following summer. Also he mentioned how bear skins, sealskins and narwhal tusk implements were traded with people further south to take to the west coast to exchange for ironware. On one occasion an Angmagssalik umiak made the whole journey, taking 4 years over the round trip. Another local type of trade which occurred in Alaska was between inland and coastal Inuit. Here, exchange allowed groups to specialize on one set of resources, yet to have access to the other (Oswalt, 1967).

Overall the exchange movements in the Arctic ensured an interchange of goods and ideas over surprisingly large areas. Good evidence of this comes from the fact that the pre-contact east Canadian Inuit knew of the twelfth-century Norse settlements in Greenland (Petersen, 1962). Unfortunately it is not yet possible to synthesize the fragmentary movements mentioned above into an overall trading system.

Migrations

Longer-term movements occurred when local Inuit groups migrated permanently. A well-documented example is the last migration of Baffin Islanders to Greenland which took place in the 1850s. It is likely that they were the Inuit group of 12 who met McClintock in the ship *Fox* near Devon Island (Rasmussen, 1908; Petersen, 1962). They followed the traditional route across the southern end of Smith Sound. Interestingly the migration reintroduced the kayak and the bow and arrow to the polar Inuit of northwest Greenland, who had lost the use of both, though they had heard of them.

There is evidence of large-scale migrations in the immediate period before historic contact. Oswalt (1967) mentioned examples of marked southward movements in Alaska, while the Norse sagas tell of a southward movement of 'skraelings' in Greenland. Similar movements took place in Arctic Canada. As noted earlier, it is tempting to relate this large-scale southward migration to the climatic deterioration of the Little Ice Age and its effect in reducing the availability of game in the remoter north.

NODES

Inuit settlements were a compromise between the advantages gained from concentration — which allowed specialization, communal hunting, security, social intercourse — and the disadvantage which followed from such concentration — which was the risk of overstretching sparsely distributed resources. The common pattern among the 'eastern' Inuit was for a group of 25–30, consisting of one or several families, to operate as a unit, moving their settlement every 8 weeks or so. Each winter they congregated in groups of about 120. Figure 9.8 shows the location of one group's settlement sites in one year as they followed the annual cycle (Balikci, 1968). Camps 1 and 2 were in company with other groups and concerned with winter hunting of seals at breathing holes. Camp 3 was concerned with spring hunting of seals at seal holes, Camp 4 with summer fishing at a stone weir, Camp 5 with autumn hunting of caribou and Camp 6 with late autumn fishing through river ice. It may seem anomalous that at the time of greatest stress in winter, the concentration of groups is most marked. However Freeman (1967) suggested that this was the time of year when the advantages of collective hunting at seal holes were at a maximum. Also one might add that the festiveness of these winter gatherings helped to while away long hours of darkness.

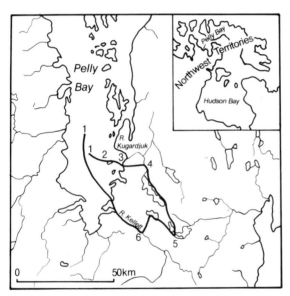

FIGURE 9.8
The annual movement of the Arviligjuarmiut, a Netsilik sub-group in 1919. After Balikci (1968).

The sites of settlements varied according to their purpose. Thus access to smooth ice in winter and to good sea hunting in summer was crucial. The stress on sea resources produced a settlement pattern which is anomalous to the land-bound peoples of mid-latitudes. Instead of locating coastal settlements in sheltered inlets as in Europe the opposite was the case. Settlements were on promontories, or better still on small islets. Any piece of rock big enough for a tent or house was enough. Islands commonly supported more camps than promontories. The reason for this pattern is that a camp location was chosen in relation to access to sea resources and, apart from its role as a solid base for tents, the less land around the camp the better. Hence the prime value of small islands which offered hunting in all directions. It is interesting that similar settlement patterns existed in Mesolithic Britain and for similar reasons (Ralston, personal communication, 1981). Inuit camps associated with caribou hunting and inland fishing were obviously exceptions to this rule and here location was determined above all by proximity to migration routes.

A typical Inuit house consisted of sleeping platforms in the main house with a sunken entrance doubling up to form a larder and shelter for the dogs. The actual design of the house varied according to the number of occupants and their relationship. Families with close blood links shared one platform, while good friends shared separate platforms in one house. Less close friends shared a common entrance (Figure 9.9)

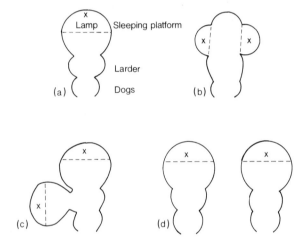

FIGURE 9.9
Conceptual diagram of different house layouts. The lamps represent family nuclei: *(a)* extended family, e.g. one sleeping platform shared with newly married daughter and husband; *(b)* two very friendly families; *(c)* families of good friends; *(d)* other friends. Spacing of separate houses reflects closeness of these other friends. After Guemple, personal communication (1978).

while still less close friends had separate houses, and so on. An important principle with far-reaching implications is that the social links within the group were reflected in the housing design. What is more, the regular migrations meant that the houses were rebuilt regularly and reflected recent changes in social relations. Thus, following a tiff between friends who shared one house, the next move would allow both to build separate houses.

Inuit winter houses tended to be partially excavated into the ground with stone walls and a roof of sods propped up by whalebones, wood, or in the case of small houses, cantilevered stones (Figure 9.10 and 9.11). The entrance tunnel was low, trapping a pocket of cold air which prevented draughts but permitted ventilation. In the central Canadian Arctic, winter stone houses gave way to the use of snow houses in the climatic deterioration of the Little Ice Age before historic

FIGURE 9.10   Winter house in Thule photographed by T. Thomsen in the summer of 1909.
Reproduced with the permission of the National Museum of Denmark,
Department of Ethnography.

contact (Schledermann, 1976) (Figure 9.12). This was probably because
in a time of stress it was necessary to be more mobile and to hunt over
a wider area than was possible from one centre. Since snow houses
melted in summer and stone houses also deteriorated into a quagmire,
the Inuit relied on skin tents in summer (Figure 9.13).

NETWORKS

In the absence of permanently modified routes it is not easy to find
examples of the routes used by the Inuit. Nonetheless it is clear that
all movements − including migrations, trade journeys and annual
movements − followed clearly demarcated routes. Moreover these
routes were sometimes represented as relief maps on pieces of wood
and reflected the features that were relevant to the traveller. For
example the two wooden maps sketched in Figure 9.14 display a piece
of coast north of Angmagssalik. The longer piece displays a chain of
offshore islands and stresses features that would be apparent to a boat
traveller. Comparison with the real coastline shows how absolute size
and space has been suppressed. The shorter piece of wood represents
the mainland coast adjacent to the islands, the right-hand side representing the northern part and the left-hand side (when rotated) the
southern part. A groove round the base of a peninsula demonstrates
a land portage which would be used by sledges or kayaks if ice conditions offshore were unsuitable. Again the absolute shape and spacing
of the fjords is not represented on this map.

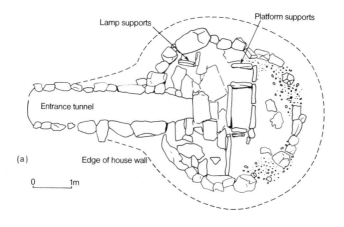

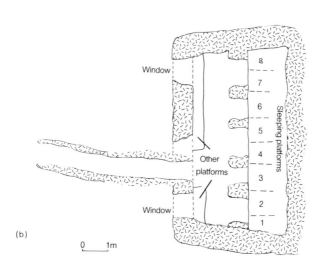

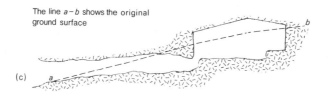

FIGURE 9.11   (a) Generalized plan of a Thule winter house in north-central Canada, based on
archaeological excavations. After Dumond (1977). (b) and (c) Communal
winter house of stone and sods with a roof supported by wood in Angmagssalik
area, as described by Holm (1914). The house held 38 people, and different
families slept on different parts of the sleeping platform.

FIGURE 9.12   Igloos at Oopungnewing, Baffin Island in 1860—62. From Hall (1865).

FIGURE 9.13   Skin tents in Angmagssalik in 1908. Photograph by Th. Krabbe, reproduced by permission of the National Museum of Denmark, Department of Ethnography.

FIGURE 9.14
Two wooden relief maps of
the coastline near
Angmagssalik. A fuller
explanation is given in the
text. After Thalbitzer (1914).

One of the most commonly used lines of travel by sledge was along the ice-foot on the shore. Except on exposed coasts where ice floes may break up the ice foot, it forms a flat surface between the irregular land on the one side and the jumbled floes associated with tidal movements on the other (Chapter 6). An insight into likely network patterns can be seen on maps associated with the Inuit Land Use and Occupancy Project in Canada where routes used for trapping are indicated. If one ignores the inland bias introduced by the growth of trapping in the days since European contact, one still sees the importance of these coastline routes. Occasionally an inland route across a neck of land may be used to cut off a long coastal diversion. The sites of such short cuts may be recognized on maps by the Inuit prefix Itivdl-.

Superimposed on regular routes were movements in pursuit of game. Rather thoughtlessly I tended to regard these as random until confronted with an example of the precision involved in hunting (Figure

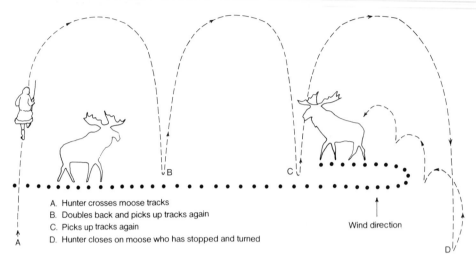

A. Hunter crosses moose tracks
B. Doubles back and picks up tracks again
C. Picks up tracks again
D. Hunter closes on moose who has stopped and turned

Wind direction

FIGURE 9.15   The applied geography of catching a moose. After Osgood (1936).

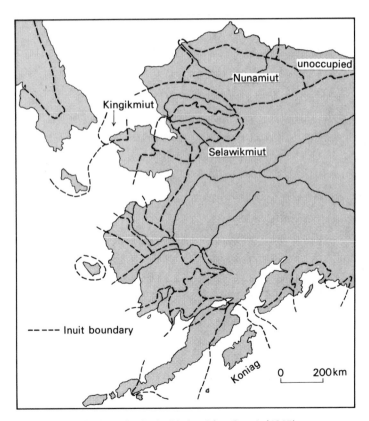

FIGURE 9.16   Former Inuit territories in Alaska. After Oswalt (1967).

9.15)! Although taken from an example of a sub-arctic Kutchin hunter, the illustration makes the point that successful hunting is a highly developed spatial skill.

SURFACES

Inuit society was subdivided into subgroups each strongly bound to territory. In the central Canadian Arctic the territory might support some 200 people in all, most of whom would meet together in winter and subdivide again next summer (though in slightly different groups). Overall, this often represented a population density of 1 per 100 km² or less. There was completely free movement within a territory and none was privately owned, not even the area occupied by a house. It is this background which explains the habit, which today is sometimes disconcerting to a European, whereby an Inuit just walks into a house uninvited and sits down to watch for hours on end. The lack of feeling of ownership of a territory meant that the Inuit would not defend it. Nonetheless, the people in the world outside the territory were seen as hostile.

Figure 9.16 shows some Inuit territories in Alaska. The map brings out the coastal locations of most territories and also the way in which inland territories focus on river basins. In pre-contact times, the territories supported larger than average groups ranging in size from 300 in the case of the Selawikmiut in an inland situation to a maximum of 6500 in the case of the Koniag in the relatively lush sub-arctic land of coastal southern Alaska. Population densities varied from a maximum of 30 per 100 km² in the case of the Koniag to 1 per 100 km² in the case of the interior Nunamiut. The main feature of Figure 9.13 is the increase in density from an average value of 2 per 100 km² in the north to an average of 6 per 100 km² in the south. Superimposed on this trend is a tendency for coastal territories to support denser populations than inland territories. Thus the Kingikmiut on one flank of Bering Straits had a density of 16 per 100 km², whereas the mainly interior Selawikmiut had a density of only 2 per 100 km². The most favoured territories were those on islands and peninsulas with enhanced access to sea resources.

The functioning of the spatial system

Although there are obvious regional variations, certain characteristics of Inuit society were common to most of the area. These are important not only in themselves but also because of the way they differ from basic precepts of intrusive society.

SOCIAL ATTITUDES

A common outsider's view is to pity and admire the Inuit for their life of continual hardship. However Sahlins (1968, 1974) made the point that seen in a different light hunters and gatherers can be viewed as part of the original affluent society. Having modest material needs they needed to work no more than 18½ hours per week for sustenance. The rest of the time was commonly spent sleeping or partaking in festive occasions. Not only have the Inuit long struck strangers as being of a happy disposition but they were able to achieve such feats as bringing up children without resorting to beating. Even the well-known trait of not worrying about the morrow and wasting food in orgies of over-eating can be re-interpreted as reflecting a supreme confidence in their way of life. These points are made in order to show that the outside view of the poverty of the Inuit is precisely that − an outside view. There are certainly no grounds for thinking that the Inuit themselves felt deprived. Now perhaps there is a danger of over-reacting and ignoring their hardships. Undoubtedly from time to time there were famines and people did die as a result (Balikci, 1968).

An important feature of Inuit society was the way in which it was communistic in the full sense. Not only was the land communally owned, but so also was game. Even if killed by an individual, a seal would be shared throughout the community. People too were regarded as a communal resource and sometimes a constraint. Thus children were adopted and exchanged in response to need. Spouses might be exchanged freely, for example, if a man's wife was pregnant and he needed another companion on a trip. If a hunter was successful then he might have more than one wife. Infanticide was common, especially among female babies. Old women who could no longer contribute to the community were sometimes left behind when the group moved on. As befits a communistic society, leadership was unostentatious and by advice and example rather than by persuasian or force. Normally respect for an individual was in proportion to his skill. Persuasion (and education) was regarded as unnecessary because people were born with certain qualities which could not be changed. Material possessions were not numerous. This reflected the nomadic way of life where surplus possessions were a burden. Everything had to go easily onto a sledge or into an umiak. One feature of Inuit society which will not please half the readers of this book was the low status conferred on women. Women were at the beck and call of men and treated as little more than vital possessions.

SPATIAL VARIATION AMONG INUIT SYSTEMS

The discussion so far in this chapter has centred around examples from different parts of the Inuit Arctic. As a result any spatial variation over the area as a whole has been mentioned only in passing. There were marked variations in traditional Inuit systems and these are worth highlighting.

Inuit culture was most complex at each extremity of its range in Alaska and Greenland and simplest in between, in the central Canadian Arctic archipelago. This variation is reflected in overall population densities which attained values of 6 per $100\,km^2$ in Alaska and the fjord systems of West Greenland but were often less than 1 per $100\,km^2$ in the central Canadian Arctic. It was also displayed by settlement types. In Alaska and the Greenland fjords permanent or semi-permanent villages consisting of wooden or stone houses were the rule. In some densely populated areas the villages were fully occupied all the year round, while in other areas villages were full in winter but supported only a skeleton population in summer. In the Canadian Arctic, however, settlements in both summer and winter were smaller and temporary; indeed winter settlements were built of snow. A final contrast was the absence of whale and kayak hunting in the central Canadian Arctic in contrast to both Alaska and Greenland.

The contrast between the central Canadian Arctic on the one hand and Alaska and Greenland on the other is likely to reflect a contrast in resources related to the climatic deterioration of the Little Ice Age (Dumond, 1977). Whereas in the warm period in the centuries following A.D.1000 the Thule culture spread throughout the Arctic and was based on the hunting of whales, the subsequent deterioration obliterated the whales from the ice-infested straits of the central Canadian Arctic. Thus the population was forced to abandon communal whale hunting in favour of seal hunting from ice. The resulting reduction of the available resources was accompanied by a change to a more mobile way of life and a reduction in population density.

Another broad pattern was for there to be an increase in the complexity of Inuit life from north to south. This is seen in Alaska where there was an increase in population density, absolute numbers, in territories and village size from north to south (Giddings, 1968). It was also mirrored in Greenland where the simple lifestyle of the polar Inuit around Thule contrasted with the complex fjord settlements of the southwest. This variation is characteristic of marine and terrestrial ecosystems and it seems likely that the human systems reflected the productivity of the ecosystem. Also, like the ecosystem, the human systems were dynamic and migrated north and south in response to climatic change.

THE INUIT COMPARED WITH OTHER HUNTERS AND GATHERERS

Among other hunters and gatherers of the world the Inuit were different in that they depended more on hunting than other groups. Lee (1968) pointed out how the main food supply of most other groups came from gathering fruit, vegetables and shellfish. In the Arctic the poverty of the terrestrial environment and the ice infestation of the shore zone ruled out these possibilities (at least on an important scale) and as a result hunting was the mainstay.

In most other respects the Inuit were similar to other hunters and gatherers in marginal environments. Lee and Devore (1968) noted some general characteristics of such societies, namely: hunters and gatherers lived in small groups of generally less than 50 souls; they moved around a lot; the overall population densities were sparse and generally between 1 and 10 per 100km^2; personal property was minimal; resources were shared; no food surpluses were accumulated and there was no territorial possessiveness. All these characteristics apply to traditional Inuit society. Moreover, in terms of population density the Inuit spanned the whole range with some favoured Alaskan territories attaining densities higher than usual. However if the sea area was included as part of the Alaskan territories this contrast would not be so marked.

Contrasts between Inuit values and those of western 'intrusive' society

Much of the remainder of the book is concerned with the human geography of the existing inhabitants of the Arctic. A key issue is the way in which the indigenous peoples have adapted to a dominant, intrusive, urban and industrial society. In order to understand the interrelationships it is obviously crucial to appreciate the values of the Inuit system and the way they differ from those of the western 'intrusive' system. A comparison of the two is revealing and goes a long way towards explaining present apparently intractable problems.

There is an important contrast between the spatial layout and role of nodes in the two systems. Inuit village plans reflected social relationships and the spacing and design of houses was correlated with the social links between different families. In contrast, intrusive villages tend to be laid out regularly on a grid-iron pattern of roads. Again, many Inuit village plans were updated every 2 months or so and thus were constantly adjusting to changing social conditions in the group. In contrast, intrusive village plans tend to be permanent over a time-span of several years and cannot respond to changing social conditions effectively. Inuit houses were open plan, while intrusive houses generally have separate bedrooms and living rooms; it is hardly surprising to find that an Inuit family moving into an intrusive house would often quickly knock down interior walls. Several families often occupied one house in Inuit villages while one house per family is characteristic of intrusive villages; the separation of Inuit families into different houses reduces social cohesion. Finally, the Inuit settlements rarely exceeded a few hundred in population size, while intrusive urban centres may be measured in thousands. In practical terms this meant that an Inuit moving to an urban centre was confronted with Inuit from other 'hostile' territories. The problems arising may be compared to ethnic strains within intrusive society.

The approach to territory between the two systems is also fundamentally different. The Inuit did not lay claim to the ownership of land or resources and this had an important implication in giving flexibility to the spatial organization of society. In contrast ownership of land and resources is a key concept in intrusive society. The very concept of private houses and private mines is quite foreign to the Inuit.

The internal functioning of the two systems is also fundamentally opposed. The Inuit laid little stress on material goods while in intrusive society they are an important key to status. Inuit women had a low status compared to women in intrusive society. The result has been that Inuit women have been quick to accept the ways of intrusive society and their whole-hearted participation has aggravated strains among Inuit men who see their traditional role threatened. In Inuit society leadership depended on example and personal skill, while in intrusive society it depends on the election of representatives who are not necessarily the most skilled in the community. This has made it difficult for elected representatives to gain trust and be effective. Educational attitudes are different. The Inuit believed that you were born as you are and that therefore there was no need for formal teaching, while in intrusive society education is often seen as the key to success. Finally, the Inuit were used to irregular, short hours of hunting separated by long periods of rest, while intrusive society stresses the value of long, regular hours of work.

Even a simple account of comparisons between Inuit and intrusive systems gives some indication of the profundity of the problems presented by the juxtaposition of the two. In effect, when confronted by the intrusive system, an Inuit is forced to abandon his long-held beliefs and habits and has to learn all over again. In the chapters that follow it will be seen that the difficulties facing such a person are frequently overwhelming and that this has profoundly affected the modern spatial systems in the Arctic.

Further reading

Balikci, A. 1968: The Netsilik Eskimos: adaptive processes. In Lee, R. B. and Devore, I. (editors) *Man the Hunter*. Aldine, Chicago, 78—82.

Birket-Smith, Kaj 1936: *The eskimos.* Methuen, London.

Dumond, D. E. 1977: *The Eskimos and Aleuts.* Thames & Hudson, London.

Holm, G. 1914: Ethnological sketch of the Angmagssalik Eskimo. *Meddelelser om Grønland*, 39 (1), 1—147.

Kemp, W. B. 1971: The flow of energy in a hunting society. *Scientific American*, 224 (3), 104—15.

CHAPTER TEN

Greenland and Svalbard

Introduction

Greenland and Svalbard have in common the fact that they are both experiencing development by Scandinavian countries: Denmark in the case of Greenland and Norway in the case of Svalbard. Together, they provide an interesting insight into the Scandinavian approach to development. This insight is made all the more interesting by the similarities and contrasts between the two areas. They are similar in that they are both well-glacierized islands with relatively warm west coasts and cold east and north coasts. There are three main contrasts. First, Greenland is larger than Svalbard. Second, Greenland is physically part of North America, while Svalbard is part of Eurasia. Third, Greenland has an indigenous Inuit population, while Svalbard has none. Since these contrasts prove to be so fundamental, it is helpful to look at the human geography of each area separately.

GREENLAND

The subcontinent of Greenland is inhabited by no more people than would fit into a small European or American town. It is twice the size of Alaska and in a European context would stretch from north of Oslo to the northern coast of Africa (Figure 10.1). The population is around 50000 (50643 in 1981).[1] In this chapter the treatment of Greenland follows the lines explained in Chapter 1 (pages 10—11). First, there is an assessment of the actual and perceived constraints and resources of the natural environment. These act as independent variables which influence the human spatial system. Second, the main elements of the human spatial system are identified. The main body of

[1] Statistics are derived from annual government statistics, e.g. *Grønland, 1980* (Ministry for Greenland, 1981).

the chapter then looks at the system as a whole in terms of its evolution over time and the way it functions today. The final section draws some conclusions about the spatial system as an aid to comparison with other polar areas.

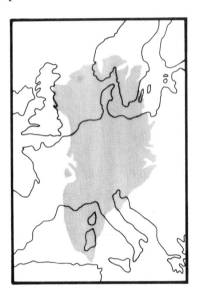

FIGURE 10.1
Greenland, superimposed on Europe to demonstrate its size, is the home of 50000 people.

Physical constraints and resources

The main constraint placed upon human affairs is ice. Greenland's central heart is an ice sheet, while her coast is surrounded by permanent or seasonal sea ice (Figure 10.2). As a result, the ice-free area forms a broken ring of land many thousands of kilometres long but rarely more than a few kilometres wide. The ring is frequently dissected by fjords or pinched out in places where the ice sheet extends to the sea. The ice-free ring is best developed in the north, in part of the east and along the southern half of the west coast. There is a crucial contrast in sea ice conditions between these areas. While the northern coast is never free of ice, the eastern coast is partially free of ice for a brief time in summer, while the western coast is free of ice either seasonally or throughout the year.

The inland ice sheet and sea ice in Greenland provide firm constraints upon a self-supporting way of life. The ice sheet offers no realistic resource and thus rules out effective use of some 84 per cent of

FIGURE 10.2   (Opposite) The main constraints and resources of the physical environment and the main elements of the human spatial system in Greenland.

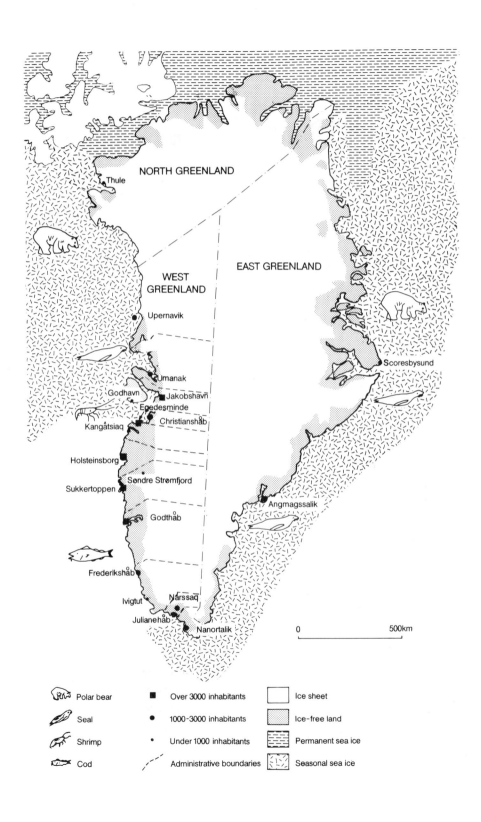

NORTH GREENLAND

Thule

WEST
GREENLAND

EAST GREENLAND

Upernavik

Scoresbysund

Umanak

Godhavn

Jakobshavn

Egedesminde

Christianshåb

Kangåtsiaq

Holsteinsborg

Søndre Strømfjord

Sukkertoppen

Angmagssalik

Godthåb

Frederikshåb

Ivigtut

Nårssaq

Julianehåb

Nanortalik

0   500km

	Polar bear	■	Over 3000 inhabitants		Ice sheet
	Seal	●	1000-3000 inhabitants		Ice-free land
	Shrimp	•	Under 1000 inhabitants		Permanent sea ice
	Cod	‒‒‒	Administrative boundaries		Seasonal sea ice

Greenland's land area. Sea ice is a constraint in that it prevents accessibility both to the coast and to living marine resources. The permanent sea ice off North Greenland rules out access by all except the world's most powerful ice-breakers. Also, its continuous presence means that living sea resources are poor and stretch to little more than bears (Chapter 6). The seasonal loosening of the East Greenland sea ice means that access to the shore is possible by ice-strengthened freighter for 4–10 weeks in summer (Figure 10.3). Also, the fragmented sea ice

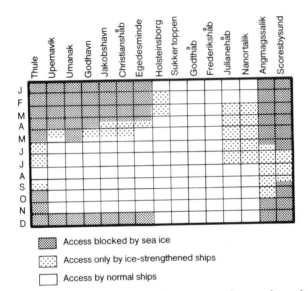

FIGURE 10.3
The duration and intensity of sea ice conditions and their effect on the accessibility of harbours. After Royal Greenland Trade Department.

provides a suitable environment for seals, while the southward drift carries polar bears down from the north. The west coast ice conditions have important spatial and seasonal variations. In the south in spring and early summer, East Greenland pack ice drifts round the southern tip of Greenland and can impede navigation in the Julianehåb area between March and July. In the northern part of the west coast the sea is affected by sea ice which builds up *in situ* in winter and, for example at Umanak, lasts from December to May, thus preventing easy sea access. In the central western area over a distance of some 700 km there is no sea ice at all during the year. In terms of living resources, seals are associated with the pack ice in northern and southern West Greenland. In between is a rich fishing area with cod and salmon thriving in an area of offshore banks which benefit from the mixing of cold East Greenland water with warmer Atlantic water. Also noteworthy are dense concentrations of shrimps which find especially favourable sites for growth in the cold enclosed waters of the fjord basins of Disko Bay.

The terrestrial resources are poor in comparison with living marine resources, although new mineral discoveries could quickly shift the balance in their favour. As shown in Chapter 2, Greenland consists of a fragment of the North American shield and is known to have deposits of such minerals as iron, lead, zinc, nickel and uranium. Also, the Palaeozoic sediments of North and East Greenland and offshore in western and eastern Greenland hold potential for oil, gas and coal. Finally, Tertiary basalts related to the tectonic break-up of Greenland are associated with 100 million tons of low-grade coal on Disko Island. The living terrestrial resources comprise wild caribou in West Greenland, musk ox in northeast Greenland and near Søndre Strømfjord in the west, foxes and hares. Also in the southern Norse part of Greenland around Julianehåb there is sufficient grass for grazing by sheep. No trees grow in Greenland and the cultivation of crops in the open air is effectively ruled out on climatic grounds.

Figure 10.4 is an attempt to conceptualize the natural resources and constraints of the environment from a Greenlander's point of view.

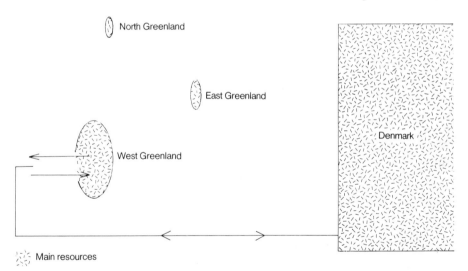

FIGURE 10.4   A conceptualized view of Greenland's resources.

Since most Greenlanders live in the west, it has a western Greenland bias. Seen from here, North and East Greenland are remote, 'ice-olated' and relatively unimportant. West Greenland is viewed as a long thin zone with access to long-term viable resources in only one area — the ice-free coast. Here, too, is access to the biggest resource of all — Denmark, the mother country, which tends to be seen as a land of infinite bounty.

The human spatial pattern

PEOPLE

Of the 50000 people living in Greenland, some 41000 are called Greenlanders, a name used to describe the indigenous Inuit and their descendants. The remainder, some 9000, are mainly Danish. The two populations have distinctive age characteristics. The indigenous Greenland population is youthful, with half the population under 20 years of age and a large proportion of teenagers (Figure 10.5). The Danes

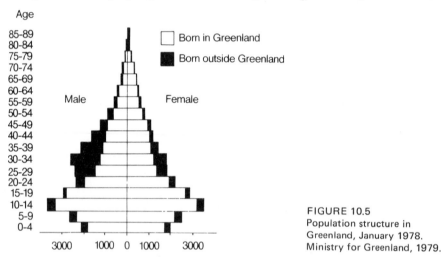

FIGURE 10.5
Population structure in
Greenland, January 1978.
Ministry for Greenland, 1979.

tend to be older with largest numbers in the 30—40-year-old age range. Unlike the Greenlanders, the Danish population has more males than females.

NODES

In 1980 the population was distributed in about 140 settlements, including 18 towns (77 per cent of the total population), 102 villages (20 per cent) and 20 radio or weather stations (4 per cent). The settlements are peripheral and lie on the outer coast of Greenland or along coastal fjords. Most of the settlements are in West Greenland which accounts for 90 per cent of the total population (compared with 6 per cent in East Greenland and 1.5 per cent in North Greenland).

The main towns in West Greenland form a string along the coast. Approximately in the middle of the string lies the largest centre of Godthåb with 9077 people. Four other towns, Holsteinsborg, Sukkertoppen, Egedesminde and Jakobshavn, each have over 3000 inhabitants, and they too are in the central part of the populated west coast. Three other West Greenland towns have populations of less than 1000 and are classified as towns merely because they are the centres of administrative districts. The towns in East and North Greenland are small and more isolated. Thule is 650km from its nearest Greenland neighbour and supports just over 400 people. There are two isolated towns in East Greenland; Scoresbysund boasts less than 400 people, while Angmagssalik has just over 1100 inhabitants.

Morphologically, the towns in Greenland fall into two main types. The smaller towns for the most part consist of brightly painted, small wooden houses haphazardly scattered on the sides and summits of exposed rock knolls near a harbour. Umanak is an example (Figure 10.6). The nucleus of the town is the harbour where boats vie with icebergs for moorings (Figure 4.12). Here is the Royal Greenland Trade Department pier and warehouse, the supermarket, a few battered vehicles and, at a discrete distance, the administrative building, school, hospital and church. Several roughly graded roads radiate from the harbour for several hundred metres and beside these are scattered

FIGURE 10.6   Umanak in West Greenland.

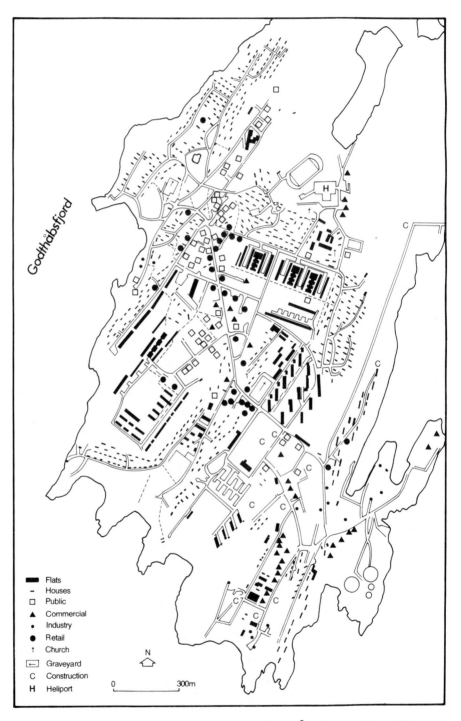

Godthåbsfjord

Flats
Houses
Public
Commercial
Industry
Retail
Church
Graveyard
Construction
Heliport

N

0   300m

FIGURE 10.7   Land-use and the settlement pattern of Godthåb. After A. Wilkin, 1980.

houses. These include the larger houses occupied by Danes, the standard detached Greenlanders' two-up—two-down houses and a few small flats. The interiors of the houses are warm, well fitted out with Danish mail-order furniture, luxuriant indoor plants and high-quality radios, while walls are frequently decorated with family photographs and portraits of the Danish royal family. In between the houses are the dogs tethered in lines, fish-drying racks and pipes for summer distribution of water.

The larger towns in the southwest have additional variety in that a new planned part has grown up beside the haphazardness of the old (Figure 10.7). Modern multi-storey blocks of flats, hotels, supermarkets, fine road networks, taxis, buses, television, open spaces, deep sea and inshore fishing boats, fish-processing plants and modern harbour facilities abound (Figures 10.8 and 10.9). Often the only feature to

FIGURE 10.8
The new and old in a West
Greenland supermarket.
Royal Danish Ministry for
Foreign Affairs.

distinguish a block of flats from any other in the western world is the seal meat hanging to dry outside many windows.

FIGURE 10.9
New and old housing.
Photograph by Ib Tøpfer.

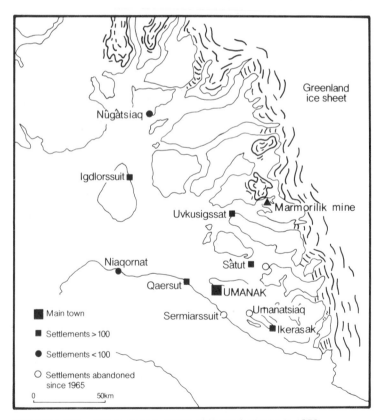

FIGURE 10.10   The town and villages of Umanak district in 1978.

The villages in Greenland, with generally 50–200 inhabitants, are tributary to the various towns. Thus, in 1980 Umanak with a population of 1175 had seven villages in its hinterland with a mean size of 163 people (Figure 10.10). The villages are scattered on small islands or along the shores of the fjord network at distances from Umanak of 20–120 km. Generally, the number of tributary villages is highest in the northern and southern extremes of the west coast area and lowest in the middle. Thus, in 1980 there were ten associated with both Nanortalik in the south and Upernavik in the north, while there were only two villages tributary to both Godthåb and Holsteinsborg in the middle (Table 10.1). The proportion of the population living in outlying villages in each district varies in a similar way. Whereas in 1980 over half the population in Nanortalik and Upernavik Districts lived in the outlying villages, in Godthåb and Holsteinsborg Districts the comparable figure was less than 5 per cent.

TABLE 10.1   *1980 population of towns and districts and the number of outlying villages*

Town	Population	Population of district	Number of tributary villages*	Percentage living in outlying villages
Godthåb	9077	9561	2	5
Holsteinsborg	3976	4201	2	5
Christianshåb	1771	1877	1	6
Godhavn	941	1012	1	7
Egedesminde	3196	3495	2	9
Jakobshavn	3648	4062	4	10
Sukkertoppen	3008	3926	3	13
Julianehåb	2594	3056	10	15
Frederikshåb	2237	2619	3	15
Narssaq	1723	2064	8	16
Scoresbysund	391	496	2	21
Thule	409	771	5	47
Nanortalik	1402	2801	10	52
Umanak	1175	2503	7	53
Angmagssalik	1114	2618	7	57
Upernavik	844	2089	10	60
Kangâtsiaq	411	1162	4	65

The towns are inversely ranked according to the percentage of the population living in outlying villages.
*   Villages with less than five inhabitants excluded.

The outlying villages are less well endowed than the towns. For example, in the Umanak district the village centre may comprise a ramshackle pier, a maze of communal fish-drying racks, a large village hall, small fish-processing plant and shop. Further away and sometimes linked only by paths are houses generally smaller than those in Umanak itself and including a proportion whose outside walls consist of turf and stone. Each house has its sledge, fish-drying rack and dogs, while in summer near the sea is a kayak or small dinghy (Figure 10.11). Services are limited and water commonly obtained from grounded chunks of glacier ice along the shore.

FIGURE 10.11   A scene from an outlying village, Umanak district, showing fish drying racks, kayak and sod house. V. Haynes.

NETWORKS

Most of the main towns in Greenland are linked by frequent flights by helicopter or fixed-wing aircraft. These are subsidized and widely used. For example in 1979 there were over 70000 air passenger movements within Greenland. These internal services radiate out from Søndre Strømfjord, which is directly linked several times weekly to Copenhagen, and to a lesser extent from Narssarssuaq which is reached via Reykjavik in Iceland. The helicopters link the west coast towns while fixed wing aircraft link Søndre Strømfjord with Godthåb, East Greenland and Narssarssuaq.

In addition, there is an efficient sea-going ferry service which plies between as many coastal towns in West Greenland as are ice-free in the prevailing season. In practice a ship calls in at a coastal settlement every few days in summer. In 1979 ship passenger movements amounted to 47 000. Cargo imports, carried mainly in Royal Greenland Trade Department ships from Denmark, arrive directly at the port of destination, when ice-free, or at the ports of Godthåb and Holsteinsborg, from which they are transhipped up and down the west coast by coaster when ice conditions allow. Exports to Denmark have a similar but reversed flow. East Greenland is served by ship directly from Denmark.

Perhaps the most significant point about Greenland's network is what is or has been missing. There are no roads linking towns within the country. Furthermore, until recently there was no regular international flight to North America. A service to Frobisher Bay in Arctic Canada was first introduced in May, 1981.

The evolution of the spatial system

Greenland is unusual for the western world in that it has evolved in a protected economic environment. The country has been under Danish rule since 1721 and the main effect has been that the spatial system has been closed in relation to the outside world. This has meant that the impact of diffusion waves of economic exploitation, so dramatic in the North American Arctic, has been suppressed, at least until recently. In turn, this has allowed the change from an indigenous to an intrusive spatial system to proceed more gradually and over a longer time-span.

Before looking at the main phases of evolution, it is useful first to recognize the basic trends of the change from an indigenous to intrusive spatial system. The starting point in the early eighteenth century was an Inuit population of 7 000 which depended on hunting and fishing and lived in small coastal villages (Fristrup, 1965). Then as now the population was concentrated mainly along the coast of West Greenland. The arrival of intrusive society has been associated with two main trends. The first is that the population has grown, slowly at first, but at an ever-increasing rate, especially in the years following the Second World War when the rate of increase was 4 per cent (Figure 10.12a). Only in the early 1970s has this burst of growth slowed down. The second trend has been for the population to concentrate in the towns at the expense of the outlying villages (Figure 10.12b). Whereas in the early twentieth century less than 25 per cent of the population lived in towns, in 1980 the figure had risen to 80 per cent. The implication of this was the burgeoning growth of the towns as well as the abandonment of outlying villages.

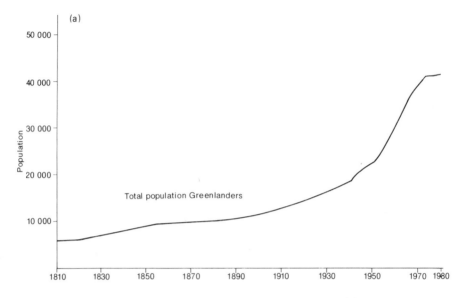

FIGURE 10.12(a)
Population trends in
Greenland, 1810–1980.

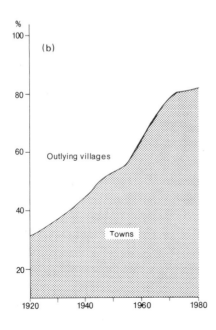

FIGURE 10.12(b)
The proportion of
Greenland's population
living in towns, 1920–80.
Various sources.

The implications of the two trends are of fundamental importance. A rise in population means that there are more mouths to feed. At the same time the concentration of people in permanent settlements hits at the very foundation of a hunting way of life, where success is dependent on a dispersed or nomadic population. Concentration means that hunters quickly reduce the catch in the vicinity of the town and run short of food. Unless alternative ways of subsistence can compensate for the decline of the hunting catch, then poverty quickly strikes. Danish attempts to deal with this fundamental and long-term problem are of considerable interest. Three distinct phases can be distinguished, each reflecting a distinctive shift in policy, which in turn has affected the structure and functioning of the spatial system as a whole. It is proposed to look at the effects, firstly, of these three phases and, secondly, of the externally derived diffusion waves of recent decades.

NO PROFIT, NO LOSS – THE COLONIAL ERA

With the exception of temporary whaling stations such as at Godhavn, the first European settlement near Godthåb followed the arrival of the missionary Hans Egede in 1721. After some early years when the missionaries and traders undermined local Inuit beliefs and introduced various devastating diseases, the country settled down to a period of protective colonial rule. This began in 1774 when the Royal Greenland Trading Company was set up and soon given a monopoly of trade to and from Greenland and within the country (Strøm Tejsen, 1977). This vast monopoly survived until the 1950s. The guiding principle was that Greenlanders should maintain their hunting way of life but move towards a more commercial lifestyle by selling part of their catch. In return, they received selected goods at artificially controlled prices. Some goods, such as alcohol, were banned. Shielded from the abrasive world of free trade, the long-term aim was gradually to raise the economic and social standards of Greenlanders until they could withstand open competition with the rest of the world. The Royal Greenland Trading Company was set up as a non-profit-making organization and it reinvested any returns in Greenland.

The population growth until the 1940s closely reflected the improvement in the standard of living of the Greenlanders and the expansion of health and educational services. The concentration of population in the towns seems to have reflected a long-term tendency to move towards the security and commercial opportunities of the trading posts established by the Royal Greenland Trading Company. Typically, such stations were set up in locations with both good harbours and access to the villages in the fjord hinterlands. Umanak is a good example of such a location at the centre of a fjord complex (Figure 10.10). Extreme poverty of the population at such town centres was avoided through welfare schemes and by employment of Greenlanders by the Company, but at various times the problems were very severe.

Two extra factors can be identified as accentuating the drift to the towns. The first was the setting up of Moravian missions which concentrated followers around them (Armstrong *et al.*, 1978). This aggravated problems in the years up to the middle of the nineteenth century. A second factor of some relevance in the twentieth century was climatic change. The warming in the first half of the century reduced the amount of sea ice off West Greenland (Chapter 7) and the numbers of seal declined while those of cod increased. A comparison of seal catches in 1904–05 and 1961–62 shows how seal catches in the southwest declined sharply (Figure 10.13). This hit the hunting populations of the villages in particular, and was an extra stimulus encouraging migration to the larger coastal towns. The towns seemed all the more attractive because they offered the chance of a fishing way of life from a centre well-positioned for offshore fishing for cod. Climatic change is often represented as the main cause of excessive population concentration, but a longer perspective suggests it was merely an added aggravation.

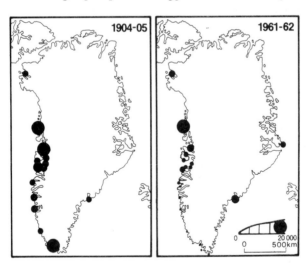

FIGURE 10.13
The changing location and quantity of seals caught in Greenland in the 1900s and 1960s.

An interesting Danish response to the problem this century was, apart from social welfare programmes and some help with the fishing industry, an attempt to encourage activities which re-dispersed the population. Thus, in 1924 they established the new hunting settlement of Scoresbysund, hoping that it would expand in response to the exploitation of the adjacent fjords. Also, in 1906 sheep farming was introduced into the former pastures of the old Norse settlements, mainly around Julianehåb, and has since been in the hands of Greenlanders. The limited fortunes of these two ventures when compared with Greenland's problem as a whole may be judged from the small size of Scoresbysund today, and the fact that less than 1 per cent of Greenlanders depend on sheep farming today.

ECONOMIC CONCENTRATION: 1950s TO MID-1970s

Greenland was effectively independent of Denmark during the Second World War and instead received protection and assistance from the U.S.A. The experience was stimulating and introduced new dimensions to the formerly protected Greenlander. Pressure for a change in the former colonial status led the *Greenland Commission of 1948* to recommend extensive political reforms as well as a programme of investment. A provincial council of Greenlanders was set up to vet all new laws and after 1953 Greenlanders elected two members to the Danish Parliament. Equally fundamental was investment in the existing settlements in terms of transport, schools and health. The attack on the scourge of TB was especially successful and in the late 1950s Greenland had a population increase of 4 per cent, one of the highest in the world at that time.

In the light of this explosive population growth, the *Greenland Committee of 1960* was charged with the problem of recommending a policy for Greenland. Dramatically, they recommended the wholesale concentration of population and investment, a policy which has had profound implications for the modern spatial structure of Greenland. Noting and rejecting the cheapest solution, which was to move all Greenlanders to Denmark, the Commission considered that 'Aid towards self-assistance must be the guiding line in strengthening Greenland's commerce' (Greenland Commission, 1964, p. 1). They then made two recommendations which evolved into official Danish policy. They were:

(1) A significant improvement of the standard of living in Greenland will depend on a continued concentration of the population whereby a larger proportion of the inhabitants will settle in urban districts. Only in this way will it be possible to provide the necessary sources of income and to make school facilities, social services, etc. available to a reasonable extent.

(2) The mainstay of Greenland trade must be the all-seasonal marine fisheries. In consequence hereof future developments

> will primarily pivot on the open-water towns: Godthåb,
> Frederikshåb, Sukkertoppen and Holsteinsborg. These centres
> provide the best opportunities for fishing on a large scale and
> at all seasons of the year. Second in importance from an eco-
> nomic point of view will be the shrimp centres at Disko Bay
> (Ministry for Greenland, 1967, p. 2).

These two recommendations followed study of the development of
other comparable countries such as Iceland and a review of Greenland's
resources. In the 1960s the cod catch was expanding rapidly off West
Greenland and yet Greenlanders were accounting for only 10 per cent
of the total catch because of a lack of deep-sea vessels. There seemed
obvious prospects for a larger Greenlandic share, which in time might
lead to a self-sustaining economy.

Investment soared. In 1966–70 no less than 60 per cent of Greenland's total state investment was in the four open-water towns as
opposed to a mere 5 per cent in the four main hunting district towns
of the periphery. Outlying villages in the whole of Greenland received
only 3 per cent of the investment, and the villages near the growth
towns often nothing. There was a vast increase in housing in the open-
water towns ready for the anticipated immigrants, as well as in hospitals,
schools, technical colleges, fishing boats, fish-processing plants, utilities,
harbours, ship maintenance yards, etc. Efficient and subsidized sea
ferries and helicopter flights were provided between towns in order to
facilitate flows of people. Schools emphasized Danish language teaching
and reorientated towards an industrial society (Bornemann, 1977;
Cram, 1978). Skilled workers necessary for the developments poured
in from Denmark, attracted by financial incentives for working in
Greenland.

It is difficult to over-emphasize the effect of this phase of planned
concentration on the spatial structure in Greenland. Within the space of
a few years the whole of Greenland became affected by the processes
involved in constructing a modern urban infrastructure in West Greenland. The growth of the main centres was dramatic (Figure 10.14).
Godthåb more than doubled its size from about 3 000 inhabitants in
1960 to 7 500 in 1970. The other three open-water towns and the
shrimp town of Jakobshavn doubled in size in the same period (Figure
10.15). The migration to the main growth towns drew population
from the villages. Not only did the number of village inhabitants fall,
but in many cases smaller villages were abandoned. Umanatsiaq is an
example which was abandoned in 1969 (Figure 10.14). Altogether in
Greenland in the years between 1960 and 1978, 85 villages were

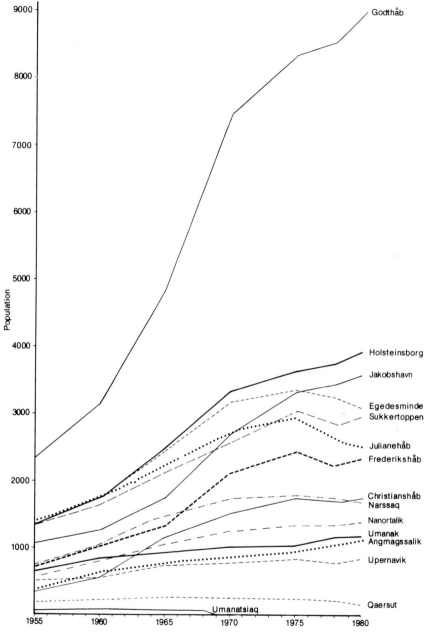

FIGURE 10.14   Population trends in selected settlements in Greenland, 1965–80. The primary growth point of Godthåb is compared with open-water towns such as Holsteinsborg and Frederikshåb, the shrimp centre of Jakobshavn and the hunting town of Umanak. Umanatsiaq and Qaersut illustrate the fortunes of two outlying villages in the Umanak area, one successful and one unsuccessful (see Figure 10.10).

abandoned, a figure representing about one-third of the total. Most of these were in the areas surrounding the main growth towns.

By the 1970s there were two Greenlands. The growth towns were areas of economic opportunity where a person could raise his or her standard of living. The other Greenland was starved of investment and economic opportunity and the young were forced to migrate seasonally or permanently to the open-water towns if they wished to raise their standard of living. The spatial pattern of the two Greenlands is illustrated by the relative dependence of each district on either fish or hunting products (Figure 10.16). The greater the dependence on fish, the more the district gained from economic development. Conversely, the greater the dependence on hunting products, the less the district benefited. The towns in the middle of the west coast fishing districts gained most. The benefits fell off dramatically from these cores and, indeed, in the hunting districts the effects were adverse.

These peripheral hunting districts were classic Downward Transitional Areas as envisaged by Friedmann (1966). A survey of Umanak District in 1968 by Aberdeen University students revealed most of the characteristics highlighted by Friedmann and came to rather depressing conclusions (Sugden, 1969). The area was dependent on subsistence hunting and fishing. The standard of living was low and services rudimentary. With a poor resource base and a burgeoning population, out-migration rates were high and many families had sons or daughters working in southern fishing centres. Social demoralization was evident and Greenlanders felt at a disadvantage when compared to the Danes,

FIGURE 10.15   Aerial view of Jakobshavn in winter. Sea ice fills the harbour in the foreground. Royal Danish Ministry for Foreign Affairs.

especially over differential rates of pay given for the same job, depending on one's country of origin.

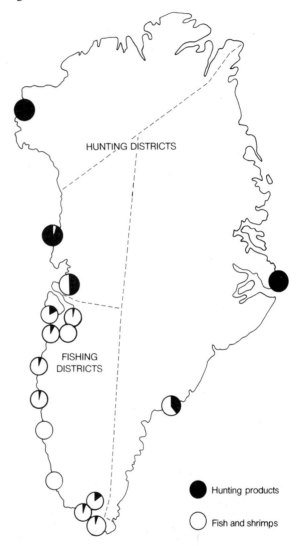

FIGURE 10.16
The division into hunting and
fishing districts based on the
value of hunting and fish
products. Data for 1978 from
Ministry for Greenland, 1979.

SOCIAL REACTION: AGAINST CONCENTRATION

Perusal of the graphs of population growth and of the percentages living
in towns (Figure 10.12) shows that the trends of concentrated development which were accelerating in the 1960s had slowed down or had
even reversed in the mid-1970s. In 1978 for the first time in centuries

the trend in migration to the towns from the villages was actually reversed (Ministry for Greenland, 1979). Moreover, the population of some towns such as Egedesminde, Frederikshåb and Sukkertoppen declined (Figure 10.14). In 1978 Greenland's total population declined, mainly in response to a sharp drop in the number of Danes in the country. These changing trends reflected a social reaction to the Danish policy of concentration. The migration policy broke up families, separated those of working age from their elders and sometimes children. The emphasis on Danish in schools (necessitated by the shortage of Greenlandic-speaking teachers) and the incursion of many thousand Danes led to an alienation whereby Greenlanders sensed they no longer controlled their own destiny (Pjettursson, 1969; Petersen, 1975). Familiar problems arose with growing drunkenness, violence, suicide and political protest (Figure 10.17). Resentment focused around the treatment of peripheral villages. At an international conference on Arctic Oil and Gas in Le Havre in 1973, I vividly remember a Greenlandic-made film about the forced abandonment of the village of Qutdligssat in 1972. This spotlighted the crude injustice felt by the people at the social upheaval, and dramatized the implications of a policy of economic concentration. Mounting concern succeeded in bringing Greenlanders home rule in 1979.

FIGURE 10.17   An appeal to reduce the alcohol problem from a campaign begun in 1969. The Greenlandic and Danish captions read 'Incidentally, athletes should set a good example for others — also outside the sports ground! Young people especially, should do something about the alcohol problem!' Bornemann, 1975.

Had the cod catch expanded as hoped, the overall plan of concentrated development might have worked and stemmed the rising tide of social protest. But the total catch has never exceeded that in the peak year of 1961 in spite of an investment in fishing boats which has greatly increased Greenland's share of the catch. In the mid-1970s the total catch for the Davis Strait area west of Greenland was only one-fifth of the catch in 1961. It is impossible to know precisely why the cod catch has decreased. In part it is likely to be the result of over-fishing, in part the result of the recent climatic deterioration and its effects on offshore currents (Chapter 7). The failure of the cod fishing has meant that the growth of the open-water towns was less than expected, while the population of the towns in the hunting districts has remained larger than expected (Table 10.2). Fortunately, the shrimp fishery expanded instead and this is reflected in the larger population than expected in the shrimp town of Jakobshavn.

TABLE 10.2   *Town populations: predictions based on the 1960s policy of concentration and the actual figures*

	Predicted 1975 population	Actual 1975 population
Open-water towns	22 400	17 483
Shrimp towns	7 000	8 847
Towns in sealing districts	2 400	3 595

Bereft of an economic lynch-pin, Danish policy shifted back towards a more socially acceptable policy, or even 'non-policy'. The reduction in the number of Danes, an increase in the number of Greenlandic-speaking teachers, a more equal distribution of investment among all towns, as well as outlying villages, and the agreement on home rule were the main changes.

EXTERNALLY ORIGINATING DIFFUSION WAVES

Before analysing the way Greenland's spatial system functions today, it is important to examine the impact of waves of resource exploitation generated from outside Greenland and Denmark. In other parts of the Arctic such waves have played a fundamental role in determining the nature of the spatial system. In Greenland, however, the impact is subdued.

The first wave instigated during the Second World War and rein-forced during the cold war of the 1950s was military, and originated in the U.S.A. as Greenland became involved in the defence of continental North America. The result was the creation of a U.S. air base at Thule in 1951–52 and four Distant Early Warning (D.E.W.) line radar stations one on either coast and two on the ice sheet, all in the vicinity of the Arctic Circle (Figure 8.17). The effect on the spatial system of the rest of Greenland has been limited because the military bases are self-supporting and mixing between military personnel and Greenlanders has been discouraged. This principle was so important that the original Inuit settlement at Thule was physically moved to avoid contact with the air base of the same name. The main effect of military activity on the civilian system is the existence of the airfield at Søndre Strømfjord which is a U.S. air base also used by internal and international Green-landic civilian flights.

A second wave of exploration and exploitation of minerals and fossil fuels, generated by world demand, has affected Greenland in the 1970s. As yet, the effects on Greenland's spatial structure are minimal. For example, in 1980 a Canadian-owned lead–zinc mine at Marmorilik employed only 184 people, of whom only 34 were Greenlandic. Other minerals have been discovered, such as an iron ore deposit under the edge of the ice sheet near Godthåb (pp. 86–7), a molybdenum deposit in the Werner Mountains near Mesters Vig in East Greenland and some 6000–10000 tons of uranium ore near Narssaq. However, all are uneconomic at present and await exploitation. An initial enthusiastic rush to drill for oil on the continental shelf off the ice-free coast of West Greenland by international concerns in 1976 and 1977 has appa-rently drawn a blank and hopes are now focused on eastern and northern Greenland. Again, oil exploration has had little effect on the spatial structure of Greenland.

The functioning of the spatial system

Study of the evolution of Greenland's spatial structure implies that progress towards the build-up of an urban core was arrested in the late 1970s. There was a pause while various options were considered. In order to gain a clearer perspective on these various alternatives, it is useful to examine the current processes at work. As in later chapters, comparison with the network model of Taaffe, Morrill and Gould (1963) and the core/periphery model of Friedmann (1966) adds useful insights.

NETWORKS

At first sight there is no similarity between Taaffe, Morrill and Gould's network model and the infrastructure of towns and transport links in Greenland. Rather than an inland pattern, there is a line of coastal towns. Yet the contrast is of great interest and use of the model allows the reasons for the contrast to be appreciated.

In early colonial days in Greenland the coastal trading centres were analogous to Stage I of the network model and were concerned with tapping resources in their respective hinterlands. According to the model, one would have expected competition to occur between these ports and the one with first access to inland resources to gain at the expense of the others. In Greenland, however, the ice sheet has ruled out inland resources and thus no interior link has evolved. But the process of competitive growth of the coastal towns has still occurred. A crucial advantage was gained by those four open-water towns of Godthåb, Sukkertoppen, Holsteinsborg and Egedesminde which had access to fishing grounds unimpeded by seasonal pack ice, as well as by Jakobshavn which was close to the shrimp resource. Exploitation of these locational advantages has allowed these West Greenland towns to grow and also to develop good interlinking routes. The central location of the open-water towns, and especially Godthåb, in relation to the populated west coast has been an additional factor encouraging their growth.

One can argue from the above that the processes underlying the functioning of the west coast infrastructure are analogous to those applying to Stage II of the network model, where a process of competition has caused differential growth among the coastal towns. The contrast is that in Greenland the natural environment has constrained the spatial pattern and prevented expansion into the interior.

CORE/PERIPHERY

In terms of Friedmann's model, Danish policy in the 1960s and 1970s was to develop part of the Resource Frontier Region which was Greenland into a core area capable of self-sustaining growth. The transformation of the spatial structure necessary to achieve this was arrested for social and economic reasons in the mid-1970s. It is important to discover whether this pause is likely to be permanent and lead to the creation of a different spatial structure, or whether it merely represents a pause in the longer-term drive for concentration. Useful perspective may be obtained by comparing Greenland with the characteristics of a Resource Frontier Region and then looking at recent trends in population and investment. The conclusion is that Greenland has progressed a long way from being a raw Resource Frontier Region and that processes of spatial concentration have picked up once more. The headings in the next few paragraphs list the main characteristics of Resource Frontier Regions and they are taken from Friedmann (1966). Consideration of these in turn allows Greenland to be compared with the model (see Table 1.2).

1. Dependent on one economic resource, usually minerals. Unlike most Resource Frontier Regions, Greenland is not highly dependent on minerals. This means that it is less susceptible to changes in the fortunes of a single commodity and is thus able to plan ahead with greater confidence. Lead and zinc ore and sales of stock-piled cryolite accounted for 39 per cent of Greenland's exports by value in 1979 (Figure 10.18),

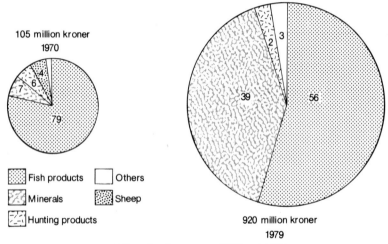

FIGURE 10.18   The value of Greenland's exports, 1970 and 1979.

while fish products accounted for 56 per cent. The contribution of fish products is broad-based in that the catch depends on three cornerstones -- shrimps, cod and other varieties — which are partly complementary (Figure 10.19). These figures suggest an encouraging degree of diversification.

2. Investment is commonly foreign. Individual projects in Greenland such as the Canadian-owned Marmorilik mine and the exploration for oil by international companies are foreign-owned and this implies, as Friedmann argued, that the Resource Frontier Region has little control

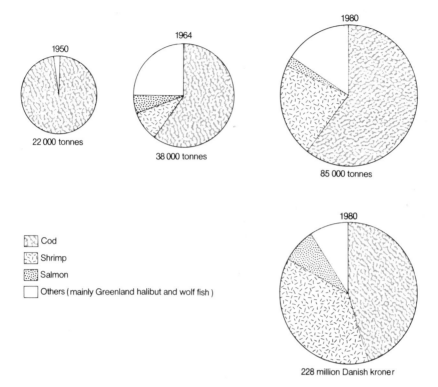

1950
22 000 tonnes

1964
38 000 tonnes

1980
85 000 tonnes

1980
228 million Danish kroner

Cod
Shrimp
Salmon
Others (mainly Greenland halibut and wolf fish)

FIGURE 10.19   The changing composition of Greenland's fish catch, 1950—80, and a breakdown of its value in 1980.

over their development. Nevertheless, the direct impact of such mines
on Greenland's spatial structure is slight and this has been according to
government policy. The main dependence is in the level of revenues
received by Greenland and accounts for little more than a third of total
receipts (38 per cent in 1979).

*3. Conflict between the economic goals of industry and the social
goals of government.* This has proved to be the crux of the problem
in Greenland. Although the conflict has surfaced within government
circles, rather than between industry and government, the very
intensity of the conflict illustrates the difficulty of achieving economic
growth in some areas while maintaining adequate standards in the periphery. The social problems of concentration were always recognized
and, indeed, in 1968 the Ministry for Greenland produced a pamphlet
justifying the short-term problems as being necessary for the long-term
benefit of the people as a whole (Christiansen, 1968). Social problems
were to be tackled after self-sustaining economic growth had been
achieved. In actual practice, the social problems grew to such an extent

that they were tackled before self-sustaining economic growth was achieved.

4. *Centred on a town with limited functions which may not achieve the critical size for self-sustaining growth.* The creation of open-water towns was to be the key to development in Greenland. A massive effort was made to build up the size of the towns as quickly as possible and to diversify activities in order to attract further economic growth. This policy seems to have been largely successful and can be illustrated by figures relating to occupations and the number of private firms. In 1976 over one-third of all Greenlanders depended on administration and service industries for a living (Table 10.3). Next in importance were

TABLE 10.3   *Population dependent on various economic activities, 1976 (percentages)*

	Greenlanders	Danes
Administration and services (schools, transport, commerce)	39	56
Fisheries	14	2
Manufacturing	12	7
Building and construction	10	23
Hunting	6	0
Sheep farming	0.7	0
Mining	0.4	3
Other and unemployed	18	9
	100	100

fisheries (12 per cent) with manufacturing (mainly fish-processing plants) and building construction also important. It is interesting to note that only 6 per cent depended on hunting for subsistence while sheep farming and mining each supported less than 1 per cent of Greenlanders. As would be expected, over half the Danes in Greenland were concerned with administration and services and most of the remainder with building and construction. These figures suggest considerable diversity of occupations. The number of private firms is also impressive. Following growth in the preceding two decades, in 1974 private firms made up two-thirds of the total in Greenland. Although many were small, in 1979 almost two-thirds of the salmon, one-third of the shrimp and one-quarter of the cod catch was purchased by

private concerns. Most frozen fish went to the U.S.A. and the remainder
to Europe.

The implications of the figures above are that the main Greenland
towns have progressed a long way from being raw Resource Frontier
towns. It is significant that Godthåb, Holsteinsborg and Jakobshavn
continued to grow right through the slow-down of the 1970s and that
the rate of growth has accelerated since. Perhaps they have crossed an
important threshold in terms of size and diversity. Godthåb in particular is better regarded as an extension of the core rather than part of
the Resource Frontier.

5. High cost of labour and transport. This still applies in Greenland.
Skilled labour from Denmark attracts premium wages. This reflects
both the level of expertise required, which is unavailable in Greenland,
and incentive payments. It is illustrated in the case of the Marmorilik
mine where it has proved necessary to bring in 92 per cent of the labour
force in spite of a strong policy to employ local labour. The high costs
of transport due to distance and difficult conditions are estimated to
double the cost of building in Greenland (Rosendahl, 1968).

The cost differential within Greenland is suppressed by the policy of
the Royal Greenland Trade Department which maintains uniform prices
throughout the country. As will be seen in future chapters, this provides a contrast with Alaska and Arctic Canada.

6. Special social structure — transient, male, single. This is true only
of the Danish population, many of whom work in Greenland for only
a few seasons or years. Many are single and male. However, Figure 10.5
demonstrates that there are also many Danish families (particularly
among teachers and administrators) and this ameliorates the worst
social problems. Probably this reflects the long history of administration
and education in Greenland.

The conclusion to be reached from this comparison of Greenland
with the core/periphery model of Friedmann is that, although several
characteristics of a Resource Frontier Region persist, nevertheless
there are significant differences which reflect progress towards the
creation of an economically viable core area centred on a limited number of towns. As significant as the achievement is, the process is far
from complete. After all, the economy is far from self-sustaining. In
1979 the value of exports was only 63 per cent that of imports. Furthermore, there is still a massive subsidy received from Denmark, one
which amounted to 27 000 Danish kroner per Greenlander in 1978.

Predicting the future spatial system

In 1978, when trends of economic concentration had been arrested or even reversed and when Greenland was about to embark on home rule, it seemed that the future would see the creation of a different spatial structure with more emphasis on the peripheries and less on the growth towns. One could have predicted the stabilization or decline of the main open-water towns and a new lease of life for the hunting districts and the remote villages. After all, such trends had already appeared. In 1975—77 core towns like Egedesminde and Sukkertoppen lost population while peripheral towns like Umanak and Angmagssalik grew. Also in 1978 for the first time in centuries the net flow of migrants from village to town was actually reversed. With plans of self-sustaining growth originating from within Greenland shelved, there were hopes that the great costs of such a decentralized policy could be financed by mineral and oil discoveries, especially the latter. One wonders whether a major oil discovery, as yet elusive, would have allowed Greenland to create a future spatial system with a higher proportion of its population in villages and less in core towns than now.

In the meantime, the trends towards continued concentration seem to have re-emerged. The rate of growth of the three largest towns of Godthåb, Holsteinsborg and Jakobshavn has picked up since 1978 (Figure 10.14). Sukkertoppen and Frederikshåb, two of the original open-water towns which were losing population in 1975—78 are growing again. The proportion of Greenland's population living in villages has fallen once more and the figure of only 10 per cent for 1980 is the lowest achieved this century. This trend towards a new phase of urban concentration can be inferred from details of public investment. Table 10.4 compares the proportion of the total public investment in Greenland received by selected towns and hunting districts during 1966—70 (the time of the initial drive for concentration) and in 1979 (the latest figures available at the time of writing). These figures reveal that, although the villages received a higher proportion of investment in 1979 than in 1966—77, nevertheless the total was only 8 per cent as compared to a massive 71 per cent devoted to towns. Furthermore, investment in the key growth towns is increasing. Godthåb, Holsteinsborg and Jakobshavn all took a higher proportion of investment in 1979 than in 1966—70 and Godthåb alone took almost one-third the total Greenlandic sum. The main change of emphasis seems to be that the number of core towns is being trimmed to include only those with greatest advantages in terms of natural resources and location. Thus, Frederikshåb and Sukkertoppen are losing at the expense of the three largest towns. There has been relatively little change in the status of the towns in the hunting districts over the period in terms of investment.

TABLE 10.4   *Comparison of the proportion of total investment allocated to growth centres and the periphery, 1966—70 and 1979*

Type of settlement	Town	Proportion of the total public investment in Greenland (%)		
		1966—70	*1979*	*Trend*
Open-water towns	Godthåb	29	31	+
	Holsteinsborg	10	11	+
	Sukkertoppen	9	4.5	—
	Frederikshåb	10	0.7	—
Shrimp	Jakobshavn	6	9	+
Hunting district as a whole	Umanak	2	3	+
	Angmagssalik	3	3	
All towns		83	71	—
All villages		2.5	8	+

Although the evidence is limited and the time-scale too short to reach firm conclusions, it does seem that the three major towns of West Greenland are poised for continued growth. Godthåb is developing on the basis of the fishing industry and its adminstrative and service functions for Greenland as a whole. It is likely to gain an important additional transport function when, as planned, its airport is extended sufficiently to receive intercontinental flights, thus by-passing the airfield at Søndre Strømfjord (Ministry for Greenland, 1977). Holsteinsborg's future rests on its being the most northerly ice-free port and well positioned to tap the northern fishing banks. Its fish-processing industries are thriving. Jakobshavn suffers from ice problems, but thrives because of its position close to shrimps, which provide the basis of a catching and processing industry (Figure 10.20).

Perhaps it is fair to predict that the core of Greenland will focus increasingly on the largest town of Godthåb and its increasingly efficient links with Jakobshavn and Holsteinsborg. Interestingly, the next fixed-wing airport is planned for Jakobshavn and this will greatly reduce costs and increase the capacity of air transport between the town and Godthåb. One might expect comparable improvements in coastal transport by sea and for Holsteinsborg also to become increasingly integrated into the coastal axis. The scenario presented here is one of a linear axis of coastal towns focused on the main centre of Godthåb. Although the axis north of Godthåb seems destined for most growth, it is important to add that the axis also extends south to the fishing towns of southwest Greenland.

FIGURE 10.20
Shrimp processing at Jakobshavn. Photograph by Ib Tøpfer.

The role of the remainder of Greenland's settlements is not so clear. The hunting districts, and indeed the fishing districts away from the main towns, have limited resources and it is difficult to envisage growth unless some mining developments arise. In the absence of such developments, their role is likely to be similar to that of the last decades in that they will be a source of migrants moving to the core towns. If so, then one might expect the size and number of outlying villages to decline, especially in those areas closer to the main core towns. The main effect of such migration from areas with limited resources is the creation of the downward spiral of opportunity so characteristic of a Downward Transitional Area. It remains to be seen whether the increased, yet still modest, investment in the villages can arrest this tendency.

Conclusion

The development of Greenland has followed the classic line expounded by Friedmann (1966). The plan has been to concentrate growth in key towns in an attempt to attain self-sustaining growth. After a hiccup in the mid-1970s the strategy seems intact, even though the emphasis between different growth towns has changed. The result is two Greenlands. The Greenland focused on a linear axis of coastal towns in the west is well on the way to forming a viable core area. The remainder of Greenland is the periphery.

An interesting development in Greenland was the way the push for concentrated growth caused the periphery to acquire the social and economic problems of a Downward Transitional Area. Social reaction was sharp and the Danish response was to slow down the pace of change. The successful acquisition of home rule by Greenlanders was a means of gaining more control over the process of development. The quick and pragmatic response of the Danish government to the social problems is unusual in an arctic context and many would regard this as the hallmark of the Scandinavian approach to development.

The growth and diversity of activity in the main towns is impressive, especially when compared to comparable arctic areas in North America (Chapters 11 and 12). One reason for this greater progress may be that development in Greenland has had a long history and began in the eighteenth century. The adjustment from an indigenous to a modern spatial structure has taken place over centuries rather than decades.

Finally, it is interesting to reflect on the role of the natural environment in providing resources and constraints for the spatial system. The ice sheet in the centre of Greenland has effectively restricted settlement to the ice-free coastal periphery. Furthermore, the location of the axis of development within the coastal periphery has been influenced by the location of an offshore current which provided in one part of West Greenland two key resources: ice-free harbours and fish. The axis has subsequently extended northwards to Jakobshavn, and this again has been influenced by natural conditions in the fjord bottoms which form the basis of a major shrimp industry. As important as the natural environment has been in influencing the location of human activity, it is important not to over-emphasize its role. After all, as comparison with Friedmann's concepts has shown, the evolution of the spatial system has been in response to processes of development which are common to many of the world's peripheries.

SVALBARD

Svalbard is an Old Norwegian name meaning cold coast, and describes the islands at the northwestern edge of the Barents Sea (Figure 10.21).

FIGURE 10.21   Map of Svalbard, showing mining centres and ice-free land.

The main archipelago, which consists of the large islands of Spitsbergen and Nordaustlandet as well as a number of smaller islands, lies some 700 km north of Norway and only 500 km from the northeastern tip of Greenland. The islands have been under the sovereignty of Norway following a treaty signed in 1920. Under the terms of the treaty, Norway offers other signatories the same rights of economic access to resources as she enjoys. Svalbard illustrates another facet of the Scandinavian approach to the Arctic and thus complements the case of Greenland. There are differences and similarities between the two cases. Unlike Greenland, Svalbard has no indigenous people and thus development has taken on a different character. But, as with Greenland, one can see the hallmark of the pragmatic Scandinavian approach; Norway maintains sovereignty even though the bulk of the population is Russian.

Physical constraints and resources

The main archipelago is nearly 500 km from north to south and from east to west, and comprises a land area similar in size to Nova Scotia. Two-thirds of the land area is covered by glacier ice; ice caps are typical of the east, whilst valley glaciers and mountain ice fields predominate in the west. The western island of Spitsbergen has magnificent mountains which top 1700 m as well as spectacular fjords. The geology of the archipelago is complex (Winsnes, 1975); it is somewhat analogous to that of Britain. In the north and west are metamorphic rocks associated with the Caledonian orogeny, while to the east and south are flat-bedded sedimentary rocks of a wide variety of ages. The climate can be characterized as maritime Arctic. Whereas the mean annual temperature is $-3°$ to $-4°$C, winter temperatures may fall to $-35°$C while summer temperatures occasionally rise to $16°$C. What this means in effect is that snow melts from the lower ground in June and new snow may fall in late August and September. The coasts of Svalbard are impeded by sea ice, but its persistence varies dramatically from place to place. While the northern and eastern coasts of Nordaustlandlet are rarely free of sea ice even in summer, the western coast of Spitsbergen is ice-free for much of the year. In the fjords, ice persists from early autumn to May/June.

The physical characteristics mentioned above combine to give Svalbard several key resources. First, is location. Svalbard is both very far north and yet accessible by sea. This has important strategic overtones especially in view of the fact that it overlooks one flank of the U.S.S.R.'s main sea route to and from the ice-free port of Murmansk. It is also important from the tourist point of view in that high arctic splendour is easily approached by sea. Second are mineral resources. Coal occurs in the flat-lying sediments of Spitsbergen and the fjord walls have made the seams readily accessible. Other unexploited deposits of iron, asbestos, gypsum and uranium are also known, but the great hope for the future is oil and gas, particularly under the continental shelf surrounding the islands. Although nothing much is confirmed, prediction on the basis of geological affinity with the

Soviet Arctic and the North Sea implies the existence of huge reserves. Third, are biological resources. Most important have been whales, seals, walrus and fish. However, reindeer, polar bears and arctic fox have also proved attractive.

The human spatial pattern

PEOPLE

The most striking feature is that there are two largely independent human systems, one Norwegian and one Russian. In 1979 the total population of Svalbard was 3650, of whom 2460 were Russian and virtually all the remaining 1190 Norwegian.

NODES

About 1100 of the Norwegians live in Longyearbyen, a coal town owned by the Store Norske Spitsbergen Coal Company (Figure 10.22) Flats for families and single bedsitters are sprawled over a distance of 2–3 km and are all owned and maintained by the company. The Norwegian government runs a church, school and hospital. A small number of Norwegians also live at the new coal mine of Sveagruva and at a research station at Ny Ålesund, the site of a coal mine abandoned

FIGURE 10.22   Longyearbyen, looking towards new housing developments. The church is in the middle distance. Photograph by G. Nerdrum.

in 1962. The Russians live at the mining towns of Barentsburg and Pyramiden, the former of which is the larger.

NETWORKS

The main feature of the transport network is the airfield at Longyearbyen which handles flights to and from the U.S.S.R. and Norway throughout the year. The airfield, opened as recently as 1975, is the main way in which people move between Svalbard and the U.S.S.R. and Norway respectively. Movements within the islands are limited. The Russians rely heavily on helicopters which link their two settlements with each other and Longyearbyen. The mining towns rely heavily on ships both for the import of goods and the export of coal. These ships link the settlements with the respective core areas of the U.S.S.R. and Norway.

The evolution of the spatial system

Svalbard has experienced many waves of economic exploitation, but it is only in the twentieth century that they have produced permanent settlement. Following Hudson's description of abundant sea mammals in the area after his voyage in search of the Northeast Passage in 1607, there was an assault on the walruses and whales. Fuelled by a burgeoning European demand for whale oil (used for lamp fuel, lubricating oil and soap) and for baleen (used for clothes engineering), exploitation proceeded rapidly. By 1614 there were 14 Dutch and 11 British ships in the area. During the peak years of 1625—44, when hundreds of ships were involved, several nations established land stations. One example was the Dutch town of Smeerenburg (Blubber-town) which had over 1000 inhabitants and boasted a church, shops, a bakery and even cannons for defence. Smeerenburg was abandoned after 1660 when the whales had been eliminated from inshore waters. Whaling and sealing continued, though progressively less intensively, until well into the nineteenth century (Greve, 1975).

A low-intensity wave of trapping involved Svalbard in the eighteenth and nineteenth centuries. This attracted first Russian and then Norwegian trappers, who occupied winter cabins dotted round the coast. One trapper is reputed to have spent 39 winters in Svalbard.

The present wave of coal exploitation commenced in 1899, the year which marks the date of the first shipment of coal to reach Norway. Within a few years a multitude of mines was opened, but they gradually became concentrated into a few major mines during the 1920s (Figure 10.23). The mining introduced all-year-round settlements and the fortunes of the industry may be measured from the growth of the number of people employed in the mines (Figure 10.24). Progress was checked temporarily in the late 1920s, during the Second World War when all mining installations were destroyed, and again in the 1960s. Yet there has been an overall expansion and build-up of population and in 1978 some 3 000 people were employed in mining. Throughout the last 30 years the number of Norwegians has remained constant while the Russian population has tended to vary (Figure 10.24). In the 1970s the Norwegian and Russian concerns have each produced about 400 000 tons of coal per year. The progress of individual mines has varied. Longyearbyen, Barentsburg and Pyramiden have thrived, while a Russian mine at Grumant and a Norwegian mine at Ny Ålesund have closed in the post-war years. Sveagruva, exploited earlier in the century, but subsequently closed, has just gained a new lease of life and is expected to produce 300 000 tons of coal per year for at least 20 years.

FIGURE 10.23   Coalmine at Longyearbyen in 1919. Reproduced courtesy of the Royal Geographical Society.

Tourism and recreation has stimulated much interest in Svalbard and can be regarded as yet another wave of exploitation. The wave has a surprisingly long history. A hotel was running in the years 1896—1905 and catered for a succession of tourist ships. Such cruises are still important in summer and supplemented by a stream of university and school expeditions from elsewhere in Europe. The easy access by air since 1975 has further stimulated the tourist industry.

Currently, there is a wave of interest in oil and gas. The 1970s saw wells drilled by Norwegian, Russian and international oil concerns,

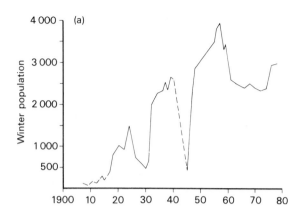

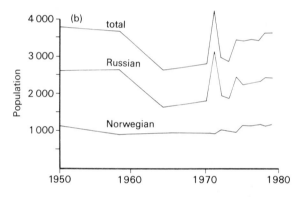

FIGURE 10.24
Population trends in Svalbard:
(a) Population employed in
coal mines during the winter
season (statistics before
1914 do not differentiate
between summer and winter).
(b) Trends in the number of
Russians and Norwegians over
the last 30 years (statistics are
ı an annual basis only
ter 1970).

ecially in the fjords of the west and on small remote islands which
red access to a wider shelf area. Although, at the time of writing,
ignificant find has yet been reported, one large discovery would
kly influence the settlement pattern and activity in Svalbard.

The functioning of the spatial system

The settlements in Svalbard are part of two spatial systems, one Russian
and one Norwegian. In spite of minimal communication between the
two, both systems fulfil a similar role in that they are mining towns on
the periphery with direct and separate links with their separate cores.
Perhaps the most useful perspective comes from comparison with
Friedmann's (1966) core/periphery model, which suggests that Svalbard
is a Resource Frontier Region with little prospect of change. In a sense
Svalbard provides a classic situation for unfettered economic development in that there is a legally prescribed equality of access to a large
number of countries. It is useful to compare features of the system

with the characteristics of Resource Frontier Regions highlighted in Chapter 1 (Table 1.2).

1. *Dependent on the export of one economic resource, usually a mineral.* This is an exact description of the Svalbard situation where coal is the sole export. This means that the settlements are completely dependent on an external demand for coal. Although this demand is conventionally conceived in economic terms, in the case of Svalbard the demand also has strategic and political overtones (as will be seen later).

2. *Investment is commonly foreign.* This is true in Svalbard, but in a rather unique way. Friedmann's point was that foreign investment in a periphery often means that a sovereign state has little control on the type of development. Russian investment in Svalbard is a case in point and the Norwegian government is able to exert control only in such matters as environmental protection. Norway has no direct control on the level or location of Russian investments.

3. *Conflict between the economic goals of industry and the social goals of government.* The problem addressed by Friedmann arises when the social goal for self-sustaining urban growth clashes with short-term economic goals. Thus, the government may be looking for the development of a permanent urban infrastructure while a company may wish to construct only temporary mining camps. This clash has not emerged in Svalbard. The political goals of both Russians and Norwegians favour the support of economic activity in its present form.

4. *Centred on a town with specialized but very limited functions which may not achieve the critical size for self-sustaining growth.* It is difficult to imagine a more specialized settlement than the mining towns of Svalbard which are, in essence, company bases, albeit with good facilities. The main diversification is in Longyearbyen. Here, the Norwegian government has recently taken over the running of the hospital, school and church from the coal company and is trying to stimulate a local town council. The level of diversification is, however, limited and designed only to provide the facilities of a normal Norwegian town. There is no sign of a concerted long-term programme of diversification and growth. At present, one can conclude that all settlements are far from the threshold of self-sustaining growth.

5. *Transport and labour costs are high.* The remoteness of Svalbard

means that transport costs are high, while the seasonal nature of sea routes introduces the extra cost involved in stockpiling coal for shipment in the summer season. Wage levels correspond more or less to mainland rates. Incentives are achieved by favourable tax rates which represent hidden costs met by the Norwegian taxpayer (Greve, 1975).

As Friedmann emphasized, these high costs discourage any economic diversification, in this case either by private or government bodies.

6. Special social structure — transient, male and single. Although there are women and children participating in family life typical of less remote areas, the proportion is low and the 'frontier' nature of the population is clear. For example, 47 per cent of the workforce of the Norwegian coal mine are single men and the average duration of employment is only 4 years (A. Orheim, personal communication, 1981).

The conclusion to be reached from this comparison with the Friedmann model is that Svalbard has many similarities with a classic Resource Frontier Region. It differs significantly in only one respect, namely the lack of a conflict between long-term social goals and short-term economic goals. This difference is important and unique in the Arctic and seems to reflect the lack of a plan for self-sustained urban growth. There are probably two main reasons for this. Firstly, there is no indigenous population applying political pressure. Had there been such a population, some of the early whaling settlements may have attracted more people and more diverse functions. This, in turn, would have carried the settlement through to later waves of exploitation, thus allowing it to develop from wave to wave. (A good site for such a long-term settlement would have been those whaling stations in the coal-bearing fjords of Spitsbergen, for example those on the southern shore of Isfjorden at Grönfjorden.) The existence of permanent settlements would have demanded different priorities in development, especially in terms of devising a socially acceptable solution beneficial to the people of the area as a whole. Such a policy is likely to have focused around plans for long-term economic development and to have caused the sorts of social and economic conflicts that have arisen in Greenland. Secondly, one is led to the conclusion that there is no need to change the *status quo*. Exploitation of the resources can be carried out effectively at the present level of activity. Any growth in activity would represent wasted investment.

So far the present wave of exploitation in Svalbard has been viewed in economic terms. If economic considerations are paramount, then it is interesting that the mining of coal can be viable in an arctic locality. At the turn of the century when Svalbard was *terra nullius* (belonging to no-one), it seemed reasonable to regard the coal mining as economic. This was the time when the rapid expansion of steamships and railways was boosting the demand for coal. The case is not so clear today and, indeed, there are several indications that the mining is uneconomic. First, the Norwegian government tops up the deficit involved in administering Svalbard; this amounted to 7 million kroner in 1975. Second, no country other than Norway and the U.S.S.R. has taken up the chance to mine coal, in spite of equal opportunity. Third, the Russian mines, with twice the number of employees as the Norwegians for the same output of coal, must be even more marginal economically. Taken together, these points would seem to suggest that there are other reasons for the coal mining in Svalbard. These other reasons are strategic (Fairhall, 1977). The U.S.S.R. is sensitive about the strategic location of Svalbard and it seems politic to accept Norwegian sovereignty but to maintain a population twice that of the Norwegians. From the Norwegian point of view the coal pays much of the cost of administering Svalbard. For both countries the *status quo* with a ban on military investments is a cheap solution to a potentially tricky strategic issue. It remains to be seen whether the arrangement can survive the strains that would be imposed by the discovery of oil or gas in the Barents Sea.

Conclusion

In common with most of the Arctic, Svalbard has experienced a long history of waves of economic exploitation. In contrast to other parts of the Arctic, the lack of an indigenous population has meant the diversified arctic towns such as those in Greenland have not materialized. Presumably for the sake of political expediency the present spatial structure so characteristic of a remote Resource Frontier Region will be deliberately maintained in the future. Perhaps this illustration of a pragmatic response to the problems of the real world is a good way to sum up the Scandinavian approach to the Arctic.

Further reading

GREENLAND

Armstrong, T., Rogers, G. and Rowley, G. 1978: *The circumpolar north*. Methuen, London. Chapter 5, 165–209.

Bornemann, C. 1976: *Greenland.* Ministry for Greenland, Copenhagen.

Ørvik, N. 1976: Northern development: modernization with equality in Greenland. *Arctic*, 29 (2), 67–75.

Taagholt, J. 1982: Greenland's future development: a historical and political perspective. *Polar Record*, 21 (130), 23–32.

SVALBARD

Greve, T. 1975: *Svalbard, Norway in the Arctic Ocean.* Grøndahl, Oslo.

CHAPTER ELEVEN

Arctic Canada

Introduction

Arctic Canada exceeds the size of the Soviet Arctic and, indeed, is the largest polar area under the control of one country. Interest in Arctic Canada springs from three main characteristics. First, it comprises a continental landmass and an archipelago, the latter presenting unique problems for access. Second, it is the only example of a continental-sized polar area developed under a western industrial way of life and thus provides a contrast with the Soviet Arctic. Thirdly, development has proceeded from a relatively small population base of 23 million Canadians, this affording an interesting contrast with Alaska and the Soviet Arctic.

The Canadian Arctic is a confusing concept to many non-Canadians, mainly because of the way in which natural and political boundaries conflict (Figure 11.1). Also history has produced a confusing political nomenclature. I have much sympathy with the student who expected Yukon Territory to be in Alaska along with most of the river of that name and failed to understand why Northwest Territories included the eastern Arctic but excluded the Yukon Territory which is in the north-west! The natural boundaries of the Arctic are effectively delimited to the south by the tree line which swings down from the vicinity of the arctic coast in the northwest, round most of Hudson Bay and across the northern Ungava Peninsula. This boundary is closely paralleled by the southern limit of continuous permafrost. It also effectively separates Inuit-occupied land to the north from Indian-occupied land to the south. The administrative boundaries of Canada do not conform to these natural boundaries. The Northwest Territories includes a large area south of the tree line along the Mackenzie River Valley and extends far to the north. Moreover, it now excludes the arctic area of Ungava, which has been part of the province of Quebec since 1921. Again Yukon Territory is often treated along with Northwest Territories as part of Canada's northland and yet most falls into the cordillera area

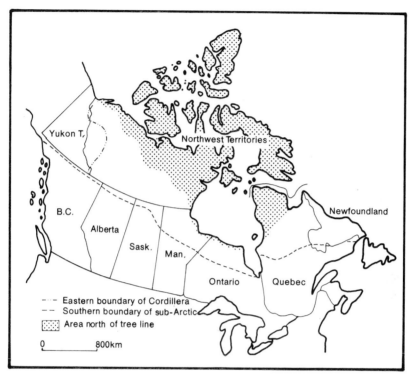

FIGURE 11.1   Natural boundaries and administrative boundaries in northern Canada.

on natural criteria. In this chapter the focus of interest is the area north of the tree line. However, in order to understand the human patterns it will be necessary to look at the Northwest Territories and Yukon Territory as a whole and to a lesser extent northern Quebec.

Physical constraints and resources

The large size of Arctic Canada can be viewed both as a resource and a constraint (Figure 11.2). Canada is the world's second-largest country and the Yukon and Northwest Territories account for more than 40 per cent of its area. Put another way, the area north of the tree line is 2.6 million km² or nearly 11 times the size of the United Kingdom. To travel from southern Hudson Bay to northern Ellesmere Island is 3400 km, a distance sufficient to get a traveller to Cuba in the opposite direction. The distance from eastern Baffin Island to the Alaska border is 3500 km: this would get a traveller as far as Sweden in the opposite direction. The absolute size of Arctic Canada is all the more formidable

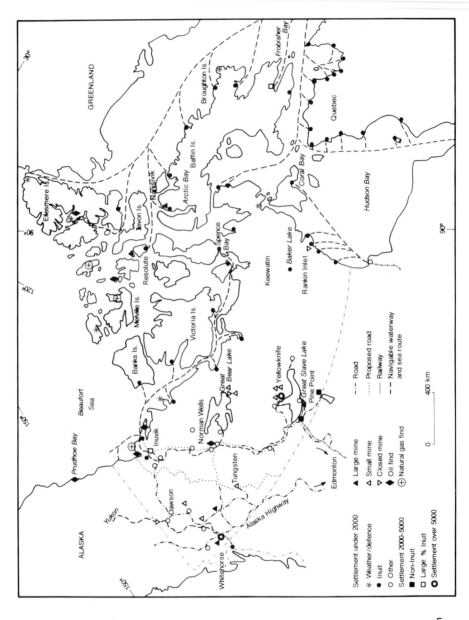

FIGURE 11.2
The pattern of the human
system in Arctic Canada.

in the context of the location of Canada's population, 90 per cent of which is compressed into a 300 km wide band adjacent to the United States' border (Scott, 1975), while less than 0.25 per cent live in the Yukon Territory and Northwest Territories.

The geological core of the Canadian Arctic is the Laurentide shield which encircles Hudson Bay (Chapter 2). For much of its area it is a rugged glacially scoured lowland dotted with lakes (Figure 4.13). In the east it forms an uplifted rim and it is here in Labrador and Baffin Island that one finds spectacular plateaux, fjords and mountains. The shield is flanked to the west and north by Palaeozoic sediments which underlie much of the Mackenzie River basin and the Arctic islands. In the west, including part of the Mackenzie Valley and Yukon Territory, are the northern cordillera, which form a series of broad valleys, barren plateaux and mountains. Glaciers are restricted to the highest uplands in the cordilleras and the uplifted rim of the eastern Arctic.

These broad geological patterns provide a basis for predicting the location of major mineral resources in Arctic Canada (Figure 11.3).

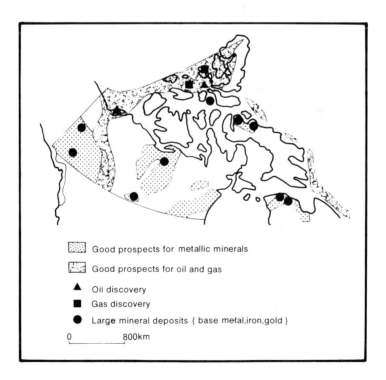

FIGURE 11.3   Mineral resources in Arctic Canada showing major known resources. After Tough (1972) and McLaren (1975).

Within the shield areas are zones of mineralization on either flank of Hudson Bay, on the western edge near the Mackenzie Valley and in north Baffin Island. Major deposits of iron, asbestos and lead/zinc are already known to exist in certain of these areas. The cordillera region has major deposits of gold, copper, iron, lead and zinc. Oil and gas prospects are best where the Palaeozoic sediments are deepest. There are two main basins in the north and west. In the Mackenzie Delta/Beaufort Sea basin, estimates by the Department of Energy, Mines and Resources in 1976 gave a 90 per cent probability of reserves of 580 million tons of oil and 1.1 million m^3 of gas. In the Sverdrup basin in the Arctic islands the same source estimated reserves to be 220 million tons of oil and 680 billion (thousand million) m^3 of gas. If expectations are fulfilled then the Mackenzie/Beaufort Sea field will be a major oil field by international standards and the Arctic islands a major international gas field. A third promising zone for oil and gas which is currently the scene of much exploration is the continental shelf off Baffin Island and Labrador.

The living resources of the area of northern Canada are not vast. There is a large tundra area of low-grade pastureland suitable for caribou and musk-ox. A disadvantage of the tundra from the point of view of potential reindeer herding is that much of it is remote from the forest edge or isolated on islands. Thus it does not offer the advantage of the Soviet tundra which can be exploited in summer by herds which shelter in the forest in winter. On the other hand there are numerous rivers, lakes and a long coastline which provide the basis for fishing and the exploitation of sea mammals.

The Canadian Arctic has certain advantages of access by water. In the west the Mackenzie River provides a 2 700 km long waterway which can be used by barges and tugs for 4 months in the summer. The Yukon River between Whitehorse and Dawson is also navigable. Although the presence of one good inland waterway does not compare favourably with the Soviet Arctic (see Chapter 13) it does give the western Canadian Arctic advantages of inland access not shared by the eastern Canadian Arctic. On the other hand, the eastern and northern Arctic is well served by straits which provide sea access briefly in summer. Hudson Bay is accessible by normal freighter for 3 months each year while the eastern stretches of straits further north are accessible by ice-strengthened freighters for 1—2 months. The straits in the northern and northwestern Arctic islands are rarely free of ice. Ice-breaker support is routinely required throughout the eastern Arctic during the shipping season.

Apart from distance, the main constraint on human activity in Arctic

Canada is the climate. The winter is long and cold, the summer often fleeting. Winter temperatures can fall to −50°C for long periods. This is below the temperature normally found critical for operating and maintaining machines and dominates all activities (p. 58). Most aircraft, for example, are not operated when surface temperatures drop below −40°C. Strong winds from the Arctic basin sweep across the area and in the central and eastern Arctic, where wind speeds are high, windchill is exceedingly severe. Summers are short, especially in the east; winter snow does not melt until the end of June and the lakes remain frozen until the end of July. Autumn is approaching in the Arctic islands by late August and in Hudson Bay by late September. The summer in the eastern Arctic is dogged by mist and rain and temperatures rarely reach 15°C. In the western Arctic away from the coast, summer temperatures may sometimes exceed 30°C and the summer is sunny. Summer days are long and above 64°N there is continuous daylight for several months, a feature which permits an intense period of activities such as construction. Two points concerning the climate are of major significance. Firstly, compared with the Soviet Arctic the winters are more severe and the summers cool and short. Secondly, the climate of the western Canadian Arctic is less severe than that of the east; this contrast, which can be inferred from the more northerly latitude of the tree line, is the result of a more continental summer and a less windy winter.

The human spatial pattern

PEOPLE

About 43 000 people lived in Northwest Territories in 1981 (Figure 11.4). Approximately 36 per cent of these lived north of the tree line while 64 per cent lived south of the tree line. About 33 per cent of the population of Northwest Territories is Inuit (*c*. 15 500 in 1979). This compares with a figure of approximately 21 per cent for Indians and those of mixed Indian blood and *c*. 41 per cent for immigrants from the south. With few exceptions the Inuit live north of the tree line while the Indians live to the south. In addition to the Inuit in Northwest Territories there are over 4 000 in Quebec and 1 000 in Labrador (Table 11.1). Approximately 33 per cent of the Inuit population lives in the Baffin region, and here as in other Inuit areas, they account for some 80–90 per cent of the total population. The population of Yukon Territory is about 25 000; 75 per cent are immigrant and the remainder Indian or mixed Indian blood. In 1976 there were only 10 Inuit in the whole Territory.

FIGURE 11.4
Two young inhabitants of
Northwest Territories at
Broughton Island.

TABLE 11.1   *Inuit population north of the tree line, 1978*

	Number	Mean settlement size
Western Arctic (Mackenzie, Banks Island)	2 500	500
Keewatin (western Hudson Bay)	3 570	510
Central Arctic (Victoria Island to western Baffin Island)	3 120	390
Eastern Arctic (Baffin Island, Foxe Basin Grise Fiord, Resolute Bay)	6 930	410*
Northern Quebec	4 250	386
Labrador	1 000	420
TOTAL	21 370	

*   Excluding the large settlement of Frobisher Bay.

NODES

The people of Northwest Territories live in small isolated settlements (Figure 11.2). In 1979 44 per cent of the population lived in towns of over 1 000 people and the remainder in villages or hamlets. Most towns are in the western Arctic where 75 per cent of the population are urban (Fenge *et al.*, 1979). These are strung out along the Mackenzie River and its associated Great Bear and Great Slave lakes, and include the main town of Yellowknife, the capital, with 22 per cent of the total

Territories' population. With nearly 10000 people, Yellowknife is about three times larger than its nearest rival (Table 11.2). Only two of the towns, Frobisher Bay and Baker Lake, are north of the tree line. Frobisher Bay is the main town in the eastern Arctic and has an Inuit population of around 1600 and a non-native population of around 1000. It lies at the head of a deep-sea inlet surrounded by bleak ice-scoured shield. There is an airport, a dock which experiences phenomenal tides and a rudimentary network of gravel roads. The town is a curious mix of two worlds. On the one hand, there are standard wooden Inuit houses surrounded by heaps of personal belongings (Figure 11.5). On the other hand there is a futuristic school which seems a cross between a space station and a Lego building-brick creation (Figure 11.6). Also there is a central service complex with hotel,

FIGURE 11.5
Houses flanking a
utilidor, Frobisher Bay.

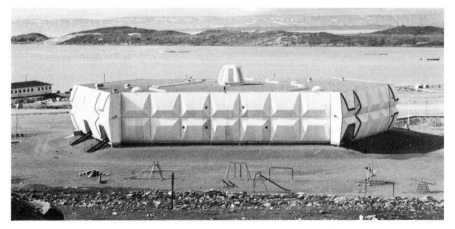

FIGURE 11.6   The school at Frobisher Bay.

post office and shops. Utilidors wind their way between most buildings. Frobisher Bay is unusual in that it is a relatively large town with a majority Inuit population. Most other towns in Northwest Territories are peopled mainly by non-natives.

TABLE 11.2 *Size and trends of main population centres (over 1000 people), Northwest and Yukon Territories*

	Population 1979	Change from 1977
Northwest Territories		
Yellowknife	9918	—
Hay River	3345	—
Inuvik	2892	—
Frobisher Bay	2454	+
Fort Smith	2234	—
Pine Point	1719	—
Rae Eazo	1367	—
Baker Lake	1017	—
Fort Simpson	1000	—
Yukon Territory		
Whitehorse	16476	+
Faro	1660	+
Dawson City	1153	+

Most Inuit in Northwest Territories, Quebec and Labrador live in small villages which are scattered along the coasts. Usually the population of such settlements is between 50 and 900 with a mean size of around 400–500 (Table 11.1). The settlement of Broughton Island is an example (Figure 11.7). In 1978 it consisted of 348 people, of whom 335 were Inuit. Again there is an airstrip, church, hotel, school and a limited road network. In the village is a Hudson Bay Company Store stocked annually by the visit of a ship. There is a village cooperative which markets Inuit products and carvings as well as catering for sewerage, water and garbage. Sewerage means 'honey bags' (polythene bags) which are collected regularly. Water comes from a lorry which backs up to each house. Fuel is delivered to tanks outside each house. In 1975 nearly half the labour force of 72 was employed full time in administration, services or by the D.E.W. line radar station on the other side of the island (Gaunt, 1975). An Inuit is manager of a private pool hall. About 60 people (most adult males) are involved in hunting and in 1974/75 a total of 4731 seals, 15 polar bears and 334 foxes were

FIGURE 11.7   A street scene at Broughton Island.

caught and their skins sold to the cooperative or Hudson Bay Company
for a value of $91 000 (Figure 11.8). Skidoos, motor boats and rifles
are the means of hunting. There are less than 20 non-Inuit in the village.
These include Hudson Bay Company personnel, doctors, some teachers
and nurses, administrators, researchers and engineers associated with
the diesel power generator. The non-native D.E.W. line station personnel live out of the village at the station.

FIGURE 11.8   The cash economy at Broughton Island.

NETWORKS

Unlike Greenland there is overland transport in the Canadian Arctic to complement air and water networks (Figure 11.2). It is, however, restricted to the Mackenzie area of Northwest Territories and Yukon Territory. A road network strikes north from Edmonton and links together the southern complex of towns around Great Slave Lake (e.g. Yellowknife and Hay River) and pushes part-way down the Mackenzie Valley. In the Yukon the road pattern comprises a series of spurs from the Alaska Highway which runs obliquely through the region. One spur, the Dempster Highway, crosses to Inuvik in Northwest Territories. Railways have only penetrated in three separate locations in the south where they are access routes of fundamental importance. The Whitehorse–Skagway railway links Yukon Territory with the sea, while the Pine Point railway runs to Edmonton. A third railway reaches Churchill on Hudson Bay. The Mackenzie River and associated lakes provide a major artery of communication with 3860 km of scheduled inland routes. Tugs push barges with capacities of up to 1500 tons, taking 9 days for the 1780 km downstream trip from Hay River to the delta and 12 days for the return (Bone, 1972). In the 1970s the traffic involved in each summer season was more than half a million tons. It serves not only the Mackenzie Valley itself but also provides a spring-board for coastal traffic in the western Arctic.

Sea access routes are shown in Figure 11.2. They are used from late July to early October in the south. In the western Arctic, barges sup-ported by ice-breakers distribute supplies as far east as Spence Bay as well as westwards into Alaska. The main re-supply operation in the eastern Arctic is based at Montreal. Ships have to comply with varying regulations regarding ice strengthening. Normal ships can be used in the south but increasingly ice-strengthened ships are necessary towards the north. The settlements on the western shore of Hudson Bay are commonly supplied by ships plying from the southern railhead of Churchill. At present it is rare for ships to sail between the eastern and western Arctic along the line of the Northwest Passage, although the journey by the tanker *Manhattan* in 1969 may yet be an augury of things to come.

Air routes are shown in diagrammatic form in Figure 11.9. The basic structure is for a series of commercial airlines to fly into the Arctic from southern Canadian centres (Courtney, 1971, 1980). Thus Nordair flies from Montreal to Frobisher Bay and on to Resolute while Transair flies from Winnipeg, Pacific Western from Edmonton and C.P. Air from Edmonton and Vancouver. The north–south trunk

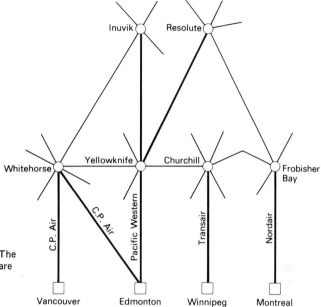

FIGURE 11.9
Simplified diagram of
scheduled air routes in
northern Canada, 1979. The
main north—south links are
in the hands of different
regional airlines. After
Courtney (1980).

FIGURE 11.10
Twin Otter at Broughton
Island. This type of plane
is commonly used for local
flights.

routes are flown by modern jets. From the main northern centres there
is a basically hub-and-spoke series of local flights to small settlements.
These may be scheduled or charter flights by small aircraft (15–40
seats) which are highly sensitive to inclement weather (Figure 11.10).
All passenger movements in the eastern Arctic are by air.

The evolution of the spatial system

The evolution of Arctic Canada's spatial system is the story of the
impact of a succession of waves of diffusion emanating from outside

the area (Figure 11.11). The starting point was the Inuit spatial system dependent on self-sufficiency. The Inuit population in the Canadian Arctic originally numbered 20000 and was scattered in discrete territories centred usually on coastal settlements (Chapter 9). Immediately prior to European contact the Inuit occupied all coasts north of the tree line, except for the Queen Elizabeth Islands in the far north which were uninhabited. The waves of diffusion, all associated with the incursion of intrusive society, have submerged the Inuit spatial system and instead progressively replaced it with a spatial structure integrated with southern Canada.

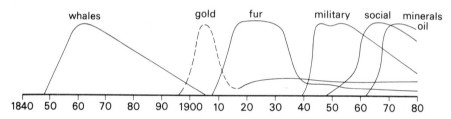

FIGURE 11.11   Waves of exploitation which have struck Arctic Canada. The dashed line indicates the Klondike Gold Rush.

There have been two dominant effects. The first has been the arrival of immigrants from outside. This is illustrated by the population graphs for both Northwest Territories and Yukon Territory (Figure 11.12). In the nineteenth century the native population accounted for almost all the population in the two areas. There was a short-term blip in the

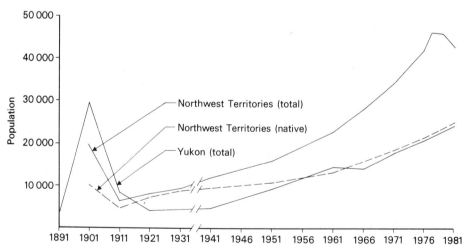

FIGURE 11.12   Population trends in Northwest Territories and Yukon Territory, 1890s to 1981.

Yukon during the Klondike gold rush at the turn of the century when non-natives swarmed into the area, but numbers soon fell back and the populations of both areas were close to their nineteenth-century totals in the 1920s. Then, beginning in the late 1930s in Northwest Territories and in the 1940s in Yukon Territory, there began a progressive rise in population up to the present day. Northwest Territories saw the sharpest increase in the early 1970s followed by a decline in the late 1970s, while Yukon Territory has experienced continual growth. The trends of the native population are illustrated by the graph for Northwest Territories. Following a decline in the late nineteenth century, the native population stabilized in the 1920s and has continued to grow at an increasing rate to the present day. It is still growing and the rate of increase is 2–2.5 per cent.

The second effect has been the growth of towns. In the nineteenth century the native population lived in small villages and there were no towns. Such a situation continued to apply in the 1930s. Only since the Second World War when there has been progressive population growth have towns sprung up. By 1976 half the population of Northwest Territories lived in towns, while over 60 per cent of Yukon's population lived in Whitehorse (Fenge *et al.*, 1979). As will be seen, the towns were generally established and settled by incomers at locations with good transport links to the south.

The earliest contact between the Inuit and the explorers of the Northwest Passage (Chapter 8) had relatively little impact on the native way of life or on numbers (Fournier, 1975). The first significant wave of exploitation involved whaling. In the 1860s American and British whalers penetrated most of the eastern Arctic. The American whalers tended to overwinter in areas like Hudson Bay, while the British tended to be seasonal, summer visitors. By 1890 whaling extended to the western Arctic, but by 1907 the industry had collapsed as whales had been almost exterminated. The effect of the whalers upon the Inuit was dramatic. The practice of overwintering tended to attract the Inuit and encouraged their concentration into permanent rather than temporary settlements. This increased pressure locally on hunting resources, while at the same time the game itself, notably the whale, but also caribou and musk-ox in coastal areas, was virtually exterminated by the whalers. The devastating long-term effect of such a reduced food supply was countered briefly by the introduction of firearms for the Inuit, but in the end this hastened the extermination of local game. Starvation or dependence on the whalers for food was accompanied by epidemics of influenza, smallpox, the common cold and alcoholism. The Inuit population was decimated and, for example, in 1910 there were only 130

Mackenzie Inuit alive out of an original total of around 2000 (Lotz, 1975). The legacy of whaling was a few coastal settlements, such as Kivitoo on eastern Baffin Island, a severly depleted Inuit population and the introduction of new habits such as tobacco-chewing and tea-drinking; in Broughton Island today a Scottish scone or 'bannock' is still a popular Inuit meal. The whalers did not affect the Canadian Arctic uniformly, but were concentrated on the shores adjacent to seasonally ice-free seas. One major centre of diffusion was in the west in the vicinity of the River Mackenzie Delta and along the shores of Amundsen Gulf and its eastern continuation. The other was in the east and centred on the shores of Hudson Bay and the east coast of Baffin Island.

The vacuum left by the whaling was filled a few years later by a second wave associated with the exploitation of furs, notably that of the arctic fox. Although the Hudson Bay Company had been buying furs throughout the sub-Arctic for over 100 years, it was not until after 1910 that it established a network of trading posts north of the tree line. These were established on both flanks of Hudson Bay and Hudson Strait as well as along the Mackenzie River and coasts in the western Arctic. The price of furs made such an expansion worthwhile and the boom lasted until the late 1930s with a peak price achieved in 1926. The trade lasts to this day but is well below capacity (Elkin, 1976). The effect of the fur boom was to set up nuclei for permanent settlements, each complete with a Hudson Bay Company store and a R.C.M.P. 'mountie' to supervise hunting regulations. It also encouraged the Inuit to change from a subsistence way of life to a cash economy. In return for furs the Inuit purchased hunting equipment and, inevitably, increasing quantities of 'foreign' packaged foods. The main effect on the Inuit spatial system was to change the nature and purpose of the traditional nomadic pattern. Whereas movements were traditionally in pursuit of subsistence needs, now they became increasingly concerned with trapping and shooting fur-bearing animals. Some Inuit families were attracted to the settlements permanently and centred their hunting activities in the surrounding area. Other groups retained their nomadic way of life but came to depend on a regular visit to the settlement.

The only other pre-Second World War boom of note was concerned with minerals, notably gold. Its importance is that it established the first stages of a modern land-based infrastructure, albeit in the sub-Arctic. The Klondike gold rush of 1898 saw 30000 people flood into Yukon Territory and in 1900 Dawson City with 25000 inhabitants was the largest city in western Canada. The population dropped as the placer deposits along the Yukon River were exhausted. Legacies of this gold rush were the towns of Whitehorse and Dawson, the Whitehorse–Skagway railway and the discovery of other mineral deposits in the western sub-Arctic. These latter were exploited in a small way in the 1930s; for example, uranium and radium were mined near Great Bear Lake, the first mine in Northwest Territories, and gold was mined at Yellowknife in 1934. Mining had little effect north of the tree line.

The Second World War saw the arrival of the first of a series of diffusion waves of a different scale and intensity. Affecting the whole of the Canadian Arctic, they resulted in the creation of the present-day urban and communication infrastructure which reflects the integration of the Arctic with the main population centres of the south. The war saw the building of air bases such as Frobisher Bay to facilitate the Allies' air staging routes to northwest Europe, as well as radio and weather stations (Judd, 1969). The Japanese threat after 1941 saw dramatic changes in the west. The Alaska Highway was built to connect Alaska with the rest of the U.S.A. by land, while oil was obtained from Norman Wells, piped to Whitehorse for refining and thence to Alaska. Winter roads were established in the Mackenzie Valley and a chain of air bases developed to service the northwest air staging route to the wartime ally, the Soviet Union. Later, in the 1950s the D.E.W. line chain of radar stations was distributed across Arctic Canada and involved 23 000 people in the construction of stations and airstrips such as that at Broughton Island (La Fay, 1958; Chasen, 1967) (Figure 8.17). The importance of the D.E.W. line has declined but it is still manned. These military activities were largely unrelated to Arctic Canada itself. They were instigated by the U.S.A. for continental defence and indeed the U.S. military population outnumbered Canadian residents in the high Arctic by at least three to one (Judd, 1969). The D.E.W. line was part of a defensive scheme which includes Alaska and Greenland and even Europe. The main effects of the military diffusion wave on Arctic Canada were profound. The result was the creation of a land and air route infrastructure in the western Canadian Arctic and a pattern of aircraft supported nodes in the eastern Arctic. Further, and most important, the wave stimulated the next Canadian-inspired 'social' wave.

Surprised by the casual attitude of the United States towards Canadian ownership of the Arctic, and also awakening to the low standard of living of the Inuit within Canada's border, the post-war years saw a diffusion wave of social interest affect the Arctic (Judd, 1969). Health was the first concern and was tackled with the construction of hospitals, X-ray and vaccination programmes in the late 1940s. Schools were next. The first school was founded in 1947 and by 1965 there were 51 schools and by 1970 there were 60. Many of these, especially higher secondary schools, operated as boarding schools with one 9-month 'winter' term each year. After the realization that in 1964 many one-room houses held five to eight people, in 1965 a big programme of housing was instigated. The centre of Northwest Territories' government was moved from Ottawa to Yellowknife in 1967, causing the population of the latter town to double to 7000 by 1970. In 1961 the town of Inuvik was completed on virgin land in the Mackenzie Delta to provide the normal facilities of a Canadian town. It was designed not only as a base for development and administration, but as a centre to bring education, medical care and new opportunity to the people of the western Arctic. It also maintained the distinction between the thoroughly serviced housing used mainly by non-native immigrants and lower-quality native homes. Since 1959 cooperatives have been encouraged in order to involve Inuit participation in trade and commerce (Sprudz, 1967), and housing corporations have been established to employ local people to upgrade housing.

This interest in the social welfare of Arctic Canadians was dramatic and its effects continue to the present day. The emphasis was on improving facilities in the main nodes and, in the case of Inuvik, even involved the creation of a new node from scratch. Centralized social services encouraged migration towards the main settlements. One of the most important centralizing factors was the secondary school at which pupils boarded for long periods of time. These were sited at the main settlements and not surprisingly many Inuit families moved to the settlements to be near their children (Brody, 1977). In the years 1966–71 the number of outlying villages in Northwest Territories fell by 87 or almost half (Elkin 1976). The development of a southern-orientated blend of education taught by southern teachers meant that the young Inuit were trained for administrative, commercial and industrial jobs typical of southern Canada. In the case of the Inuit in Quebec this involved a proposal to teach another completely foreign language – French. Above all, the pace of change for the Inuit was rapid. In effect they were offered an urban way of life within a time-span of no more than three decades.

A separate diffusion wave has struck Arctic Canada within the last decade and a half – the exploitation of petroleum and minerals. The first oil well in the high Arctic was drilled by Pan Arctic in 1961 at Winter Harbour, an anchorage previously surveyed only by Edward Parry in 1819–20. So powerful are the bonds of pre-existing infra-structure on the location of subsequent activity, that Pan Arctic simply took the nearest possible site to the known nineteenth-century anchorage and drilled a hole (Currie, 1975)! The Prudhoe Bay oil discovery on the north slope of Alaska in 1969 stimulated feverish activity in adjacent areas of Arctic Canada. The years 1970—75 saw $500 million expenditure in the Mackenzie Delta and Arctic islands as oil companies explored for oil and gas. The number of wells drilled increased to a peak of 83 in 1973 in Northwest Territories (Armstrong *et al.*, 1978). Some of the early hopes were disappointed and oil exploration activity fell off in the late 1970s, although there are still high hopes for the offshore fields in the Beaufort Sea. The effect of the oil exploration on the spatial infrastructure has not yet been significant. Air communications to nodes like Resolute Bay grew and have since declined, but such activity has been self-contained, using specially chartered tankers and Hercules aircraft based on southern centres. Rea Point on Melville Island is now the new logistics base for gas exploration.

Exploration for and exploitation of other minerals peaked in the 1960s (Chrétien, 1973; Oil and Mineral Division, 1970) and is now high once more. The 1960s saw several mines open in the Mackenzie—Yukon area — lead/zinc at Pine Point (1964) and Ross River (1969), copper near Whitehorse (1967) asbestos near Dawson (1967), tungsten at Tungsten (1964). The only mine north of the tree line during this period was at Rankin Inlet where nickel was mined in the years 1957—62. Significantly the late 1970s and early 1980s have seen the first mines established in the eastern Arctic since Frobisher's ill-fated attempt to mine gold in the late 1570s (p. 204)! The impact of this wave of mining in the eastern Arctic has as yet been slight. Arctic Bay has been upgraded to cope with the nearby Nanisivik mine and a small number of Inuit are employed in the mine.

The functioning of the spatial system

It is the purpose of this section to follow the description of the main elements of the spatial system and its evolution with an analysis of the functioning of the system as a whole. The network model of Taaffe, Morrill and Gould (1963) and the core/periphery model of Friedmann (1966) add important insights when trying to understand the processes responsible for the present spatial structure.

NETWORKS

Strict application of Taaffe, Morrill and Gould's model to the Canadian Arctic would imply that the eastern Canadian Arctic, where a series of coastal settlements depend on ship-borne supplies from Canada's core, can be regarded as illustrating the early Stage I of colonial route development (Figure 1.4). Few of these coastal ports provide access to the interior except the airports of Frobisher Bay and Resolute. Instead they are outposts dependent on their summer relief ships. A similar case can be made for the western Arctic where a number of coastal settlements rely on ships in summer. However, to restrict Taaffe, Morrill and Gould's model to coastal access from the west and east is probably to overlook its potential contribution when applied to Arctic Canada as a whole. In terms of former colonial countries, such as Nigeria, the coast was the main line of access from which penetration took place. In the case of Canada the main line of access is not the ice-bound seas but the south. Here there is an east—west axis with the bulk of Canada's population comprising a string of cities stretching from Montreal in the east through Winnipeg and Edmonton to Vancouver in the west. It is perhaps more useful to regard this east—west zone with its railways, roads and airways as the main line of access to the north. If one accepts this 'coast' for the purposes of arctic development, then some interesting parallels emerge (Figure 11.13). The predominant feature is that the communication pattern is analogous to Stage II in that there are inland routes penetrating to nodes in the interior. Cross-links characteristic of Stage III are rare except in the Whitehorse area of Yukon Territory.

The north—south air routes centred on different regional airlines are a classic illustration of a Stage II pattern and causes frustrations to anyone wishing to cross the area from east to west. In 1975 I wished to fly from Broughton Island on the east coast of Baffin Island to Coral Harbour on Southampton Island which is just west of Baffin Island. The only scheduled route was to return to Montreal by Nordair, fly to Winnipeg on Air Canada and then back to Coral Harbour on Transair. Not surprisingly the high cost of such a long diversion in time and money was a powerful disincentive! It could be argued that the fact that three airlines fly into Resolute is demonstration of lateral links in the network. It is true that one can cross the network via Resolute, but it involves a major diversion. The choice of Resolute as a northern terminus owes more to its being a convenient airfield in the north and the fact that travellers wish to travel from south to north rather than across the network. The dominance of the southern core areas as controls on the alignment of air routes and the lack of cross-links is illustrated in an international context by any traveller wishing to hop across to Greenland from Arctic Canada. Until 1981 scheduled air routes involved a flight south to Montreal and thence to Reykjavik in

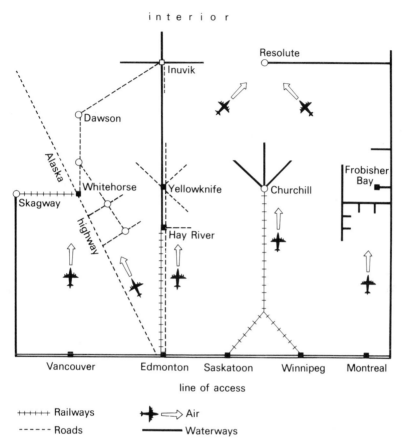

FIGURE 11.13   Schematic diagram of northern Canada's infrastructure seen from a southern line of access.

Iceland or even Copenhagen in Denmark before returning to Greenland! It is difficult to imagine a better example of the effects of routes wholly orientated between core and periphery than this.

The waterway networks reinforce the Stage II pattern. Originating from railheads in the south, the Mackenzie River system and the Churchill route all run essentially north–south, while the east is served by a separate link from the core of Montreal. There is no regular cross-link. Roads are scarce in the Arctic proper. They have little effect on accessibility except in the Mackenzie/Yukon area. Here the proposed Mackenzie Highway duplicates the north–south waterway and air routes and reinforces the Stage II pattern. Only in the Yukon are there signs of interconnections between the inland lines of penetration, for example in the road linking Dawson City with Inuvik and several loops round Whitehorse. But even here the most important route is the railway to the coast at Skagway, which fulfils the familiar colonial role of exporting minerals.

Accepting the east–west zone of populated southern Canada as a 'coastline', then development of the Arctic can be seen as a series of inland lines of communication to northern nodes. Towns well linked to the south such as Yellowknife, Inuvik, Frobisher Bay and Whitehorse have become the main northern centres. There is little communication between them. It could be argued that this classic Stage II stage simply reflects a 'colonial' stage of development concerned with the export of raw materials to the world's core areas. Whereas this is perhaps the main factor, there is the additional factor of provincial boundaries which have accentuated the pattern. Inter-provincial rivalry has ensured that independent lines of north–south penetration are encouraged and lateral connections discouraged (Wonders, 1970). In this context it is interesting to record an idea which surfaced in the early 1970s: that of a corridor of towns, railways and roads extending from east to west from Newfoundland to Whitehorse. The corridor would link the northern terminals of the existing lines or their extensions and would terminate at northern ports (Rohmer, 1970). The idea has not progressed. If this proposal for better cross-communication in mid-Canada has not prospered, then a more advanced network of cross-links in the Arctic proper would seem to be even further from being achieved.

The main anomaly in the broad Stage II infrastructure is the more developed road network in Yukon Territory. A major reason for this greater development was the construction of the Alaska Highway which suddenly provided Yukon with greater access to the south (Fournier, 1975). When in 1965 the Canadian government embarked on schemes to encourage economic development in the north, they decided to build on the existing road network and create loop roads and provide subsidies for the building of spurs to potential mines in the same area (*Polar Record*, 1967a). This gave a boost to the Whitehorse area which in turn encouraged more development. It is interesting to reflect that the initial stimulus came from a road built across the area for strategic reasons which were largely unrelated to northern Canada but to North America as a whole. It was Yukon's good fortune that the Alaska Highway happened to go through its territory.

CORE/PERIPHERY

Comparison of Arctic Canada with Friedmann's concepts of a Resource Frontier Region and a Downward Transitional Area yields evidence which confusingly suggests that both types coexist. This paradox is clarified when one discovers that characteristics of a Resource Frontier Region apply to the non-native intrusive society while the characteristics of a Downward Transitional Area apply to Inuit society. In Arctic Canada both coexist with varying degrees of interplay and it is worth recounting the characteristics of each by comparison with Friedmann's model (Table 1.2).

Resource Frontier Region: non-Inuit Arctic Canada
1. Dependent on the export of one economic resource, usually minerals. This applies in the case of Northwest Territories. In 1976 minerals accounted for 92 per cent of the total revenue. In comparison tourism contributed only 5 per cent and furs, fish and Inuit craft products just under 3 per cent. The value of metal mining in the Northwest Territories in 1979 was $420 million. This came from seven mines, of which only Nanisivik in northern Baffin Island was north of the tree line, although a lead/zinc mine on Little Cornwallis Island should be producing by 1982. All minerals are sent to core areas outside the north. Many Yukon minerals go via Skagway to Japan or Germany while much of the lead/zinc ore in Baffin Island goes to Europe. Many other minerals go to the United States or southern Canada and the same is likely to be the case with any future petroleum products. This dependence on minerals means that the economy of Arctic Canada is heavily dependent on the fortunes of world markets.

2. Investment is commonly foreign. The mining in Northwest Territories supplies world markets and the firms involved are usually multinational in character. International and European interests have provided 82 per cent of the investment in the Nanisivik mine (*Polar Record*, 1974) and such a figure is typical of many northern mines. U.S. and Japanese investment is important in the west, while in the petroleum field it was estimated that, in 1971, 95 per cent of the exploration in the Arctic was foreign-owned (Wonders, personal communication, 1971). The implication of this dependence is that Canada can exert only limited control over the economic exploration of her arctic territories.

3. Conflict between the economic goals of industry and the social goals of government. Ever since the days of whaling it has been clear that the short-term exploitation of raw materials by outsiders has been detrimental to the well-being of permanent residents. Any economic benefits have been only of short-term benefit and in some cases even this is doubtful. In the case of whaling the Inuit livelihood was destroyed and disease killed many people. Today the conflict is more subtle, but nonetheless often as devastating. Brody (1977) showed how the offer of wage employment by, for example, a mining company, attracts some Inuit who thereby cease to hunt for a living and become dependent on employment. Even those who choose to remain hunters suffer through a cruel paradox. While those *with* employment can afford new skidoos, motor boats and rifles and can hunt more efficiently — if only in their spare time — full-time hunters rely on a decreasing amount of game, and struggle with less effective hunting techniques. Brody argues that the latter are in effect forced into wage employment. The body blow to both groups comes when, as in the case of Rankin Inlet, the mine closes, leaving in its wake high expectations and no economic means of fulfilling them.

According to Friedmann's ideas this situation leads to a clash of interests between private industry and the government which would be concerned with long-term settlement and economic development of the area. A conflict between social and economic goals, such as occurred in Greenland, might have been expected in Arctic Canada some years ago. However, it is only in the last decade that awareness of long-term social problems has come to the fore. Perhaps the lack of earlier concern reflected two factors. First there has been a tendency to assume that economic development would eventually lead to long-term social development. Second, and probably more important, the government's central concern has been to stimulate any economic activity of whatever type. It is at least arguable that most of Arctic Canada proper has until recently been beyond the frontier of resource development, and that initial government efforts must necessarily be concerned with priming economic development. Seen in this light one appreciates the government's role in offering financial incentives for exploration and road building (Oil and Mineral Division, 1970; *Polar Record*, 1967a and 1967b) and investing in the Nanisivik mine (*Polar Record*, 1974).

4. Centred on a town/city with specialized but very limited functions which may not achieve critical size for self-sustaining growth. With the exception of Yellowknife, the capital, most towns in Northwest Territories are small and dominated by one activity. It is possible to type towns according to their single dominant function; for example, administrative towns such as Inuvik, mining towns such as Pine Point and Rae Eazo, and towns which are important nodes in northern communications, such as Frobisher Bay and Hay River. With the exception of Yellowknife the towns are small and it is sobering to realize that

Frobisher Bay, the largest town in the Arctic, has only 2 500 inhabitants. The small size of the towns means that they cannot support much diversified economic activity. In this respect they are at a disadvantage compared to Greenland towns, which can muster four of over 3 000 inhabitants each, and as will be seen later, Soviet Arctic towns with populations of tens of thousands of inhabitants. The problem of achieving self-sustaining growth from such a slim base is illustrated by the decline of Dawson city from a peak population of 25 000 in 1900 to less than 1 000 today. And Dawson city in its heyday had sufficient flair to support sophisticated productions at the Palace Grand Theatre! Of towns in Northwest Territories, perhaps only Yellowknife with its administrative and communication functions is well placed for long-term growth.

5. Transport and labour costs are high due to remoteness and high level of technology. This applies in Northwest Territories. In 1959 an analysis suggested that the costs of mining in the Arctic doubled the cost of copper ore compared with the south of Canada (Dubnie, 1959). There seem several reasons for this. One, as suggested by Friedmann, is the sheer distance from southern markets which means that transport costs of any product are bound to be higher than for the same product in the south. Another reason is introduced by the physical environment. Winter cold and permafrost make operating costs inland higher, while ice problems north of 70°N add 25 per cent to shipping costs compared to the southern Arctic (Marsden, 1972). Also the cost of flying in the Canadian Arctic is high and comes as a shock to any visitor used to Trans-Atlantic or domestic U.S.A. air fares. This is partly because each carrier is given a virtual monopoly on its routes and partly because military and civilian flights are handled separately and thus duplicate each other wastefully (Armstrong *et al.*, 1978).

Labour costs are high because most economic activities depend on immigrant labour from the south which commands high wages for work in remote areas. This pattern may be inferred from the characteristics of the population structure of non-natives in Northwest Territories, which shows a bulge of people of young working age between 20 and 35 years (Figure 11.14). The dependence on immigrant labour is also demonstrated by the observation that the total percentage of native employment in mining in the Territory in the early 1970s was only 4—12 per cent (Chrétien, 1973).

Together high transport and labour costs conspire to raise the cost of living in the Arctic. Figure 11.15 shows the cost of living differential in Arctic Canada in 1978 compared to that of southern cities. The cost

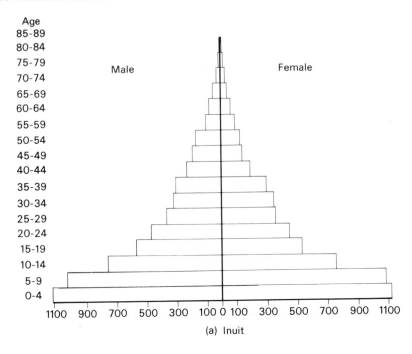

(a) Inuit

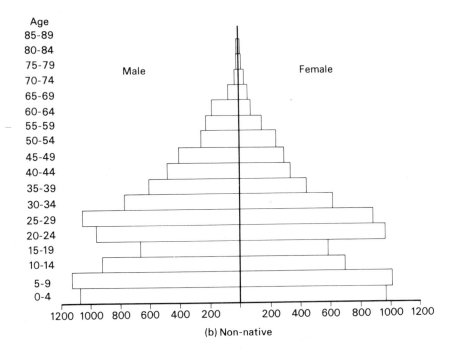

(b) Non-native

FIGURE 11.14   Population pyramids showing age structure of *(a)* Inuit and *(b)* non-native populations, Northwest Territories, 1971.

surface is a close reflection of accessibility. The lowest differential is in the Mackenzie Valley where, in the Yellowknife area, costs are only 25 per cent higher than in the south. The differential in the eastern Arctic is greater and is over 60 per cent compared to the south. It rises towards the north and in Grise Fjord the cost of living is almost double that of southern Canada.

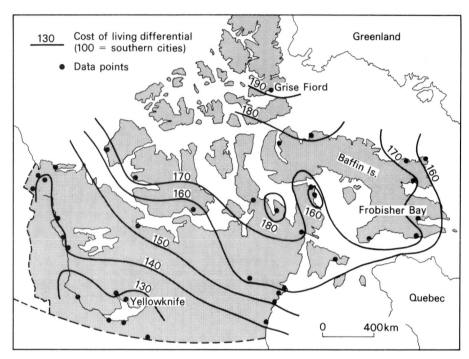

FIGURE 11.15   The cost of living differential in Northwest Territories, 1978, based on government employee consumption patterns. The comparison is with the southern centres of Edmonton, Winnipeg and Montreal.

The significance of this differential is of course profound. As Friedmann stressed, it places the arctic periphery at a major disadvantage compared to Canada's core when it tries to diversify the economy as a step to long-term economic development. Within Arctic Canada the east is particularly disadvantaged.

6. Special social structure: transient, male and single. The high percentage of single males is implied by the inequality between the sexes in the Northwest Territories as a whole (Figure 11.14). In 1971 there were only 83 women for every 100 men in Northwest Territories. Most incomers have regarded themselves as temporary residents only, drifting in to seek work and passing on in a while (Wonders, 1972). The operation of shift work on a 3—4 week basis is a modern version of the same tendency. In this case it is common for men to spend their leave in southern centres or even resorts like Hawaii and to spend only their working shifts in the Arctic. Such work patterns do not encourage a sympathetic attitude towards the Arctic, its people or its local settlements. In particular they strike at the very heart of any attempt to create an arctic community whose inhabitants are committed to the long-term success of that community.

Comparison of the intrusive spatial system in Arctic Canada with Friedmann's model suggests that many processes at work in a Resource Frontier Region are operating in intrusive Arctic Canada. Before going on to consider various possible strategies for development, it is important to look at the situation affecting the Inuit settlements in Arctic Canada. The conclusion here is that few economic benefits have spread to the Inuit. Rather the reverse; they have experienced processes characteristic of a Downward Transitional Area. Again it is useful to summarize the main characteristics.

Downward Transitional Area: the Inuit settlements
Almost every criterion mentioned by Friedmann was characteristic of Inuit Arctic Canada in the 1970s:

1. It was an old subsistence area of low productivity and indeed could only support subsistence hunting by a sparse, preferably nomadic, population.

2. The standard of living was low. In 1966 the mean income of the Inuit peoples was one-sixth the national average (Fournier, 1975) while as recently as 1976 the per capita income of settlements in Keewatin was less than half the national average. In 1970 Inuit income in Northwest Territories was about one-third that of the southern incomer.

3. The resource base was declining. A combination of over-concentration of people in large settlements, over-hunting by non-natives and natives, environmental disturbance of the domain of some key game animals by industry and the allocation of land for industrial, military or national park uses was reducing the resource base.

4. Fertility, mortality and out-migration rates were high. The flat base of the population pyramid in Figure 11.14 reflects a youthful Inuit population, with a median age of 16 years. The birth rate hovered between two and three times the national rate in the 1970s. In 1966 Inuit life-expectancy was 10 years shorter than for a non-native Canadian (Fournier, 1975). Out-migration occurred from small villages to the main towns.

5. *There was social demoralization.* The depth of feeling is clear to anyone reading the reports of Inuit viewpoints, mentioned for example in the Berger Report on the proposed Mackenzie Valley pipeline (Berger, 1977) or in conference proceedings (Pimlott *et al.*, 1973). The gist of the complaint was that Inuit views were not respected, particularly the view that the maintenance of the cultural values associated with a hunting way of life were incompatible with economic development and southern educational values.

6. *Services were inadequate.* The bad housing conditions of the immediate post-war years have been rectified to some extent but most Inuit still rely on the primitive 'honey-bag' sewerage system. Also limited services were built in to new showpiece settlements such as Inuvik.

7. *All the above were aggravated by ethnic differences.* The clarity of the contrast between the well-being of native and intrusive peoples in Arctic Canada and the obvious inequalities between the two has fostered ethnic grievances. This was illustrated by the creation of an Inuit pressure group — Inuit Tapirisat, in 1971 — charged with representing Inuit views in negotiations with the government.

It is clear from the above that Inuit Arctic Canada in the 1970s was similar in many respects to a Downward Transitional Area. Far from economic development improving the lot of the native population, it was instead introducing new problems which were aggravating existing economic and social problems.

So far it has been assumed that both the intrusive Resource Frontier Region and the Inuit Downward Transitional Area extend over the whole of the Canadian Arctic, but are distinguished only on ethnic grounds. However, the differences have a complex spatial expression at a variety of scales. At the scale of Northwest Territories as a whole there is a contrast between east and west. The west, and particularly the Mackenzie Valley, is urban and holds the majority of non-natives. This is the Resource Frontier Region. The larger east, on the other hand, is largely Inuit and is the Downward Transitional Area. This includes the coastal settlements of Hudson Bay, Baffin Island and Quebec, as well as those in the central Arctic area of northern Keewatin. The contrast is also seen at the scale of an individual settlement, especially in the more developed centres. The Resource Frontier Region is represented by the comfortable and often well-serviced non-native areas, while the Downward Transitional Area is represented by the crowded, poorly serviced native area, which in some cases in the late 1960s formed squatter settlements (Lotz, 1965).

It remains to ask why Arctic Canada has evolved this particular type of dual spatial economy. Government policy has closely followed the lines suggested by Friedmann in an attempt to turn a Resource Frontier Region into a self-sustaining extension of the core. In retrospect it can be seen that whereas many aspects of the policy were successfully pursued, other crucial requirements have not been met. The main requirements identified by Friedmann are listed in Table 1.2 and it is useful to consider them. On the positive side the creation of a regional development authority was one of the first actions in planning post-war development of Northwest Territories. This was the setting up in 1953 of a special ministry, the Department of Northern Affairs and National Resources, to concentrate on administration and development of the north. In 1967 this Federal concern was backed up by a re-vamped local Northwest Territories government in Yellowknife. The fundamental requirement of a modern urban infrastructure with good communications to and from the core was implemented and, indeed, has been the main thrust of government planning, especially the provision of centralized services in the main nodes and subsidies for road-building in the west. The need for a diversified economic base has been only partially successful. Efforts have concentrated on the provision of government-paid jobs (which accounted for half the jobs in Northwest Territories in 1979) and the creation of cooperatives to support Inuit initiatives, for example in the sales of carvings, furs etc. and the provision of fuel.

On the negative side there have been several failings. First, the requirement of a reduced cost of living has not been met. The 1978 differentials shown in Figure 11.15 are either equal to or higher than the differentials in 1972. Secondly, towns have not quickly achieved a size which allows continued growth. All towns other than Frobisher Bay declined in size in the years 1977—79 (Table 11.2). Second, and even more important, the creation of an integrated and stable sense of community has been elusive. Rather the reverse has occurred as native groups have objected to the policy of development. With the benefit of hindsight it is possible to see that it was the very policy of providing improved and centralized social services which has done as much as anything to aggravate the problem. The centralization of services, in particular the schools, attracted people to the main centres. The greater concentration of people overstretched hunting resources and forced people to accept welfare payments to live (Fried, 1963). The loss of traditional values closely bound up with a hunting way of life hit at the very basis of Inuit culture (Gourdeau, 1973 and Chapter 9). Demoralized and lacking in confidence, Inuit migrants found their children educated by non-native teachers and seduced by southern values. Growing up with a poor grounding in Inuit culture and incapable of hunting, these children were trained for administrative and industrial jobs which were just not available. Awash in a foreign culture, an outcast of both Inuit and intrusive culture, it is hardly surprising that the Inuit found themselves in a downward spiral of decreasing aspirations.

Solving the contradictions – towards Inuit control

The situation in Arctic Canada at the moment is in a state of flux. On the one hand the majority of Canadians feel they have the right to develop the resources of the Arctic for the benefit of all. On the other hand the Inuit feel they have rights to the land and the resources and should be free to influence the character of exploitation, even preventing it if it conflicts with their needs. The different viewpoints are clearly illustrated by official ministerial speeches (Chrétien, 1973), the native responses (Charley, 1973) and reviews (Brody, 1974). The 1970s have seen the push for native claims with the key issue being the ownership of land (Faulkner, 1978). In 1978 the 4200 Inuit in northern Quebec negotiated an agreement which gave certain ethnically defined rights but also much power of self-government which depends on a voting majority in municipal government. In effect the agreement provides rights to certain land areas around existing settlements, an Inuit development corporation to administer money obtained in the agreement, and influence over local health, education, planning, justice, transport, economic development and environmental issues. The Inuit Tapirisat of the remaining Canadian Arctic submitted a claim in 1977 which calls 'for the right of the Inuit to self-determination, constitutional recognition and continued assurance of the right to exist as an independent culture within Canada *and* the formation of a new territory and government within Canadian confederation along the lines of Inuit political institutions' (Faulkner, 1978, p. 14). At the time of writing the claim is being considered. These claims are in effect calling for more control by the local Inuit of the process of northern development. It represents the sort of selective closure called for by Friedmann and Weaver (1979) when they appealed for local political and economic autonomy (Table 1.3). Nevertheless it leaves open the other fundamental issue — self-reliant economic growth. The problem is how to support a growing population with rising aspirations. Exploitation of mineral resources would seem to be a necessary part of development and yet the problem is to avoid the devastating effects so often associated with it.

Perhaps there is already a trend towards development of mineral resources by a form of economic apartheid, which is attractive to both sides (Armstrong *et al.*, 1978). For economic reasons the scale of modern extraction is vast and highly dependent on outside capital and advanced technology. There are signs that mines such as that on Little Cornwallis Island could be exploited with scarcely any direct impact on Inuit settlements, which are far removed from the site. The mine can be efficiently staffed by shift workers who are flown in from outside for a 1—4 week period, a technique commonly employed by oil companies, for example in the European North Sea. The advantage to the Inuit is that they can obtain royalties from the mine. With local control the choice of how to spend the royalties can be made by the people on the spot rather than by paternalistic administrations in the south.

The interest of this possibility is that it suggests a completely different strategy for the creation of an efficient spatial system. Rather than aim for the creation of a permanent and growing urban infrastructure, the emphasis shifts to something quite different. The modern mines now become viewed as temporary, and can be envisaged as bases which are closed when the resource runs out. Instead, the permanent infrastructure focuses on native villages relying on local resources. In such a scenario one can look forward to a large number of small settlements dispersed widely throughout the coastal Arctic. The need for an integrated hierarchy of settlements covering the whole of the Arctic is no longer important. It is notable that in line with such a trend the total population of Northwest Territories has been in decline since 1977 (Figure 11.12).

As idealistic as such a future sounds, there are very real problems remaining. Not the least is how to rebuild a culturally satisfying way of life for arctic Inuit in a world which is so interdependent. The problem is that relatively traditional Inuit occupations are influenced by southern markets. For example, the well-meaning ban on the import of whale products into the United States in the 1970s has prevented the import of Inuit whalebone carvings and restricted the market, even though sales elsewhere have done well and reached $1.9 million in 1979. Again, the world outcry about the killing of harp seals off Newfoundland in the early 1970s caused demand for all sealskins to plummet. Inuit hunters in the Canadian Arctic saw prices for the skins of ring seal drop from over $20 per skin to $2 per skin (Butters, 1973). Such examples show how difficult it is to achieve selective closure.

Conclusion

Arctic Canada has been influenced above all by *laissez faire* governmental attitudes which laid the area open to the world cores for exploitation of resources. Whales, gold, furs, oil, gas and now other minerals have been extracted for the benefit of world markets, while the strategic location of the area has seen it enveloped into the United States' defensive umbrella. A colonial north–south-orientated, urban infrastructure has been developed by modern intrusive society to facilitate the utilization of such resources. Improved social services have reinforced this trend since they have been centred on the main nodes. The local Inuit were first ignored in the rush of development and clearly suffered from its effects, notably the destruction of their way of life and the lack of a viable alternative. Abandoning outlying villages in favour of the towns they found themselves at an economic disadvantage when competing for modern 'intrusive' jobs. Inuit opposition to the trend of development flowered in the 1970s and an interesting change in approach is evolving. Rather than aiming to integrate the whole area into one permanent and self-sustaining intrusive spatial system, the emphasis is shifting towards temporary mining towns related to the intrusive system and with the permanent infrastructure focusing on the Inuit system.

Wider perspective on the Canadian Arctic comes from comparison with its immediate neighbour – Greenland. In Greenland evolution proceeded within artificially protected colonial borders which shielded the Inuit from the worst short-term effects of waves of economic exploitation. Also, development has taken place over a far longer time-period. But two other contrasts are also of interest. In post-war Greenland social and economic policies were integrated and the people were encouraged to migrate to where the jobs were being created. In Canada economic and social developments were divorced. While social developments and the resulting concentration of population were taking place in the eastern Arctic, financial incentives and road-building were taking place in the Mackenzie Valley and Yukon Territory. Another contrast with Greenland concerns the role of internal political boundaries. Canada has been plagued by inter-provincial rivalry which makes long-term planning of the Arctic as a whole almost impossible. Whereas Greenland could be planned as a whole, the Inuit in northern Quebec were asked to learn French, and provincial airlines, especially Nordair, competed to tap the Arctic for the benefit of their respective provinces.

In Greenland the natural environment had a firm influence on the form of the human spatial system. In Arctic Canada the influence is less obvious but still significant. Perhaps the main effect can be attributed to the contrast between the more favourable environment of the western Arctic and the more difficult environment of the eastern Arctic. Had the natural environment of Arctic Canada been uniform from east to west, one would have expected a more developed infrastructure in the east because this is the part closest to Canada's main metropolitan centres of Montreal and Toronto. The opposite has occurred. The greater distances, the more severe climate, and the difficulties presented by the archipelago in the east have hindered development. One result has been the evolution of a sparser and more costly infrastructure which is more dependent on air travel than in the west.

Further reading

Berger, T. R. 1977: *Northern frontier, northern homeland: The report of the Mackenzie Valley pipeline inquiry.* vol. 1. Ministry of Supply and Services, Canada.

Brody, H. 1977: Industrial impact in the Canadian north. *Polar Record*, 18 (115), 333–9.

Courtney, J. L. 1980: Arctic airport construction: the Canadian experience. *Polar Record*, 20 (126), 253–9.

Fournier, J. T. 1975: Repenser de développement arctique Canadien: population, environnement, resources. In Malaurie, J. (editor), *Arctic oil and gas: problems and possibilities.* Mouton, Paris, 769–823.

Judd, D. 1969: Canada's northern policy: retrospect and prospect. *Polar Record*, 14 (92), 593–602.

Wonders, W. C. (editor) 1972: *Studies in Canadian geography: the North.* University of Toronto Press, Toronto.

CHAPTER TWELVE

Alaska

Introduction

Alaska provides an opportunity to view the direct impact of the United States on arctic development. The traditional American commitment to the exploitation of resources coupled with the pioneer ethic of minimum governmental interference makes the comparison with other arctic regional systems of particular interest. The word 'Arctic' needs some explanation in an Alaskan context. Common parlance in Alaska often restricts the term Arctic to the tundra north of the Brooks Range, an area amounting to about one-fifth of the total area of Alaska. Whereas this definition is useful in describing the area of central interest to this chapter, it is perhaps unduly restricting. In the first place, tundra vegetation covers much of western coastal Alaska (Figure 12.1) and indeed forms the habitat of past and present Inuit peoples practising an essentially arctic way of life (Figure 9.16). In the second place, the pattern of human development in Alaska reflects the operation of the state as a whole. Understanding development in any one part demands some appreciation of the workings of the whole. Thus for the purposes of this chapter discussion will range over Alaska as a whole but with the focus on the north. Little attention is paid to the cool temperate penhandle of southeastern Alaska.

Physical constraints and resources

The great size of Alaska was brought home to me when I was benighted in the wilds after failing to accomplish what was, in retrospect, a hopelessly ambitious hitch-hiking tour. The apparently short hop from Anchorage to Valdez took over 12 hours driving (rather than the 4 hours I had allowed). The Aleuts were somewhat more perceptive than me when they named the area 'Alaska', meaning 'The Great Land'. Alaska's 1.52 million km^2 comprises one-fifth of the total area of the United States. On a map of Europe Alaska would reach from London

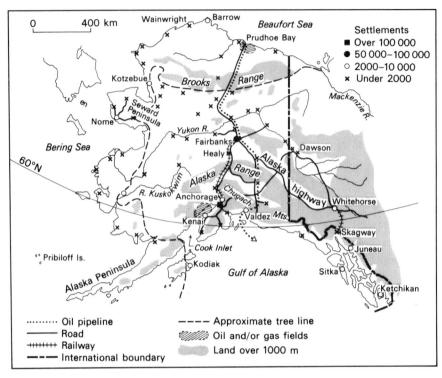

FIGURE 12.1   Regional patterns in Alaska.

to Copenhagen in the north and from Lisbon to Athens in the south. The great size is obviously a major resource in its own right as well as a constraint. There are marked environmental contrasts within Alaska. In the south are two major mountain belts. Emanating from the St. Elias Mountains on the Canadian border with peaks of 5800 m, the Chugach Mountains (2000–4000 m) are a backdrop to the arcuate southern coast. They form the backbone of the Kenai Peninsula and disappear below sea level before reappearing in the guise of Kodiak Island. Further north the Alaska Range with its culminating peak of Mount McKinley (6178 m) swings round to the north of Anchorage before running along the axis of the Alaska Peninsula and the Aleutian Islands. These mountains are dramatically steep and lavishly endowed with the spectacular glaciers which adorn many a glacial textbook. Situated near the junction of two tectonic plates, they are also the scene of dramatic earthquakes such as that in 1964 (Figure 2.12). Lying athwart the main moisture-bearing winds, these mountain ranges experience high snowfalls. The coast itself is humid and relatively mild for its latitude. Seasonal pack ice is rare except in embayments like Cook Inlet.

North of these mountain barriers is interior Alaska, an extensive area of lowland and gently rolling uplands. Large rivers such as the Yukon and Kuskokwim trend southwestwards parallel to the grain of the uplands. The area is continental sub-arctic in character. Except along the west coast beside the seasonally ice-bound Bering Sea, a forest cover is typical of lowlands. Mean temperatures at Fairbanks range from −25°C in January to 16°C in July. Precipitation is light, permafrost common and winter ice fogs troublesome. Northward again is the bleak Brooks Range, which forms a clear boundary between sub-Arctic and Arctic (Figure 2.3). Formerly glaciated jagged peaks rise starkly to altitudes of 2830 m. Few glaciers exist today in the mountains, largely because of the lack of moisture. Finally, in the extreme north is the Arctic Slope. Flat, poorly drained, underlain by continuous permafrost and subject to a maritime arctic climate, it is a bleak environment (Figure 5.12). Barrow can only muster 17 frost-free days in a year.

The physical environment seems to offer an unusually rich set of resources. A compilation of areas with good mineral and fossil fuel prospects includes most of Alaska (Figure 12.2). The main mountain ranges are known to contain gold, copper, platinum, nickel, tin, silver, lead and zinc, all of which have been mined in the past. Known gold reserves exceed 3000 tons. Large copper reserves occur at Bornite (500 million tons) and near Nabesna. Huge iron deposits exist on the west side of Cook Inlet and Nushagak. Tin occurs on the Seward Peninsula. Further exploration is likely to reveal many other large deposits of these and other minerals. Oil and gas reserves seem enormous. Estimates of the recoverable reserves from the North Slope oil province range from 7–20 billion tons of oil as well as 8.5 trillion m³ of natural gas. In the Cook Inlet oil province reserves are estimated at 200 million tons of oil and 5 trillion m³ of natural gas (Armstrong *et al.*, 1978). In addition, there are several other promising oil provinces on land and offshore. Coal reserves, too, are huge. The most extensive deposit of over 100 billion tons is north of the Brooks Range and includes some bituminous coal. Taken together with other fields, Alaska's known reserves are 130 billion tons but possibly 5–10 times as much remains to be discovered (*Alaska Statistical Review*, 1980).

Renewable resources of note are the fisheries associated with the 9000 km of Alaskan coast and extensive continental shelves. The most important coasts for fishing are in the Kodiak and Aleutian island areas but in the north and west bowhead whales and seals are seasonally abundant. Fur seals thrive in the Pribilof Islands where the 1.75 million which breed there annually provide an important resource, though one which is diminishing in importance. Timber is a major resource in cool

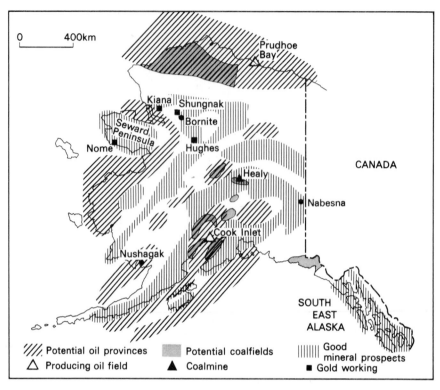

FIGURE 12.2   Potential and existing mineral and fossil fuel resources in Alaska. Various sources.

temperate Alaska, especially in the southeast. In the north and west the timber gives way to tundra grazing lands suitable for reindeer (although domesticated animals occur only on the Seward Peninsula).

Another Alaskan resource is scenery and wildlife. The spectacular mountain backdrop and sea inlets of the south coast and the wilderness of interior Alaska are an attraction for tourists. Even the glaciers are trained to perform feats for visitors. The Columbia Glacier near Valdez calves to order at a signal from a ship's siren!

Finally, Alaska's relative location is a resource of some significance. While much of the state is arctic and sub-arctic, it is relatively accessible compared, for example, with Arctic Canada and the Soviet Arctic. On the one hand it is approximately equidistant from the northern hemisphere's main industrial centres of Europe, Japan and eastern North America; by sea it is closest to Japan. On the other hand, Alaska is an arctic territory with an ice-free southern coast accessible to normal shipping; in this latter respect it is similar to West Greenland.

The human spatial pattern

PEOPLE

In 1980, 400000 people lived in Alaska. This is some eight times more than in Greenland and nine times more than in Northwest Territories. About 336000 were classified as non-native and represent immigrants to Alaska and their descendants. The majority of these immigrants have come from the rest of the U.S.A. or the *Lower 48* as it is called in Alaska. They comprise the intrusive society. The remaining 64000 were classified as native. Three-fifths of this latter group, or just under 40000, were Inuit.

NODES

Unlike Greenland and Arctic Canada there is a pronounced urban hierarchy in Alaska. Nearly half the population of the state lives in Anchorage which is a major city of 173000 people.[1] Sprawled out in the rectangular grid-iron pattern typical of many western United States' cities, it lies near an inlet named after James Cook. Today there is an international airport, a high-rise downtown area, extensive suburbs and heavy motor traffic. Perhaps the essential character of the city is best illustrated by the catchphrase that it is 'the northernmost city in the Lower 48'. Fairbanks is the second most important centre with 48600 inhabitants. The atmosphere is that of frontier town with chain stores cheek by jowl with bars displaying names such as 'The Mad Russian'. There are also attractive suburbs (Figure 12.3). In 1971 an

FIGURE 12.3
Suburbs in part of
Fairbanks.

[1] All figures in this chapter are for 1980, unless otherwise stated.

unpretentious two-storey building had a sign of equal size attached to the roof which proclaimed the existence of the *International Hotel*. Fairbanks is unique in that it is the only important town in Alaska which is not situated on the coast. Other smaller Alaskan towns of note include the capital, Juneau, in temperate southeast Alaska with 19 500 inhabitants and the oil port Valdez (3 000) in south-central Alaska.

In the north and west of Alaska the population lives in a number of small coastal towns and villages. The larger local centres, a few thousand strong, include small towns like Bethel (3 576 people), Nome (2 300), Kotzebue (2 000) and in the far north Barrow (2 200). Nome, with its gravel roads, wooden houses leaning because of permafrost disturbance, and wooden poles sagging beneath a tangle of overhead wires, is almost a caricature of a Hollywood frontier town. Barrow and Kotzebue are less fortunate and many of their wooden houses are dilapidated and without water and sewerage (Figure 12.4). It is worth recalling that these towns, though small by Alaskan standards, are similar in size to the towns in Arctic Canada and Greenland. The villages in the north and west are mainly scattered along the coast and comprise small clusters of wooden houses with limited services. The villages usually have 100–400 inhabitants.

FIGURE 12.4
Sub-standard housing in
Kotzebue.

The native and non-native peoples are not scattered evenly throughout the Alaskan nodes. At one extreme non-native peoples are concentrated in the main towns; thus in 1980 they comprised 95 per cent of the population of Anchorage and 94 per cent of the population of Fairbanks. At the other extreme, the 200 small coastal villages in Alaska are largely peopled by natives; for example Wainwright on the North Slope mustered only 33 non-native people out of its population of 405. In between are the larger centres on the coast, such as Nome and Kotzebue, where between a quarter and a third of the population is non-native. These figures draw attention to a fundamental contrast in Alaska. While the two largest centres of Alaska are associated with the intrusive society, the rural peripheries are essentially native; in the case of the north and west these natives are Inuit. However, the percentage figures obscure one important fact, and that is that in absolute terms the number of natives in Anchorage and Fairbanks is significant and indeed together the cities contain one-fifth of the native population of Alaska.

NETWORKS

Alaska's land communications are shown in Figure 12.1. A road and single-track railway link Anchorage in the south with Fairbanks in the interior. The road runs to Prudhoe Bay on the North Slope although the northern part is not open for public use. The road network is linked to the rest of the United States via the Alaska Highway which runs through Canada. The roads are well paved considering the relatively light traffic they are asked to bear. Nome has a small radial network of roads extending inland. The main point of importance is that the majority of Alaskan settlements are not linked to the road or railway networks. The west and north coasts are particularly isolated from this point of view. The lack of roads is compensated for by air and water routes. Regular jet flights carry passengers from Anchorage (and to a lesser extent Fairbanks) to the main outlying centres, from which there is a radial series of local flights by air taxis and other small planes to outlying villages. Anchorage is reputed to have the highest number of pilots in the world for its population, and this claim is easily believed by anyone seeing the serried ranks of float planes on special marinas. Heavier cargo destined for the western and northern settlements normally goes by sea during the summer months and is sent from larger Alaskan ports or sometimes directly from Seattle (Gray, 1980; Maybourn, 1976). Regular ferry services ply between certain coastal settlements in south-central Alaska and in southeast Alaska, but not between the two areas. Finally, there is the oil pipeline linking Prudhoe Bay with Valdez (Figure 12.5). Running in tandem with the road for its 1284 km length, the pipeline is expected to transmit 1.5 billion barrels of oil per day throughout the 1980s and 1990s, and perhaps beyond. The oil is pumped into tankers at Valdez and most is taken to the west coast of the *Lower 48* for refining.

FIGURE 12.5   The Trans-Alaska pipeline in the vicinity of the Yukon River. The zig-zag
configuration is to allow for thermal contraction and expansion. The heat
exchangers on top of the piles serve to keep the ground frozen and firm.
Sohio photograph.

The evolution of the spatial system

A look at the evolution of the present Alaskan human system gives a
useful perspective on the present-day pattern of development. The
story is one of the impact of a succession of waves of diffusion emanating from the world's core areas (Figure 12.6). These waves, associated
with the arrival of the intrusive society, have had the effect of progressively adding a spatial infrastructure which effectively links Alaska
with the rest of the U.S.A. and the outside world. The first few diffusion waves were associated with Russian exploits and commenced in
the 1740s. In 1867 Alaska was purchased from Russia by the United
States. It was then run as a United States colony until 1959 when
Alaska became a fully fledged state.

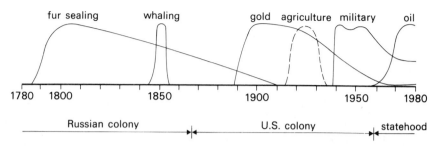

FIGURE 12.6 Main economic diffusion waves which affected northern and western Alaska.

Before the arrival of the Russians Alaska had a native population of around 62000 living in small permanent and semi-permanent villages. The Inuit were the most numerous and their numbers in the coastal west and north were around 28000 (Chapter 9). In addition, there were some 16000 Aleuts in the Aleutian Islands, some 7000 Athapascan Indians in wooded interior Alaska and 12000 Indians in southeast Alaska. The main feature of native Alaska was the existence of small villages scattered along the coasts and main rivers. Each village was surrounded by a discrete territory which provided the basic resources for survival (Figure 9.16). In the case of Inuit Alaska the basis of life was mainly marine and focused on fish and the seasonal migrations of sea mammals along the coast. The bowhead whale in particular was of exceeding importance for the Inuit of northern Alaska for both economic and cultural reasons. As explained in Chapter 9, the number of Inuit decreased and the spacing of the settlements increased towards the north in sympathy with a decline in resources in the same direction.

The first diffusion wave to strike this self-subsistence native Alaska was the quest for fur seal and sea otter pelts which peaked with Russian hegemony in Alaska in the years 1770–1867 and continued until the early twentieth century. The effects were concentrated in the Aleutian and Pribilof Islands where permanent trading settlements were established. A catastrophic effect was the decimation of the Aleut population as a result of disease, forced migration and enslavement. The original population of 16000 was reduced to just over 2000 by 1840 (Kresge *et al.*, 1977). The effect was the destruction of the rural village structure. Elsewhere in Alaska this early wave had little impact and it seems that there were rarely more than 500–700 Russians in Alaska throughout the period and these were mostly in Kodiak and Sitka (Armstrong, 1972).

A second diffusion wave struck Alaska in the years 1847–53 as whalers swept up the west coast of Alaska and along the northern coast. Although short-lived, the wave had a devastating but localized effect on north-western Alaska. The Inuit population in coastal villages suffered badly from disease and from the destruction of their economic and cultural livelihood, the bowhead whale. At the same time a few of the coastal settlements grew in importance as they acquired trading functions and attracted Inuit from surrounding areas. The increased concentration of the Inuit, coupled with the introduction of more powerful hunting weapons, followed the familiar pattern and exhausted local hunting resources. The disruption of the Inuit spatial system was so severe that in the aftermath of this wave in the late nineteenth century the coastal Inuit of northwest Alaska experienced wholesale starvation.

The first two diffusion waves had catastrophic effects in two coastal areas but had little impact in the interior of Alaska. Subsequent diffusion waves in the late nineteenth century and up to the present day began a process of change whereby an urban and transport infrastructure began to develop in the interior (Rogers, 1962). The growth of towns and transport links was not steady or even progressive. The pattern changed in response to each wave of external exploitation. This can be illustrated by looking at the fortunes of the four main towns throughout the period (Table 12.1). In 1900 Nome was the largest town in Alaska and Juneau the second. Neither Anchorage nor Fairbanks existed. In 1939 Juneau was the largest town and Fairbanks second. Nome had dropped into insignificance. By 1970 Anchorage had more than 100000 inhabitants and this amounted to 41 per cent of Alaska's total population. Fairbanks was second and Juneau, the capital, third. This pattern has been accentuated during the 1970s.

TABLE 12.1   *The relative fortunes of the four main Alaskan nodes*

Town	Population			
	1900	*1939*	*1970*	*1980*
Anchorage	0	3500	126333	173017
Fairbanks	0	4430	45864	48663
Nome	12400	1500	2500	2301
Juneau	1864	7390	13556	19528

Each wave since the late nineteenth century has been accompanied by an influx of outsiders. Although some such immigrants often left Alaska after the wave passed its peak, many others stayed and there has been a progressive increase in population. Numbers grew from a few hundred in 1880 to about 40000 in 1900–10. Numbers then slowly declined until the Second World War but just managed to exceed the numbers of natives which were stabilizing at around 30 000 after a decline throughout the previous century. Since the Second World War there has been a sharp rise in the number of immigrants (Figure 12.7).

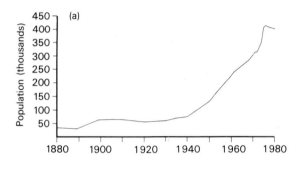

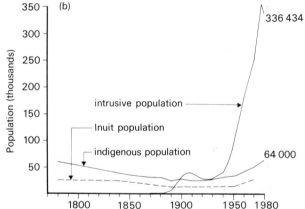

FIGURE 12.7
Population growth in Alaska:
(a) total population
(Harrison, 1979); (b) indigenous, Inuit and non-native
population.

A wave of lasting economic importance was associated with gold mining. Following gold strikes in Juneau and the Klondike in the 1880s/1890s, gold was discovered in Nome in 1898 and saw the imme-diate growth of a gold rush town. A few years later in 1906 Fairbanks developed after the discovery of gold in river terrace alluvial gravels. The Nome workings were rapidly exhausted (although they have been reopened recently) and the isolated town soon declined and indeed had only 800 inhabitants in 1920. In Fairbanks, gold provided a mainstay until the onset of the Second World War. The significance of the two towns is immense. Nome was the first town supplied regularly by ship on the western coast while Fairbanks was the first sizeable town to grow up in the interior. It depended for its trade and supplies on barge traffic up and down the Yukon River from the west coast.

Other diffusion waves influenced pre-Second World War Alaska. In retrospect one of the most significant was an attempt at agricultural colonization in the 1920s and 1930s. Although the numbers involved were small, this wave saw the building of the pioneering Alaska Railroad from Anchorage to Fairbanks. Anchorage was chosen from virgin land to be the coastal terminus and Fairbanks, the only interior town, was the obvious inland terminus. Although the railway was not an important transport artery its existence proved significant later on.

The explosive growth of population which followed the Second World War was associated with the two waves of exploitation which are important today — military activity and oil. The military wave had dramatic effects. In 1937 there were 298 military personnel in Alaska. In 1943 the figure was 152000. After a sharp decline in the immediate post-war years the 'cold war' saw numbers stabilize with an average of 50000 throughout the 1950s. In 1952 no less than 52 per cent of the total labour force in Alaska was on the military payroll. Since then numbers fell to 34000 in 1960 and the decline continued to a level of 24000 in 1979. The military wave of exploitation was fuelled by strategic considerations concerned with the defence of the U.S.A. as a whole. In the Second World War there was the threat posed by the Japanese, and actual fighting in the western Aleutians. In the cold war in the 1950s there was the need to defend this vulnerable salient of the U.S.A. against a possible manned bomber attack from the Soviet Union. Today, in the era of intercontinental missiles, the crucial role of Alaska has diminished to some extent, although a continued military presence seems assured.

The effect of the military diffusion wave was to create the main bones of modern Alaska's inland infrastructure. The population of Anchorage and Fairbanks grew, the former explosively. By 1960 Anchorage's population reached 65000, a figure 20 times higher than its 1939 total. The railway was rebuilt and extended southwards through the mountains to the ice-free ports of Whittier and Seward. Roads were improved and new ones like Glenn Highway and the Alaska Highway built to link the network with the rest of the U.S.A. Airfields were modernized and new ones constructed. D.E.W. line stations were built and air bases established. Throughout the period Alaska gained from an influx of people, wages and construction jobs. Also native peoples were affected by the construction activity and began to migrate to the main urban centres.

The discovery of oil on the Kenai Peninsula near Anchorage in 1957 heralded the start of the current oil boom. Production began in 1960 and within a decade the oilfield population doubled. However, a quantum leap occurred with the discovery of oil at Prudhoe Bay in 1969. Following delays in completing the pipeline to Valdez, the line was opened in 1977. Within 2 years the oil from Prudhoe Bay flowing along this pipeline was accounting for 91 per cent of Alaska's total oil production (Figure 12.8).

FIGURE 12.8   Aerial view of the northernmost pump station at Prudhoe Bay. The pipeline disappears southwards over the lake-studded tundra. Sohio photograph.

The main effect of the oil discoveries has been to develop the main cities of Anchorage and Fairbanks and to improve and extend existing transport links. The early years of production in the Kenai Peninsula saw Anchorage's population grow in the decade 1960—69 by 38 per cent to a total of 114000. Exploration and oilfield development on the North Slope involved a massive flow of goods and people through Anchorage and Fairbanks. In April 1969 Fairbanks airport handled more freight than any other air terminal in the world, while a winter road was hastily pushed northwards to Prudhoe Bay (Johansen, 1970). A further boom in activity affected the same axis during the construction of the pipeline when 21000 people were employed during the peak of construction. The net effect has once again been to accentuate the dominance of Anchorage. It is now the undisputed administrative centre of oil operations and, for example, houses the head offices of oil companies like Sohio—B.P. Alaska and Atlantic Richfield. The population grew by a staggering 45 per cent in the years 1970—78. The vast majority of this growth was associated with the support sector, involving trade and service industries, transportation, public utilities and finance as well as the expansion of local government including education, health and administration (Kresge *et al.*, 1977). Fairbanks too has grown as a result of the massive construction effort, and, to a lesser extent, maintenance activity. Its population grew by 30 per cent in the years 1970—78. The pipeline and accompanying road accentuate

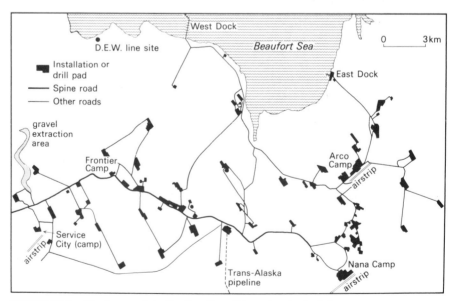

FIGURE 12.9   The layout of the Prudhoe Bay oil base showing buildings, production facilities, roads and jetties. After Sohio map.

and extend Alaska's communication network, although there is an extension of the pipeline east of Anchorage to take advantage of the ice-free port of Valdez. Prudhoe Bay is a permanent oil base on the North Slope with a population of *c.* 1500 where employees are flown in and out on varying schedules for intensive shifts (Figure 12.9). Native peoples have been increasingly attracted to the opportunities and diversions offered by Fairbanks and Anchorage (Dept. of the Interior, 1974). In spite of an overall population decline since the boom associated with pipeline construction, it is interesting to see that the highest growth areas in Alaska in 1970–78 were all associated with oil. Whereas Alaska's overall population grew by 37 per cent in this period, the Anchorage, Kenai, Valdez and North Slope areas grew by 47 per cent (Harrison, 1979). Areas off the axis of development grew at much slower rates. Increases of under 20 per cent were characteristic of much of the west coast, while Upper Yukon east of the pipeline actually declined.

The functioning of the spatial system

The purpose of this section is to follow the description of the main elements of Alaska's spatial system and its evolution with an analysis of how the system functions. As in earlier chapters, the network model of Taaffe, Morrill and Gould (1963) and the core/periphery model of Friedmann (1966) add important insights into the processes responsible for the present spatial structure.

NETWORKS

Figure 12.10 is an idealized diagram of the surface transport structure in Alaska. The west and northwestern coast resembles Stage I of Taaffe, Morrill and Gould's model in that there are a number of small towns which have limited land links and look to the sea instead. Most cargo arrives by coastal steamer or by ships plying directly from Seattle. The larger centres such as Bethel, Nome and Barrow play a distribution role in that they tranship goods onto small barges which supply smaller settlements in their respective local areas. At present none of the coastal towns has an inland link which could be expected to give it an advantage over the others. This comparison of western and north-western Alaska with Stage I of the network model must be treated with care. This is because the comparison ignores the effect of air transport which accounts for most passenger movements (Gray, 1980). Air transport links the main coastal settlements with Anchorage and/or Fairbanks.

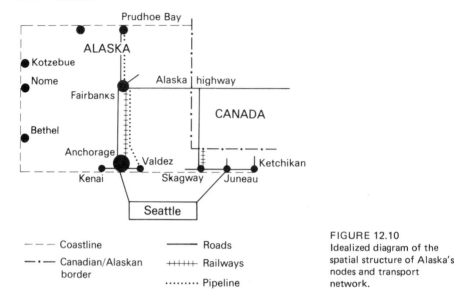

FIGURE 12.10
Idealized diagram of the spatial structure of Alaska's nodes and transport network.

Yet the pattern of air travel reinforces the separateness of the main local centres in that there are few flights along the coast. Instead the links are directly with the core and in this sense the analogy with Stage I of the network model is appropriate.

South-central Alaska demonstrates a classic Stage II development where the coastal port of Anchorage, with access to the main line of inland communication, has emerged as the prime Alaskan city. Anchorage became the southern coastal access point for the terminus for an inland line of communication to Fairbanks, a town exploiting an inland mineral deposit. Both towns began to grow, Anchorage's locational advantages on the coast leading to faster growth. This basic communication line developed further with subsequent waves of activity. The military wave strengthened it literally by rebuilding the railway, but also by extending it through the coastal mountains to Whittier and Seward. Also, the selection of Anchorage as the main military headquarters helped provide the diversification which further enhanced its dominance. Finally, the oil wave extended the axis to the north, dramatically benefiting both Anchorage and Fairbanks in terms of population growth and the diversification of activities. Now the Anchorage–Fairbanks link involves the railroad, the busiest long-distance road in Alaska and frequent air flights. One exception to the progressive growth of Anchorage occurred in the case of Valdez in the south, which was chosen as a safe ice-free port for the export of oil in the 1970s.

Implicit in Taaffe, Morrill and Gould's model is the idea that the coastal ports will be in competition with each other and that the victor will be the one which first becomes the terminus of a line of penetration into the interior. The Alaskan situation provides a variation on the theme in that existing coastal nodes such as Valdez were by-passed when the initial pioneering railway was built. In this case the site of Anchorage offered sufficiently powerful topographic advantages for a railway to outweigh other considerations. In other respects, however, the Alaskan situation closely follows the model in that the inland line of penetration has been extended and the interior node expanded to tap resources in the interior.

The Stage I and II transport network is typical of a colonial type of development when separate parts of the network are orientated to an external core rather than with each other. In Alaska this is illustrated not only by the lack of land links between different parts of Alaska, but also by air and sea links. For example, there are more flights from Anchorage to Seattle and from Juneau to Seattle than there are between Anchorage and Juneau. This is in spite of Anchorage being the biggest city and Juneau the capital. Also, while there are regular marine links between coastal towns within both southeastern and south-central Alaska, there are no links between the two areas. Rather, as with air traffic, each area is linked by sea with Seattle. The 'colonial' pattern is also illustrated by the pattern of commodity flows into and out of Alaska (Figure 12.11). In these cases western, south-central and south-eastern Alaska are operating independently with relation to the outside world. The importance of the links between the south-central Alaskan axis of development and the Lower 48 and the Far East are particularly noteworthy.

The next major development in the transport network is likely to lie outside Alaska's control. For a decade there has been a debate as to how the natural gas beneath the North Slope (and future oil discoveries) may best be transported to the main markets which lie in mid-western and northeastern U.S.A. Seen on a continental scale the proposals ranged between three main possibilities (Figure 12.12). The simplest, and the one employed for the oil, is to pipe the gas to Valdez, transport it by tanker to the markets of the west coast of the Lower 48, and then take the surplus by pipeline towards the east. An alternative was pioneered by the ice-breaking tanker *Manhattan*, which successfully traversed the Northwest Passage and demonstrated that petroleum products could be moved directly by sea from source to the area of highest demand. The third alternative, of which there were several variants (Coombs and Madden, 1978), was to combine with Canada and run a pipeline directly to the markets or to the existing pipeline

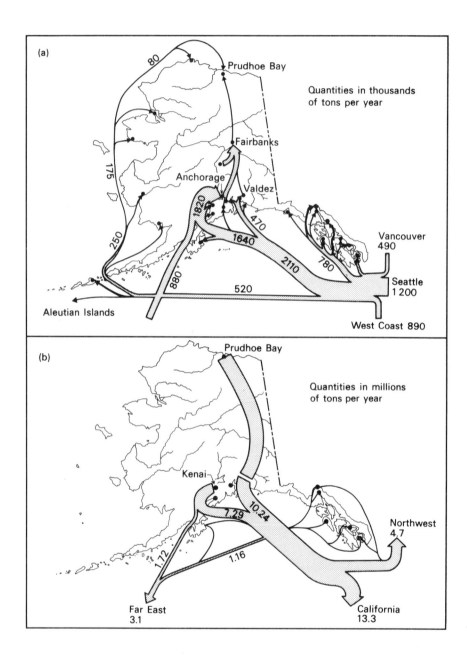

FIGURE 12.11 *(a)* Major inbound commodity flows and *(b)* major outbound commodity flows in 1977. The inbound flow comprises general cargo while the outbound flow is mainly oil and gas. The different parts of Alaska are linked with the core areas of western North America and the Far East rather than with each other. After Gray (1980).

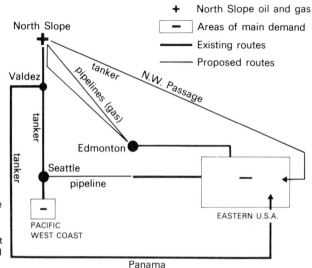

FIGURE 12.12
The various routes that have been discussed for shipping petroleum products from Alaska to the area of highest demand in the mid-west and northeastern U.S.A.

network in Alberta. It is interesting to see that the latter proposal has won through and the current plan is to run a gas pipeline from the North Slope to Fairbanks alongside the existing oil pipeline, and then beside the Alaska Highway to the south. This direct high-priority continental link will have the effect of by-passing south-central Alaska, although the construction phase is likely to cause further growth in Anchorage and Fairbanks.

CORE/PERIPHERY

Additional perspective on the operation of Alaska's spatial system comes from comparison with Friedmann's concepts of a Resource Frontier Region and a Downward Transitional Area. In a nutshell the central axis based on Anchorage and Fairbanks, which was a Resource Frontier Region as recently as the 1950s has become a core area with firm prospects of self-sustaining growth. The northern part of the axis, the extension to Prudhoe Bay, is now the Resource Frontier Region. The economic development of the central axis has caused familiar social problems and produced conditions in the native periphery of Alaska which, until recent and dramatic changes, was a classic Down-ward Transitional Area. It is worth examining the situation in more detail in order to gain a more balanced view of the processes underlying the present sharply changing situation within Alaska. To do so it is proposed to compare the main features of Friedmann's model with the situation in Alaska. As in earlier chapters the comparison is made point by point following Table 1.2.

Alaska compared with the concept of Resource Frontier Region
1. Dependent on the export of one economic resource, usually minerals.
This is true of Alaska today and particularly of the main Anchorage–Fairbanks axis: 78 per cent of Alaska's total product in 1979 depended on oil and gas (*Alaska Statistical Review*, 1980). Most of this was petroleum which was shipped by pipe and tanker to the Lower 48 as well as some gas which went to Japan. The overriding dependence on oil is illustrated by the small components related to other sectors for which Alaska is famous; for example, 18 per cent for the fishing and fish processing industry, 3 per cent for all other minerals and 0.5 per cent for timber and agriculture combined. When one appreciates that most of these other contributions come from the southwest and southeast coasts of Alaska, then it is clear that the reliance of the Anchorage/Fairbanks axis and northern Alaska on oil and gas is even more complete. This dependence on one product, particularly one so sensitive to political upheavals, means that the economy of Alaska is heavily dependent on the fortunes of world markets and politics.

2. Investment is commonly foreign. One of the points stressed by Friedmann was that the dominance of foreign investment in a peripheral area meant that the periphery could do little to control economic development. This has obviously been true earlier in Alaska's history when earlier booms of exploitation were controlled entirely by enterprises based outside the state. The same is true today. Much of the investment in the North Slope is foreign, and for example one of the partners in the first oil strike was British Petroleum. The remainder of the investment in oil and gas is 'foreign to Alaska' in that it is in the hands of international and American Companies with an eye on the national U.S. market. Since 1960 Japanese investment in Alaska has grown dramatically. In 1970 20 per cent of Japan's total overseas investment was in Alaska, and the impact is illustrated in the steady growth of trade with Japan since then. In 1979 Japan took 81 per cent of Alaska's foreign exports. Most Japanese investment so far has been in fisheries and timber products (although petroleum products are of growing importance).

   A new factor is that Alaska now reaps hundreds of millions of dollars in revenues from oil and gas sales. This provides the opportunity for Alaska to play an increasing role in investment and reduces the dependence on foreign investment.

3. Conflict between the economic goals of industry and the social goals of government. One could suggest that there ought to have been a conflict, but the economic orientation of federal and state governments in Alaska until the 1970s meant that the conflict was simply ignored. Nevertheless the familiar ingredients for conflict were always present. The waves of exploitation which struck Alaska for over 100 years were beyond the control of the Alaskan government. The military wave has waxed and waned in response to the perceptions of continental security held in the Pentagon. Even the last oil wave, which occurred after the achievement of statehood, was initially a response to the national U.S. market conditions (Reed, 1970). Rather than tackling the problems of inequality that accompanied these waves, many Alaskan policies went out of their way to encourage developments in the already booming areas and ignored the native peripheries. As recently as 1975 such an approach was being defended on the ground of economic efficiency (Fitzgerald, 1975).

As a result the problems of the native periphery multiplied. In the 1950s and 1960s numerous reports pointed out the problems of poverty associated with 'Native Alaska'. In 1954 Alaskan natives were found to be 'victims of sickness, crippling conditions and premature death to a degree exceeded in very few parts of the world.... Here are found 90% of Alaska's tuberculosis deaths; here more than 10 per cent of all infants die during the first year of life' (Alaska Health Survey Team, 1954; quoted in Rogers, 1969, p. 448). Again: 'Native Alaska is in fact one of the backwashes of our economy. Its members share with other poor the immobilizing effects of lack of education, lack of skills, racial discrimination, ill health and malnutrition' (Rogers, 1969, p. 450). Statistics bear out the validity of these judgements. The median native income in 1970 was one-third of the median wage of non-natives (Darnell, 1979); 35 per cent of native families were living in a state of poverty in 1969 (Kresge *et al.*, 1977); 90 per cent of all native housing was grossly substandard; and in 1973 no Inuit house in Barrow had piped water or sewerage (Morehouse and Leask, 1980). Most substandard houses were still occupied in the late 1970s (Kruse *et al.*, 1980). In 1970 life-expectancy was only three-fifths the national average (Gazaway and Thompson, 1975). Unemployment ranged from between 80 and 90 per cent in winter to perhaps 25 per cent in summer. In the 1970s the contrast between the comfortable suburbs of Fairbanks with their confident, dynamic residents, and the huts of Inuit villages containing demoralized inhabitants was difficult for a visitor to understand (compare Figures 12.3 and 12.4).

In terms of Friedmann's model, the Inuit periphery of the 1970s was a classic Downward Transitional Area. Each of Friedmann's criteria applied:

(1) The area was an old subsistence area of low productivity.
(2) The standard of living was low.
(3) The resource base was declining as the growing population exhausted staple hunting products and hunting restrictions were introduced (Kruse *et al.*, 1980).
(4) Fertility, mortality and out-migration rates were high (Milan, 1970). Younger people were moving to larger local towns as well as to Anchorage and Fairbanks (Figure 12.13). Also, the population was growing rapidly (Hippler, 1976).
(5) Social demoralization was rife and apparent to any visitor, especially in the larger Inuit settlements.
(6) Services were blatantly inadequate. Water, sewerage and electricity were often absent, not to mention libraries, high-schools and hospitals.
(7) All the above were aggravated by the ethnic difference between the prosperous non-native Alaskans and the poor native Alaskans.

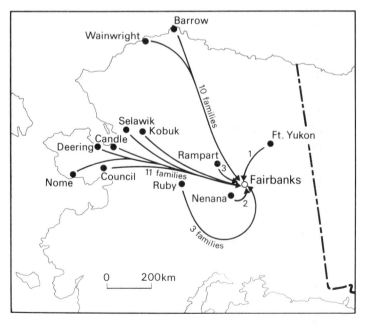

FIGURE 12.13   The migration of Inuit families to Fairbanks. Such migrations have accompanied the development of Anchorage and Fairbanks. After Milan and Pawson (1975).

The problems associated with Inuit Alaskans have sometimes been regarded as unrelated to the development of Alaska. However, it was the intrusive society which destroyed the basis of the native economy by hunting whales, introducing efficient firearms and a money economy (Harrison and Morehouse, 1970). Also by raising material expectations and providing a largely inappropriate educational curriculum, the Inuit were poorly prepared for the modern skills needed in industry and administration (Darnell, 1979). Thus in terms of Friedmann's model, the downward spiral of Alaska's periphery was related to the success of the core in attracting immigrants from outside. What is surprising is that such a major differential between core and periphery could develop without more obvious official concern for the well-being of all Alaskans. It seems to represent a classic example of untrammelled capitalist growth unconcerned with social justice. As will be seen later, the social problems of the periphery were not tackled until there was direct political protest (Harrison, 1973).

4. *Centred on a town/city with specialized but very limited functions, which may not achieve the critical size for self-sustaining growth.* There is no doubt that Anchorage, with its large population and varied governmental and commercial activities, is a metropolitan city. In the 1950s Fairbanks could have been regarded as a town of limited functions but again its present size and varied functions, including the University of Alaska, are impressive. One would suppose that both cities have achieved sufficient size and variety of functions to ensure their long-term future. Indeed the contrast between the Resource Frontier Region model and these two cities serves to emphasize just how successful they have been in transforming their status and how they have become extensions of the world's urban cores.

The northern end of the axis is a different matter. A few years ago it was fashionable in certain quarters to think of thriving cities of 10000—50000 inhabitants on the North Slope (see Rogers, 1971) and in his 1967 inaugural address former Governor Walter Hickel called for a railway to the arctic coast (Kresge *et al.*, 1977). The reality of today is the highly specialized oil camp of Prudhoe Bay with 1500 people (Figure 12.14). The base is linked to the south by air and by a gravel road which is restricted to the public. So far, there is no sign of any process which will cause the camp to expand into a self-sustaining settlement and, indeed, it is likely to close when the oil runs out. One must conclude that in the capitalist Alaska of today Prudhoe Bay is too remote and the threshold population of an oil camp too small to justify investment in long-term sustained growth. As will be seen this forms an interesting contrast with the Soviet Arctic where plans for long-term sustained growth of arctic mining towns are common.

FIGURE 12.14   Sohio's modern base at Prudhoe Bay houses 474 workers on a week-on, week-off shift. The inside of the base is superbly equipped with swimming pool, indoor garden, etc. Sohio photograph.

5. Transport and labour costs are high due to remoteness and high level of technology. High costs are characteristic of Alaska. The impact is felt immediately by any visitor from the Lower 48 if they buy a bottle of beer or stay in a hotel. Official statistics show that in 1970 costs in Anchorage were 50 per cent higher than in the rest of the U.S.A. The differential had narrowed by 1979 when costs in Anchorage were only 36 per cent higher, but this is still a significant handicap. The implications for the diversification of the economy in Alaska are profound. As Kresge *et al.* (1977) noted: 'It has been cheaper to produce goods in larger, more efficient plants in the Lower 48 and then ship them to the state, rather than produce them in small, high-cost plants within Alaska', (pp. 65–6). Thus only recently a new brewery in Anchorage was set up but failed. In the more remote areas where costs increase dramatically, then the problem is even more acute.

6. Special social structure: transient, male, single. This has long been true of the non-native immigrant population. Among non-natives in 1900 there were nine men for every woman. Similar or worse figures apply to extreme situations such as Prudhoe Bay today and in areas swamped by construction workers. On an Alaskan scale, however, the differential is much less and in 1970 there were only 1.2 males for every female. Indeed, the population age structure for the state is not too unlike that of the United States as a whole. Much of the non-native population is transient. The 23 000 military personnel frequently spend only a few years in Alaska before being transferred elsewhere. Oil workers and construction crews are particularly mobile and indeed are moved around the world as necessary. In 1970 nearly half (43 per cent) of all non-natives in Alaska had moved to the state within the previous 5 years. There are signs now that the above pattern is changing. Surveys suggest that an increasing number of people are moving into permanent homes and jobs (Baring-Gould, personal communication, 1981).

Comparison of south-central and arctic Alaska with Friedmann's model suggests that the cities of Anchorage and Fairbanks have successfully negotiated the transition from a Resource Frontier Region to a state of development. They are now core regions. This conclusion is all the more striking when one recalls that Anchorage did not exist in 1912. In common with this successful transition many other characteristics of Resource Frontier Regions, such as population instability and the high level of foreign investment, are being modified. Other important characteristics such as the dependence on one resource still apply, and represent a potential problem for the future. In retrospect one can see that the development of the Anchorage—Fairbanks axis has closely followed classic lines as listed by Friedmann (see Table 1.2). Emphasis has been on the creation of an urban spatial system and as quickly as possible. The economic base within the cities has become diversified and has included such specific acts as the creation of a university campus in each centre. The high cost of living has been reduced. The need for a regional development authority to promote long-term development was met in part by the achievement of statehood in 1959; one reason for the pressure for statehood was the desire by Alaskans to have more control of economic development (Kresge *et al.*, 1977).

The main problem associated with this development has been the plight of the native periphery. In Alaska of the 1970s the priorities were for economic development and not socio-economic equality.

Towards the self-dependence of the periphery

Had this chapter been written in 1970 it would have ended on the above note. However, the 1970s have seen a change so dramatic that in historic perspective a new era in Alaska's development may be seen to have commenced. The Alaska Native Land Claims Settlement Act of 1971 was in effect an act of statehood for native Alaskans (Harrison, 1972). The background is well described by Rogers (1969) who mentioned how in 1966 a united front of eight formerly separate native organizations put forward a claim by right of aboriginal use and occupancy to a vast area of Alaska. This eventually stopped oil development in its tracks and had much to do with the 5-year delay in building the Prudhoe Bay–Valdez pipeline. The 1971 Act gave the native groups rights to land and money as well as a measure of local control. In return for withdrawing aboriginal claims, the native peoples will eventually have received (over 11 years) title to 176 000 km² of land (and minerals), grants totalling \$462 million from Federal Funds and a further \$500 million from 2 per cent of the annual royalties received by Alaska from minerals. Also, the Act organized native Alaska into 12 regional corporations with the purpose of promoting their economic and social development (Figure 12.15).

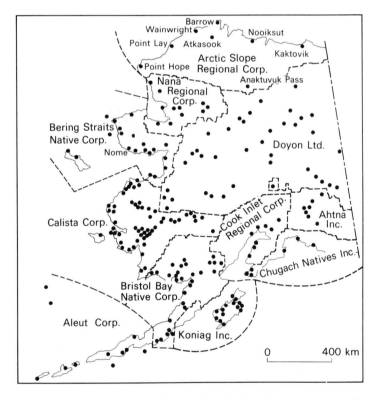

FIGURE 12.15　Distribution of native villages and the Regional Corporations established by the 1971 Alaska Native Claims Settlement.

The full impact of such an act is far-reaching. The Arctic Slope Regional Corporation will eventually receive 1.6 million hectares of land and $52 million. But more than this the native political movement that led to the 1971 Act also led to the setting up of a North Slope Borough, a unit of local or regional government with independent powers of taxation and regulation. Extracting property taxes from the Prudhoe Bay oil companies the Borough raised no less than $150 million extra in 1972–79. In 1980 alone the Borough planned to raise $74 million, 70 per cent of which was to come from property taxes and the remainder from other state and federal sources. This amounts to $20000 per resident!

It is difficult to over-emphasize the significance of these developments for the North Slope Inuit. Almost overnight they have become powerful members of a profit-making business corporation typical of western society. They have surmounted the crucial obstacle of achieving a return flow of capital from the core to the periphery – one of the key problems identified by Friedmann and Weaver (1979). They are now free to invest the money in the North Slope area according to local wishes. The first step by the Borough has been to launch a $500 million capital investments programme mainly for schools, roads in the settlements, water and sewerage. Not surprisingly the Borough has been able to employ most adults on the North Slope, most of the men in construction (Morehouse and Leask, 1980). The problem is to reconcile investment with long-term goals. But the basis of this future is difficult to foresee. As the Mayor of the Borough said: 'I am very concerned about the long term economic impact of oil and gas development upon our Arctic community. We are riding the crest of a high economic wave, and I fear about where it will deposit us, and how hard we will land' (Hopson, 1976, quoted by Morehouse and Leask, 1980).

The lack of skills in jobs associated with modern industrial society, the lack of resources and the extremely high costs associated with life on the North Slope make the prospects of self-sustaining economic growth bleak. Perhaps the beginnings of an alternative long-term scenario can be inferred from a recent survey of the North Slope settlements (Kruse *et al.*, 1980). In a nutshell this survey implied that traditional village activities were thriving. In spite of full employment (mainly in construction), 70 per cent of those interviewed participated in hunting, while 80 per cent of the households depended partly on hunting products for food. Significantly the younger generation was as interested in hunting as older generations. Perhaps there is scope for a future where oil revenues can be used first to improve and then to sustain a village life focused on hunting. If this proves to be the

case, then the whole thrust of Alaskan development which has previously been based on extending an urban spatial system into the
periphery will have been reversed. Instead of the growth of larger
centres there would be a resurgence of small-village life which is so
well suited to hunting. If this interpretation of current trends is correct,
then Inuit Alaska will be developing on similar lines to Inuit Arctic
Canada, though via a separate route.

Lest the above paragraphs be taken to imply that the problems of
the periphery are over, it is important to stress that the North Slope
is in the unique position of taxing a large producing oilfield. Other
Inuit peripheries are not so fortunate and, according to Kresge *et al.*
(1977) are unlikely to become so in the near future. In other parts of
peripheral Alaska, the revenues accruing to the native corporations
are more modest and the pace of change is likely to be slower.

Conclusions

Alaska has experienced a succession of externally generated diffusion
waves of exploitation similar in kind and duration to those experienced
in other polar lands. The present Alaskan boom depends on the production of petroleum. Prospects for the continuation of petroleum
exploitation are good. Existing North Slope reserves are expected to
last 2–3 decades and there are numerous other potential oilfields.
Furthermore, new mineral waves are likely as U.S., Japanese and
European interests are attracted to known minerals in a relatively
accessible land.

The more recent waves have had the effect of building an urban
spatial system centred on Anchorage as the coastal port and Fairbanks
as the interior node, a pattern which closely conforms to a colonial
model of spatial evolution. It is interesting to note that this process of
development has proceeded across the grain of some of the world's
most formidable mountain barriers as well as a very sensitive earthquake zone. This seems surprising when one realizes that an alternative
navigable waterway exists from the west coast via the Yukon River to
the main interior node of Fairbanks. It is tempting to conclude that
the natural environment has played a relatively minor part in influencing spatial development and that, rather, the pattern is related to
contrasts in distance from the core area of Seattle, with the south
coast being more accessible than the west coast. However, although
relative accessibility is an important factor, the natural environment
has also influenced the spatial pattern significantly. Thus seasonal sea
ice off the Yukon mouth and along the river prevented year-round

access from the west and favoured access from the south coast. On a smaller scale in the 1970s the deep ice-free port of Valdez offered better facilities for an oil terminal than the shallower waters of Anchorage and became the terminus for the trans-Alaska oil pipeline. Conversely early in this century the choice of Anchorage as a terminus for the initial Alaska railroad was influenced by its relatively favourable natural advantages on land compared, for example, to such sites as Valdez. From this one can conclude that, although influenced by the natural environment at a variety of scales, the spatial system in Alaska has evolved in a broadly similar fashion to that in other colonial areas.

An important principle to emerge in Alaska is the way the existence of a spatial structure has helped to channel subsequent developments. Out of all the potential oilfields in Alaska which could have been explored (Figure 12.3), it is interesting that the first modern find was within sight of the largest node, Anchorage. Further, the second commercial find at Prudhoe Bay was the closest North Slope location to the inland spur of Fairbanks. The pipelines are also influenced by access routes. The oil pipe followed existing routes where possible, while the proposed gas pipeline will run alongside the existing Alaska Highway rather than directly via the Mackenzie Valley as was proposed (Coombs and Madden, 1978). Again, the only coal mine in Alaska, at Healy, is located on the Anchorage–Fairbanks railway. Although it is one of Alaska's smallest fields, its location is crucial to its development. Presumably in future one can expect minerals near the existing infrastructure (or along the coast) to be exploited first.

The economic waves have attracted immigrants into Alaska on a large scale, especially since the Second World War. This has had a major influence on the dynamism and population structure of Alaska and is in stark contrast to both Greenland and Arctic Canada. One reason for this immigration is the importation of the American frontier ethic with its vision of opportunity for those who take a chance. The importance of this dream in luring people to Alaska is apparent when one talks to many non-native Alaskans. Another factor is the relatively favourable natural environment. Most immigrants have moved to the cool temperate or sub-arctic regions of Alaska. In such areas the environment is positively welcoming if compared with the climates of some American mid-west towns. However, this view of widespread immigration does not apply to the Arctic proper. There are notably few immigrant Alaskans on the Arctic Slope other than those working shifts on the oil installations. So in this latter region the contrast with Arctic Canada and Greenland is not so apparent.

Economic development in Alaska has taken place in an unfettered American capitalist environment, where economic exploitation has been seen almost as a duty. This dominance of economic goals and eclipse of social goals allowed development to create a crude imbalance whereby the immigrant half of the state prospered at the expense of peripheral native Alaska. In the 1970s Alaska offered a glimpse of the problems that accompany development of polar regions for economic reasons alone. The most radical lesson to come from Alaska is the dramatic turn-around in native Inuit fortunes in the late 1970s. From a position of weakness, Alaskan Inuits have leapfrogged to a position of strength. Cashing-in on economic development they are reaping the benefit in oil property taxes which they are able to spend locally to achieve their own social and economic goals. The surprise is that such a radical change in native fortunes occurred so rapidly. It reflects an unusually favourable set of circumstances. On the one hand the extreme poverty of the periphery gave the political protest movement, when it emerged, depth and conviction. On the other hand the 1971 Act was advantageous to *all* major interests in Alaska. The Federal government wanted to see the oil flowing for strategic reasons, the state itself wanted the tremendous royalties from the oil while the native groups wanted money and land. In other words the agreement was reached on the crest of a wave of economic exploitation with discussion focused on the issue of how to share out the future bonanza. Perhaps it will prove to be the watershed in the evolution of the spatial system in peripheral Alaska, in that it may mark the replacement of an urban strategy of development by a more locally controlled village strategy.

Further reading

Gray, J. 1980: Alaska's unique transportation system. *Alaska Review of Social and Economic Conditions*, 17 (2), 2–28.

Harrison, G. S. 1972: The Alaska Native Claims Settlement Act, 1971. *Arctic*, 25 (3), 232–3.

Harrison, G. S. and Morehouse, T. A. 1970: Rural Alaska's development problems. *Polar Record*, 15 (96), 291–9.

Kresge, D. T., Morehouse, T. A. and Rogers, G. W. 1977: *Issues in Alaska development.* Institute of Social and Economic Research, University of Alaska, University of Washington Press, Seattle.

Kruse, J., Kleinfeld, J. and Travis, R. 1980: *Energy development and the North Slope Inupiat.* Man in the Arctic Program, University of Alaska.

Morehouse, T. A. and Leask, L. 1980: Alaska's North Slope Borough: oil, money and eskimo self-government. *Polar Record*, 20 (124), 19–29.

CHAPTER THIRTEEN

The Soviet Arctic

Introduction

The Soviet Arctic illustrates a completely different philosophy towards development. Its study affords the possibility of contrasting a centrally planned, communist approach to the Arctic with the decentralized, capitalist approach characteristic of the American Arctic. This chapter first describes the physical constraints and resources in the Soviet Arctic and the present spatial system. This is followed by discussion of the evolution and functioning of the system which reveals both contrasts and similarities with other arctic areas; whereas the level of activity is much higher, many of the problems encountered are familiar. The reasons for any similarities and contrasts are discussed in the final part of the chapter.

A problem immediately confronting anyone studying the Soviet Arctic is that of definition. Physical and human criteria are very divergent (Figure 13.1a). The tundra, which coincides with the zone of reindeer herding, is a thin strip of land fringing the north coast and broadens only in the far east. The southern limit of continuous permafrost is quite different and in the east it extends close to the Chinese border while in the west it excludes areas well north of the Arctic Circle. Human geographical definitions are different again (Armstrong, 1974). In the Soviet Union the term 'Far North' is used to describe a somewhat bigger area than either of the above physical definitions and comprises 11 million km². Whereas this human definition often coincides with administrative boundaries, it does not always do so and, indeed, it cuts across the major economic regions of western Siberia, eastern Siberia and the Far East (Figure 13.1b). For the purpose of this chapter the Arctic will be accepted as the area of tundra and this will form the main focus of attention. However, the wider area of the 'Far North' will be employed for some statistical purposes while, for the analysis of the function of the Arctic regional system, it will be necessary to extend even further south.

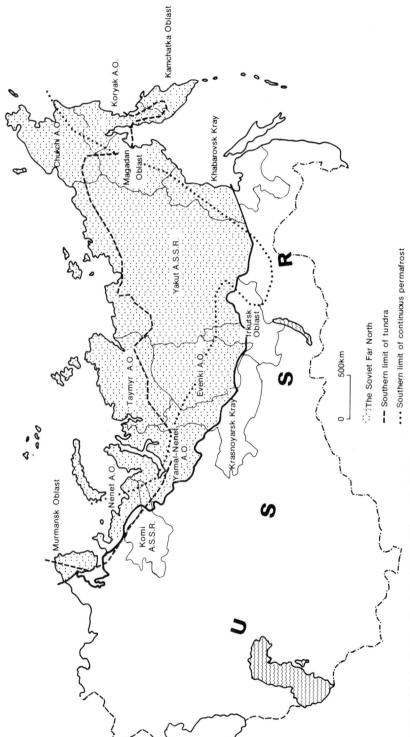

FIGURE 13.1(a)   The Far North in the U.S.S.R. and its component administrative units contrasted with some natural boundaries for A.O. stands for Autonomous Okrug and A.S.S.R. for Autonomous Soviet Socialist Republic.

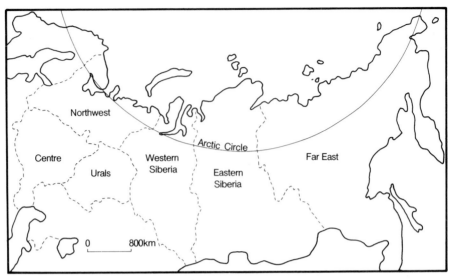

FIGURE 13.1(b)   Major economic regions involving the Soviet Arctic.

Physical constraints and resources

The Soviet Arctic is huge and extends in an east–west direction for 7000 km. This is almost halfway round the world in terms of longitude and as Hooson (1966) wryly remarked, it forms part of a vast realm on which the sun scarcely sets. As such it presents a number of resources for exploitation as well as constraints on human occupation.

The main natural resources apart from space are minerals, tundra and rivers. The minerals relate to the broad structural scenario illustrated in Figure 2.4. Although it is impossible to forecast the resources accurately, one can point to three regional associations, namely: (a) the shield minerals of the Kola Peninsula and of the uplifted Angara shield in the Noril'sk area east of the River Yenisey; (b) the oil, gas and coal of the flat-lying sediments of the plain of western Siberia and the basins and coastal plain of northeast Siberia; and (c) tin and gold associated with the fold mountains of the Far East (Figure 13.2). Perspectives on these resources may be gained by comparison with the American Arctic. All three tectonic types occur in the American Arctic and in this sense the areas are comparable; shield minerals occur in Arctic Canada and minerals associated with folded mountains in Alaska, while oil and gas occurs around the Laurentian shield especially along

FIGURE 13.2   (Opposite) The Soviet North — major minerals, settlements and transport routes.

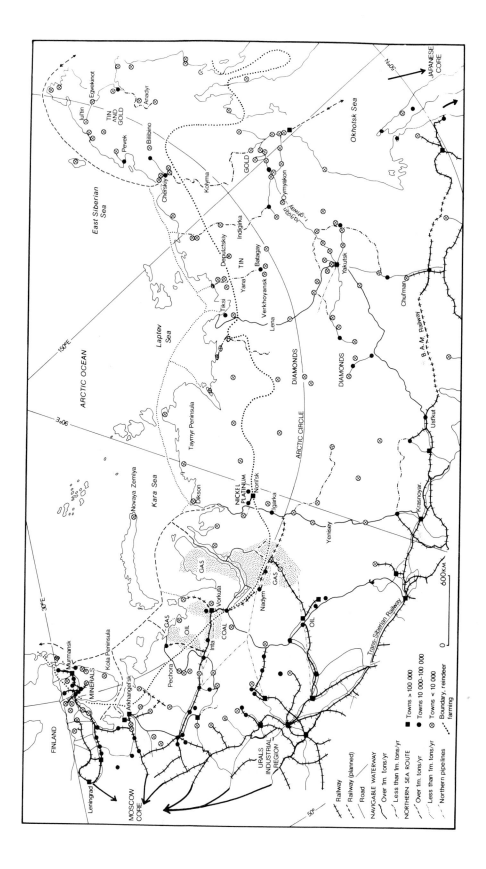

FINLAND

Leningrad

MOSCOW
CORE

50°

URALS
INDUSTRIAL
REGION

Trans-Siberian Railway

Krasnoyar'

Yenisey

Igarka

Nadym

OIL

GAS

GAS

COAL

Inta

Vorkuta

Pechora

OIL

GAS

Arkhangel'sk

Murmansk

Kola Peninsula

MINERALS

30°E

Novaya Zemlya

Kara Sea

Dikson

NICKEL
PLATINUM
Noril'sk

Taymyr Peninsula

90°E

ARCTIC OCEAN

Laptev Sea

Tiksi

Yana' TIN

Verkhoyansk

Lena

Batagay

Depudziskiy

Indigirka

East Siberian Sea

Cherskiy

Kolyma

GOLD

150°E

ARCTIC CIRCLE

DIAMONDS

DIAMONDS

Yakutsk

Chul'man

B.A.M. Railway

Ust'kut

Bilibino

Pevek

Iul'tin

Egvekinot

Anadyr

TIN
AND
GOLD

Oymyakon

Aldan (River)

Okhotsk Sea

50°N

JAPANESE
CORE

600km

0   600km

Railway

Railway (planned)

Road

NAVIGABLE WATERWAY

Over 1m. tons/yr

Less than 1m. tons/yr

NORTHERN SEA ROUTE

Over 1m. tons/yr

Less than 1m. tons/yr

Northern pipelines

■ Towns > 100 000

● Towns 10 000–100 000

⊗ Towns < 10 000

Boundary, reindeer
farming

the northern coast. However, the extent of the likely oil- and gas-bearing rocks in the Soviet Arctic is greater than in the American Arctic and already arctic gas discoveries account for 80 per cent of the U.S.S.R.'s proven total reserves. Vast additional resources are thought to lie beneath the offshore continental shelf.

The barren tundra is not normally perceived as a resource because conditions are too severe to allow cultivation. However, the tundra is exploited by migrating animals such as the reindeer and by hunting. Also the large arctic rivers are important for fishing. The shape of the tundra zone in relation to the rest of the Soviet Union is advantageous in that it forms a relatively thin strip of land with relatively easy access from the southern forested zone. This is in major contrast to much of Arctic America where north—south distances within the tundra zone are greater and broken by straits.

The rivers of the U.S.S.R. are sometimes termed Siberia's tragedy in that they drain water away from the southern arid lands rather than towards them. But this northward flow is highly advantageous to the Arctic in that it provides a grid of seasonally navigable rivers linking the Arctic with more temperate zones to the south. Also tributaries provide an approximately east—west network of links. Although problems arise in the spring when the middle reaches thaw while the northern channels are still choked with ice, the larger rivers can be navigated for periods of around 170 days in the south and 110—140 days in the north and east. Most rivers can take barges of around 2 000 tons capacity while the Lower Yenisey is deep enough to accommodate ocean-going vessels. In comparison Arctic America can boast only one north—south river, the Mackenzie, although admittedly the straits of the Canadian archipelago offer comparable waterborne access to large areas.

The natural constraints to life in the Soviet Arctic are familiar. The cold temperatures experienced by such towns as Verkhoyansk and Oymyakon are legendary and this creates real problems of air pollution, mobility and extra costs of living (Chapter 3). Nonetheless absolute temperatures are misleading in that they imply a marked east—west contrast in the Soviet Arctic. If windchill values are used, then the higher wind speeds in the Kola Peninsula make the winter climate much more severe than would be expected from their temperatures alone, and the east—west contrast is less marked. Also windchill values over the Soviet Arctic as a whole are lower than for much of Arctic Canada. In addition the relatively long Siberian summer with high temperatures is a major compensation which allows crops to be grown in sheltered basins as far north as the tree line. Also it allows periodic sunbathing

(Figure 13.3). This is a far cry from the brief summer of the eastern Canadian Arctic.

FIGURE 13.3   Summer temperatures in Noril'sk can sometimes reach 40°C. In the background is the copper smelter built in the 1940s. Copyright Novosti Press Agency.

Permafrost is all-pervasive within the tundra zone but there is a strong contrast between the area of discontinuous permafrost west of Novaya Zemlya and the continuous permafrost to the east. The permafrost of the U.S.S.R. presents more of a problem than in the American Arctic, mainly because it incorporates more ground ice, especially in the extensive formerly unglaciated coastal areas of northeastern Siberia.

Year-round sea access to the northern arctic coast is impeded by pack ice, except in the far west. Periods of unimpeded access range from most of the year in the west to 4½ months in the Kara Sea and 3 months in the East Siberian Sea. Although the ice does not always clear in the vicinity of the Taymyr Peninsula, the ice is less persistent than in the American Arctic archipelago and, moreover, the ice that does build up is younger. This means it is thinner, less disturbed and less tough than in the Beaufort Sea.

Topography presents remarkably uneven constraints to human activity in that there is a fundamental contrast between the uniformity of the western arctic plains, interrupted only by the north—south Ural

Range and the ruggedness of the area east of the Yenisey. Whereas the east presents scenery akin to that of Alaska, the west provides few topographical barriers to surface transport and is a plain unequalled in Arctic America.

It is useful to summarize the discussion of the natural resources and constraints in the Soviet Arctic by comparison with the American Arctic. Bearing in mind the many imponderables, Table 13.1 tentatively suggests that in many significant respects the natural environment of the Soviet Arctic offers more resources and is less of a constraint to human affairs than that of the American Arctic (Armstrong, 1963/64). This is an essential stepping stone from which to examine the human activity in the area.

TABLE 13.1   *Contrasts in the relative advantages of the North American Arctic and Soviet Arctic in terms of natural resources and constraints upon human activity. On balance the Soviet Arctic has many advantages*

	Arctic America	Soviet Arctic
Mineral fuels	−	+
Tundra access	−	+
Rivers	−	+
Windchill	−	+
Permafrost	+	−
Coastal pack ice	−	+
Topography	−	+

The human spatial pattern

The population living in the Soviet Arctic is much larger than that in other Arctic areas. There are several cities with populations of over 100000, and many towns with tens of thousands of inhabitants. The level of development is such that it is useful to distinguish four different components of the Arctic spatial system; namely

(1) the Kola Peninsula;
(2) the Vorkuta--Lower Ob' region;
(3) the Noril'sk complex; and
(4) the more scattered developments of northeastern Siberia.

The population, nodes, networks and flows of each are described below. Details of the whole area are shown in Figure 13.2.

THE KOLA PENINSULA

Figure 13.4a shows the main features of this shield region. Murmansk with 381 000 people is the largest centre and sprawls for 16 km along

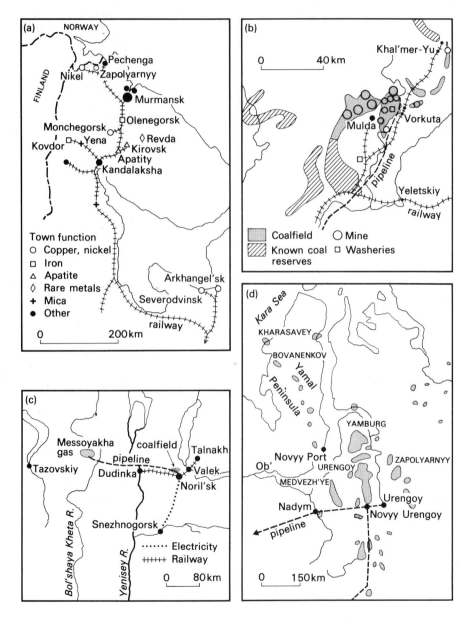

FIGURE 13.4 *(a)* The Kola Peninsula region. *(b)* The Vorkuta coalfield complex. *(c)* The Noril'sk complex. *(d)* The main gas fields in the Lower Ob'—Yamal Peninsula area.

FIGURE 13.5   A view of Murmansk. Copyright Novosti Press Agency.

the side of an ice free inlet (Figure 13.5).[1] As a fishing port it accounts
for 13 per cent of the Soviet fish catch (Shabad, 1978a). It is heavily
involved in ship repairing and 30 per cent of the workforce is employed
in metal working (Selyakov, 1979). It is a major port both for exports
outside the U.S.S.R. and as the western terminus of the Northern Sea
Route. Also in the Murmansk area are a major naval base and a centre
for the Soviet Delta-class submarine fleet (Østreng, 1977). The city is
connected to the south by a railway completed in 1916 and a major
road completed only in 1968. Strung out along the railway or on small
feeder lines is a belt of towns each with a population of the order of
20 000–45 000 persons. Most of these towns were originally founded in
the 1930s. Typically these are single-industry towns, lying in shield
terrain and based on mines and ore concentrators. For example,
Zapolyarnyy mines nickel and copper, concentrating this before further
shipment, while Kovdor and Olenegorsk mine iron and the Kirovsk–
Apatity area apatite. The natural and architectural setting of these
towns is sometimes bleak and it is no surprise to find that Makhrovskaya
et al. (1977) noted that over half the population go south for their
annual holidays. Some towns are gaining additional functions and
prestige buildings. Apatity, for example, is the centre of the Kola
branch of the Academy of Sciences, while Monchegorsk is a centre of a
smelting industry. Overall the density of population in Murmansk
Oblast as a whole is the greatest in the Arctic (6 per km^2) and is 45 per
cent of the average for the Soviet Union as a whole (Figure 13.6). 95

FIGURE 13.6   Population density in the Far North, 1979. Statistics are shown only for areas
wholly lying within the Far North.

---

[1]   Figures for 1979 (Bond and Lydolph, 1979).

per cent of the population consists of immigrants from the south and their descendants.

The Kola Peninsula towns are linked to the industrial core of the U.S.S.R. by rail. Makhrovskaya *et al.* (1977) suggested that as much as 90 per cent of the products of the region are sent south. This includes nickel, whose quantities are large by world standards, apatite, which is the basic raw material for 80 per cent of total Soviet phosphate fertilizer production, copper and iron amounting to 15 and 5 per cent of total Soviet production respectively (Shabad, 1977a, 1978b, 1979a).

THE VORKUTA–LOWER OB' REGION

There are two main components in the area, one older and based on coal at Vorkuta, and the other based on current developments in oil and gas.

Vorkuta is a coal town which, with its satellites, numbers over 200 000 inhabitants (Figure 13.4b). It is linked to the south by a railway. In 1975 the Vorkuta coalmines, together with those further down the railway at Inta, produced 24 million tons (5 per cent of the Soviet total) and much of this was sent 1750 km to the Cherepovets blast furnaces north of Moscow (Shabad, 1978b). Coal production is expanding slowly.

The discovery of natural gas in the 1960s in the arctic lowlands of the Lower Ob' and east of the lower Pechora River has stimulated much construction activity. Figure 13.4d shows the location of the main finds in the Lower Ob'–Yamal Peninsula area. Centres like Novyy Urengoy have burgeoning populations, half of whom are involved in construction and half in the gas industry. Pipelines have been built to the European U.S.S.R. One system runs southwest from the giant Urengoy and Medvezh'ye fields 3000 km to Moscow. Another runs southwards through the western Siberian oilfields which are being developed from the south. A railway has been built from the Trans-Siberian Railway north to Urengoy. Exploration and drilling in the Yamal Peninsula are being carried out from the sea. Interestingly the approach was made in winter using ice-breakers, and the supplies loaded onto fast ice near the shore (Shabad, 1977b). Exploitation has been remarkably rapid. In 1970 gas from the Arctic accounted for 9 per cent of the Soviet total and in 1980 it was 40 per cent (Shabad, 1981).

THE NORIL'SK COMPLEX

Noril'sk and its surrounding small towns have a population of 180 000 (Figure 13.4c). The complex mines and processes nickel, copper, cobalt and platinum. The main town includes several multi-storey prestige buildings and is the home of educational and government institutions as well as of other industries (Figure 13.7). Perhaps the

FIGURE 13.7   The main street in Noril'sk. Copyright Novosti Press Agency.

most remarkable feature is the way this city thrives on the very margin of the open tundra in a location 1 500 km from other comparable industrial centres. The ore concentrates are carried by rail to Dudinka, a port on the river Yenisey, from which they are shipped to the industrial cores of the U.S.S.R. Whereas most trade from Noril'sk has traditionally utilized the Yenisey and the link with the Trans-Siberian Railway at Krasnoyarsk, an interesting new development has accompanied the recent growth of Noril'sk since 1970. Some ore concentrates are being sent by ship via Murmansk to be smelted at Monchegorsk. This flow amounted to 1 million tons in 1978 and in the same year 10 new ore carriers were ordered for this route, implying its future expansion (Shabad, 1978c). The shipments are achieved with massive nuclear and conventional ice-breaker support which has almost succeeded in extending the shipping season to 12 months (Yazykova, 1977). In spite of these developments, nickel smelting is also being expanded at Noril'sk. The power needs of Noril'sk are met by a 200-km gas pipeline from the west and a hydroelectric line from the south which supplement coal mined near the city.

NORTHEASTERN SIBERIA

There is no single centre in northeastern Siberia nearly as large as the centres already described. There are clusters of towns numbering 2000–20000 people scattered along the coast or along major rivers. Commonly they comprise a nucleus of two-storey concrete buildings with perhaps a spread of wooden houses surrounding them. Surface transport links are sparse and restricted to rivers or winter roads. The rivers are smaller than those in western Siberia and do not have the advantage of a link with a railway in the south (Figure 13.2). Instead, two of them, the Indigirka and Kolyma, link with the Magadan Highway by means of spur roads. The Magadan Highway is partly unsurfaced and interrupted by unbridged rivers. Winter roads extend the road network and, for example, there is a seasonal link between Deputatskiy and the Magadan Highway. Other roads push inland to towns from coastal settlements, for example to Iul'tin from Egvekinot. Air transport is important in such a remote region and most towns are linked to Yakutsk or Magadan by scheduled flights.

The *raison d'être* of these small towns is mineral exploitation. Deputatskiy and other towns on the Yana River mine tin, as also does Iul'tin. Gold mining is the justification for other towns such as Bilibino and Pevek. One of the Soviet Union's main gold mining complexes is in the upper Kolyma valley (Figure 13.8). Cherskiy on the mouth of the Kolyma River operates as a transhipment point (Sallnow, 1981). It has grown from a settlement of 10 wooden houses in 1961 to a town with a population of over 10000 today as mining operations have expanded. Tin is sent to the industrial centres of the U.S.S.R. westwards via the Northern Sea Route or southwards to the Trans-Siberian Railway. Apparently the tin produced in the Arctic accounts for half of the total U.S.S.R. production. The gold from northeastern Siberia also accounts for about half the U.S.S.R.'s production, which is itself approximately one-seventh of the total world production.

This description of northeast Siberian mining activities has ignored the complementary reindeer-herding industry. Altogether there are some 2½ million reindeer reared for meat and hides and tended by indigenous peoples (see Figure 8.2). The reindeer are raised on state

FIGURE 13.8   Gold dredge in northeastern Siberia. Copyright Novosti Press Agency.

farms which are also responsible for fur. Mowat (1970) described how in the late 1960s, Nizhne–Kolymsk State Farm was 87000 km² in extent and supported 36000 deer. It also had departments for fishing, fur-raising and trapping. It supported 2840 people, 90 per cent of whom were native and 10 per cent Russian. The headquarters was in Cherskiy and included a staff of 37, mostly holding university degrees and mostly of native origin. Most other employees lived in three small settlements, but moved from these when hunting or tending the wandering herds of reindeer. Sometimes the moves were made by the farm's aircraft. The different native groups tended to specialize in different functions, with the Evenki responsible for fur trapping and the Chukchi for the herding (Figure 13.9).

Reindeer-herding and trapping is most important in eastern Siberia but exists in all of the Soviet Arctic. Armstrong *et al.* (1978) considered that the total amount of reindeer meat produced in 1971 (over 40000 tons) would in theory be sufficient for 5 per cent of the needs of the total population of the U.S.S.R.

The evolution of the spatial system

Three main stages in the evolution of the Soviet Arctic can be recognized. Firstly there is the stage of indigenous utilization; secondly a series of commercially instigated waves of exploitation; and thirdly, since 1917, the wave of Soviet development.

FIGURE 13.9   Helicopter visiting outlying camp in Evenki A.O. Copyright Novosti Press
Agency.

The population of the Eurasian Arctic under the first indigenous
occupation is difficult to estimate. Suffice to say that in 1959 there
were about 270000 indigenous peoples in an area roughly approximate
to the Soviet Far North, with *c.* 30 000 in the tundra and northern
fringe. This total was similar to that in 1926, a time when the indigenous peoples still practised a traditional way of life. Perhaps it is
reasonable to use this figure of 30000 as a rough estimate of numbers
living in the tundra before the Russian conquests. This population
consisted mainly of nomadic reindeer herders but also included permanent coastal settlements relying on marine resources especially in the
richer Bering Strait and Barents Sea areas.

The waves of commercial exploitation are associated with the
Russian colonization of the north (Armstrong, 1965). The Arctic west
of the Urals was exploited by fisherman, hunters and trappers from

about the mid-eleventh century and these were the people whose competitive northern products put the Norse settlements of Greenland out of business. But the arctic area east of the Urals was not touched until the sixteenth century. Then in a remarkable burst of activity fur trappers expanded from the Urals to the Sea of Okhotsk in the years 1580–1640 (Figure 8.10). They were seeking sable, ermine and silver fox. Experiencing a slight hold-up in the Bering Sea area as the riches there were exploited, the wave swept through Alaska and even into California in the late eighteenth century. The main effect of this wave of commercial exploitation was to set up a network of trading stations, usually along the river transport routes of the time. Thus the town of Mangazeya was built on the River Taz between the Ob' and Yenisey in 1601. It comprised a fort, cathedral, court and even a smelter using ore from Noril'sk. The furs were obtained in the form of tributes from native peoples and from trappers who moved out to a series of widely dispersed camps every winter. Ships came in by river from the south and from the sea to the north carrying all imported goods, especially grain. At its height the town handled 100 000 sables per year (Belov, 1977). Mangazeya lasted only 70 years before its demise. Other more lasting trading settlements were Urengoy and Yakutsk.

The wave of fur exploitation was notable for several reasons. First, it traversed the north very swiftly. The reasons for this are not entirely clear. One reason must have been that the traders and even those responsible for collecting the tributes were received cooperatively by the native peoples; perhaps because anything was better than the previous misrule by princes of the previous Tartar Empire. Other possible reasons were the lack of competition with other nations, the fine network of navigable rivers and the fact that the fur-bearing animals were quickly exterminated in any one area, necessitating a further move. A second point of interest is the comparison with the fur-seeking waves of the North American Arctic. The Russian wave tapped the Arctic some 200 years earlier, and thus ensured earlier contacts between the indigenous and intrusive societies. Also the wave was apparently accompanied by less consolidation with less permanent trading settlements than in the American Arctic. This latter contrast may reflect the slim administrative network required to hold the trading posts, which in turn was due to the lack of opposition by indigenous groups and the lack of competition with other nations. Another reason may be the apparent contrast between nomadic inland peoples and coastal population. The nomad was unable to settle in one place permanently if he wished to stay with his herds; settling in a town necessitated a complete break with the traditional way of life. The

coastal-based hunter, used to semi-permanent villages, could successfully turn to trapping and operate from the trading post, and thus the
change was easier to make. It is certainly interesting to see that the
coastal Inuit of northeastern Siberia were attracted to towns more than
nomadic reindeer herders (Leont'yev, 1977).

The October Revolution of 1917 marked the official beginning of
the wave of Soviet interest in the north. However, beset with world
opposition and internal problems, it was not until the later 1920s that
serious attention was turned to the Arctic. 1926 was the year in which
the U.S.S.R. officially claimed its sector of the Arctic. Since then there
has been a dramatic drive towards development. This is clearly illustrated by the population trends shown in Figure 13.10. Growth has
been phenomenal, starting in the 1920s at Murmansk and in the 1930s
diffusing elsewhere. The growth is everywhere associated with towns
and the rural population has been relatively little affected. This is illustrated by the flat graphs for the rural Nenet A.O. in the western Arctic
and Koryak A.O. in the east (Figure 13.10a). In the Far North between
1926 and 1976 the immigrants have advanced from being a minority of
one in four in relation to the indigenous population to being a majority
of four to one. The growth shows no sign of faltering. Absolute growth
is still highest in the main towns in the Kola Peninsula, Yakutsk and
other industrial centres (Figure 13.11a) but there is a change in the
rates of growth. The Far East seems to be experiencing higher rates of
growth than the average for the north as a whole (Figure 13.11b).
Indeed rates of growth here are comparable to those of the new gas
field complexes in the lower Ob'.

There are several reasons for this dramatic Soviet drive to develop
the Arctic and it is useful to consider the main motives. Some are (or
were) undoubtedly idealistic and based on Lenin's ideas of communism.
One tenet was that capitalism leads to inequalities and to the development of exploited peripheries. Communism on the other hand should
lead to even growth (Hunter, 1957). The Arctic was thus seen as a
periphery in need of development. Further, the argument was developed
in Soviet newspapers of the 1920s that the very difficulties presented
by the Arctic provided a test case whereby the superiority of communism could be demonstrated (Bierman, 1978). After all, the American
Arctic under capitalism was completely undeveloped at the time. A
second tenet was that ethnic minorities should receive help after the
years of corrupt misrule under the Tsars. This implied that the indigenous peoples of the north should be helped to improve their lot. Other
tenets held at the time have a less political tone. One was the desperate
need for the Soviet state to be fully self-sufficient in raw materials,

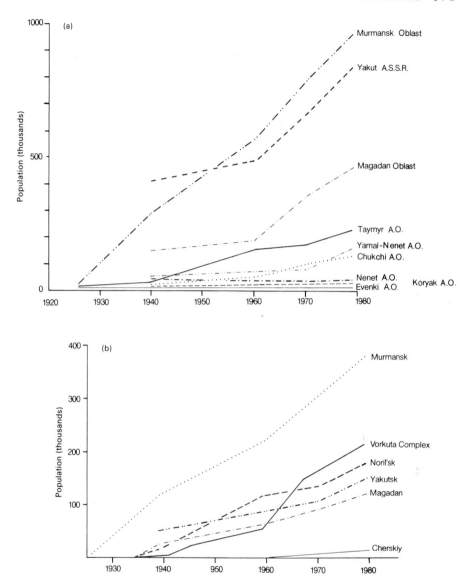

FIGURE 13.10   Population growth in the Soviet era: *(a)* in different parts of the 'Far North'; and *(b)* in selected northern towns.

because of the hostility with which it was faced by the west. Thus minerals in short supply were needed, whatever the cost. Although this belief in self-sufficiency sometimes took on the guise of a communist ethic, it is interesting to reflect that one of the minerals exploited was gold, which has been used for the wholly capitalistic purpose of raising

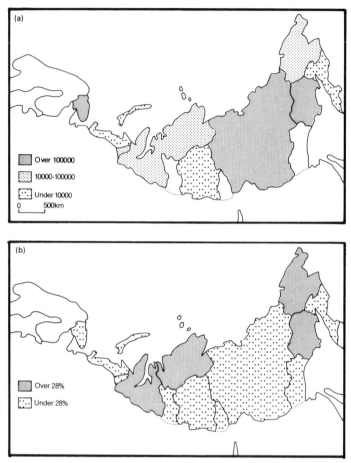

FIGURE 13.11   *(a)* Absolute population increase in administrative units wholly in the Far North, 1970–79. *(b)* Population trends in administrative units wholly in the Far North 1970–79. The shading indicates rates above or below the average for the Far North as a whole, which was an increase of 28 per cent.

money in the open world markets! Finally one can point to the final tenet which was the importance of strategy and defence. In the era of aeroplanes the Arctic was a frontier facing a potential enemy. Nothing that has happened since has changed this view. Taken together these tenets provided powerful justification for the development of the Arctic. They were the basic driving force which has sustained development to the present day.

The seven decades of Soviet development can be separated into significantly different phases. The first idealistic phase of the late 1920s and early 1930s saw the creation of civil divisions based upon the distribution of different indigenous peoples. Thus many of the administrative divisions (Figure 13.1a) have names that broadly encompass groups like the Chukchi, Koryak, Yakut, Evenki and Nentsy. The measure of control over local affairs is perhaps higher than believed by the average westerner, although of course it does not allow central decisions from Moscow to be ignored. Unfortunately such an idealistic beginning soon ran into trouble because a nomadic way of life was regarded as unworthy of a communist state and there was wholesale forced collectivization, mobilization and mergers of different groups.

The second notable phase was the tyrannical phase of forced labour which began in the early 1930s and continued in the harshest form until the 1950s. Some 'corrective' labour is still thought to occur but on a vastly reduced scale to that of the Stalin era. There is little need to dwell on the type of labour camp and the appalling conditions, which are well known from the works of Solzhenitsyn (1974, 1975) and Conquest (1979). Official documents testify to the starvation rations, only marginally in excess of those given to guard dogs, and to the death rate which seems to have been around 30 per cent. The Arctic had its full share of such camps. The Vorkuta coalmining district was founded on forced labour and estimates suggest that the Vorkuta camp complex held up to 1 million inmates. Noril'sk was another complex where development relied on forced labour. Perhaps the most notorious camps were those of Kolyma. Set up under the name of Dal'stroy, owned by the N.K.V.D. (Secret Police) it was administered from Magadan. Not only was the city itself built by forced labour, but exploitation of the gold placer deposits of the Kolyma valley relied on prisoners. Prisoners arrived in Magadan and were transferred via the Northern Sea Route to the Kolyma River, sometimes with terrible losses as ships were lost in the ice. Around ½ million prisoners are believed to have worked in the Kolyma complex at any one time and over 1 million may have died there.

The last decades comprise a different phase and have seen development progressing under practices which are more common in the capitalist world. Financial and other incentives are offered to attract people into the Far North. Although such incentives have long been in operation they became the norm in the late 1950s. Wage increments apply to all the Far North, with especially high rates in Chukchi A.O. and Koryak A.O. (Figure 13.12). The system is devised so as to reward people who stay more than a few years and can mean a doubled basic wage after 5 years. In addition there are other benefits such as a cost-of-living allowance and free travel. Since 1960 indigenous labour has also been able to qualify for these increments.

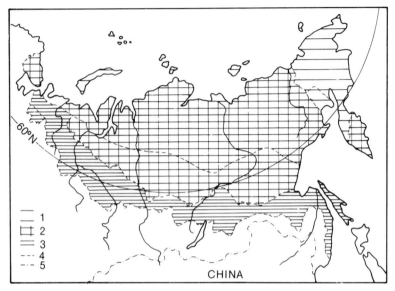

FIGURE 13.12   Wage increment zones in the Soviet north, since 1968:
   (1) 10 per cent increments every 6 months to maximum of 100 per cent;
   (2) 10 per cent increments every 6 months (for 3 years) and then every year
        up to a maximum of 80 per cent;
   (3) 10 per cent every year to a maximum of 50 per cent;
   (4) 1960 boundary of the Far North;
   (5) Political boundary (Armstrong *et al.*, 1978).

The functioning of the spatial system

Perspective on the location of development in the Soviet Arctic and its nature may be gained by comparison with more widely applicable models of development, for example, the network model of Taaffe, Morrill and Gould (1963) and Friedmann's core/periphery model (1966). To point to similarities with such models is not to suggest that they necessarily explain the patterns of the Soviet Arctic. But comparison does land some insights into the process of development.

NETWORKS

Figure 13.13 shows a topological representation of the major route structure and urban nodes in the Soviet North. Relative importance is indicated where possible, for example, in the case of node size and the relative importance of water routes. However, the diagram is not a complete representation of the pattern and several reservations must be noted. Railways are much more important than roads and indeed

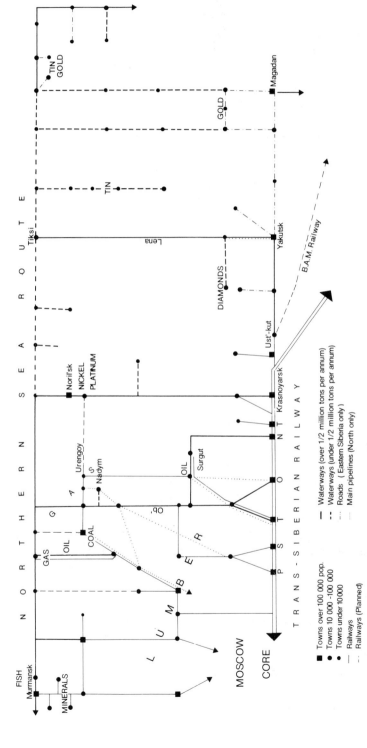

FIGURE 13.13   Topological diagram of the transport network of the Soviet north and major nodes.

roads have been excluded altogether in the west where they tend to duplicate railways. Also air transport is excluded. If it were included it would tend to emphasize the importance of such 'southern' centres as Yakutsk and Krasnoyarsk, and also add some long cross-links, especially in the north and middle. Nonetheless the topological diagram does afford a basis for analysing the pattern.

In terms of Taaffe, Morrill and Gould's network model, the pattern can be envisaged as one which is being opened up from two 'coastlines'. In the north the coastline is real in that penetration is from a series of ports associated with the Northern Sea Route (Figure 13.14). In the

FIGURE 13.14   The Northern Sea Route in the Kara Sea in spring. Copyright Novosti Press Agency.

south the 'coast' is represented by the major artery and access route of the Trans-Siberian Railway. In the east the Trans-Siberian runs too far south to be an effective springboard for exploitation of the Arctic and here the southern 'coast' is represented by the major east—west stretch of the Lena and its rail and road links to the Trans-Siberian Railway to the west and the port of Magadan in the east. Lines of communication have tended to penetrate 'inland' from nodes on both these 'coasts' and allowed development to proceed in both the Arctic and sub-Arctic.

The importance of these two 'coasts' is easily demonstrated by those statistics that are available. In 1978 Noril'sk was involved in a trade of around 5 million tons through its port of Dudinka. Two million tons went via the Yenisey mouth and the Northern Sea Route to Murmansk (Polar Record, 1979). The remaining three million tons travelled via the Yenisey to the Trans-Siberian Railway at Krasnoyarsk (Figure 13.15). Again in the mid-1970s 80—85 per cent of the goods

FIGURE 13.15   The Yenisey River south of Noril'sk. Copyright Novosti Press Agency.

reaching the Yakut A.S.S.R. entered by means of the Trans-Siberian Railway and were transhipped via the upper Lena at Ust'-Kut (Shabad, 1979b). This volume is close to capacity and further increases are being made up via greater use of the Northern Sea Route via Tiksi, where a deepwater pier opened in 1980. The Kolyma river settlements are supplied mainly from the Northern Sea Route, about half arriving from the east and half from European Russia.

There are important gaps in both 'coastlines'. The southern coastline is effective from Moscow to Yakutsk. Between Yakutsk and Magadan, however, the poor road and absence of bridges makes transport difficult. This can be demonstrated by the fact that 36 per cent of the supplies entering the Kolyma Valley area come via Ust'-Kut and the Lena mouth to the Kolyma mouth rather than taking the direct southern road route (Belinsky, 1978). The Northern Sea Route is also somewhat uneven as an access route. In effect there are two segments. The western route, focused on Murmansk, effectively links ports west of the Yenisey and, somewhat less intensively, Tiksi on the Lena delta. The eastern section is supplied from Soviet Pacific ports and is largely self-contained. Few ships traverse the route from end to end.

During the Soviet era there have been interesting changes in emphasis between the northern and southern lines of access. In the 1930s the emphasis on arctic development was clearly focused on the Northern Sea Route. This is demonstrated by the existence of Glavsevmorput (Main Administration of the Northern Sea Route), an organization charged with development of the sea route and *all* of Siberia north of 62°N. Presumably development from the north alone was deemed unsuccessful for in the post-war years emphasis has moved to the southern zone of access. For example, the Trans-Siberian Railway was extended to Ust'-Kut in the 1950s, thus opening up the Yakut A.S.S.R. from the south. Also official economic regions have tended to link various parts of the Arctic with regions to the south (Figure 13.1b). For example, the Northwest Region includes Arkhangel'sk while western Siberia, eastern Siberia and the Far East extend from the Arctic coast to the southern border of the U.S.S.R.

Viewed in terms of Taaffe, Morrill and Gould's model of route development, the eastern Soviet Arctic is classic Stage II with inland feeders extending north and south from 'coastal' nodes to inland nodes. Such lines of penetration are associated with the exploitation of minerals which are shipped out via the coastal 'port'. There is limited communication between inland centres, at least in terms of freight. In the western Arctic the major north–south routes are still apparent. Older lines run to major towns such as Murmansk. Newer north–south lines have been built from the Trans-Siberian Railway northward, such as the branch through Tobol'sk and Surgut to Novyy Urengoy. But in the western Arctic as a whole intermediate nodes assume some importance and cross-links are also beginning to occur, as in Stage III. A classic example of the growth of intermediate nodes is the string of mineral towns along the north–south Murmansk railway line. Examples of cross-routes associated with burgeoning towns comes from the West Siberian gas field towns, for example Nadym and Novyy Urengoy.

Interestingly one can also recognize routes associated with the postulated Stage IV, when high-priority cross-links develop over and above the initial route structure. One can point to the Vorkuta Railway which was completed in wartime to supply coal to the Moscow core. In this case enemy occupation of other Russian coalfields made the link of the utmost national priority. Current examples are some of the gas pipelines from the Nadym and Novyy Urengoy areas, which cut across the north–south lines and run directly and diagonally from the source of supply to the main Soviet centre of demand near Moscow.

CORE/PERIPHERY

Perspective on the characteristics of the Soviet Arctic as a whole is achieved by comparison with Freidmann's concept of a Resource Frontier Region. Friedmann's model was evolved to deal specifically with a capitalist economy and use of the model in a communist economy is obviously fraught with dangers. However, the insights it affords are striking. As in earlier chapters, points of comparison are taken from Table 1.2.

1. Dependent on one economic resource, usually minerals. Most development in the Soviet Arctic is dependent on one resource, usually minerals. As Friedmann stressed, this means that the economies of industrial complexes, even quite large ones, are highly dependent on the fortunes of a single product. Only in the Kola Peninsula area is there real diversification and this is restricted to the port of Murmansk.

2. Investment is commonly foreign. Foreign investment in the exploration of resources would seem to be ruled out in view of the Soviet Union's belief in the merits of self-sufficiency and a closed economy. However, foreign investment exists. A good example concerns Japan in the Far East. A Japanese company has provided credit for developing a coalfield near Chul'man served by a spur off the B.A.M. Railway in exchange for some of the coal. There are other such agreements. In the

1970s there was talk of plans for U.S. cooperation in exploiting the gas fields of Arctic Siberia.

Nevertheless, the significance of the role of foreign investment in Friedmann's view was that it took control of economic development out of the hands of a sovereign state. This is clearly not the case in the Soviet Union and thus this particular characteristic of a Resource Frontier Region does not apply.

3. Conflict between the economic goals of industry and the social goals of government. In the U.S.S.R. the conflict between industry *per se* and wider governmental social goals was settled in 1917. Nevertheless the conflict between political/economic goals on the one hand and social goals on the other is very striking. Indeed the use of forced labour for nearly three decades can be envisaged as the ultimate demonstration of this fundamental conflict. Even today the key problem of an acute labour shortage in the Arctic continually crops up in Soviet literature and again demonstrates the difficulty of harmoniously developing the economic potential of a remote region while creating a contented social milieu.

4. Centred on a town/city with specialized but limited functions, which may not achieve critical size for self-sustaining growth. The creation of self-contained towns to exploit specific resources is the key characteristic of Soviet Arctic development (Slavin and Agranat, 1977). The Kola Peninsula towns and Noril'sk are urban islands in a bleak and unpopulated landscape. So self-contained is the urban development, that it has been policy to discourage contacts and interchange between urban inhabitants and indigenous peoples carrying on a pastoral way of life. Although there has been much written about the ideal of economic diversification, progress in this sphere has been limited and most towns are avowedly 'one-resource' towns.

The impressive size of Soviet Arctic towns compared to other arctic areas might seem to suggest a stage of self-sustaining growth has been achieved. Whereas this is perhaps true of Murmansk, Noril'sk and a few of the larger transhipment ports, the picture in other towns is not so clear. At present there is an active debate about the best way to tap arctic resources. Whereas policy until recently has been to aim for permanent towns in even the most remote areas, there is increasing use of temporary dormitory towns, which, rather like remote camps, are run by shift workers from permanent centres in the south (Armstrong, 1976; Slavin and Agranat, 1977). In this case the town is moved or abandoned when the resource runs out. The system already operates on a small scale within state reindeer farms and, indeed, has been used with some success in the West Siberian oil and gas fields.

5. Transport and labour costs are high due to remoteness and high level of technology. Costs are high in the Soviet Arctic. Selyakov (1979) estimated social infrastructure costs to be 3.5–5 times higher than in the south and production costs 3–5 times higher. Slavin and Agranat (1977) considered construction to be up to three times as expensive. Labour is expensive, as can be inferred from the special incentives offered for work in the Arctic (Figure 13.12). It is these high costs which have made it difficult to carry out successful plans for economic diversification within arctic towns.

6. Special social structure — transients, male, single. The Soviet Arctic suffers from the familiar problems created by an abnormal social structure. Males are dominant in the population and commonly comprise 70 per cent of the total population (Khodachek, 1974). Many of these are single. Most people living in the Arctic are immigrants from the south, the figure approaching 95 per cent in the Kola Peninsula area (Makhrovskaya *et al.*, 1977). Turnover of population is high and indeed the higher the wages the stronger the incentives to 'get rich quick' and return to the south (Sallnow, 1977). The annual figure of population turnover for the Far North as a whole is 40 per cent and once approached 200 per cent in the West Siberian oilfields (Armstrong, 1970). Only Noril'sk has a low turnover (13 per cent which is comparable to the U.S.S.R. as a whole. Magadan is notorious for high rates of turnover. As Friedmann stressed, the problems presented by such a special social structure make it difficult to build attractive and permanent settlements.

Summarizing the points raised by comparison with the characteristics of Resource Frontier Regions, one can say that there is a basic contrast between the eastern and western Soviet Arctic. The eastern Soviet Arctic has virtually all the characteristics of a Resource Frontier Region. The western Arctic, especially around Murmansk and Noril'sk, has dropped some Resource Frontier Region characteristics. These two cities can perhaps be regarded as successful outposts of the Soviet core. The area around each city, however, is still in a stage of resource development and thus the 'core' extends little way beyond the city boundaries. Thus both cities differ from Friedmann's goal of an integrated hierarchy of central places. Superimposed on this basic east–west division is a north–south division. Generally the narrowness of the economic base increased from south to north (Slavin and Agranat, 1977). Thus the Resource Frontier Region is most obvious along the Arctic coast and is more diluted as one passes southwards into the sub-Arctic.

Although still dependent on extracting resources, the Soviet Arctic is more developed than other arctic areas. It is interesting therefore to note that Soviet policy has followed the lines recommended by Friedmann (Table 1.2). The idea of a regional development authority fitted readily into a Soviet approach and one recalls the example of Glavsevmorput in the 1930s. There has been a huge investment in urban centres and modern transport links, especially to and from the core. The drive for economic diversification has occurred, although at the cost of great inefficiency (Selyakov, 1979). The high cost of living has been subsidized by higher wages. Finally, the scale of investment and the growth of the towns suggests that there was indeed a rapid thrust to achieve the hopes of self-sufficiency. These similarities between Soviet practice and Friedmann's model lead to the conclusion that the processes of development in the Soviet Arctic have been similar to those in the western world. The main difference, and an important one, has been the subdued role played by foreign investment.

In view of the similarity of parts of the North American Arctic with Downward Transitional Areas, it is worth asking whether such regions exist in the Soviet Arctic. In North America such areas are associated with indigenous peoples who are suffering from the process of development through the breakdown of their traditional way of life and their inability to capitalize on the new industrial life. Unfortunately there is little hard evidence on which to base an opinion about the Soviet North. In the 1930s the indigenous population apparently went through a difficult period. This was the time of forced collectivization, forced removal to permanent villages, and was accompanied by a sharp decline in reindeer numbers. Presumably at this time the indigenous population was suffering through the imposition of an alien economic intrusive system. Subsequently, however, the signs are more favourable. The indigenous resource base seems to be stable, at least to judge from the roughly static number of reindeer over the last few decades (Armstrong *et al.*, 1978). The population explosion resulting from the superimposition of modern medicine on high fertility and mortality rates seems not to have occurred in the Soviet Arctic. For example, the population increase of Soviet indigenous peoples in the years 1959–70 was 14–15 per cent, compared to 40 per cent in Alaska (Armstrong *et al.*, 1978). The standard of living appears reasonable now that the value of reindeer meat has been raised to an attractive level and, since 1960, indigenous people have qualified for northern increments. In terms of political organization, the main indigenous groups have administrative units of their own, although this is not very significant in view of the vast Russian majorities in many of them. In the case of the larger groups like the Yakut, they fill administrative and scientific posts (St. George, 1969). In 1970 most indigenous peoples had primary and secondary education, though admittedly standards were lower than elsewhere in the U.S.S.R. Relatively few indigenous peoples are employed in the newer intrusive industries (Figure 13.16).

FIGURE 13.16   Ekonda, a trading post in Evenki A.O. used for the purchase of furs from hunters and deer breeders. Copyright Novosti Press Agency.

Perhaps this apparent Soviet success can be attributed to the policy of encouraging indigenous peoples to exploit the resources of the tundra. It was recognized that this was a contribution to resource exploitation that was best done using indigenous skills (Gurvich, 1973). The net effect seems to have been to preserve a viable basis for an indigenous way of life in the Arctic. Nevertheless, this apparently favourable conclusion is based on very little evidence. It is quite plausible that Downward Transitional Areas, which are obviously alien to successful communist planning, are simply not allowed to feature in Soviet statistics.

Conclusion

The models employed above allow one to draw two sets of conclusions about the Soviet Arctic. In the first place there are strong regional contrasts within the Arctic both from east to west and from north to south. In the second place the Soviet Arctic is more highly 'developed' than any other polar area. The purpose of this final section is to discuss the reasons for these differences.

The greater development of the Soviet western Arctic compared with the eastern reflects distance from the main industrial core of the Soviet Union as well as the existence of railways (Slavin and Agranat, 1977). It is interesting to recall that the Murmansk railway was completed before the 1917 revolution and was the only railway reaching the Arctic at the time. In contrast the eastern Arctic was barely approachable by sea and certainly not by land. The Trans-Siberian Railway had recently been completed but offered access to the rivers of the western Arctic only. Given these relative advantages, it is hardly surprising that minerals were first sought in the west. Until recently two-thirds of Soviet investment in the Arctic was in the west (Slavin and Agranat, 1977).

Initially certain minerals such as nickel were critical to the Soviet economy but, as the transport network improved, less valuable minerals could be tapped economically. Good examples are the coal at Vorkuta and more recently the iron ore at Kovdor and Olenegorsk which are both products of low unit value in terms of arctic exploitation. Meanwhile the east struggled to develop minerals of high unit value. Faced with costly transport to a distant core, only gold, diamonds and tin (which has been in critical short supply in the U.S.S.R.) have justified the high costs of development. The importance of accessibility to the core can be illustrated by the observation that minerals which exist in both east and west have been tapped only in the west. One example is coal. Figure 13.17 shows how the largest coal reserves lie in the eastern Arctic. Yet the only fields tapped are those closest to Moscow. Similarly, oil and gas are known to be abundant in the east, for example in the Lena basin; yet it is policy to develop those deposits closest to the industrial core first and to gradually eextend eastwards as these run out (Slavin and Agranat, 1977). These examples illustrate how the type of development is influenced by the position of the periphery in relation to the larger spatial system of which it is a part.

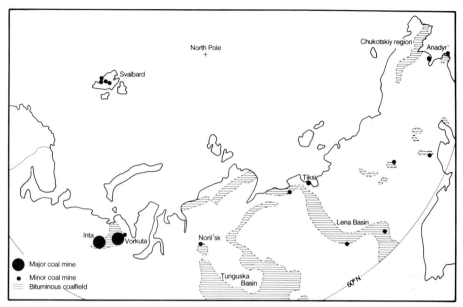

FIGURE 13.17   Coalfields in the Soviet north, demonstrating the huge reserves in the east which are untapped.

The map showing rates of growth (Figure 13.11) carries the implication that a change in emphasis in arctic development could be taking place. Slavin and Agranat (1977) wrote that in the late 1970s there had been a change whereby two-thirds of the investment in the Far North was now going to the east. Perhaps this implies that Soviet planners feel that the future of the western Arctic is secure and that the east needs help. Or perhaps it reflects strategic worries about eastern neighbours. Whatever the reason, the distance from the western industrial core presents major economic problems. In this context it will be interesting to see to what extent the nearby industrial core of Japan takes a role in development.

The second regional contrast within the Soviet Arctic, that of a narrowing economic base towards the north, is a pattern wholly consistent with development from the south. The pattern of economic regions and commodity flows shows the dominance of the southern access routes and centres as springboards for arctic development. Nevertheless it seems that the drive for all-year-round navigation along the western sector of the northern sea route in an attempt to ensure year-round access to Noril'sk reflects a shift of emphasis (Shabad, 1979a). This will reduce the Arctic's dependence on the south and could lead to a reorientation of the spatial system. Interestingly, this drive for year-round navigation is proceeding in spite of worsening ice conditions over the last few years (Chapter 6).

The reasons for the high level of development in the Soviet Arctic in comparison with other arctic lands are impossible to decide with any certainty. However, it is possible to point to advantages held by the Soviet Union.

(1) Long-term economic development is more easily achieved under a Soviet system than in a capitalist society. Working on the basis of a series of 5-year plans it is possible to integrate political, economic and social goals, and ignore problems of short-term lack of profitability. Long-term goals are less easily achieved under a free capitalist economic system. For example, it is difficult to envisage the huge long-term build-up of an ice-breaker fleet in Russia over 30 years taking place in a coherent fashion in Arctic Canada, or the willingness to accept years of loss-making in order to create large arctic cities.

(2) A second advantage following from the above concerns the state control of labour. Forced labour is the ultimate in such control, and allowed workers to be provided wherever and whenever needed. It may seem uncharitable to hark back to the use of forced labour, especially since it is widely acknowledged to have been highly inefficient when judged in cold economic terms (Negretov, 1977). Nevertheless it is a fact that complexes such as Vorkuta and Noril'sk were created by forced labour. One wonders whether a coalfield in the Arctic could have justified exploitation on economic grounds alone – at least in the 1930s. And a huge question mark must hang over Noril'sk. Nickel and copper were useful minerals but far from the only source of supply in the U.S.S.R. in the 1930s. Their strategic importance increased during the Second World War when alternative supplies in the Kola Peninsula found themselves in the war zone, but they have attracted attention ever since. Although one factor is undoubtedly the high quality of the ore, it is difficult to see convincing economic arguments for the development of such an isolated complex. However, in terms of a prison complex, isolation has an obvious advantage! Overall it is difficult to escape the conclusion that the use of forced labour created complexes which by the 1950s were of such a size as to be worth maintaining to the present day, in spite of their isolation.

(3) The decision to employ railways in arctic development seems to have been justified by events. The Murmansk Railway is a classic example of how an area can be opened up by the railway, and the

link between the Trans-Siberian Railway and the Lena was also fundamental in changing the pace of development in the Yakut A.S.S.R. The Soviet faith in railways is borne out by new or recent ventures such as B.A.M. and the Urengoy Railway. Stress on building a long-term transport network is perhaps easier under the Soviet system. Nevertheless it is clear that Soviet planners recognize the vital importance of creating an infrastructure before development (Slavin and Agranat, 1977).

(4) The population density in the Soviet Arctic immediately preceding development was higher than, say, in the Canadian Arctic. Excluding the indigenous population who have not been involved in development, Armstrong (1963/64) estimated that immediately before the October Revolution there were 40000–50000 Russians in an area north of the Arctic Circle in the west and north of 60°N in the east. This provided a firmer base for development than in Arctic America. Among the many reasons for this contrast, one can perhaps point to the probable importance of the longer history of settlement in the Soviet North (Armstrong, 1970).

(5) Finally, one cannot escape the conclusion that the natural environment in the Soviet Arctic is more favourable for development than elsewhere in the polar lands. The balance of natural environmental advantages over the American Arctic has been mentioned in Table 13.1. In addition one must add the fact that the Soviet industrial core is closer to its Arctic periphery than is the case in North America. If one confines one's attention to the remote and more comparable eastern Soviet Arctic, then the contrast with the North American Arctic is much less apparent.

Perhaps it is appropriate to end this chapter with the thought that the spatial pattern of development in the Soviet Arctic may take on a different form in future. For over 60 years the aim has been to create a permanent and economically diversified urban infrastructure, and there has been some success in the Murmansk and Noril'sk areas. This policy has proved uneconomic and there now seems to be a change of emphasis whereby development is carried out only to the level required to extract needed resources. This involves the greater use of temporary resource settlements with labour flown in and out of the settlement for particular shifts. Such a tendency marks a convergence between Soviet practice and that common in the North American Arctic. It implies that future development in the Soviet Arctic will involve the use of small settlements tightly linked to southern centres, rather than the creation of further large towns and an ambitious railway network.

Further reading

Armstrong, T. E. 1965: *Russian settlement in the North.* Cambridge University Press, Cambridge.

Armstrong, T. E. 1970: Soviet northern development, with some Alaskan parallels and contrasts. *Institute of Social, Economic and Government Research, University of Alaska, Fairbanks,* 2, 1–37.

Belinskiy, B. V. 1978: Aspects of water transport in the Soviet northeast. *Polar Geography*, 2 (1), 28–41.

Makhrovskaya, A. V., Vaytens, M. Ye., Panov, L. K. and Belinskiy, A. Yu. 1977: Urban planning and construction in the Kola north, I. *Polar Geography*, 1 (3), 205–16.

Negretov, P. I. 1977: How Vorkuta began. *Soviet Studies*, 29 (4), 565–75.

Savoskul, S. S. 1978: Social and cultural dynamics of the peoples of the Soviet north. *Polar Record*, 19 (119), 129–52.

Selyakov, Yu, G. 1979: Locational factors of machine manufacturing in the Soviet north. *Soviet Geography*, 20 (5), 310–21.

Slavin, S. V. and Agranat, G. A. 1977: Problems in the development of the north. *Polar Geography*, 1(1), 1–8.

CHAPTER FOURTEEN

Antarctica

The regional geography of Antarctica is of interest for three main reasons:

(1) unlike the continental fringes which make up arctic lands, the Antarctic is a continent lying wholly within the polar regions;
(2) it affords a unique opportunity to compare the human systems in the Arctic with those in another polar region;
(3) it is unique in that it represents multinational settlement of a continent.

To be comparable with the treatment of distinctive political systems in the Arctic, the continent should perhaps be described by the different political sectors shown in Figure 8.18. However, this is inappropriate in the case of Antarctica because these sectors are barely meaningful. This is partly due to the multinational approach to the continent and partly to the low stage of development which characterizes each sector. Also there would be the added difficulty of describing the political system operating in the unclaimed sector! It is more meaningful to look at the continent and its surrounding seas as a whole. In this way the basic similarities between the sectors and the degree of international independence emerges.

Physical constraints and resources

The main resource is a land mass 1½ times as large as the U.S.A., while the main constraint is that over 98 per cent of the continent is buried beneath ice. The area of ice-free ground is only about the size of the state of Montana, yet is scattered in small oases throughout the continent. More specifically, the natural constraints include inaccessibility of bedrock through the ice; low temperatures, including the coldest temperature ever measured on earth ($-88°C$ at Vostok) as well as generally high windchill values; high altitude of the interior which induces mountain sickness (Figure 2.7); net snow accumulation which buries any buildings; a coast with access seasonally or permanently impeded by pack ice; a deeper than average continental shelf (400–800 m compared with the global mean of 133 m, which is the result of the existing isostatic depression); and remoteness from the industrial cores of the northern hemisphere. These constraints have a distinct spatial expression and Figure 14.1 is an attempt to portray the antarctic environment in a way that is relevant to human activity. There are several distinctive areas.

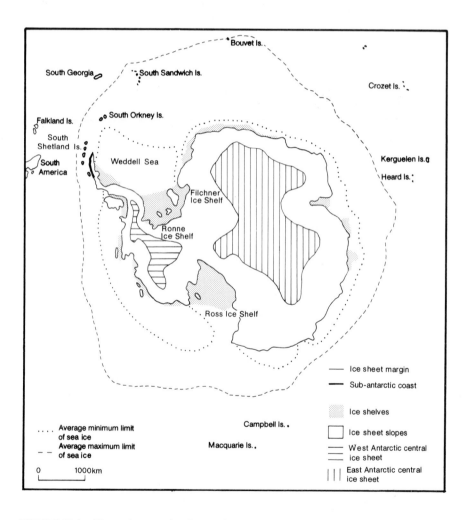

FIGURE 14.1   The main natural regions and constraints on human activity in Antarctica. After the ideas of Markov *et al.* (1970).

1. The central ice sheet areas are remote, high, flat, smooth expanses of soft snow. The most extreme example is in East Antarctica and has an altitude above *c.* 3 150 m, little wind and, as a result, loose surface snow. Aver'yanov in 1963 described how on a tractor traverse in 1958 'a metal drum of gasoline fell from the sledge and under the tracks of a tractor which followed the sledge and was pushed into the snow to a depth of over 1.5 m, without receiving a single dent' (Markov *et al.*, 1970, p. 330). Snowfall is light and temperatures 30°–40°C colder than comparable arctic latitudes (Chapter 3). The West Antarctic central area is above 1 700–2 000 m and since it is traversed by cyclones, is subjected to winds which create small snow sastrugi (corrugations on the ice sheet surface). Here the snow is firmer, while temperatures and altitude are less restricting than in East Antarctica.

2. The ice sheet slope is a zone whose altitude varies between 200 m and 3 150 m in East Antarctica and *c.* 200 m and 1 700–2 000 m in West Antarctica. Downslope katabatic winds are characteristic and snowfall higher. This is the zone of snow transport with deflation in the higher parts and deposition common at lower altitudes. Sastrugi are common and wind speeds on the lower, steeper ice sheet slopes commonly reach gale force.

3. The ice sheet margin is a zone of shattered ice where outlet glaciers and ice domes accelerate as they discharge onto the shore or into the sea. This thin linear strip around the Antarctic is a formidable hazard and the problems created for surface transport by its crevasses were well illustrated by the 1957 Commonwealth Trans-Antarctic Expedition, as it moved through crevasses from the Filchner Ice Shelf to the grounded ice sheet (Figure 4.17; Fuchs and Hillary, 1958).

4. The ice shelves themselves, which fringe over one-third of Antarctica's coastline, are another distinctive environment. Once the terminal cliffs are bypassed, the ice shelf surfaces tend to be smooth except in the vicinity of grounding points. Snowfall is high near the calving cliff. A problem is the high rate of movement which means that any building travels 1–3 km per year and eventually ends up in an iceberg, as for example happened with the remains of Camp Michigan (p. 86).

5. The sub-antarctic coast. Offshore pack ice conditions affect the relative accessibility of the coastline to shipping. Though less tough than arctic pack ice, antarctic pack ice is mixed with icebergs and differential movement of the two ice types can lead to unpredictable disturbances. Winter access is difficult anywhere except in the case of the sub-antarctic islands, but in summer the eastern and southern coasts of the embayments of the Ross and Weddell Seas become clear of sea ice for a few weeks, while the northwest coast of the Antarctic Peninsula is clear for some months. While the sea ice clearance in the Ross and Weddell Seas is primarily a wind effect, that in the Antarctic Peninsula is primarily due to mild summer temperatures. For this reason it is helpful to regard the northwest coast of the Antarctic Peninsula as sub-Antarctic. As such it has many similarities with the sub-antarctic islands lying between the continent and the Antarctic Convergence, namely the South Shetland, South Orkney and South Sandwich Islands, South Georgia, Bouvet, Heard and Macquarie Islands and Kerguelen. Here summer temperatures are above zero. However, all are bleak with upstanding massifs swathed in ice and cloud. The temperature range throughout the year is generally small with snow likely all the year round. The more southerly coastlines are ice-bound for part of the year.

The resources in Antarctica arise from the intrinsic riches of the continent and surrounding oceans themselves, and also from the position of the continent in relation to other continents. At the time of writing (1980), the main discoveries include coal and iron (Figure 14.2). The coal was discovered in the Transantarctic Mountains by scientists of Shackleton's *Nimrod* expedition in 1908 and they wrote enthusiastically of 1.25 billion tons of coal. However, although it has been used by local expeditions, the main resource is of low quality, occurs in thin seams and would require tricky transport to the coast. At present it is of no economic use. Iron ore is known in the Prince Charles Mountains where a 100 m thick deposit may extend for 120 km (Mitchell and Tinker, 1980). The ore body (35–38 per cent iron) would be large enough to satisfy world demand for the next 200 years, but vast resources are already known in more accessible areas of Australia and Canada, so this too is unlikely to become economic for a long time.

Recent years have seen much talk of further mineral potential in Antarctica (Holdgate and Tinker, 1979). Resources are assessed on the basis of predictions made by comparison with those parts of Gondwanaland which were originally adjacent to Antarctica (Chapter 2, Figure 2.9). Oil has attracted most interest. The sedimentary basins underlying the Ross, Weddell and Bellingshausen seas are thick, and exploratory drilling has already found natural gas traces in all these areas. Based on this and other circumstantial evidence, it seems likely that large reserves of oil and gas exist, and official reports mention

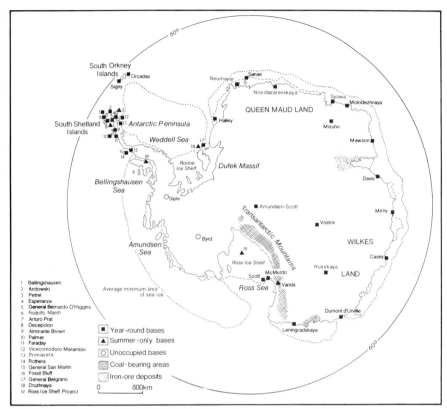

FIGURE 14.2   Antarctica: bases, transport routes and main terrestrial resources, 1980–81.

figures for recoverable oil of tens of billions of barrels, or the same order of magnitude as those in Alaska. Other oil company sources give figures of 50 billion barrels or more for the Ross and Weddell Sea basins alone (Mitchell and Tinker, 1980). Land minerals sufficiently large to be classified as deposits have not yet been found. Occurrences of copper, chromium, gold and other minerals are too small. However great interest has been shown in the Dufek Massif (Figure 14.2). Here there is a layered igneous complex similar to that near Sudbury in Ontario, the Bushveld in South Africa and the Stillwater in Montana, which contain rich deposits of platinum, copper, chromium and nickel. Finally, ice is a possible resource as a water supply for southern hemisphere cities in dry areas. Large icebergs break off annually into the southern ocean, and engineering concerns believe they can tow icebergs and deliver them economically (Weeks, 1980).

The marine resources of the antarctic seas are large and relate to the large sea areas involved and the seasonal richness of the seas (Chapter 6).

In view of dwindling fish stocks in other regions of the world, the antarctic resources seem very attractive. As discussed in Chapter 6, the main possibility is krill. Estimates of an annual sustainable yield as high as 100–150 million tons make krill potentially the world's largest single source of protein. There are also three potentially exploitable fish, the tooth fish (*Dissostichus mawsoni*), herring (*Pleuragramma antarcticum*) and cod (*Notothenia rossi*). The possible magnitude of the fish resources is illustrated by calculations of maximum sustainable yields of 50 000 tons round South Georgia and 77 000 tons round Kerguelen (Mitchell and Tinker, 1980). Other sub-antarctic island groups such as the South Shetland and South Orkney Islands could also support fisheries. An annual whale catch of 1–1.5 million tons is probably sustainable (Gulland, 1970). while according to the 1972 Convention for the Conservation of Antarctic Seals, annual quotas of crabeater seals (175 000) leopard seals (1 200) and Weddell seals (5 000) are fully sustainable. Probably fur seals and elephant seals could be harvested regularly now that their numbers have recovered from destructive earlier over-exploitation (Figures 6.18 and 6.19).

Finally, the antarctic environment is a tourist resource. The dramatic scenery, unique wildlife, aura of adventure and wilderness have attracted tourists on a regular basis since 1956. Interestingly, tourism is currently the only commercial activity on the antarctic mainland. The nature of the resource favours both cruises by ship, especially in the Antarctic Peninsula area, and overflights for example in the Transantarctic Mountain area (Figure 14.3).

The position of Antarctica on the globe can be viewed as a resource in a variety of contexts. One unfortunate consequence of its isolation is that it seems an attractive place to dump nuclear wastes. An early suggestion to encase wastes in the ice sheet has been rejected, but pressures to use the shield rocks of East Antarctica are likely to persist (Zeller *et al.*, 1976). Its isolation gives Antarctica several unique resources from a scientific point of view (Crary, 1962). Its central location in the oceanic hemisphere of the world makes it fundamental for understanding worldwide natural systems, for example oceanic and atmospheric circulation. Its proximity to the south magnetic pole makes it important for geomagnetic studies of the ionosphere and aurora which often require simultaneous observations in both north and south hemispheres. Again the isolation makes Antarctica of unique interest for biologists; of especial interest is the evolution of an ecosystem without the impact of indigenous man.

Location and isolation also have important strategic implications (Hanessian, 1964). The presence of a land mass in an otherwise watery

FIGURE 14.3   Tourist scenery on the western coast of the Antarctic Peninsula.

hemisphere is strategically significant. Nations of the southern continents are only too aware of the proximity of a southern continental shore which would be a threat if in unfriendly hands. Also, maritime nations are aware of the strategic significance of Drake Strait — the only direct open-sea passage between the Atlantic and Pacific. Having said this, however, the Antarctic is in a less critical strategic location than the Arctic.

The human spatial pattern

PEOPLE

The population of Antarctica south of 60°S is around 800 in winter and rises to over 2000 in the summer. The numbers involved are much smaller than these for areas of comparable size in the Arctic. Also, the make-up of the population is quite different. There are no indigenous peoples; instead there is an intrusive population which, unlike the Arctic, is concerned with scientific rather than economic 'exploitation'. The population is remarkable for its preponderance of males, which is 100 per cent on many bases all year round. Other bases such as McMurdo normally support a number of women in summer, while the Argentinian base of Esperanza has a number of wives and children in residence. Turnover of population is high. Most people work in Antarctica for periods varying between 1 summer and 2 years. 'Summer charlies' are frequently scientists or technicians who work in Antarctica for a specific job, usually arriving in October–December and leaving in February–March. Longer-term residents may man a base all the year round, spending 1 or 2 years in the South.

NODES

In 1980/81 the winter population in the Antarctic (south of 60°S) was confined to 35 bases (Figure 14.2). These are maintained on a year-round basis with some such as Signy existing since 1947. Of the 35 bases, Argentina had 7, U.S.S.R. 7, U.K. 4, U.S.A. 4, Australia 3, Chile 3, Japan 2, and New Zealand, Poland, South Africa, France and West Germany 1 each. The distribution of the bases is striking: 12 were in areas classified as sub-Antarctic on Figure 14.1, while 23 were in the Antarctic zone proper. Of these 23 bases no less than 18 were coastal; only 5 stations lay in the interior and one of these, Siple, was abandoned after the 1981/82 season. In addition to the permanent bases there are additional summer bases. Examples are the U.K. base at Fossil Bluff on Alexander Island and the U.S. Ross Ice Shelf Project camp used in the late 1970s.

The permanent bases are situated in two main environments. Most are built on rock near the coast. Others are built on ice; five on the ice sheet interior and four on ice shelves. McMurdo Station is the biggest Antarctic base and is built on rock (Figure 14.4). A visitor to the base receives a booklet entitled *Your Stay at McMurdo Station, Antarctica.* The booklet enthusiastically introduces the base

> McMurdo Station is Antarctica's first city. Founded in 1956, it has grown from an outpost of a few buildings to a complex logistic staging facility of more than 100 structures. Year-round population is approximately 50 persons with the summer...popu-lation jumping to nearly 800.... Greater McMurdo includes a 'downtown' area, science and support facilities, and an outlying airport (Williams Field). From Williams Field, flights not only span the continent but maintain McMurdo's contact with the outside world.

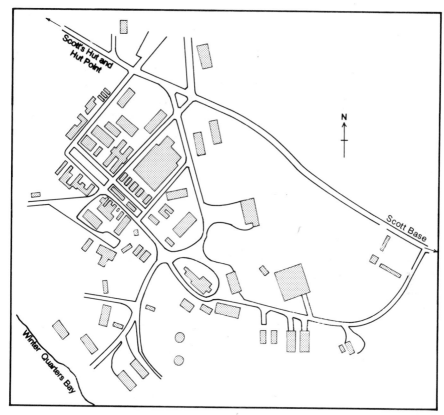

FIGURE 14.4   Street plan and buildings of McMurdo Station, 1978/79. From a pamphlet given to visitors.

There are telephones, a regular bus service to the airport, scientific laboratories, recreation facilities, a *'Mammoth Mountain Inn'*, hospital, post office and a chapel. In the 1960s the station even had its own nuclear-powered generating station.

Rothera is a British base established to further the earth sciences in the southern Antarctic Peninsula area. It is perhaps more typical of medium-sized antarctic bases. Winter parties of scientists and supporting staff are 10–12 strong, while in summer perhaps 40–50 work from the base. Situated on a raised beach, the base consists of several wooden buildings (Figure 14.5). Smaller buildings are for stores, generator, garage, etc., while the main living quarters are in a comfortable two-storey building. The facilities include a kitchen/dining room, bar/living room, library, toilet/shower room, offices, photo laboratories, radio room and bunk rooms. Snow drifts build up in the lee of the huts and the raised beach foundation only emerges briefly in February and

FIGURE 14.5   The U.K. Rothera base, typical of medium-sized bases in Antarctica.
Photograph by C. W. M. Swithinbank.

March. The main function of the base is to act as a seasonal field centre for Earth scientists.

Amundsen—Scott station at the South Pole is an example of a new base built on ice. The original structures had been buried and were collapsing under the strain of the accumulating thickness of snow. When the new Amundsen—Scott base was built in 1974—75 the old base, which was 17 years old, lay beneath 10—15 m of snow. The new base was constructed below the surface in excavated trenches, 244 m long, roofed with an arch and a geodesic dome 50 m in diameter and 15 m high. The individual buildings are scattered in the generally milder climate of the trench. Such a system avoids the problem of drifts quickly submerging huts built on the surface. However it presents problems for instruments studying meteorology and upper atmospheric conditions, and a solution is to construct specialized buildings on stilts which can be extended year by year or jacked up.

The life of an antarctic base is highly seasonal. The seasonal rhythm dominates all activities. The wintering parties tend to become closely knit groups who fear with some trepidation the invasion of impatient summer visitors (MacPherson, 1977). The visitors in turn are bemused by the in-jokes and sometimes unintelligible language which has evolved on the base during the winter! The seasonality is perhaps most marked in the case of a base like Halley, whose summer is shattered only by a brief 1—2-week visit of a ship.

NETWORKS

The coastal bases are supplied wholly or largely by sea. An example is Rothera base. In February the base is relieved by an ice-strengthened ship such as R.R.S. *Bransfield* which frequently has to free the last remaining sea ice before unloading. Fuel is piped into bladder tanks and other stores unloaded by lighter (Figure 14.6). Base personnel are changed and the ship disappears until the following February. Some nations, such as the U.S.A., use ice-breakers to ensure the reliable arrival of cargo vessels to their bases. Since bases are owned by individual nations, the logistic back-up is wholly in the hands of that nation. Thus British bases are relieved by British ships, Argentinian bases by Argentinian ships, and so on. There is logistic cooperation in that the British have carried stores to the U.S. Palmer station on the Antarctic Peninsula, and that personnel may travel with other national ships or planes, but this is very limited and usually reserved for emergencies.

FIGURE 14.6
R.R.S. *Bransfield* preparing to unload fuel at Rothera, 1979.

Several countries supplement sea routes to their coastal bases with the use of aircraft to carry passengers to and from the continent. The most important air transport user is the U.S. which has long flown wheeled aircraft into McMurdo in the early summer. The U.S.S.R. has recently begun to follow the lines of U.S. practice and Molodezhnaya is beginning to duplicate the intercontinental role of McMurdo. Chile and Argentina also fly people into the Antarctic, but the scale of operations is far smaller.

Transport links within the Antarctic continent rely heavily on aircraft. The U.S. runs the most developed network and its interior stations and temporary camps are serviced regularly from McMurdo by large, ski-equipped aircraft and numerous helicopters. Similar though smaller operations exist elsewhere. Thus in the case of Rothera, ski-equipped aircraft fly personnel from an ice-free harbour in the northern Antarctic Peninsula to an airstrip near the base in November and then distribute small mobile parties of 2–4 in the southern Antarctic Peninsula area in the months November–February. The main exception to the use of aircraft for inland travel has been the Soviet use of tractor trains to relieve Vostok each summer, although increasing reliance is being placed on aircraft.

The evolution of the spatial system

The evolution of the settlement pattern in Antarctica reflects the impact of waves of interest emanating from the world's core areas similar to those which affected the Arctic. However, the response has been very different. In particular, one can highlight the late arrival of permanent settlement and the lack of social facilities that go with a mixed community of men, women and children.

Like the Arctic the Antarctic has experienced early waves of economic exploitation (Figure 14.7). The first in the early nineteenth century involved the pursuit of fur seals; hundreds of boats from America and Britain rampaged through the sub-antarctic islands (Chapter 8; Bonner and Laws, 1964). Exterminating the quarry within a few seasons, the sealers either moved on or engaged in the extraction of oil from elephant seals (Crowther, 1970) and in cases like Macquarie Island even from penguins. While elephant seals have been a target in islands like South Georgia until the 1960s, the fur seals experienced further sporadic attacks in the late nineteenth century and have only begun to recover again in the last 20–30 years. The effect of sealing was to establish settlements on shore. In southerly islands like the South Shetland Islands groups of men would be left ashore for the summer while they clubbed fur seals to death and boiled down the blubber of elephant seals in pots. With luck they would be picked up before the winter, but sometimes groups were forced to overwinter in crude huts. Remains of these stone and whalebone huts and other relics can be seen to this day in the South Shetland Islands (Figure 8.13). Remains from these days have also left their mark on South Georgia. Grytviken (Boiler Bay) was so called by Nordenskjöld in 1902 when he discovered seven abandoned pot boilers inscribed with the name of 'Johnson and Co., London'

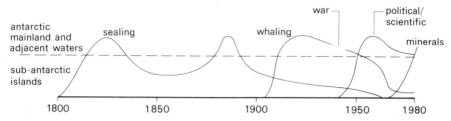

FIGURE 14.7   Waves of exploitation emanating from the world's cores which have affected
Antarctica. The diagram gives an idea of how much they affected the
sub-antarctic islands and the continental mainland.

(Nordenskjöld and Andersson, 1905). It seems that temporary winter settlements existed from time to time in the sub-antarctic islands as various sealing expeditions overwintered. One of the main points of significance to emerge from these early sealing exploits is that, in spite of the large numbers of temporary settlements exploiting such resources, none became permanent. Each settlement was abandoned as soon as the seals were exhausted, usually within a year or so.

Whaling arrived in the sub-Antarctic in 1904 when Captain Larsen, who had visited South Georgia with Nordenskjöld, established a whaling station at Grytviken (Figure 14.8). In 1905 a whaling factory

FIGURE 14.8   The whaling station at Grytviken. The church is just visible on the right. The
whaling station was established in 1904 and used until 1965. Photograph by
Gordon Thom.

ship was anchored in the South Shetland Islands and within 3 years antarctic whaling produced more oil than the rest of the world's whaling industry together. By the beginning of the First World War there were six land stations in the Falkland Islands Dependencies (South Georgia and land now included in British Antarctic Territory). Most were at the head of bays in South Georgia, but one was in the sheltered harbour of Deception Island in the South Shetlands (Figure 14.9). This latter station was responsible for the arrival for the first time of a significant overwintering antarctic population south of 60°S (Figure 14.10). Also there were 21 floating factory ships (Tønnessen, 1970). The latter used to anchor in a sheltered bay and flense whales alongside the ship. The procedure is well described by Villiers (1925) who was on the first expedition which took whaling to the Ross Sea area of Antarctica. In 1925 the introduction of the stern slipway meant that whaling factories were no longer restricted to land bases and the production of whale oil soared as the industry exploited all antarctic waters (Figure 14.11). A glut in 1930/31 resulted from the deployment of 38 factory ships and 184 catchers, and stimulated the need for control of production. This was achieved some years later by the expedient of introducing quotas measured in 'Blue Whale Units'. One Blue Whale Unit was equal to two fin whales, 2½ humpback whales, six sei whales or to an appropriate combination of these. The result of such a system was the over-exploitation of the largest species first (the blue whale), followed by successively smaller species like the fin whale and the sei whale. The successive over-exploitation of larger species meant that oil production fell while the numbers of whales caught remained close to 40000 until the early 1960s. Since then there has been a dramatic decline associated with over-exploitation and more rigid species restrictions introduced by the International Whaling Commission (Gulland, 1976; Brown, 1980). Increasing efficiency of catching techniques has meant that the number of factory ships has declined sharply (Table 14.1). In 1979/80 there were only three ships operating in the whole of the Antarctic. The decline has

TABLE 14.1   *Whale factory ships*

Dates	Total	British	Norwegian	Japanese	Soviet	Dutch
1930/31	38	11	27	0	0	0
1959/60	20	3	8	6	2	1
1969/70	6	0	0	3	3	0
1979/80	3	0	0	1	2	0

FIGURE 14.9   Whalers Bay, Deception Island, 1966. The remains of the whaling station can be seen on the shore in the foreground. The former U.K. Deception Island base is to the right in the middle distance.

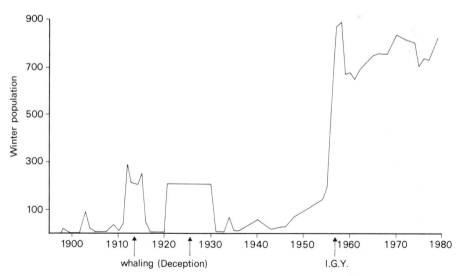

FIGURE 14.10   Total wintering population in the Antarctic south of 60°S from the first over-wintering expedition in 1898 to the present day. After Dubrovin (1966) and various other sources.

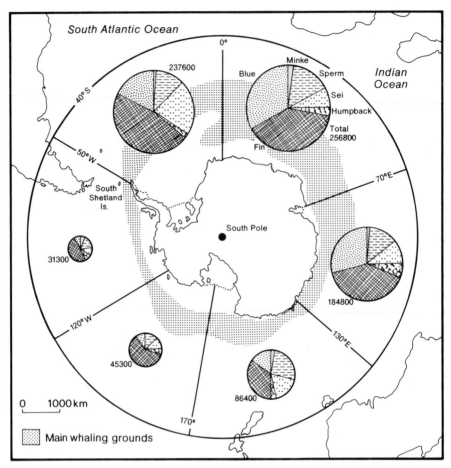

FIGURE 14.11   Main whaling grounds and catch by International Whaling Commission statistical area, 1931—76. After *Polar Atlas* (1978).

seen the termination of Norwegian and British whaling; utilizing whale oil only, and devoid of a human market for whale meat, the European nations could not compete with the Japanese who were able to sell the meat economically. Tønnessen (1970) states that in the 1960s the Japanese earned four times more from a Blue-Whale-Unit than Norwegian whalers. The fortunes of the whaling industry have left their mark on the land stations. The glut in the market in 1931/32 saw the permanent closure of the Deception Island station and four others in South Georgia. Land stations survived in South Georgia until the 1960s and the last at Leith Harbour closed after the 1965/66 season.

The significance of the whaling industry for the Antarctic is that

semi-permanent stations with up to 100–200 men were established
in the most favoured areas. In South Georgia such stations existed
for some 60 years with interruptions only during the two world wars.
An employee was commonly retained for 18 months and overwintered
at the settlement. Facilities were primitive and a doctor visiting
Stromness in the 1950s was quite appalled at the filth and low standard in a hospital which was far inferior to a military field hospital
(Robertson, 1956). Nevertheless, Grytviken had a church and common
rooms, and libraries were not unknown. Moreover, there were the
trappings of administration. South Georgia supported two customs
officers, a policeman, three radio operators and four meteorological
officers, and through them the British government extracted royalties
and maintained control. These administrative functions in the more
southerly Deception Island station were more skeletal. Nevertheless a
magistrate was resident until the closure of the station in 1931.

Thus one can conclude that the wave of exploitation associated with
whaling had the effect of establishing settlements in the most favoured
parts of the sub-Antarctic. The main control on the location of the
settlements was access to the rich whaling grounds in the vicinity of
the islands of the Scotia arc (Figure 14.11). Other islands such as
Kerguelen also successfully supported whaling stations for some years.
Within these islands good sheltered harbours and limited pack ice were
the key attractions. The fjords of South Georgia (Figure 14.8) and the
unusually well-protected and heated volcanic crater of Deception Island
were particularly well-suited to settlement (Figure 14.9). Nevertheless,
in spite of the growth of administrative functions the settlements
closed when the whaling declined. The only exception is at King Edward
Point near Grytviken. Here a British scientific base has taken over some
of the existing buildings.

A third wave of settlement in Antarctica can be recognized as being
stimulated by strategic considerations and occurred in the later years
of the Second World War. This was the first wave to affect the Antarctic
proper, though limited to the most favourable parts of the Antarctic
Peninsula. The United Kingdom became uneasy about its Antarctic
territory when Chile and Argentina made political claims for similar
and overlapping sectors of the Antarctic and sent naval vessels to the
area. Thus in order to maintain surveillance and to ensure the security
of Drake Passage for allied shipping, two military bases were established in 1944, one on Deception Island and one on Wiencke Island
near the coast of the Peninsula. In 1945 another was established on
the tip of the Peninsula at Hope Bay (Dater, 1975). All were transferred to civilian hands after the war to become the Falkland Islands

Dependencies Survey (F.I.D.S.). Chile and Argentina then established bases in the same area. There ensued a period of considerable diplomatic fencing which was typified by the sudden appearance of huts, claims in cairns, etc. as each nation tried to demonstrate its 'effective occupation' of the sector. The political machinations are well demonstrated by extracts from the diplomatic exchanges following an incident when Argentinians fired over the heads of a British party landing at Hope Bay in February 1952. The British Ambassador in Buenos Aires wrote: 'Hope Bay is a British base which has been occupied for five years continuously and there are British properties and British graves on the shore….' Further, the Argentine party 'adopted a most threatening attitude'. In reply the Argentine Foreign Minister explained that '…Hope Bay is situated in Argentine antarctic territory'. Further, the action by the 'commander of the naval detachment at Hope Bay… could, in principle, only be regarded as an excess of zeal in the defence of the national territory of the Republic' (*Polar Record*, 1954). Another flurry of exchanges followed when both Argentina and Chile erected huts on the airstrip (and football pitch!) of the British Deception Island base in 1953 (Figure 14.9). Other countries were involved in the strategic posturing. One of the aims of the U.S. 1946–47 Operation Highjump in the unclaimed area of Antarctica was to consolidate U.S. sovereignty as a basis for future claims (Hanessian, 1964), while an expedition led by Commander Ronne and fully backed by the U.S. government established a base next to the F.I.D.S. Stonington Base in 1947/48 (Dater, 1975). Australia, worried by international tensions, established Mawson Base on the mainland in 1954–55. One of the aims of this Australian National Antarctic Research Expedition was 'to maintain Australian and British interests in Antarctica' (Hanessian, 1964).

The wave of strategic interest stimulated the initial settlements of Antarctica in the 1940s and 1950s and the resulting pattern is illustrated in Figure 14.12a. The relationship of the bases to political sectors may be appreciated by comparing Figure 14.12 with Figure 8.18. The cluster of settlements in the Antarctic Peninsula area coincides with the zone of conflicting claims. However, ease of sea access is also likely to explain the extraordinary density of bases in this sector. The Australian base of Mawson, the only one in East Antarctica, is on the coast south of Australia. It is worth noting that the total population involved in this phase of settlement was less than 100 (Figure 14.10).

Antarctica was rescued from a future of international conflict by the International Geophysical Year in 1957. This wave of scientific

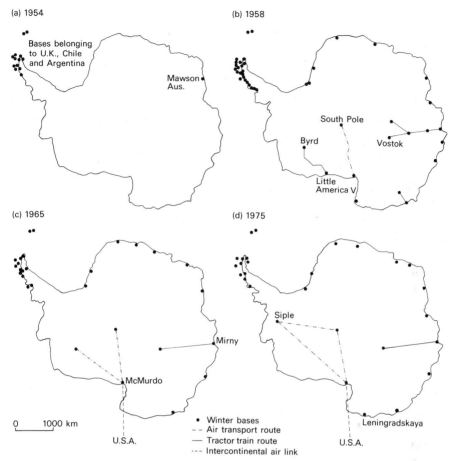

(a) 1954

Bases belonging to U.K., Chile and Argentina

Mawson Aus.

(b) 1958

South Pole

Byrd

Vostok

Little America V

(c) 1965

0   1000 km

U.S.A.

Mirny

McMurdo

(d) 1975

Siple

Leningradskaya

U.S.A.

• Winter bases
-- Air transport route
— Tractor train route
--- Intercontinental air link

FIGURE 14.12   The location of all-year-round bases in Antarctica: *(a)* 1954 (before the International Geophysical Year); *(b)* 1958 (during the International Geophysical Year); *(c)* 1965 and *(d)* 1975.

interest established the basic settlement pattern of today. The idea of the I.G.Y. arose in scientific circles and was an attempt to coordinate new geophysical techniques on a world scale. Its particular concern was with the upper atmosphere and meteorology. The period 1st July, 1957–31st December, 1958 was suitable because it coincided with a period of high sunspot activity. At its peak the project involved 30 000 scientists and technicians from 66 nations managing more than 1 000 stations girdling the Earth. The Antarctic was uniquely important to such a project because of its crucial position near the South Magnetic Pole and its role as one of the world's great heat sinks. The importance of the Antarctic contribution was accepted by various nations interested in Antarctica and an amazingly successful and huge multinational enterprise was set in motion. Thirteen nations established scientific bases in Antarctica, pushing the overwintering population almost to 900 people. By 1957 the U.S. had established South Pole Station, Byrd Station in interior West Antarctica and three coastal stations. The Soviets occupied five ice sheet stations in East Antarctica inland from the coastal stations of Mirny and Oazis. Australia, Chile, Argentina and Britain expanded existing bases or added new ones. The Commonwealth countries collaborated to pull off the Transantarctic Expedition (Fuchs and Hillary, 1958). Norway, Belgium, Japan, France and New Zealand built new stations on the coast of East Antarctica. Figure 14.12b represents the settlement pattern during the height of the I.G.Y. year. The distribution clearly shows that the basic scientific requirement of a scatter of bases throughout Antarctica was achieved, and there is no doubt that this goal was important in favouring the overall distribution and also an important factor in ensuring the great success of the venture. Nevertheless it would be wrong to underestimate the political and strategic considerations which were still important and doubtless had much to do with the ready acceptance of the project by all governments. The U.S. Amundsen—Scott base at the South Pole was not situated for scientific reasons but because of the obvious political implications of a base at the point where all political claims met. Again the East/West cold war attitudes of the time were mirrored in Antarctica. The Russians were confined to East Antarctica while the U.S. scattered its bases strategically throughout West Antarctica. One purpose of siting Ellsworth base on the Weddell Sea coast was to forestall the construction of a Russian base there (Hanessian, 1964).

As explained in Chapter 8 the success of the I.G.Y. led to the Antarctic Treaty of 1959 which came into force in 1961. The scientific cooperation of the I.G.Y. and results were demonstratably valuable, and further international cooperation offered the politically attractive device of side-stepping the controversy surrounding claims. Thus the decision was reached by most contributing nations to carry on scientific observations. Whereas some withdrew, for example Belgium, others rationalized their base structure to produce a slimmer infrastructure better suited to longer-term aims appropriate for an international continent for science. The maps in Figure 14.12c and 14.12d illustrate these changes, which focus in the reduction of duplicate bases, particularly in the Antarctic Peninsula area and among the Russian interior stations. Also changes in the location of bases took place probably for a combination of scientific and political reasons. Thus the site of Siple station was chosen on scientific grounds to be the conjugate magnetic station of Roberval, Quebec. On the other hand the decision to rebuild

Amundsen-Scott station on the South Pole rather than try another more suitable scientific location was presumably political. The Soviets have expanded their sphere of influence to a much wider area in Antarctica, including the Antarctic Peninsula area. This could be interpreted in political as well as scientific terms.

In Figure 14.7 the strategic wave is shown to be subsumed by the wave of scientific interest in Antarctica. Strategic and scientific motives are largely in agreement in favouring an international continent with political claims frozen, and it is difficult to separate the two issues today. After all, governments go to great lengths to establish 'effective occupancy' through the common device of running post offices at scientific bases, (Figure 8.19), and such rarer occupations as executing marriage ceremonies, registering births and erecting provocative signs (Figure 14.13).

Perhaps it is worth registering surprise that the number of bases has not decreased more sharply. One can argue that on scientific grounds

FIGURE 14.13
The sign which greeted visitors to the Argentine base of Esperanza in 1979.

alone one would have predicted a decline. Much basic mapping is complete, while increasingly sophisticated remote sensing techniques reduce the need for much ground survey and field observation. Again, automatic ground stations could, and do, carry out routine monitoring and transmit their data to satellites. Further, many scientific programmes can be carried out efficiently and economically from temporary summer camps, as for example in the case of the Ross Ice Shelf Program. The expected decline in numbers of permanent bases has occurred in selected cases, for example in relation to U.S. and U.K. activities (Figure 14.14). The fact that it has not occurred elsewhere presumably points to the underlying importance of strategic and political considerations. Be that as it may, one can conclude that scientific and political considerations acting in concert have maintained a relatively stable settlement pattern for over 20 years.

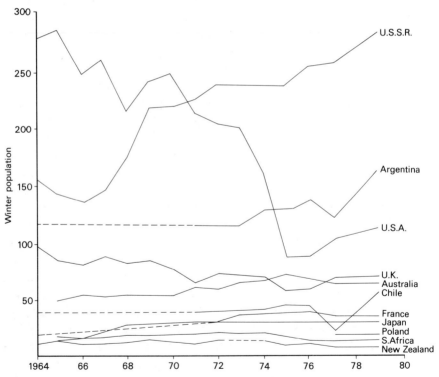

FIGURE 14.14   Total overwintering population in Antarctica by nationalities, 1964—79.

The final economic wave is shown in Figure 14.7 as affecting the sub-Antarctic and, increasingly, the continent proper. Economic exploitation is already taking place in antarctic waters while the realization that oil is within reach has increased awareness of economic potentials. The exploitation of antarctic waters includes minke whales, fish and krill. Since 1961 increasing quantities of krill have been harvested by Japan, Poland, West Germany and Chile and is marketed as paste, boiled or raw krill, krill fingers and mince (Mitchell and Tinker, 1980). In 1978 the catch amounted to 200000 tons. Fish were first caught commercially by Soviet ships round South Georgia in 1969 and round Kerguelen in 1971—74. Although there are signs that the South Georgia grounds were over-fished in 1970, East German and Polish fleets have since joined the fishery and the catch is expanding rapidly (Mitchell and Tinker, 1980). In 1977 some 30—40 ships caught almost 280000 tons in all. There is no exploitation of minerals yet. However, the potential for oil and gas in the offshore basins has already attracted commercial enquiries now that technological problems are overcome; drilling has been successfully accomplished in the Arctic in the difficult pack ice conditions of the Beaufort Sea, while in 1979 ocean drilling was successfully undertaken at depths of over 1500m. Submarine terminals and storage tanks used to fill visiting tankers are quite feasible.

It is not clear how this recent wave of economic interest has affected the settlements in Antarctica. The marine exploitation is from factory ships and does not involve land stations, except in a supervisory or surveillance capacity. The prospect of oil exploitation cannot be demonstrated to have affected the settlements yet. However, it has focused attention on an issue which will be crucial to the successful renegotiation of the Antarctic Treaty during the late 1980s. There are signs of increasing nationalism from claimant countries like Argentina, Chile, Australia and New Zealand. This can be seen in political statements, as well as in increases in the numbers of certain nationals in Antarctica (Chile, Argentina), in plans to increase operations (Australia) or to initiate them (West Germany). The role of economic exploitation is clearly stated in Russian geological programmes (Avsyuk and Kartashov, 1975) and it seems that the Soviet summer base of Druzhnaya on the Weddell Sea coast, which was used for a few years in the 1970s, was positioned specifically to explore the possibilities for oil in the Weddell Sea and the potential of the Dufek Massif for other minerals.

In summary, the history of Antarctic settlement is punctuated by waves of interest from the world's cores. These waves are very similar to those experienced in the Arctic in both type and duration. However, the effect has been for settlements to be temporary and to rise and fall with the amplitude and strength of the wave.

The functioning of the spatial system

Perspective on the operation of the Antarctic settlement system may be gained by comparison with the models used as yardsticks in an Arctic context. In the case of the network model of Taaffe, Morrill and Gould (1963), Antarctica provides an interesting field laboratory for the study of the evolution of a settlement pattern from scratch. Friedmann's concept of a Resource Frontier Region (1966) is likewise illuminating, even in such an extreme situation.

NETWORKS

There appears to be a similarity between the ring of coastal bases on the coast of Antarctica and Stage I in Taaffe, Morrill and Gould's model. The bases can be envisaged as ports tapping local resources (scientific in nature) and with little communication inland or with each other. However, such an analogy must be treated with care, especially since, unlike the case of the model there is no indigenous population or economy in Antarctica.

The location of the coastal bases in Antarctica reflects factors operating at different scales. Political/strategic/economic factors affect the general location on the coastline of Antarctica. Claimant states have bases in their perceived national territory while non-claimant states choose sites of some international significance; for example, the U.S.S.R. has bases in a number of different political sectors. A second factor is accessibility in terms of pack ice: 56 per cent of the coastal bases occur along the 18 per cent of the Antarctic coastline that is seasonally ice-free. The seasonally ice-free Antarctic Peninsula has obvious advantages to countries without ice-breakers such as the U.K. and Poland. Also, the ice-free parts of East Antarctica are fully utilized. McMurdo station was located mainly because of its easy access in terms of limited sea ice, while the string of bases on the eastern shore of the Weddell Sea exploit a moat of summer clear water. The importance of easy access is illustrated by the absence of bases on the ice-impeded western shore of the Weddell Sea and also on the ice-infested coasts of the Bellingshausen and Amundsen Seas. Operating at a more local scale site conditions play a role. Coastal rock sites are most favoured. They have obvious advantages of permanence in that they do not become submerged by snow (if care is taken to avoid large snowdrifts building up around the buildings). Where rock is unavailable on a given stretch of coast then ice shelves have to be utilized. In these cases the bases need replacement every 10 years or so as they become too deep or calve off the continent in an iceberg. An example of the role of site conditions is illustrated in the case of Druzhnaya. The lack of a suitable site meant the base was moved 200 miles east of the planned location.

Stage II of Taaffe, Morrill and Gould's model has clearly evolved in the operations of the two largest powers, the U.S.A. and the U.S.S.R. Interior bases have been established to exploit scientific or political objectives. In each case a supply transport route has been established from a suitable coastal base and this coastal base has grown in importance. McMurdo is the clearest example. Originally McMurdo was never envisaged as a scientific site, and it was intended purely as a logistics base to supply the South Pole station (Dater, 1966). It had advantages of sea access and air strips which could be used by international wheeled aircraft (sea ice) and by intracontinental aircraft fitted with skis (ice shelf). After the I.G.Y., McMurdo captured the functions of the adjacent coastal base, Little America V, and became fully responsible for supplying Byrd Station, scene of the momentous drill hole right through the ice sheet. Today it supports Amundsen–Scott Station and numerous summer parties in the adjacent Transantarctic Mountains. The Soviet example is less clear but the original coastal base of Mirny first grew in importance as the access port to interior Russian stations. Now, however, the role is being lost to Molodezhnaya which can take intercontinental air flights via South Africa, and in recent years the latter base has grown at the expense of Mirny. Yet another evolving pattern concerns the Argentine base of Vicecomodoro Marambio. Its role as an air terminal for flights from South America made it Argentina's largest base in 1977.

The level of development of the transport network has important implications concerning the function of the whole system. This is best illustrated by the contrast between the Stage II air-supported U.S. logistics and those less developed systems of other countries. The greater efficiency of the U.S. operation allows a greater seasonal contrast in that more scientists fly in for the summer only. Thus the summer population on U.S. bases is eight times higher than the winter complement. In most other national efforts the summer population is only 2–3 times higher than the winter population. Also the U.S.A. rely on wheeled landings on sea ice at McMurdo, while ship-based operations rely on the ice breaking up. Thus U.S. summer programmes tend to begin earlier in the year and last for a longer time than those of other nations.

Stage III of the Taaffe, Morrill and Gould model did not apply to Antarctica in the 1970s. There was little effective transport between bases of different nations. To have such transport would involve a measure of international cooperation of sufficient importance to override purely national considerations. In this context it is interesting to see the air bus proposal put forward by the U.S.A. in 1973 (Smith and Dana, 1973). The idea was to use McMurdo and Vicecomodoro Marambio as intercontinental terminals approached regularly by wheeled or ski-equipped Hercules aircraft (Figure 14.15). From these

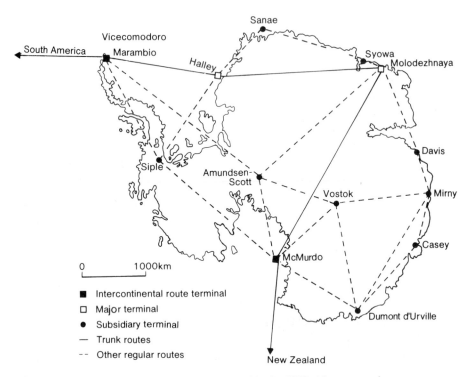

FIGURE 14.15   The network of routes envisaged in the 1973 airbus proposal.

bases ski-equipped Hercules were to fly regular schedules to intracontinental terminals, including as a minimum requirement, Halley and Molodezhnaya. A number of secondary bases could also be served by Hercules. Smaller planes would distribute personnel and supplies to other bases or field camps in the appropriate sectors. A regular system of flights on such a network would have had three advantages:

(1) intercontinental access in summer to all of the Antarctica;
(2) intercontinental travel in winter to selected locations;
(3) enhanced international cooperation.

Such a system would have been an immense boon to scientific work in Antarctica, which is so often crippled by the length of time wasted in travelling to and from an antarctic field area by ship. Its successful introduction would have involved the sacrifice of a degree of national autonomy by all nations concerned. Sadly, the proposal has not yet come to fruition and one is left with the uncomfortable feeling that in the 1970s concern for national activities outweighed the interests of science *per se.*

CORE/PERIPHERY

There is no sign that any nation in Antarctica is striving for permanent settlement based on self-sustaining economic development. Thus it may seem superfluous to discuss Antarctica in terms of Friedmann's model of development, which pre-supposes such a goal. Nevertheless, Antarctica is an extreme example of a periphery and as such may allow new perspectives to be gained. If, for example, it can be demonstrated that Antarctica is an extreme version of a Resource Frontier Region, then at least one learns of some of the problems likely to be involved in any broad economic development. It is with this aim in mind that, as in earlier chapters, Antarctica is compared with the characteristics of a Resource Frontier Region (as listed in Table 1.2).

1. Dependent on one economic resource, usually minerals. Although minerals have not yet been exploited, Antarctic bases owe their existence to the exploitation of one resource—science. Earlier, the whaling stations were unmistakably based on one resource. Such a dependence implies that settlements are highly susceptible to changes in the need for that resource — as the ghost whaling stations bear mute witness (Figure 14.8).

2. Investment is commonly foreign. Friedmann's point was that the host nation did not have control over development if the resources were being tapped by foreign concerns and that this made long-term planning difficult. A similar idea is relevant to Antarctica. If the future of Antarctica as a unit is considered, then one of the major problems will be to coordinate 'foreign' investment which is so susceptible to changes of circumstances at the core. Thus, cuts in the U.K. and U.S. Antarctic programmes in the early 1980s, which were taken for internal political reasons, modify the infrastructure in Antarctica. The closure of Siple by the U.S. and the proposal to axe summer cruises by H.M.S. *Endurance* by the U.K. are two examples.

3. Conflict between the economic goals of industry and the social goals of government. This is not a problem in Antarctica. In the Arctic social problems associated with development have commonly revolved round the indigenous population. The lack of such a population in Antarctica makes such a concept irrelevant.

4. Centred on a town/city with specialized but very limited functions, which may not achieve critical size for self-sustaining growth. The larger antarctic bases can be regarded as extreme examples of settlements with specialized but very limited functions. Nonetheless the small size of the bases serves to illustrate how remote is the prospect of normal towns in Antarctica. The total population of the whole continent in winter is less than 1 000.

5. Transport and labour costs are high due to remoteness and the high level of technology. An analysis in 1969 suggested that costs per man in a coastal station like McMurdo amounted to U.S.$23 000 per man per year and at an inland ice sheet station U.S.$102 000 per man per year (Potter, 1969). At the time these costs exceeded those in all except the highest technology chemical and mining industries, a situation which probably still applies today. If so, then mineral and fuel extraction in Antarctica seem the main economic possibilities. The same study concluded that sea transport costs varied from about twice to ten times the costs in temperate regions, depending on the ice-breaker support needed. Air transport was estimated as 3–5 times greater than U.S. air freight costs and 30–40 times greater than U.S. rail freight costs. Put another way fuel obtained from the U.S. in the 1960s increased in value 3–4 times by the time it reached Antarctica. These figures serve to emphasize the extreme disadvantages that would be faced by any economic activity other than mining in Antarctica.

6. Special social structure — transients, male, single. The all-male Antarctic base consisting of personnel wintering for one or two seasons is a classic and extreme case of the special social structures experienced in remote Resource Frontier Regions. The prospect of normal mixed settlements with separate family houses is distant indeed.

The conclusion to be reached from this comparison of Antarctica with Friedmann's model is that many of the characteristics of a Resource Frontier Region do apply, only in a most extreme fashion. The comparison highlights the problems that would be faced if a broad strategy for economic development were ever to emerge. On the other hand there are indications that some mining activities could be economic at the present day.

Contrasts with the Arctic

The preceding sections allow comparisons to be made with the Arctic. The main and obvious difference is that the level of Antarctic development is exceedingly low. There seem to be four important reasons for this state of affairs.

First, although the intrusive waves of economic exploitation which struck Antarctica were similar to these affecting the Arctic, the result was different. The crucial contrast with the Arctic has been the lack of continuity from wave to wave which allows a settlement to grow stage by stage and develop more than one function. The nearest approach to this in Antarctica has been the whaling settlement of Grytviken, where a scientific base using the former administrative buildings has maintained continuity of settlement since the whaling activities ceased. The reason for the lack of continuity probably relates to the lack of an indigenous population. In the Arctic such peoples were attracted to settlements for trade. The presence of families and children then led to the arrival of churches, missions, schools, shops and the full panoply of administration. These other functions carried some settlements from wave to wave so that stage by stage they grew. In Antarctica the settlements never knew such continuity. It was precisely the lack of such church, educational and medical facilities which so surprised the doctor visiting Stromness whaling station in the 1950s (Robertson, 1956). It is probably fair to suggest that it is the lack of an indigenous population in Antarctica which has fostered the characteristic, one-purpose, base settlement staffed by a largely male population. Furthermore, it is these characteristics which have made them so temporary.

The second reason closely follows from the first. It is that the lack of an indigenous population has meant that there has been no pressure for development from local inhabitants. Further, the intrusive powers have felt no moral obligation to embark on a programme of development, such as occurred, for example, in Greenland.

The third reason is pertinent today. It concerns the political uncertainty in Antarctica. Industrial concerns are not going to invest in Antarctica unless they can be assured of security and economic benefits. The present freezing of political claims makes any such assurance impossible to give.

The fourth reason for the low level of development is likely to be remoteness and the difficulty of the environment, although this is probably overplayed. In the continental interior the difficulties of exploiting sub-ice minerals are huge and costs immense. In coastal Antarctica, however, costs and environmental conditions would seem comparable to parts of the Arctic already being exploited. In these cases lack of development probably reflects the other factors.

Finally it is interesting to note a curious similarity between development in the Arctic and Antarctica. It comes from the national nature of Antarctic operations which means that the continent is evolving as a series of independent enclaves. The settlement structure has not yet begun to evolve as a single integrated antarctic system. This is reminiscent of the Arctic where, for example, the adjacent territories of Arctic Canada and Greenland are evolving quite separately. Nevertheless it comes as something of a disappointment in view of the hopes of an international approach to Antarctica. In a nutshell development is multinational rather than international.

The future spatial system in Antarctica

It may seem irrelevant to waste the reader's time on a discussion of the future of Antarctica. However, in this case I believe it is important for as many people as possible to contemplate the choices facing Antarctica. The future of Antarctica will come up for renegotiation when the existing Antarctic Treaty completes its term in 1991. There is a risk that the real advantages to be gained from the international scientific cooperation embodied in the 1959 Treaty will not withstand the pressures for economic exploitation and that there will be no replacement Treaty. Moreover any such breakdown may partly reflect the complacency of scientists and the general public who genuinely believe that the international approach is secure. As has been implied at several stages in this chapter, the image of international scientific cooperation often seems dangerously brittle. The scientific image has happened to suit political motives.

The benefits flowing from the Antarctic Treaty are immense. In place of the slide into political and even military rivalry which seemed only too likely in the early 1950s, the Antarctic Treaty has substituted an atmosphere of peace and cooperation. Potential political conflicts have simply been frozen. The original 12 signatories and countries which have acceded to the Treaty subsequently have found themselves bound together by a series of worthwhile goals. The continent has been the preserve of peace; it avoided the ravages of the cold war and incidentally was the first post-war multinational treaty of importance to involve the Soviet Union. Cooperation in scientific programmes, and the free exchange of information among scientists, has led to spectacular and fundamental advances in the earth sciences, the marine sciences, atmospheric sciences, and glaciology. Great progress has been made on the conservation of terrestrial and marine living resources and, for example, many sites of special scientific interest have been highlighted and protected. In 1980 a convention on the conservation of antarctic marine living resources was finally agreed. This latter agreement involves controls on the ecosystem as a whole and especially on the exploitation of krill, fish, seals and whales (Edwards and Heap, 1981). There is administrative machinery whereby international cooperation takes place, for example the Scientific Committee on Antarctic Research (S.C.A.R.). This impressive list of achievements is by no means comprehensive, and other benefits are discussed by the late Brian Roberts (1978).

The problem as the Treaty comes up for renegotiation is that the lure of rich resources may cause nationalist instincts to override the benefits of international scientific cooperation. The problem is highly complex and national viewpoints are very divergent. On the one hand there are the claimant countries who wish to benefit from the exploitation of minerals in 'their' territory. Perhaps their viewpoint can be summarized by an Australian statement at the ninth Antarctic Treaty meeting in London in 1977 to the effect that resource arrangements 'must include tangible benefits for the claimant states'. On the other hand there are the rights of non-claimant states active in Antarctica such as the U.S.A. and U.S.S.R. A U.S. government statement in 1975 emphasized the right of non-claimant countries 'to commence mineral resource activities at their will'. Finally there is a wider international dimension. To the majority of countries in the world, the Antarctic Treaty nations are seen as an exclusive club and there is increasing articulation of the view put forward by the United Nations in 1970 that Antarctic resources are 'the common heritage of mankind'.

Faced with this background the choice is obviously difficult. One extreme is to ban mineral development altogether. This is unlikely to get international support if only because it would seem to be a conspiracy among the developed countries which was acting against the interests of developing countries who need the resources. Another extreme is to allow claimant countries full rights to land and offshore resources. This would be unacceptable to non-claimants. Moreover it is likely to lead to friction between rival claimants in the Antarctic Peninsula area. This would be an unedifying end to the Antarctic Treaty. An intermediate position seems the only chance. Somehow the agreement must benefit claimants, non-claimants active in Antarctica and the wider community, and yet preserve the benefits that come from international scientific cooperation and environmental control.

Given the impossibility of a diplomatic conjuring trick that would suit everyone, Roberts (1978) made the elegant suggestion that claimant nations should simply waive their ownership claims to the resources but not their territorial claims. This would allow the territorial claims to be frozen for the duration of another treaty. Exploitation would then be carried out under the environmental controls of the Antarctic Treaty by any company which so wished. Royalties could be paid via a licence to exploit a given resource. In order to satisfy the legitimate demands of the wider international community, royalties could be used to promote additional international research in Antarctica for the benefit of all. Roberts recognized that such an arrangement would smack of control by an exclusive club and suggested that the Antarctic Treaty signatories made moves to become recognized as trustees working as representatives of the United Nations as a whole. To describe one suggestion is not to eliminate the possibility of alternative scenarios. However it does serve to highlight the dangers presented to the multinational approach to Antarctica by the discovery of minerals.

The future human spatial system in Antarctica will depend on the choice that finally emerges. One scenario, and an optimistic one, is that the international aspects of Antarctica will thrive. In such a case one can look forward to the development of an integrated infrastructure, perhaps along the lines of the U.S. airbus proposal, with McMurdo and a location in the northern Antarctic Peninsula (such as Vicecomodoro Marambio or one of the South Shetland Island bases) emerging as the main nodes. These nodes would acquire extra logistic functions as they channelled scientists in and out of Antarctica. Perhaps, if international progress triumphed, the number of outlying bases would decline, especially in the overcrowded Antarctic Peninsula area. The main nodes would also be likely to form the centres of economic and environmental monitoring activities; in addition to good access by air, both nodes would be accessible by sea and both are close to the potential oilfields.

Another scenario, and a pessimistic one, is that national rivalry in Antarctica will grow. Rather than an integrated continental infrastructure, one would expect the preservation and development of separate and competing national spatial systems. There are likely to be more bases and they are likely to remain small and highly specialized. Economic activities would be competitive among nations and would inevitably lead to defensive measures. Probably there would be a growth of bases which are little more than military outposts.

At present the spatial system in Antarctica reflects a compromise between the processes of international idealism and national interests. In a nutshell it reflects a national approach yet one that is cooperative. One hopes that renegotiation of the Antarctic Treaty can be seen as an opportunity to promote the true international development and conservation of Antarctica and avoid the dangers of national rivalry.

Further reading

Dater, H. M. 1966: Organizational developments in the United States Antarctic Program, 1954–65. *Antarctic Journal of the United States*, 1, 21–32.

Dater, H. M. 1975: *History of Antarctic exploration and scientific investigation.* American Geographical Society, Antarctic Map Folio Series 19.

King, H. G. R. 1969: *The Antarctic.* Blandford, London.

Mitchell, B. and Tinker, J. 1980: *Antarctica and its resources.* Earthscan, London.

Roberts, B. B. 1978: International cooperation for Antarctic development: the test for the Antarctic Treaty. *Polar Record*, 19 (119), 107–20.

Smith, P. M. and Dana, J. B. 1973: Airbus: an international air transportation system for Antarctica. *Antarctic Journal of the United States*, 8, 16–19.

Note added in proof

The military confrontation which broke out in South Georgia in 1982 seems to reinforce the warning sounded in this chapter.

CHAPTER FIFTEEN

Conclusion:
Towards Principles of
Polar Regional Geography

In an attempt to put the regional geography of the polar regions in a wider context, this chapter is structured around a series of generalizations or principles which emerge from study of the area. The hope is that such generalizations will add perspective, challenge assumptions and raise new questions. Perhaps too they may pose questions about areas outside the polar regions.

Natural environment

1. *The image of the polar regions as a cold waste hostile to man is a temperate viewpoint.*
This popular image is a far cry from that of the indigenous peoples. To a hunter the area offers many possibilities; in particular, the large herds of single species which collect seasonally in polar seas and on land are a rich resource. As suggested in Chapter 8, in Upper Palaeolithic times the tundra was apparently a choice area for contemporary mankind and associated with the flowering of culture. Even the idea of extreme polar cold needs to be qualified. The coldest part of the northern hemisphere in terms of absolute temperature is in the sub-Arctic, while the summer temperatures of continental tundra areas can frequently exceed 30°C. Parts of the Antarctic, too, are warmer than commonly supposed and even part of the antarctic continental coast would appear mild to a Canadian or northern Scandinavian.

2. *The ecosystems of the polar regions are not as 'fragile' as popularly supposed.*
It has tended to be assumed that the small number of species and slow growth rates of polar ecosystems makes them fragile. This view has

received support from the rapid changes in population numbers which can occur following disturbance. However, it is normal for numbers to fluctuate widely. Indeed it is the flexibility provided by such oscillating behaviour which has provided polar ecosystems with their resilience and ability to survive such dramatic upheavals as repeated Ice Ages. An additional argument used in support of fragility is that disturbance of permafrost leads to irreversible changes. However, experience suggests that the effects are confined to those areas with a high proportion of ground ice and that even in such areas new stability is attained within a few years (Chapter 5). To state the above is not to decry the need for care. After all, man may have wiped out the woolly mammoth some 10 000 years ago using far less sophisticated weapons than are available today.

3. *The polar regions are particularly sensitive to environmental change.*
There seem two main reasons for this. In the first place the amplitude of natural environmental fluctuations is higher in parts of the Arctic than elsewhere. As an example one can point to the temperature fluctuations in Franz Josef Land over the last half-century (Chapter 7). This sensitivity is related to the strong dependence of arctic temperatures on the northward flow of warm air and ocean water in the North Atlantic; small perturbations in these flows can have a major effect in the Arctic. In the second place, small temperature fluctuations can have an exaggerated effect on the distribution of ice in the polar regions. Sea-ice extent varies from year to year and can make the difference between a good and a bad summer along a particular coast. Sea-ice variations also have important biogeographical effects. For example, whales were able to thrive in the Canadian straits during the Climate Optimum about 5 000 years ago, but are unable to exist there today under present ice conditions. The same sensitivity applies to ice sheets. Since the last glacial maximum the Laurentide ice sheet crossed the threshold of survival and disappeared. The adjacent Greenland ice sheet did not cross the threshold and still exists. One suspects that only a small environmental change is necessary either to remove the West Antarctic ice sheet or even to rebuild the Laurentide ice sheet.

4. *The physical resource base on land is similar to that in other parts of the world, except that effective agriculture is impossible.*
The implication to be drawn from the theory of plate tectonics is that the probability of mineral discoveries in the polar regions is as high as anywhere else on earth. Broad structural considerations suggest that the Antarctic is comparable to South America in mineral resources while

the Arctic may have rather more oil than is average for the world as a whole (Chapter 2). The inability to plant crops has been a fundamental constraint on human activity. Whereas, during man's stage of hunting and gathering, the Arctic was in the forefront of human evolution, after the Neolithic farming stage, it progressively fell back.

5. *The marine resource base is unusually rich in sub-polar waters in summer, but is hardly tapped around Antarctica where the sustainable yield amounts to twice the world's fish catch.*

The mixing of waters of different characteristics and upwelling provides minerals, while the long summer daylight of polar latitudes provides the basis for a plankton boom. This resource is exploited by animals such as whales and seals which migrate to polar seas in summer and are easy to catch. Following the decline of whale numbers in the Antarctic, there is a vast surplus of krill, their former staple food. The maximum sustainable yield of krill is though to be twice the world fish catch of the late 1970s, but it is only tentatively exploited at present. Whaling was and is one way of tapping this resource. It seems doubtful whether the world can afford to neglect this major resource.

Development

6. *The human spatial systems in the Arctic reflect the impact of intrusive waves of economic development superimposed on an indigenous system.*

All arctic areas except Svalbard supported indigenous populations subsisting on local resources. Waves of economic exploitation have intruded into the Arctic from the world's cores. Such waves have been stimulated by the needs of the core, and any products have been extracted for the use of the core. This is best illustrated today by oil and other minerals which are streaming from the Arctic to the North American, European, Soviet and Japanese cores. Former economic waves of diffusion have punctuated the evolution of the polar regions. Seals and whales have been the cause of economically motivated waves into the coastal Arctic, while furs from land animals attracted the exploitation of arctic land areas. Strategic and political waves of interest in the polar regions have been instigated by the need to defend the interests of the core. Finally, even the history of geographical exploration and the Vikings' colonization of Greenland can be seen as a series of waves responding to the activities of the core.

7. *Modern spatial systems in the polar regions have been influenced both by the presence and type of indigenous system and by the political approach of the intrusive system.*

Unlike the Arctic, the Antarctic had no indigenous population and this is probably the most important factor influencing the contrast in settlement styles between the two areas; whereas towns exist in the Arctic, the Antarctic can boast none. The lack of an indigenous population meant that there could be no spontaneous growth of towns by immigration and thus no pressure or need for further development (Chapter 14). The type of indigenous system may also have influenced modern spatial systems, although its role is less clear. Within the Arctic the main contrast was between the hunting Inuit cultures of North America and Greenland, with a sparse and isolated coastal population, and the reindeer-herding cultures of Arctic Asia, with a denser population exploiting the interior and with contacts with the south. Perhaps the greater population density and the pre-existing contacts with the south has made it easier for Arctic Asians to participate in modern urban development.

The contrasts between the communist, paternalistic and capitalist approaches to arctic development by the Soviet Union, Denmark and North America respectively, are fascinating. When measured strictly in terms of the level of the existing infrastructure, the arctic territories of each may be ranked with the Soviet Union first, Denmark second, and Alaska and Canada third. The Soviet system of long-term planning supported by massive investment over decades, or longer if necessary, is well suited to large-scale arctic development. Losses can be sustained for much longer than is possible in a capitalist system. Investment in the Northern Sea Route stands out not only because of its vast scale but also because much of it preceded economic development. The same is true of the railways which are planned on a large scale to help initiate development. It is difficult to imagine an all-year-round Northwest Passage route being created by the U.S. or Canadian governments unless economic demands made it necessary; in the capitalist Arctic, planning has tended to follow economic exploitation. The paternalistic Danish approach lies in an interesting intermediate position. It has allowed Greenland to be artificially protected from the wider world and this, in turn, has allowed medium-term plans of infrastructure development to be carried out successfully.

It must be emphasized that the level of the infrastructure in an area is not the same thing as a measure of success. It could be that an urban infrastructure is not the best way to develop the Arctic (see point number 13).

8. *The Taaffe, Morrill and Gould model of infrastructure evolution (1963) helps explain the reasons for the location of development, namely,*

   (a) *penetration 'inland' takes place for economic and political reasons,*

   (b) *the shape of the infrastructure depends on the shape of the area and the 'coastline' of access,*

   (c) *Stage II occurs when one resource is exploited, Stage III when the base is broader. Natural gas seems to justify links running directly between source and market reminiscent of Stage IV.*

(a) Penetration 'inland' has taken place for economic reasons. Examples of this are oil exploitation at Prudhoe Bay in Alaska and in western Siberia, and metal and ferrous minerals in eastern Siberia and the Yukon. 'Inland' penetration for political/strategic motives can be illustrated by Amundsen–Scott base at the South Pole in Antarctica, by the military developments in Alaska and Arctic Canada as well as by the construction of administrative towns such as Inuvik in northern Canada. These reasons are identical to those discovered to to be important in Nigeria by Taaffe, Morrill and Gould. Indeed the main difference is that, whereas the tapping of agricultural resources was important in Nigeria, it has had no part to play in the polar regions. On the other hand, early trading posts exploiting fur are a close analogy, and they were sited on lines of communication in positions to exploit local resource areas.

(b) The influence of the shape of an area of development and its relationship to a line of access is a point which is not always easy to study objectively. Perhaps Figure 15.1 is too obvious to merit

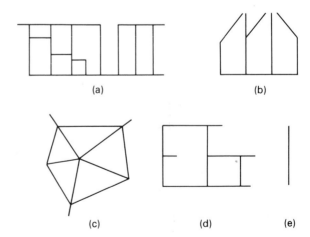

(a)   (b)

FIGURE 15.1
Contrasting shapes of
emerging transport infra-
structures: *(a)* Soviet Arctic,
(b) Arctic Canada,
(c) Antarctica, *(d)* Alaska
and *(e)* Greenland.

(c)   (d)   (e)

serious attention! However the contrast between the rectangular grid-like pattern of communications in Siberia and the conical pattern of air routes in Arctic Canada could be due to the shape of the respective areas; north—south lines of communication are the main means of communication in box-like Siberia, while in the case of Canada these 'inland' centres happen to coincide at the site of Resolute and Inuvik simply because the arctic north is narrower than the south. Using similar arguments one might suggest that, given further development, the circular outline of Antarctica will ensure a radial or triangular network of routes, while box-like Alaska could be well served by a rectangular grid. A single axis is adequate for Greenland's strip of development.

(c) The simplest communications infrastructure with lines running inland from an external 'coastline' dominate in those areas where one or two resources are being exploited. One can point to several instances in eastern Siberia where a simple Stage II infrastructure is associated with the exploitation of minerals like tin or gold. Further, the simple inland axis to Prudhoe Bay in Alaska is associated with the one resource of oil while in eastern Arctic Canada, where activity is concerned with either mineral exploration or administration, there is also a simple Stage II structure. In Antarctica too, the inland stations represent a Stage II infrastructure and exploit one political/scientific 'resource'. The only polar areas where a Stage III network has evolved are in western Siberia and the Yukon—Alaska area. Both areas rely on the exploitation of a number of minerals, and have an important strategic/military role. Shield minerals, fuels and fish products are exploited in western Siberia while Murmansk and other coastal ports have important strategic activities. In Alaska and Yukon Territories also, several minerals and fuels are exploited. In addition, the Alaska Highway and other cross-links were built for strategic reasons.

It could be suggested that there are tentative signs of a Stage IV transport network in that both continents contain (or soon will contain) gas pipelines which directly link source of supply with major centre of demand. Thus the Soviets have a pipe leading from the giant Urengoy gas field directly to Moscow. The North Americans will soon have a pipe which runs first south from northern Alaska and then directly through Canada towards the pipeline networks of the industrial northeast. In both cases the pipelines are conceived on a sub-continental scale. Interestingly, part of both pipelines follows the line of pre-existing routes which themselves were a response to continental strategy, the Alaska Highway in North

America (Chapter 12) and the Vorkuta railway in the U.S.S.R. (Chapter 13). The analogy of these pipelines with Stage IV must be treated with circumspection. Although the pipelines represent a considerable degree of network integration, they are not accompanied by flows of a wider range of goods and people. Thus the processes are different to those envisaged by Taaffe, Morrill and Gould (1963).

It can be argued that this book has relied on comparison with the model evolved by Taaffe, Morrill and Gould to an unhealthy extent. The danger is that its employment focuses attention on those characteristics that fit the model, and diverts attention from those that do not. In such a case it is not surprising that polar route development seems to agree with the model. To avoid such a danger the reader is encouraged to scrutinize the descriptive maps relevant to each area and to focus on the assumptions made. In spite of the risks involved, however, the model does give important insights into the processes involved in the evolution and functioning of a transport infrastructure. Concepts such as the important role played by a 'coastline' of access, the process of 'port' competition following the exploitation of 'inland' resources, and the subsequent growth of intermediate nodes and transport links help to explain many polar patterns.

9. *The role of the natural environment in influencing the location of the spatial system has varied from place to place but in general is muted.*

The strongest influence of the natural environment on spatial human activity is in Greenland. Here, the central ice sheet has been largely avoided and, instead, activity is focused on those towns which have sea access uninterrupted by sea ice and which are close to the fishing grounds. Yet even here the relative vitality of the nodes reflects their position with regard to the rest of the spatial structure. There are other examples of the role of sea ice in influencing coastal access and thereby the spatial system. In Antarctica, McMurdo was chosen as a logistics base because it offered unimpeded access to ships in summer, while it is clear that the ice-infested Bellingshausen Sea remains an obstacle to settlement to this day. On the other hand, in the Soviet Arctic sea ice has not prevented massive investment in the western portion of the Northern Sea Route in an effort to provide year-round access to Noril'sk.

The natural environment has played a relatively minor role in influencing the location of transport links on land. One of the clearest examples of this comes from Alaska where the route structure cuts right across two mountain ranges from the southern coast. This is all the more striking when one realizes that the routes ignore the seasonally navigable Yukon River, which happens to flow in an 'unsuitable' east—west direction. In this case offshore ice conditions and the fact that development sprang from the south seem to have been the most important factors. It could be argued that the north—south alignment of transport routes in the Soviet Arctic reflects the importance of major rivers and thus the natural environment. However, north—south routes also exist in the eastern North American Arctic in spite of there being no rivers. One is left to conclude that it is access from the south and the presence of markets in the south that have played the dominant role in the alignment of transport routes.

Even the location of natural resources has had less effect on the spatial system than might have been expected. Minerals are known throughout the Soviet Arctic, yet development is concentrated in the west near the main markets. Rich minerals deposits are known in several parts of Arctic Canada, yet only the most accessible are utilized. In Alaska the oilfields first to be developed were all close to the main infrastructure. Also the only exploited coalfield in Alaska happens to be the one which lies on the railway.

10. *Friedmann's concepts of a Resource Frontier Region and a Downward Transitional Area (1966) add important perspectives to the Arctic.*

The fundamental feature of the Arctic is that intrusive economic development is associated with Resource Frontier Regions, most of which are well on the way to becoming extensions of their respective national cores. The indigenous economy, which is often quite separate, is not always part of this development and, instead, displays many characteristics of a Downward Transitional Area. In places the contrast between the two economies and the two types of area is subdued, but in other places it has crystallized out spatially. One of the clearest spatial contrasts emerged in Alaska in the 1960s and 1970s when the intrusive system of Anchorage and Fairbanks prospered as a developing Resource Frontier Region, while the Inuit of the north and west found themselves part of a Downward Transitional Area; in Alaska the strong U.S. faith in the virtues of development favoured a situation where the contrast emerged starkly. In Canada the contrast was somewhat less extreme, although even here social concern to raise the standard of living helped create a contrast between urban and rural populations; the towns are mainly filled by immigrants and are typical of Resource Frontier Regions while the small indigenous villages resemble Downward

Transitional Areas. In Greenland the integration of social and economic goals was more successful, but even so a contrast has emerged between the thriving fishing towns of the southwest and the hunting periphery; in this case Danish policy responded before the periphery developed too many characteristics of a Downward Transitional Area.

The Soviet case is more difficult to assess. The new towns peopled by immigrants are clearly characteristic of a Resource Frontier Region. But the role of the native peoples is not so clear. While in some regions such as Yakutsk, native peoples are clearly involved in economic development, in other parts they seem to have been deliberately separated from it and to have been encouraged to lead an essentially traditional way of life, even if partially relying on cash products.

11. *A distinctive type of Arctic Resource Frontier Region can be characterized as follows:*
    (a) *Dependent on the export of one or two economic resources, usually minerals;*
    (b) *investment is commonly foreign;*
    (c) *conflict between the economic goals of the intrusive system and the socio-economic goals of the indigenous system;*
    (d) *centres on a town/city, with specialized but very limited functions, which may not achieve critical size for self-sustaining growth;*
    (e) *transport and labour costs are high due to remoteness, environmental difficulty and high level of technology;*
    (f) *special social structure—ethnic friction between the transient, male, single, intrusive population and the indigenous people.*

Comparison of the above with Table 1.2 shows that the Arctic Resource Frontier Region is similar in most respects to Friedmann's concept of a Resource Frontier Region. The main differences concern points (c) and (f) where the social problems have crystallized out to cause friction between the intrusive and indigenous populations. Another minor difference is the additional transport expense caused by the presence of sea ice. It is worth summarizing the main characteristics of this arctic version of a Resource Frontier Region.

(a) Arctic economies are overwhelmingly dependent on one or two resources — oil in Alaska, minerals in the Northwest Territories, minerals and fish in Greenland, gold or tin in the eastern Soviet Arctic, and a slightly more varied blend of minerals, oil and gas in the western Soviet Arctic.

(b) The importance of the external control of exploration can be seen in a historical and modern context. Whaling, fur trapping and gold mining were all a response to world market conditions and often foreigners participated directly, for example, Scottish whalers in Arctic North America. In a modern context the same is true. Japan is heavily involved in the Soviet eastern Arctic, Alaska and the Yukon. European and American companies are involved in Arctic North America and apparently, as suggested by occasional press releases, in the Soviet Arctic too. Canada is involved in mining in Greenland. However, in the day of multinational companies it is not the international origins of a company that are important, so much as the fact that all development is associated with the needs of the world's industrial cores. Market conditions at the cores determine whether or not development takes place and also the level of exploration. In this guise the Soviet Arctic fulfils the same role as the Western Arctic. It is supplying the needs of the core, only in this case it is the Soviet core.

(c) Perhaps the most important feature of arctic development has been the clash between the development ethic of the intrusive system and that of the indigenous system. The saga of economic waves sweeping into Inuit lands and causing havoc on the Inuit way of life goes back to the early fur traders and especially the whalers. Once development created nuclei for towns, the troubles began. The Inuit were tempted to change to a cash economy and, partly as a result of this, and partly because their concentration in towns destroyed hunting prospects, they were weaned from their traditional way of life. But they have not been able to participate fully in the intrusive culture and economy except at the level of trapping where their skills are legendary. Increasing frustration has led to a dramatic change in the last decade. The home-rule movement in Greenland and its achievement in 1979, the Native Land Claims Settlement Act of 1971 in Alaska and similar Arctic Land Claims among Canadian Inuit are all examples of political protest movements. Above all, they are concerned with local autonomy so that local arctic peoples can have a say in the type of development and share in its rewards. The situation in the Soviet Union is not clear. The original administrative organization of the north following Soviet accession was based partly on local groupings, but the level of autonomy is limited.

(d) The role of the town in development is best illustrated in the Soviet Arctic. Here it is policy to create isolated towns, such as Noril'sk, as centres of development. But the same trend occurred in Greenland where development was accompanied by the planned transfer of the population to four main towns. It can be seen in an extreme form in the company mining towns such as Faro in Yukon or Longyearbyen in Svalbard. The bulk of Alaska's population is in the two towns of Anchorage and Fairbanks and is yet another illustration of the tendency.

The towns are often single-purpose in their function. Whether it is the case of the fur trading town of Mangazeya, the gold mining town of Dawson, or the modern mineral towns of the Kola Peninsula, the whole town focuses on exploiting one major resource. As Wonders (1972) wrote feelingly, it is the presence of diversity such as the cultural gem of the Palace Grand Theatre at Dawson which provokes surprise.

In a historical perspective towns in the Arctic have waxed and waned with the fortunes of the resource they exploit. The eclipse of Dawson, which was a centre of up to 25 000 people, is a salutary reminder of the insecurity of one-purpose resource towns. Settlements like Prudhoe Bay, Faro, and the mineral towns of the Kola Peninsula are modern equivalents which may not survive after the depletion of their respective resources. Larger multi-purpose centres, which are normally in the southern Arctic or sub-Arctic, would seem to be a better prospect for long-term survival; for example Fairbanks, Yellowknife, and Godthåb. Yet there are historical instances of towns of this size declining into insignificance. The towns are dependent on relatively few functions and a political philosophy towards the north which favours their preservation. If the resources decline and the philosophy changes then they too could be vulnerable.

(e) High costs of labour and transport and tremendous capital investment are typical of all areas. Massive, high-level technology is involved and the costs, measured in billions, are usually beyond the comprehension of normal individuals. Perhaps the sight of the 1284 km Alaska pipeline best conveys the idea of the scale and investment (Figure 12.5). The key problem is that such technology requires labour with skills which are typically found only in the world's core areas. Thus, high-cost labour, paid premium rates to attract them away from the cores, is flown in and out in regular shifts. High wages coupled with remoteness are a powerful way to increase general living costs in the area. Most costs in the Arctic are 50—100 per cent more expensive than in the respective cores.

(f) Transient labour living in hostels, comprising a population which is often male and single, is not conducive to the creation of a settled community. There is little incentive to care for a house and its immediate surrounds, to plan for parks and pleasant walks, or to encourage family and youth activities. Instead the tendency is to turn away from the settlement and even abuse it and its indigenous people. Thus garbage and junk is left lying around and this in turn leads to further alienation from the scruffy settlement. Such centres are a shock to visitors from the south. I still have not forgotten the sight, admittedly some 20 years ago, of a lateral moraine consisting of beer cans, oil drums and worse on a glacier flowing past an East Greenland mining camp. Here, one of the world's more spectacular views was disfigured by a crude lack of sensitivity.

Still further problems appear when the settlement has an indigenous population. As described in Chapter 9, the Inuit often find many values of southern culture perplexing. Faced with the rather harsh example typical of arctic towns, they find themselves awash in an unfriendly culture and unable to master its paths to success. Capable of participating only in low-paid jobs, and losing the means or skills to hunt, their standard of living falls. With it goes self-confidence, self-esteem and morale. Alcoholism, disease and suicides take their toll. The gulf between the two cultures grows and so too does the physical fabric of the town with a superior southerner's quarter growing apart from a native slum of shacks.

This attempt to highlight a particular type of Resource Frontier Region in the Arctic is made for two main reasons. First, it is hoped that comparison with Friedmann's wider concepts will allow the processes affecting arctic spatial systems to be better understood. Second, it is hoped that the Arctic can be placed in a world perspective so that general principles can emerge more clearly.

12. *Effective transport links within the polar periphery and between the periphery and core are prerequisites for successful intensive economic development.*

Intensive development in the Arctic commonly follows the building of a transport artery. The mineral towns of the Kola Peninsula grew up along the line of the pre-existing Murmansk Railway. The search for oil and gas in Alaska looked first at areas accessible from an infrastructure created previously for military activities in Alaska. The surge of post-war mineral exploitation in the Yukon was able to capitalize on a railway inherited from gold-rush days and from the improved access offered by the wartime Alaska Highway. The above examples all relate to situations where the lines of access were inherited from pre-existing times. The Arctic also provides examples of infrastructure development being used specifically to stimulate development. It is after all one of the main ways in which a government can influence the long-term development of an area. Examples come from Greenland where one of the first acts of development was to provide efficient subsidized air and sea services to and between the four growth towns of the southwest. In the Yukon and the Mackenzie Valley areas, the government began a programme in 1965 to create better communications, especially loop roads, to bring all likely mineral resources within 320km of a road. In the Soviet Arctic massive investment in the Northern Sea Route and railways has been seen as a necessary step towards development.

Good communication with the core is important for economic development at two scales. At a world scale there is the viability of communication between the polar periphery and the world cores. At a sub-zonal scale there is the question of communication between core and periphery within each polar area. The importance of world-scale accessibility between core and polar periphery is illustrated above all by the contrasts in development between the Arctic and Antarctic; whereas most of the Arctic has been linked by land with the main land masses, the Antarctic has remained apart, separated by a tricky sea passage. A more specific example is provided by the Viking colonization of Greenland, a success which depended on effective trade with the European homeland. Also the history of exploration clearly highlights the role of effective communication — as illustrated by the contrast between Amundsen's and Scott's assaults on the South Pole (Chapter 8).

There are many examples of the effect of varying accessibility within the Arctic and Antarctic. The contrast between the high level of development in western Siberia and the low level of development in the east is essentially due to differences in access to the core. Soviet policy is to develop the most accessible resources in the west and move eastwards as they become exhausted. In Alaska the good external and internal communications offered by Anchorage gave it an advantage which has made it the largest centre. In Greenland efficient year-round communication between Godthåb and Copenhagen is a key feature of the modern development plan. In Antarctica the high level of U.S. activity compared to other nations goes hand in glove with a sophisticated air-supported logistics structure based on McMurdo Sound.

This stress placed on the important role played by the spatial infrastructure on polar development is very much in line with the recommendations made by Friedmann (1966).

13. *A form of economic apartheid may be a successful means of developing the Arctic for the benefit of both the intrusive and indigenous systems.*

There is a tendency in Alaska, Greenland and Arctic Canada for resources to be tapped by highly specialized company bases. The Prudhoe Bay oilfield, Marmorilik lead—zinc mine and proposals to exploit ore on Little Cornwallis Island are all examples. A similar procedure seems to be taking place in the oil and gas fields of western Siberia. The same has also long applied in Svalbard. The idea is to set up a base with only those services which are necessary. Employees are flown in and out of the camp on a shift basis. The advantage for the intrusive system is that it is cheaper not to have to build a permanent transport infrastructure, a settlement with service and administrative functions and housing facilities for permanent inhabitants. When the resource runs out the base camp can simply be abandoned or, better still, re-used in a different location. The advantages for indigenous peoples are (a) they need not come into contact with the base, (b) the compactness disturbs the environment to only a limited extent, and yet, (c) through a royalty system, they can gain financially. This money can be used to promote a non-urban spatial system, as seems to be evolving in Arctic Canada.

If future arctic development takes this course then it marks a fundamental shift in strategy. No longer can we expect to see the development of towns, especially on the massive scale common in the Soviet Arctic. As suggested in chapter 11, one can perhaps envisage a lower-density, dispersed, arctic population based in small towns and villages.

14. *Environmental pressure groups based in the world's cores represent another intrusive wave which can constrain arctic indigenous systems.*

A theme that has emerged, particularly in the case of the North American Arctic, is the way environmentalists seem to represent yet another externally controlled wave of southern interference. In the 1970s world-wide publicity about the harp seal slaughter of Newfoundland hit the market for all seal skins. The Inuit found the value of the ring seal skins decimated. At one stroke this removed the one prop of their cash economy — one of the few which dovetails neatly into both Inuit and southern cultures. Similar effects have been felt concerning the furs of arctic fox and polar bears. The United States' ban on the import of whale products in the 1970s hit at the market for whalebone carvings from Arctic Canada. Yet again the Alaskan Inuit resented being told by the International Whaling Commission to limit their quota of bowhead whales. This limitation (which was less damaging than the total ban sought) hits at an activity with both cash and cultural value — one which is thousands of years old.

Perhaps the moral is for a more balanced approach to worldwide conservation campaigns. At least let us not perpetrate a system which causes an Inuit person to wonder ruefully if he or she would be better off as a seal or a bird.

Antarctica

15. *The spatial system in Antarctica represents a multinational rather than an international approach.*

Here surely lies one of the greater challenges of today. The Antarctic Treaty of 1959 was a bold step but comes up for renegotiation in 1991. The vision of a continent with no national claims and with its natural and human resources utilized for the benefit of all mankind is a clear goal which has excited scientists and others for many years. I suspect many visitors to Antarctica, myself included, have been so impressed by the international cooperation on the ground and the obvious value of Antarctic studies, that they have complacently believed that Antarctica's international future is secure. If Chapter 14 on Antarctica jogs that complacency then it will have achieved more than it could hope to. The multinational compromise of the existing Treaty survives because it suits the needs of the claimant states and those such as the U.S.A. and U.S.S.R. who also work in Antarctica. There are already deep frictions within this multinational club, and between it and the rest of the world. Countries that are not members of the club, and particularly the Third World, see a powerful blend of conservationists and high technology. They fear the combination will block use of many resources, such as whales, on conservation grounds and reserve the remaining minerals for exclusive high-technology uses.

In many ways the situation parallels that in the Arctic where the indigenous peoples have gained little from exploitation of their lands by the world's core areas. A more just solution is only now beginning to emerge. In the case of Antarctica there is a chance to devise a joint solution before the major injustices arise. Perhaps a royalty system on the lines of that evolving in the Arctic could provide a solution.

Conclusion

This book has focused on the regional geography of the polar periphery of the world. The natural and human patterns in the polar regions have been viewed as spatial systems in an attempt to understand the links between process and form. Emphasis has also been placed on the interrelationships between these spatial systems at a variety of scales. It is hoped that the approach will have emphasized the complexity of the links which go to make up the spatial patterns in any area of any scale. The interrelationships exhibited by a small spatial pattern such as a tundra polygon are amazingly complex when seen in terms of the roles of climate, snow accumulation, soil materials, site history, vegetation and animals. Such complexity increases markedly as one increases the variety of regional interrelationships and also the scale of study; as a result the task of understanding seems daunting indeed. Perhaps the main conclusion to be drawn from this is that there is much to learn about the regional interrelationships of both natural and human phenomena. In turn this suggests the need for a more thoughtful and sensitive approach to the Arctic and Antarctic than has been common in the past.

References

Adie, R. J. 1965: Antarctic geology and continental drift. *Science Journal* (August), 65–73.

Alaska Statistical Review, 1980. Division of Economic Enterprise, Juneau.

Allen, M. B. 1971: High latitude phytoplankton. *Annual Review of Ecology and Systematics*, 2, 261–76.

Amundsen, R. 1912: *The South Pole*. London.

Andrée, S. A., Strindberg, N. and Fraenkel K. 1931: *The Andrée diaries*. John Lane the Bodley Head, London.

Andrews, J. T. 1970a: *A geomorphological study of postglacial uplift with particular reference to Arctic Canada*. Institute of British Geographers Special Publication 2.

    1970b: Present and postglacial rates of uplift for glaciated northern and eastern North America derived from postglacial uplift curves. *Canadian Journal of Earth Sciences*, 7, 703–15.

    1974: Cainozoic glaciations and crustal movements of the Arctic. In Ives, J. D. and Barry, R. G. (editors), *Arctic and alpine environments*. Methuen, London, 277–317.

    1975: *Glacier systems*. Duxbury, North Scituate, Mass.

Andrews, J. T., Barry, R. G., Bradley, R. S., Miller, G. H. and Williams, L. D. 1972: Past and present glaciological responses to climate in eastern Baffin Island. *Quaternary Research*, 2, 303–14.

Andrews, J. T., Davis, P. T. and Wright, C. 1976: Little Ice Age permanent snow cover in the eastern Canadian Arctic: extent mapped from LANDSAT–1 satellite imagery. *Geografiska Annaler*, 58A, 71–81.

Andrews, J. T., Guennel, G. K., Wray, J. L. and Ives, J. D. 1972: An Early Tertiary outcrop in north-central Baffin Island, Northwest Territories, Canada: environment and significance. *Canadian Journal of Earth Sciences*, 9 (3), 233–8.

Andrews, J. T. and Peltier, W. R. 1976: Collapse of Hudson Bay ice center and glacio-isostatic rebound. *Geology*, 4, 73–5.

Andriashev, A. P. 1965: A general review of the Antarctic fish fauna. In Mieghem, J. van and Oye, P. van (editors), *Biogeography and ecology in Antarctica*. Junk, The Hague, 491–550.

Armstrong, T. E. 1958: *The Russians in the Arctic*. Methuen, London.

1963/64: Northern affairs in the Soviet Union. *International Journal*, 19 (1), 40–9.

1965: *Russian settlement in the North*. Cambridge University Press, Cambridge.

1970: Soviet northern development, with some Alaskan parallels and contrasts. *Institute of Social, Economic and Government Research, University of Alaska, Fairbanks*, 2, 1–37.

1972: Russians in Alaska before 1867. *Polar Record*, 16 (102), 423–4.

1974: 'The North' in Soviet specialist literature, *Polar Record*, 17 (108), 314–18.

1976: The shift method in the Arctic, *Polar Record*, 18 (114), 279–81.

Armstrong T. E., Roberts, B. and Swithinbank, C. W. M. 1973: *Illustrated glossary of snow and ice*. 2nd edn. Scott Polar Research Institute, Cambridge.

Armstrong, T. E., Rogers, G. and Rowley, G. 1978: *The circumpolar north.* Methuen, London.

Arnborg, L., Walker, H. J. and Peippo, J. 1966: Water discharge in the Colville River, Alaska, 1962. *Geografiska Annaler*, 48A, 195–210.

Avsyuk, G. A. and Kartashov, S. N. 1975: Prospective plan for Soviet investigations of Antarctica for 1971–75: general information. In Bugaev, V. A. (editor), *The Antarctic Committee reports 1969*. Amerind, New Delhi, 230–6.

Babb, T. A. and Bliss, L. C. 1974: Susceptibility to environmental impact in the Queen Elizabeth Islands. *Arctic*, 27, 234–7.

Baer, K. E. von 1838a: On the ground ice of frozen soil in Siberia. *Journal of the Royal Geographical Society*, 8, 210–12.

1838b: Recent intelligence upon the frozen ground in Siberia. *Journal of the Royal Geographical Society*, 8, 401–6.

Baird, P. 1964: *The polar world*. Longman, London.

Balikci, A. 1968: The Netsilik Eskimos: adaptive processes. In Lee, R. B. and Devore, I. (editors), *Man the hunter*. Aldine, Chicago, 78–82.

Barker, P. F. and Burrell, J. 1976: The opening of Drake Passage. *Proceedings of the Joint Oceanographic Assembly* (Edinburgh), 103.

Barkov, N. I. 1977: Glaciological studies with the U.S. Antarctic Research Program, 1974–1975 and 1975–1976. *Antarctic Journal of the United States*, 12, 11–14.

Barr, W. 1972: Hudson Bay: the shape of things to come. *The Musk-ox*, 11, 64.

Barrie, J. V. 1980: Iceberg–seabed interaction (Northern Labrador Sea). *Annals of Glaciology*, 1, 71–6.

Barry, R. G. and Hare, F. K. 1974: Arctic climate. In Ives, J. D. and Barry R. G. (editors), *Arctic and alpine environments*. Methuen, London, 17–54.

Belinskiy, B. V. 1978: Aspects of water transport in the Soviet north-east. *Polar Geography*, 2 (1), 28–41.

Belov, M. I. 1977: Excavations of a Russian arctic town. *Polar Geography*, 1 (4) 270–85.

Benson, C. S. 1962: *Stratigraphic studies in the snow and firn of the Greenland ice sheet.* U.S. Army Snow, Ice and Permafrost Research Establishment, Research Report 70.

　1969: The role of air pollution in arctic planning and development. *Polar Record,* 14 (93), 783—90.

　1970: *Ice fog: low temperature air pollution.* U.S. Army Cold Regions Research and Engineering Laboratory, Research Report 121.

Berger, T. R. 1977: *Northern Frontier, northern homeland. The Report of the Mackenzie Valley Pipeline Inquiry.* 2 vols. Lorimer, Toronto.

Bergthorsson, P. 1969: An estimate of drift ice and temperature in Iceland in 1000 years. *Jökull,* 19, 94—101.

Bierman, D. E. 1978: Soviet territorial claims in the Arctic and their economic and political implications. *Soviet Geography,* 19 (7), 490—6.

Billings, W. D. 1974: Arctic and alpine vegetation: plant adaptations to cold summer climates. In Ives, J. D. and Barry, R. G. (editors), *Arctic and alpine environ-ments.* Methuen, London, 403—43.

Bird, J. B. 1967: *The physiography of Arctic Canada.* Johns Hopkins Press, Baltimore.

Birket-Smith, Kaj. 1936: *The Eskimos.* Methuen, London.

Blake, W. Jr. 1972: Climatic implications of radiocarbon-dated driftwood in the Queen Elizabeth Islands, Arctic Canada. In Vasari, Y., Hyvärinen, H. and Hicks, S. (editors), *Climatic changes in Arctic areas during the last ten thousand years.* Acta Univ. Oulu. Ser. A. Sci. Rerum Natur. 3, Geol., 1, 77—101.

Bliss, L. C. and Peterson, E. B. 1975: The ecological impact of northern develop-ment. In Malaurie, J. (editor), *Arctic oil and gas: problems and possibilities.* Mouton, Paris, 505—37.

Bond, A. R. and Lydolph, P. E. 1979: Soviet population change and city growth 1970—79: a preliminary report. *Soviet Geography,* 20 (8), 461—88.

Bone, R. M. 1972: The population of northern Canada. In Wonders, W. C. (editor), *Studies in Canadian geography: the North.* University of Toronto Press, Toronto, 91—116.

Bonner, W. N. 1968: The fur seal of South Georgia. *British Antarctic Survey Scientific Reports,* 56, 1—81.

　1976: Recovery of the Antarctic fur seal at South Georgia. *N.E.R.C. (National Environment Research Council) Newsjournal,* 2 (3), 4—6.

Bonner, W. N. and Laws, R. M. 1964: Seals and sealing. In Priestley, R., Adie, R. J. and Robin, G. de Q. (editors), *Antarctic research.* Butterworth, London, 163—90.

Bornemann, C. 1975: *Grønland.* Ministry for Greenland. Copenhagen. Also English version, *Greenland* (1976).

　1977: Arctic social and cultural systems. In Amaria, P. J., Bruneau, A. A. and Lapp. P. A. (editors), *Arctic systems.* Plenum Press, 103—17.

Brassard, G. R. 1971: The mosses of northern Ellesmere Island, Arctic Canada, 1. Ecology and Phytogeography, with an analysis for the Queen Elizabeth Islands. *Bryologist,* 74 (3), 233—81.

Brody, H. 1974: Priorities in northern Canada: review. *Polar Record*, 17 (106), 58–61.

1977: Industrial impact in the Canadian north. *Polar Record*, 18 (115) 333–9.

Broecker, W. S. and van Donk, J. 1970: Insolation changes, ice volumes and the 0^{18} record in deep-sea cores. *Reviews of Geophysics and Space Physics*, 8, 169–98.

Brookfield, H. C. 1973: On one geography and a Third World. *Transactions of the Institute of British Geographers*, 58, 1–20.

1975: *Interdependent development*. Methuen, London.

Brown, J. 1966: Massive underground ice in northern regions. *Proceedings of the Army Science Conference 14th–17th June, 1966*. Department of the Army, Washington, D.C., 89–102.

Brown, R. J. E. 1970: *Permafrost in Canada*. University of Toronto Press, Toronto.

Brown, S. G. 1980: Thirty-first annual meeting of the International Whaling Commission, 1979. *Polar Record*, 20 (124), 59–62.

Bryson, R. A., Wendland, W. M., Ives, J. D. and Andrews, J. T. 1969: Radiocarbon isochrones on the disintegration of the Laurentide ice sheet. *Arctic and Alpine Research*, 1 (1), 1–13.

Buckley, J. T. 1969: *Gradients of past and present outlet glaciers*. Geological Survey of Canada Paper 69–29.

Bulatov, L. V. and Zakharov, V. F. 1978: Changes in the amount of multi-year ice in arctic seas during the current cooling trend. *Polar Geography*, 2 (3), 216–18.

Bull, C. 1971: Snow accumulation in Antarctica. In Quam, L. O. (editor), *Research in the Antarctic*. American Association for the Advancement of Science, Washington, D.C., Pub.93, 367–421.

Burns, J. J. and Morrow, J. E. 1975: The Alaskan arctic marine mammals and fisheries. In Malaurie, J. (editor), *Arctic oil and gas: problems and possibilities*. Mouton, Paris, 561–82.

Butters. T. 1973: Visitors north: development of a tourist industry in the Northwest Territories. In Pimlott, D. H., Vincent, K. M. and McKnight, C. E. (editors), *Arctic alternatives*. Canadian Arctic Resources Committee, Ottawa, 132–42.

Calkin, P. E. 1973: Glacial processes in the ice-free valleys of southern Victoria Land, Antarctica. In Fahey, B. D. and Thompson, R. D. (editors), *Research in polar and alpine geomorphology*. Geoabstracts, Norwich, 167–86.

Carsola, A. J. 1954: Submarine canyons of the arctic slope. *Journal of Geology*, 62, 605–10.

Carson, C. E. and Hussey, K. M. 1962: The oriented lakes of Arctic Alaska. *Journal of Geology*, 70 (4), 417–39.

Chapman, K. 1980: *People, pattern and process: an introduction to human geography*. Edward Arnold, London.

Charley, R. 1973: The native people reply. In Pimlott, D. H., Vincent, K. M. and McKnight, C. E. (editors), *Arctic alternatives*. Canadian Arctic Resources Committee, Ottawa, 41–5.

Chasen, R. E. 1967: Distant Early Warning Systems in the North American Arctic. *Polar Record*, 13 (86), 595—6.

Childe, G. 1960: *What happened in history*. M. Parrish, London.

Childe, V. G. 1954: Early forms of society. In Singer, C., Holmyard, E. J. and Hall, A. R. (editors), *A history of technology*. Clarendon Press, Oxford, 38—57.

Chorlton, J. C. and Lister, H. 1970: Snow accumulation over Antarctica. In Gow, A. J. *et al.* (editors), *International Symposium on Antarctic Glaciological Exploration (ISAGE)*. International Association of Scientific Hydrology publication, 86, 254—63.

Chrétien, J. 1973: Northern development for northerners. In Pimlott, D. H., Vincent, K. M. and McKnight, C. E. (editors), *Arctic alternatives*. Canadian Arctic Resources Committee, Ottawa, 27—41.

Christiansen, K. 1968: *From outpost to town: The migration policy in Greenland*. Ministry for Greenland, Copenhagen.

Christie, E. W. H. 1951: *The antarctic problem*. Allen & Unwin, London.

Church, M. 1974: Hydrology and permafrost with reference to northern North America. In *Permafrost hydrology: proceedings of workshop seminar, 1974*. Canadian National Committee. International Hydrological Decade, Environment Canada, Ottawa, 7—20.

Churkin, M. 1973: Geologic concepts of Arctic Ocean Basin. In Pitcher, M. G. (editor), *Arctic geology*. American Association of Petroleum Geologists Memoir 19, 485—99.

Clapperton, C. M. 1969: The volcanic eruption at Deception Island, December 1967. *British Antarctic Survey Bulletin*, 22, 83—90.

Clapperton, C. M., Sugden, D. E., Birnie, R. V., Hansom, J. D. and Thom, G. 1978: Glacier fluctuations in South Georgia and comparison with other island groups in the Scotia Sea. In van Zinderen Bakker, E. M. (editor), *Antarctic glacial history and world palaeoenvironments*. Balkema, Rotterdam, 95—104.

Clark, G. 1952: *Prehistoric Europe: the economic basis*. Methuen, London.

1967: *The stone age hunters*. Thames & Hudson, London.

1977: *World prehistory in new perspective*. 3rd edn. Cambridge University Press, Cambridge.

Clark, G. and Piggott, S. 1965: *Prehistoric societies*. Hutchinson, London.

Clark, J. A. 1977: An inverse problem in glacial geology: the reconstruction of glacier thinning in Glacier Bay, Alaska, between A.D. 1910 and 1960 from relative sea-level data. *Journal of Glaciology*, 18 (80), 481—503.

CLIMAP Project Members, 1976: The surface of the Ice-Age Earth. *Science*. 191 (4232), 1131—7.

Coachman, L. K. and Aagaard, K. 1974: Physical oceanography of Arctic and Subarctic seas. In Herman, Y. (editor), *Marine geology and oceanography of the Arctic seas*. Springer-Verlag, New York, 1—72.

Cochard, C. 1975: Problems of drilling offshore in the Arctic: new types of platform. In Malaurie, J. (editor), *Arctic oil and gas: problems and possibilities*. Mouton, Paris, 239—62.

Colbeck, S. C. 1974: A study of glacier flow for an open-pit mine: an exercise in applied glaciology. *Journal of Glaciology*, 13 (69), 401–14.

Conquest, R. 1979: *Kolyma, the Arctic death camps.* Oxford University Press, Oxford.

Coombs, J. and Madden, C. 1978: The Mackenzie Valley and Alaska Highway gas pipeline route proposals. *Polar Record*, 19 (120), 282–5.

Corte. A. E. 1969: Geocryology and engineering. In Varnes, D. J. and Kiersch, G. (editors), *Reviews in engineering geology*, vol.2. Geological Society of America, Boulder, Colorado, 119–85.

Courtney, J. L. 1971: Air transport in northern Canada. *Polar Record*, 15 (97), 495–8.

    1980: Arctic airport construction: the Canadian experience. *Polar Record*, 20 (126), 253–9.

Craddock. C. 1970: *Geologic maps of Antarctica.* American Geographical Society, Antarctic Map Folio Series 12.

Cram, J. 1978: Northern teachers in northern schools: the Greenland experience. *Polar Record*, 19 (120), 209–16.

Crary, A. P. 1962: The Antarctic. *Scientific American*, 207 (3), 2–15.

Crowther, W. E. L. H. 1970: Captain J. W. Robinson's narrative of a sealing voyage to Heard Island, 1858–60. *Polar Record*, 15 (96), 301–16.

Currie, R. G. S. 1975: Panarctic: successful exploration of the High Arctic. In Malaurie, J. (editor), *Arctic oil and gas: problems and possibilities.* Paris, Mouton, 892–907.

Dalrymple, P. C. and Frostman, T. O. 1971: Some aspects of the climate of interior Antarctica. In Quam, L. O. (editor), *Research in the Antarctic.* American Association for the Advancement of Science, Washington, D.C., 429–42.

Darnell, F. 1979: Education among the native proples of Alaska. *Polar Record*, 19 (122), 431–46.

Dater, H. M. 1966: Organizational developments in the United States Antarctic Program, 1954–65. *Antarctic Journal of the United States*, 1, 21–32.

    1975: *History of Antarctic exploration and scientific investigation.* American Geographical Society, Antarctic Map Folio Series 19.

Dayton, P. K., Robilliard, G. A. and Devries, A. L. 1969: Anchor ice formation in McMurdo Sound, Antarctica, and its biological effects. *Science*, 163 (3864), 273–4.

Deacon, G. E. R. 1937: The hydrology of the southern ocean. *Discovery Reports*, 15, 1–124.

    1964: The southern ocean. In Priestley, R., Adie, R. J. and Robin, G. de Q. (editors), *Antarctic research.* Butterworth, London, 292–307.

Dell, R. K. 1965: Marine biology. In Hatherton, T. (editor), *Antarctica.* Methuen, London, 129–152.

Dempster, R. T. and Bruneau, A. A. 1975: Dangers presented by ice bergs and protection against them. In Malaurie, J. (editor), *Arctic oil and gas: problems and possibilities.* Mouton, Paris, 348–62.

Denton, G. H. and Armstrong, R. L. 1969: Miocene—Pliocene glaciations in southern Alaska. *American Journal of Science*, 267, 1121—42.

Denton, G. H. and Hughes, T. J. (editors) 1981: *The last great ice sheets.* Wiley, New York.

Denton, G. H. and Karlén, W. 1973: Holocene climatic variations — their pattern and possible cause. *Quaternary Research*, 3, 155—205.

Department of the Interior, 1974: *Federal programs and Alaska natives. Task 1. An analysis of Alaska Natives' well-being.* United States Department of the Interior Report 2(c).

Dietz, R. S., Holden, J. C. and Sproll, W. P. 1972: Antarctica and continental drift. In Adie, R. J. (editor), *Antarctic geology and geophysics.* Universitetsforlaget, Oslo, 837—42.

Drewry, D. J. 1975: Initiation and growth of the East Antarctic ice sheet. *Journal of the Geological Society* (London), 131, 255—73.

    1978: Aspects of the early evolution of West Antarctic ice. In van Zinderen Bakker E. M. (editor), *Antarctic glacial history and world palaeoenvironments.* Balkema, Rotterdam, 25—32.

Drewry, D. J. and Cooper, A. P. R. 1981: Processes and models of Antarctic glacio-marine sedimentation. *Annals of Glaciology*, 2, 117—22.

Dubnie, E. 1959: Some economic factors affecting northern mineral development in Canada. *Canadian Department of Mines and Technical Surveys. Mineral Information Bulletin*, M.R. 38, 21—30.

Dubrovin, L. I. 1966: Population of Antarctica. *Soviet Antarctic Expedition Information Bulletin*, 6 (2), 58, 177—9.

Dumond, D. E. 1977: *The Eskimos and Aleuts.* Thames & Hudson, London.

Dunbar, M. J. 1968: *Ecological development in polar regions.* Prentice Hall, New York and London.

    1973: Stability and fragility in arctic ecosystems. *Arctic*, 26, 179—85.

    1976: Climatic change and northern development. *Arctic*, 29 (4), 183—93.

Dunbar, M. J. and Thomson, D. H. 1979: West Greenland salmon and climatic change. *Meddelelser om Grønland,* 202 (4).

Dunbar, M. and Wittman, W. 1963: Some features of ice movement in the Arctic Basin. In *Proceedings of the Arctic Basin Symposium, October 1962.* Arctic Institute of North America, Washington, D.C., 90—108.

Du Toit, A. L. 1937: *Our wandering continents.* Oliver & Boyd, Edinburgh.

Edwards, D. M. and Heap, J. A. 1981: Convention on the conservation of Antarctic marine living resources: a commentary. *Polar Record*, 20 (127), 353—62.

Elkin, L. 1976: An outpost camp policy for the Northwest Territories, *Polar Record*, 18 (113), 184—6.

Elliot, D. M. 1972: Aspects of Antarctic geology and drift reconstructions. In Adie, R. J. (editor), *Antarctic geology and geophysics.* Universitetsforlaget, Oslo, 849—58.

El-Sayed, S. Z. 1970: On the productivity of the southern ocean (Atlantic and Pacific sectors). In Holdgate, M. W. (editor), *Antarctic ecology.* Scientific

Committee for Antarctic Research, Academic Press, London and New York, 119—35.

1971: Biological aspects of the pack ice ecosystem. In Deacon, G. (editor), *Symposium on Antarctic ice and water masses, Tokyo, 1970*, Scientific Committee for Antarctic Research, Cambridge, 35—54.

1976: Living resources of the southern ocean. *Antarctic Journal of the United States*, 11, 8—12.

Emiliani, C. 1978: The cause of the ice ages. *Earth and Planetary Science Letters*, 37, 349—52.

Erickson, A. W., Siniff, D. B., Cline, D. R. and Hofman, R. J. 1971: Distributional ecology of Antarctic seals. In Deacon, G. (editor), *Symposium on Antarctic ice and water masses*. Scientific Committee for Antarctic Research, Cambridge, 55—76.

Fairhall, D. 1977: North of Murmansk: status of oil-rich Svalbard. *Geographical Magazine*, 44 (6), 347—53.

Faulkner, J. H. 1978: *Native claims: policy processes and perspectives*. Ministry of Supply and Services, Ottawa.

Fenge, T., Gardner, J. E., King, J. and Wilson, B. 1979: *Land use programs in Canada, Northwest Territories*. Ministry of Supply and Services, Hull, Quebec, 141—4.

Ferrians, O. J., Kachadoorian, R. and Greene, G. W. 1969: *Permafrost and related engineering problems in Alaska*. United States Geological Survey Professional Paper, 678.

Fitzgerald, J. H. 1975: Long range development of Arctic areas: Alaska's approach. In Malaurie, J. (editor), *Arctic oil and gas: problems and possibilities*. Paris, Mouton, 758—68.

Flint, R. F. 1971: *Glacial and Quaternary geology*. Wiley, New York.

Fogg, G. E. 1977: Aquatic primary production in the Antarctic. *Philosophical Transactions of the Royal Society* (London), B, 279, 27—38.

Fournier, J. T. 1975: Repenser le développement Arctique Canadien: population, environnement, ressources. In Malaurie, J. (editor), *Arctic oil and gas: problems and possibilities*. Mouton, Paris, 769—823.

Foxton, P. 1956: The distribution of the standing crop of zooplankton in the Southern Ocean. *Discovery Reports*, 28, 191—236.

Fraser, F. C. 1964: Whales and whaling. In Priestley, R., Adie, R. J. and Robin, G. de Q. (editors), *Antarctic research*. Butterworth, London, 191—205.

Freeman, M. M. R. 1967: An ecological study of mobility and settlement patterns among the Belcher Island Eskimo. *Arctic*, 20 (3), 154—75.

French, H. M. 1976: *The periglacial environment*. Longman, London.

Frenzel, B. 1959: *Die Vegetations- und Landschaftzonen Nord-Eurasiens während der Letzten Eiszeit und wöhrend der post-glazialen Wärmezeit*. Akademie der Wissenschaft und Literatur, Abhandlungen der Mathematisch-Naturwissenschaften Klasse 1 (13), Mainz.

Fried, J. 1963: White-dominant settlements in the Canadian Northwest Territories. *Anthropoligica*, 5 (1), 57–68.

Friedmann, J. 1966: *Regional development policy: a case study of Venezuela.* Cambridge, Mass.

Friedmann, J. and Weaver, C. 1979: *Territory and function.* Edward Arnold, London.

Fristrup, B. 1965: *Grønlands geografi.* Gyldendal, Copenhagen.
   1966: *The Greenland ice cap.* University of Washington Press, Seattle.

Fuchs, V. and Hillary, E. 1958: *The crossing of Antarctica.* Cassell, London.

Funder, S. and Hjort, C. 1973: Aspects of the Weichselian chronology in central East Greenland. *Boreas*, 2 (2), 69–84.

Gad. F. 1970: *The history of Greenland.* Part 1. Hurst, London.

Garner, F. 1978: The vanished Norseman: mystery of Greenlanders' disappearance. *Geographical Magazine*, 50 (7), 446–51.

Gaunt, S. 1975: *Broughton Island — social statistics.* Department of Geography, University of McGill (mimeo).

Gazaway, H. P. and Thompson, M. 1975: Alaska natives in transition. In Malaurie, J. (editor), *Arctic oil and gas: problems and possibilities.* Paris, Mouton, 699–719.

Giddings, J. L. 1968: *Ancient men of the Arctic.* Secker & Warburg, London.

Gill, D. 1972: Modification of levee morphology by erosion in the Mackenzie River delta, North-West Territories, Canada. In Price, R. J. and Sugden, D. E. (compilers), *Polar geomorphology.* Institute of British Geographers Special Publication 4, 123–38.

Glaciological Data, 1978: *Arctic sea ice.* Parts 1 and 2. World Data Center A for Glaciology, Report GD-2.

Goldthwait, R. P. 1976: Frost-sorted patterned ground: a review. *Quaternary Research*, 6, 27–35.

Gordon, A. L. and Goldberg, R. D. 1970: *Circumpolar characteristics of Antarctic waters.* American Geographical Society, Antarctic Map Folio Series, New York, 1–5.

Gordon, J. E. 1980: Recent climatic trends and local glacier margin fluctuations in West Greenland. *Nature*, 284 (5752), 157–9.

Gourdeau, E. 1973: The people of the Canadian north. In Pimlott, D. H., Vincent, K. M. and McKnight, C. E. (editors), *Arctic alternatives.* Canadian Arctic Resources Committee, Ottawa, 41–5.

Gow, A. J. 1971: *Depth–time–temperature relationships of ice crystal growth in polar glaciers.* U.S. Army Cold Regions Research and Engineering Laboratory Research Reports, 300.

Gray, J. 1980: Alaska's unique transportation system. *Alaska Review of Social and Economic Conditions*, 17 (2), 2–28.

Greene, S. W. 1964: Plants of the land. In Priestley, R., Adie, R. J. and Robin, G. de Q. (editors), *Antarctic research*. Butterworth, London, 240—53.

Greenland Commission, 1964: *Extract from the Greenland Commission of 1960*. Ministry for Greenland, Copenhagen (mimeo).

Greve, T. 1975: *Svalbard: Norway in the Arctic Ocean*. Grøndahl, Oslo.

Guemple, L. 1972: Eskimo band organization and the 'DP Camp' hypothesis. *Arctic Anthropology*, 9 (2), 80—112.

Gulland, J. A. 1970: The development of the resources of the antarctic seas. In Holdgate, M. W. (editor), *Antarctic ecology*. Scientific Committee for Antarctic Research, Academic Press, London and New York, 217—23.

1976: Antarctic baleen whales: history and prospects. *Polar Record*, 18 (112), 5—13.

Gurvich, I. S. 1973: Socio-economic transformation and modern ethnical develop-ment of the inhabitants of the Siberian polar zones of the north-eastern regions. In Berg, G. (editor), *Circumpolar problems*. Pergamon, Oxford, 53—60.

Haggett, P. 1965: *Locational analysis in human geography*. Edward Arnold, London.

Hall, C. F. 1865: *Life with the esquimaux*. Sampson Low, Son & Marston, London.

Hamilton, W. 1970: The Uralides and the motion of the Russian and Siberian platforms. *Bulletin of the Geological Society of America*, 81, 2553—76.

Hanessian, J. 1964: National interests in Antarctica. In Hatherton, T. (editor), *Antarctica*. Methuen, London, 3—53.

Hansen, W. R. and Eckel, E. B. 1966: A summary description of the Alaska earth-quake — its setting and effects. *United States Geological Survey Professional Paper* 541, 1—37.

Hardy, A. C. and Gunther, E. R. 1935: The plankton of South Georgia whaling grounds and adjacent waters, 1926—1927. *Discovery Reports*, 11, 1—456.

Harrison, G. S. 1972: The Alaska Native Claims Settlement Act, 1971. *Arctic*, 25 (3), 232—3.

1973: Notes on Alaskan native electoral politics. *Polar Record*, 16 (104), 691—700.

Harrison, G. S. and Morehouse, T. A. 1970: Rural Alaska's development problems. *Polar Record*, 15 (96), 291—9.

Harrison, S. D. 1979: *Alaska population overview*. Alaska Department of Labor, Juneau.

Hattersley-Smith, G. 1974: Present arctic ice cover. In Ives J. D. and Barry, R. G. (editors), *Arctic and alpine environments*. Methuen, London, 195—223.

Hattersley-Smith, G. and Serson, H. 1973: Reconnaissance of a small ice cap near St. Patrick Bay, Robeson Channel, northern Ellesmere Island, Canada. *Journal of Glaciology*, 12 (66), 417—21.

Hays, J. D. 1978: A review of the Late Quaternary climatic history of Antarctic seas. In Van Zinderen Bakker, E. M. (editor), *Antarctic glacial history and world palaeoenvironments*. Balkema, Rotterdam, 57—71.

Hayes, J. D., Imbrie, J. and Shackleton, N. J. 1976: Variations in the Earth's orbit: pacemaker of the Ice Ages. *Science*, 194 (4270), 1121–32.

Heap, J. A. 1964: Pack ice. In Priestley R., Adie, R. J. and Robin, G. de Q. (editors), *Antarctic research*. Butterworth, London, 308–17.

   1965: Antarctic pack ice. In Hatherton, T. (editor), *Antarctica*. Methuen, London, 187–96.

Hedgpeth, J. W. 1970: Marine biogeography of the Antarctic regions. In Holdgate, M. W. (editor), *Antarctic ecology*. Scientific Committee for Antarctic Research, Academic Press, London and New York, 97–104.

Herman, Y. 1970: Arctic paleo-oceanography in Late Cenozoic time. *Science*, 169, 474–7.

   1974: Topography of the Arctic Ocean. In Herman Y. (editor), *Marine geology and oceanography of the Arctic seas*. Springer, Berlin, 73–81.

Herron, E. M., Dewey, J. F. and Pitman, W. C. III, 1974: Plate tectonic model for the evolution of the Arctic. *Geology*, 2, 377–80.

Herron, E. M. and Tucholke, B. E. 1976: Sea-floor magnetic patterns and basement structure in the Southeastern Pacific. In Hollister, C. D., Craddock, C. *et al.* (editors), *Initial Reports of the Deep Sea Drilling Project*, 35, 263.

Hippler, A. E. 1976: The demographic 'youth bulge': one reason for acculturative difficulties among Alaska natives. *Polar Record*, 18 (114), 304–6.

Hoffman, R. S. 1974: Terrestrial vertebrates. In Ives, J. D. and Barry, R. G. (editors), *Arctic and alpine environments*. Methuen, London, 475–568.

Holdgate, M. W. 1961: Biological routes between the southern continents. *New Scientist*, 239, 636–8.

   1967: The Antarctic ecosystem. *Philosophical Transactions of the Royal Society* (London), B, 252, 363–83.

Holdgate, M. W. and Tinker, J. 1979: *Oil and other minerals in the Antarctic*. Report of the Rockefeller Foundation, Bellagio, Italy, 5th–8th March, 1979. Scientific Committee for Antarctic Research/Scott Polar Research Institute, Cambridge.

Holdsworth, G. and Bull, C. 1970: The flow law of cold ice; investigations on Meserve Glacier, Antarctica. In Gow, A. J. *et al.* (editors), *International Symposium on Antarctic Glaciological Exploration. (ISAGE)*. International Association of Scientific Hydrology Publication 86, 204–16.

Hollin, J. T. 1965: Wilson's theory of ice ages. *Nature*, 208, 12–16.

Holm, G. 1914: Ethnological sketch of the Angmagssalik Eskimo, *Meddelelser om Grønland*, 39 (1), 1–147.

Hooson, D. J. M. 1966: *The Soviet Union*. University of London Press, London.

Hopkins, D. M., Matthews, J. V., Wolfe, J. A. and Silberman, M. L. 1971: A Pliocene flora and insect fauna from the Bering Strait region. *Palaeogeography, Palaeoclimatology, Palaeoecology*, 9, 211–31.

Hopson, E. 1976: *Mayor Hopson's warning to the people of the Canadian Arctic. Testimony, before Canadian Royal Commission, Mackenzie Valley Pipeline Inquiry*. Barrow, North Slope Report.

Hughes, T. 1975: The West Antarctic ice sheet: instability, disintegration and initiation of Ice Ages. *Reviews of Geophysics and Space Physics*, 13 (4) 502–26.

Hughes, T., Denton, G. H. and Grosswald, M. G. 1977: Was there a late-Würm Arctic ice sheet? *Nature*, 266, 596–602.

Hunter, H. 1957: *Soviet transportation policy*. Harvard University Press, Cambridge, Mass.

Huntford, R. 1979: *Scott and Amundsen*. Hodder & Stoughton, London.

Ives, J. D. 1957: Glaciation of the Torngat Mountains, northern Labrador. *Geographical Bulletin*, 12, 47–75.

  1962: Indications of recent extensive glacierization in north-central Baffin Island, NWT. *Journal of Glaciology*, 4, 197–205.

  1970: Arctic tundra: how fragile? A geomorphologist's point of view. *Transactions of the Royal Society of Canada*, Series 4, 8, 401–4.

  1974: Biological refugia and the nunatak hypothesis. In Ives, J. D. and Barry, R. G. (editors), *Arctic and alpine environments*. Methuen, London, 605–36.

Jensen, A. S. 1939: Concerning a change of climate during recent decades in the Arctic and Subarctic regions, from Greenland in the west to Eurasia in the east, and contemporary biological and geophysical changes. *Det Konlige Danske Videnskabernes Selskab, Biologiske Meddelelser*, 14 (8), 1–75.

Johansen, W. 1970: Winter road in northern Alaska, 1969–70. *Polar Record*, 15 (96), 352–5.

John, B. S. 1972: Evidence from the South Shetland Islands towards a glacial history of West Antarctica. In Price, R. J. and Sugden, D. E. (compilers), *Polar geomorphology*. Institute of British Geographers Special Publication 4, 75–92.

John, B. S. and Sugden, D. E. 1975: Coastal geomorphology of high latitudes. In *Progress in Geography*, 7, 53–132.

Johnson, H. M. 1953: Preliminary ecological studies of microclimates inhabited by the smaller arctic and sub-arctic mammals. *Proceedings of the Alaska Science Conference 1951*, 125–31.

Johnson, P. R. and Hartman, C. W. 1971: *Environmental atlas of Alaska*. 2nd edn. University of Alaska.

Jones, G. 1964: *The Norse Atlantic saga*. Oxford University Press, London.

Judd, D. 1969: Canada's northern policy: retrospect and prospect. *Polar Record*, 14 (92) 593–602.

Kelly, M. and Funder, S. 1974: The pollen stratigraphy of Late Quaternary lake sediments of south-west Greenland. *Grønlands Geologiske Undersøgelse Rapport*, 64.

Kemp, S. and Bennett, A. G. 1932: On the distribution and movements of whales in the South Georgia and South Shetland whaling grounds. *Discovery Reports*, 6, 165–90.

Kemp, T. 1977: The new strategic map. *Survival* (International Institute for Strategic Studies), 19 (2), 50–9.

Kemp, W. B. 1971: The flow of energy in a hunting society. *Scientific American*, 224 (3), 104–15.

Kennett, J. P. 1977: Cenozoic evolution of Antarctic glaciation, the circum-Antarctic ocean and their impact on global paleoceanography. *Journal of Geophysical Research*, 82 (27), 3843–60.

1978: Cainozoic evolution of circumantarctic palaeoceanography. In van Zinderen Bakker, E. M. (editor), *Antarctic glacial history and world palaeoenvironments*. Balkema, Rotterdam, 41–56.

Kerfoot, D. E. 1973: Thermokarst features produced by man-made disturbances to the tundra terrain. In Fahey, B. D. and Thompson, R. D. (editors), *Research in polar and alpine geomorphology*. Geoabstracts, Norwich, 60–72.

Khodachek, V. M. 1974: On the formation of population in the Far North of USSR. *Soviet Geography*, 15 (5), 288–98.

Kind, N. V. 1967: Radiocarbon chronology in Siberia. In Hopkins, D. M. (editor), *The Bering land bridge*. Stanford, 172–92.

Kirwan, L. P. 1962: *A history of polar exploration*. Penguin, Harmondsworth.

Knox, G. A. 1970: Antarctic marine ecosystems. In Holdgate, M. W. (editor), *Antarctic ecology*. Scientific Committee for Antarctic Research, Academic Press, London and New York, 69–96.

Koch, L. 1945: The East Greenland ice. *Meddelelser om Grønland*, 130, 1–375.

Koenig, L. S., Greenaway, K. R., Dunbar, M. and Hattersley-Smith, G. 1952: Arctic ice islands. *Arctic*, 5, 67–103.

Kresge, D. T., Morehouse, T. A. and Rogers, G. W. 1977: *Issues in Alaska development*. Institute of Social and Economic Research, University of Alaska, University of Washington Press, Seattle.

Krogh, K. J. 1967: *Viking Greenland*. National Museum, Copenhagen.

Kruse, J., Kleinfeld, J. and Travis, R. 1980: *Energy development and the North Slope Inupiat*. Man in the Arctic Program, University of Alaska.

Kukla, G. J. 1977: Pleistocene land–sea correlations; 1: Europe. *Earth-Science Reviews*, 13, 307–74.

Kukla, G. J., Angell, J. K., Korshover, J., Dronia, H., Hoshiai, M., Namias, J., Rodewald, M., Yamamoto, R. and Iwashima, T. 1977: New data on climatic trends. *Nature*, 270, 573–80.

Lachenbruch, A. 1962: *Mechanics of thermal contraction cracks and ice wedge polygons in permafrost*. Geological Society of America, Special Paper 70.

1968: Permafrost. In Fairbridge, R. W. (editor), *Encyclopedia of Geomorphology*. Reinhold, New York, 833–8.

1970: *Some estimates of the thermal effects of a heated pipeline in permafrost*. Geological Survey, Circular 632, Washington, D.C.

La Fay, H. 1958: DEW line: sentry of the far north. *National Geographic Magazine*, 114, 128–46.

Lamb, H. H. 1972: *Climate present, past and future.* Vol. 1: Fundamentals and climate now. Methuen, London.

1977: *Climate, present, past and future.* Vol. 2: *Climatic history and the future.* Methuen, London.

Larsen, J. A. 1974: Ecology of the northern continental forest border. In Ives, J. D. and Barry R. G. (editors), *Arctic and alpine environments.* Methuen, London, 341–69.

Laws, R. M. 1977: Seals and whales of the southern ocean. *Philosophical Transactions of the Royal Society* (London), B, 279, 81–96.

Lee, R. B. 1968: What hunters do for a living, or how to make out on scarce resources. In Lee, R. B. and Devore, I. (editors), *Man the hunter.* Aldine, Chicago, 30–48.

Lee. R. B. and Devore, I. 1968: Problems in the study of hunters and gatherers. In Lee, R. B. and Devore, I. (editors), *Man the hunter.* Aldine, Chicago, 3–11.

LeMasurier, W. E. 1972: Volcanic record of Antarctic glacial history: implications with regard to Cenozoic sea levels. In Price, R. J. and Sugden, D. E. (compilers), *Polar geomorphology.* Institute of British Geographers Special Publication 4, 59–74.

Leont'yev, V. V. 1977: The indigenous peoples of Chukchi National Okrug: population and settlement. *Polar Geography,* 1 (1), 9–22.

Lewellen, R. I. 1970: *Permafrost erosion along the Beaufort Sea Coast.* Arctic Institute of North America, Technical Report ONR-382:1.

Lewis, E. L. and Weeks, W. F. 1971: Sea ice: some polar contrasts. In Deacon, G. (editor), *Symposium on Antarctic ice and water masses, Tokyo, September 1970.* Scientific Committee for Antarctic Research, Cambridge, 23–34.

Lieth, H. 1975: Primary production of the major vegetation units of the world. In Lieth, H. and Whittaker, R. H. (editors), *Primary productivity of the biosphere.* Ecological Studies, 14, Springer-Verlag, New York, 203-215.

Limbert, D. W. S. 1974: Variations in the mean annual temperature for the Antarctic Peninsula, 1904–72. *Polar Record,* 17 (108), 303–6.

Loewe, F. 1970: *The transport of snow on ice sheets by the wind.* University of Melbourne Meteorology Department Publication 13.

Lotz, J. R. 1965: The squatters of Whitehorse: a study of the problems of new northern settlements. *Arctic,* 18 (3), 172–88.

1975: Northern alternatives. *Arctic,* 28, 3–8.

Löve, A. and Löve, D. 1974: Origin and evolution of the arctic and alpine floras. In Ives, J. D. and Barry, R. G. (editors), *Arctic and alpine environments.* Methuen, London, 571–603.

Lyons, J. B., Savin, S. M. and Tamburi, A. J. 1971: Basement ice, Ward Hunt Ice Shelf, Ellesmere Island, Canada. *Journal of Glaciology,* 10, 93–100.

McCann, S. B. and Carlisle, R. J. 1972: The nature of the ice-foot on the beaches of Radstock Bay, southwest Devon Island N.W.T., Canada. In Price, R. J. and Sugden, D. E. (compilers), *Polar Geomorphology.* Institute of British Geographers Special Publication 4, 175–86.

McCann, S. B., Howarth, P. J. and Cogley, J. G. 1972: Fluvial processes in a peri-glacial environment, Queen Elizabeth Islands, N.W.T., Canada. *Transactions of the Institute of British Geographers,* 55, 69—82.

McGhee, R. 1974: The peopling of arctic North America. In Ives, J. D. and Barry, R. G. (editors), *Arctic and alpine environments.* Methuen, London, 831—55.

Mackay, J. R. 1970: Disturbances to the tundra and forest tundra environment of the western Arctic. *Canadian Geotechnical Journal,* 7, 420—432.

1971: The origin of massive icy beds in permafrost, western Arctic coast, Canada. *Canadian Journal of Earth Sciences,* 8, 397—422.

1972: The world of underground ice. *Annals of the Association of American Geographers,* 62 (1), 1—23.

Mackintosh, N. A. 1975: *The stocks of whales.* Fishing News (Books) Ltd., London.

1970: Whales and krill in the twentieth century. In Holdgate, M. W. (editor), *Antarctic ecology.* Scientific Committee for Antarctic Research, Academic Press, London and New York, 195—212.

1972: Life cycle of Antarctic krill in relation to ice and water conditions. *Discovery Reports,* 36, 1—94.

McClaren, D. J. 1975: The geological background and petroleum potential of Arctic North America. In Malaurie, J. (editor), *Arctic oil and gas: problems and possibilities.* Mouton, Paris, 36—55.

McCulloch, D. and Hopkins, D. 1966: Evidence for an early Recent warm interval in northwestern Alaska. *Bulletin of the Geological Society of America,* 77, 1089—1108.

MacPherson, N. 1977: The adaption of groups to Antarctic isolation. *Polar Record,* 18 (117), 581—5.

Magnusson, M. and Pálsson, H. 1975: *The Vinland sagas.* Penguin, Harmondsworth.

Makarov, R. R., Naumov, A. G. and Shevtsov, V. V. 1970: The biology and the distribution of the Antarctic krill. In Holdgate, M. W. (editor), *Antarctic ecology.* Scientific Committee for Antarctic Research, Academic Press, London and New York, 173—6.

Makhrovskaya, A. V., Vaytens, M. Ye., Panov, L. K. and Belinskiy, A. Yu. 1977: Urban planning and construction in the Kola North. Part I. *Polar Geography,* 1 (3), 205—16.

Margolis, S. V. and Kennett, J. P. 1971: Cenozoic paleoglacial record in Cenozoic sediments of the southern ocean. *American Journal of Science,* 271, 1—36.

Markov, K. K., Bardin, V. I., Lebedev, V. L., Orlov, A. I. and Suetova, I. A. 1970: *The geography of Antarctica.* Israel Program for Scientific Translations, Jerusalem (Moscow, 1968.)

Marr, J. 1964: The natural history and geography of the Antarctic krill *(Euphausia superba Dana). Discovery Reports,* 32, 33—464.

Marsden, M. 1972: Transportation in the Canadian north. In Wonders, W. C. (editor), *Studies in Canadian geography: the North.* Toronto, 41—70.

Martin, P. S. 1974: Palaeolithic players on the American stage: man's impact on the Late Pleistocene megafauna. In Ives, J. D. and Barry, R. G. (editors), *Arctic and alpine environments.* Methuen, London, 669—700.

Mather, K. B. and Miller, G. S. 1967: The problem of the katabatic winds on the coast of Terre Adélie. *Polar Record,* 13 (85), 425-32.

Mawson, D. 1915: *The home of the blizzard.* Heinemann, London.

Maybourn, R. 1976: Sea lift to Arctic Alaska. *Polar Record,* 18 (113), 175—92.

Mercer, J. H. 1968: *Antarctic ice and Sangamon sea level.* International Association of Scientific Hydrology Publication 79, 217—25.

— 1973: Cainozoic temperature trends in the southern hemisphere: Antarctic and Andean glacial evidence. In Van Zinderen Bakker, E. M. (editor), *Palaeoecology of Africa and of the surrounding islands and Antarctica,* 8, 85—114.

— 1978a: West Antarctic ice sheet and CO_2 greenhouse effect: a threat of disaster. *Nature,* 271, 321—5.

— 1978b: Glacial development and temperature trends in the Antarctic and in South America. In Van Zinderen Bakker, E. M. (editor), *Antarctic glacial history and world palaeoenvironments.* Balkema, Rotterdam, 73—93.

Milan, F. A. 1970: A demographic study of an eskimo village on the North Slope of Alaska. *Arctic,* 23 (2), 82—99.

Milan, F. A. and Pawson, S. 1975: The demography of the native population of an Alaskan city. *Arctic,* 28 (4), 275—83.

Miller, G. H. 1973: Late Quaternary glacial and climatic history of northern Cumberland Peninsula, Baffin Island, N.W.T., Canada. *Quaternary Research,* 3, 561—83.

Ministry for Greenland, 1967: *Greenland on the road to 1970.* Ministry for Greenland, Copenhagen.

— 1977: Regional development programme for Greenland. Ministry for Greenland, Copenhagen (mimeo).

— 1979: *Grønland 1978.* Årsberetning, Ministry for Greenland, Copenhagen.

— 1981: *Grønland 1980.* Årsberetning, Ministry for Greenland, Copenhagen.

Mitchell, B. and Tinker, J. 1980: *Antarctica and its resources.* Earthscan, London.

Mitchell, J. M. 1963: On the world-wide patterns of secular temperature change. In *Changes of Climate.* Proceedings of the UNESCO/WMO Rome 1961 Symposium. UNESCO Arid Zone Research Series 20, Paris, 161—81.

Morehouse, T. A. and Leask, L. 1980: Alaska's North Slope Borough: oil, money and Eskimo self-government. *Polar Record,* 20 (124), 19-29.

Morris, W. R. and Peters, N. L. 1960: Inside Antarctica No. 5 — Byrd Station. *Weatherwise,* 13, 162—5.

Mowat, F. 1965: *Westviking.* Secker & Warburg, London.

— 1970: *The Siberians.* Redwood Press, London.

Murray, J. 1886: The exploration of the Antarctic regions. *Scottish Geographical Magazine,* 2, 527—43.

Myrdal, G. 1957: *Economic theory and underdeveloped regions.* Duckworth, London.

Nace, R. L. 1969: World water inventory and control. In Chorley, R. J. (editor), *Water, earth and man.* Methuen, London, 31—42.

Nansen, F. 1890: *The first crossing of Greenland.* Longman, Green, London.
  1897: *Farthest north.* 2 vols. Constable, London.
Negretov, P. I. 1977: How Vorkuta began. *Soviet Studies,* 29 (4), 565–75.
Nichols, H. 1974: Arctic North American palaeoecology: the recent history of vegetation and climate deduced from pollen analysis. In Ives, J. D. and Barry, R. G. (editors), *Arctic and alpine environments.* Methuen, London, 637–67.
  1975: *Palynological and paleoclimatic study of the Late Quaternary displacement of the boreal forest-tundra in Keewatin and Mackenzie, N.W.T., Canada.* Institute of Arctic and Alpine Research Occasional Paper 15.
Nordenskjöld, O. 1913: Antarktis. *Handbuch der Regionalen Geologie* (Heidelberg), 8 (15), 1–29.
Nordenskjöld, O. and Andersson, J. G. 1905: *Antarctica.* Hurst & Blackett, London.

Oil and Mineral Division 1970: Recent and future mineral developments in northern Canada. *Polar Record,* 15 (95), 151–66.
Ommanney, C. S. L. 1969: *A study in glacier inventory: the ice masses of Axel Heiberg Island, Canadian Arctic Archipelago.* Axel Heiberg Research Reports, (McGill University), Glaciology, 3.
Osgood, C. 1936: *Contribution to the ethnography of the Kutchin.* Yale University Press, New Haven.
Ostenso, N. A. and Wold, R. J. 1973: Aeromagnetic evidence for the origin of the Arctic Ocean basin. In Pitcher, M. G. (editor), *Arctic geology.* American Association of Petroleum Geologists Memoir 19, 506–16.
Østrem, G., Bridge, C. W. and Rannie, W. F. 1967: Glacio-hydrology, discharge and sediment transport in the Decade Glacier area, Baffin Island, N.W.T. *Geografiska Annáler,* 49A, 268–82.
Østreng, W. 1977: The strategic balance and the Arctic Ocean: Soviet options. *Co-operation and Conflict,* 12, 41–62.
Oswalt, W. H. 1967: *Alaskan eskimos.* Chandler, Scranton.

Paterson, W. S. B. 1981: *The physics of glaciers.* 2nd edn. Pergamon, Oxford.
Pavlik, H. F. 1980: A physical framework for describing the genesis of ground ice. *Progress in Physical Geography,* 4 (4), 531–48.
Payne, M. R. 1977: Growth of a fur seal population. *Philosophical Transactions of the Royal Society* (London), B, 279, 67–79.
Permitin, Yu. E. 1970: The consumption of krill by Antarctic fishes. In Holdgate, M. W. (editor), *Antarctic ecology.* Scientific Committee for Antarctic Research, Academic Press, London and New York. 177–82.
Petersen, R. 1962: The last Eskimo immigration into Greenland. *Folk,* 4 (1), 95–110.
  1975: Mining in Greenland with reference to the ethnic identity, occupational structure and territorial ownership. In Malaurie, J. (editor), *Arctic oil and*

gas: problems and possibilities. Mouton, Paris, 677—83.

Péwé, T. L. 1959: Sand wedge polygons (tesselations) in the McMurdo Sound region, Antarctica. *American Journal of Science,* 257, 545—52.

1969: The periglacial environment. In Péwé, T. L. (editor), *The periglacial environment.* McGill—Queen's University Press, Montreal, 1—11.

1975: *Quaternary geology of Alaska.* United States Geological Survey Professional Paper 835.

Pimlott, D. H., Vincent, K. M. and Mcknight, C. W. 1973: *Arctic alternatives.* Canadian Arctic Resources Committee, Ottawa.

Pissart, A. 1967: Les pingos de l'Île Prince-Patrick (76°N—120°W). *Geographical Bulletin,* 9 (3), 189—217.

1968: Les polygons de fente de gel de l'Île Prince-Patrick, *Biuletyn Peryglacjalny,* 17, 171—80.

Pitman, W. C. and Herron, E. M. 1974: Continental drift in the Atlantic and Arctic. In Kristjansson (editor), *Geodynamics of Iceland and the Atlantic area.* Reidel, Holland, 1—15.

Pjettursson, J. 1969: Bilingualism in Greenland and its resulting problems. Paper presented to Fourth International Congress on Arctic development and the future of the Eskimo Societies, Le Havre, November, 1969. Report 16, (mimeo).

Polar Record, 1954: Antarctic claims — diplomatic exchanges between Great Britain, Argentina and Chile in 1952 and 1953. *Polar Record,* 7, 212—26.

1967a: Canadian northern road network programme. *Polar Record,* 13 (85), 482.

1967b: Canadian government aid for northern mineral exploration. *Polar Record,* 13 (86), 653—4.

1974: Canada's northernmost mine. *Polar Record,* 17 (108), 310—11.

1979: The Northern Sea Route, 1978. *Polar Record,* 19 (122), 496—501.

Polar Regions Atlas, 1978: Central Intelligence Agency, Washington.

Pollitt, J. 1976: Locational aspects of some viking age farms in the vicinity of Qagssiarssuk, S.W. Greenland. Undergraduate thesis, Department of Geography, University of Aberdeen.

Popov, A. I. 1969: Underground ice in the Quaternary deposits of the Yana-Indigirka lowland as a genetic and stratigraphic indicator. In Péwé, T. L. (editor), *The periglacial environment,* McGill—Queen's University Press, Montreal, 55—64.

Porslid, A. E. 1951: Plant life in the Arctic. *Canadian Geographical Journal* 42, 120—45.

Post, A. S. 1967: *Effects of the March 1964 Alaska earthquake on glaciers.* United States Geological Survey Professional Paper 544-D.

Potter, N. 1969: Economic potentials of the Antarctic. *Antarctic Journal of the United States,* 4 (3), 61—72.

Prik, Z. M. 1959: Mean position of surface pressure and temperature distribution in the Arctic. *Trudy Arkticheskogo Nauchno-Issledovatel'skogo Instituta,* 217, 5—34 (Russian).

Rasmussen, K. 1908: *People of the polar north.* London.

Reed, J. C. 1970: Oil developments in Alaska. *Polar Record,* 15 (94), 7–17.

Reimnitz, E. and Bruder, K. F. 1972: River discharge into an ice-covered ocean and related sediment dispersal, Beaufort Sea, coast of Alaska. *Bulletin of the Geological Society of America,* 83, 861–6.

Rink, H. 1875: *Tales and traditions of the Eskimo.* London.

Riordan, A. J. 1975: The climate of Vanda Station, Antarctica. In Weller, G. and Bowling, S. A. (editors), *Climate of the Arctic.* Proceedings of the 24th Alaska Science Conference, August 1973. University of Alaska, 268–75.

Roberts, B. B. 1978: International cooperation for Antarctic development: the test for the Antarctic Treaty. *Polar Record,* 19 (119), 107–20.

Robertson, R. B. 1956: *Of whales and men.* Macmillan, London.

Rodewald, M. 1972: Einige hydroklimatische Besonderheiten des Jahrzehats 1961–70 im Nordatlantik und im Nordpolarmeere. *Deutsche hydrographische Zeitschrift,* 25 (3), 97–117.

Rogers, G. W. 1962: *The future of Alaska: economic consequences of Statehood.* Johns Hopkins Press, Baltimore.

1969: Party politics or protest politics: current political trends in Alaska, *Polar Record,* 14 (91), 445–58.

1971: International petroleum and the economic future of Alaska. *Polar Record,* 15 (97), 463–78.

Rohmer, R. 1970: *The green north.* MacLean-Hunter, Toronto.

Rosendahl, G. P. 1968: Urban development in the Arctic. *Danish Foreign Office Journal,* 58, 28–42.

Ross, J. C. 1847: *A voyage of discovery and research in the southern and Antarctic Regions, during the years 1838–43.* Vol.2. John Murray, London.

Rutford, R. H., Craddock, C., White, C. M. and Armstrong, R. L. 1972: Tertiary glaciation in the Jones Mountains. In Adie, R. J. (editor), *Antarctic geology and geophysics.* Universitetsforlaget, Oslo, 239–43.

Rydén, B. E. 1981: Hydrology of the northern tundra. In Bliss, L. C., Cragg, J. B., Heal, D. W. and Moore, J. J. (editors), *Tundra ecosystems: a comparative analysis.* Cambridge University Press, Cambridge, 115–37.

Sahlins, M. 1968: Notes on the original affluent society. In Lee, R. B. and Devore, I. (editors), *Man the hunter.* Aldine, Chicago, 84–9.

1974: *Stone age economics.* Tavistock, London.

Sallnow, J. 1977: The population of Siberia and the Soviet Far East (1965–1976). *Soviet Geography,* 18 (9), 690–8.

1981: Forbidden Kolyma. *Geographical Magazine,* 53 (4), 261–7.

Sater, J. E., Ronhovde, A. G. and Van Allen, L. C. 1971: *Arctic environment and resources.* Arctic Institute of North America, Washington, D.C.

Schell, I. I., Corkum, D. A. and Sabbagh, E. N. 1975: Recent climatic changes in the eastern North American sub-arctic. In Weller, G. and Bowling, S. A. (editors), *Climate of the Arctic.* Geophysical Institute, University of Alaska,

Fairbanks, 76–81.

Schledermann, P. 1976: The effect of climatic/ecological changes on the style of Thule culture winter dwellings. *Arctic and Alpine Research,* 8 (1), 37–47.

Schwerdtfeger, W. 1970: The climate of the Antarctic. In Orvig. S. (editor), *Climates of the polar regions,* Elsevier, Amsterdam, World Survey of climatology, vol. 14, 253–355.

Scott, J. F. 1975: Relationship between land and population: a note on Canada's carrying capacity. *Geografiska Annaler,* 57B (2), 128–32.

Scott, R. F. 1905: *The voyage of the 'Discovery'.* 2 vols, Smith, Elder, London. 1913: *Scott's last expedition.* 2 vols. Smith, Elder, London.

Sellman, P. V. 1972: Relief characteristics and variations due to snow: Barrow, Alaska. In Sellman, P. V., Carey, K. L., Keeler, C. and Hartwell, A. D. (editors), *Terrain and coastal conditions on the arctic Alaskan coastal plain.* Cold Regions Research and Engineering Laboratory, Special Report 165, 1–16.

Selyakov, Yu. G. 1979: Locational factors of machine manufacturing in the Soviet North. *Soviet Geography,* 20 (5), 310–21.

Shabad, T. 1977a: News notes. *Soviet Geography,* 18 (2), 132–9.
1977b: News notes. *Polar Geography,* 1 (1), 171–8.
1978a: News notes. *Soviet Geography,* 19 (6), 426–31.
1978b: News notes. *Soviet Geography,* 19 (4), 273–93.
1978c: News notes. *Polar Geography,* 2 (1), 53–5.
1979a: News notes. *Polar Geography,* 3 (1), 63–5.
1979b: News notes. *Polar Geography,* 3 (3), 162–3.
1981: News notes. *Soviet Geography,* 22 (4), 272–90.

Shackleton, E. H. 1909: *The heart of the Antarctic.* 2 vols. Heinemann, London. 1919: *South.* Heinemann, London.

Shackleton, N. J. 1978: Some results of the CLIMAP project. In Pittock, A. B., Frakes, L. A., Jenssen, D., Peterson, J. A. and Zillman, J. W. (editors), *Climatic change and variability: a southern perspective.* Cambridge University Press, Cambridge, 69–76.

Shackleton, N. J. and Opdyke, N. D. 1977: Oxygen isotope and palaeomagnetic evidence for early northern hemisphere glaciation. *Nature,* 270, 216–19.

Sharpe, T. A. 1975: Problems of ice and the effect of low temperatures on production installations on land. In Malaurie, J. (editor), *Arctic oil and gas: problems and possibilities.* Mouton, Paris, 268–86.

Shearer, J. and Blasco, S. 1975: *Further observations of the scouring phenomena in the Beaufort Sea.* Geological Survey of Canada Paper 75–1.

Simpson, G. G. 1947: Holarctic mammalian faunas and continental relationships during the Cenozoic. *Bulletin of the Geological Society of America,* 48, 613–88.

Siple, P. A. and Passell, C. F. 1945: Measurement of dry atmospheric cooling in subfreezing temperatures. *American Philosophical Society Proceedings,* 89, 177–99.

Slavin, S. V. and Agranat, G. A. 1977: Problems in the development of the north. *Polar Geography,* 1 (1), 1–8.

Smith, A. G. and Hallam, A. 1970: The fit of the southern continents. *Nature*, 225 (5228), 139—44.

Smith, G. A., Briden, J. C. and Drewry, G. E. 1973: Phanerozoic world maps. In Hughes, N. F. (editor), *Organisms and continents through time.* Special Papers on Palaeontology 12, 1—42.

Smith, J. 1960: Glacier problems in South Georgia. *Journal of Glaciology*, 3 (28), 705—14.

Smith, P. M. and Dana, J. B. 1973: Airbus: an international air transportation system for Antarctica. *Antarctic Journal of the United States*, 8, 16—19.

Solzhenitsyn, A. 1974: *The Gulag Archipelago.* Vol. 1.

    1975: *The Gulag Archipelago.* Vol. 2.

Sorre, M. 1952: *Les fondements de la géographie humaine.* 3 vols. Armand Colin, Paris.

Sprudz, A. 1967: Development of the co-operative movement in northern Canada since 1963. *Polar Record*, 13 (86), 597—9.

St. George, G. 1969: *Siberia: the new frontier.* Hodder & Stoughton, London.

Steadman, R. G. 1971: Indices of windchill of clothed persons. *Journal of Applied Meteorology*, 10, 674—83.

Stefansson, V. 1914: Prehistoric and present commerce among the arctic coast Eskimo. *Canada Geological Survey Museum Bulletin*, 6.

Stonehouse, B. 1965: Birds and mammals. In Hatherton, T. (editor), *Antarctica.* Methuen, London, 153—86.

Strøm Tejsen, A. V. 1977: The history of the Royal Greenland Trade Department. *Polar Record*, 18 (116), 451—74.

Sugden, D. E. 1969: Umanak, 1968: *Aberdeen University Review*, 43 (2), 112—22.

    1974: Landscapes of glacial erosion in Greenland and their relationship to ice, topographic and bedrock conditions. In Waters, R. S. and Brown, E. H. (editors), *Progress in geomorphology.* Institute of British Geographers Special Publication 7, 177—195.

    1977: Reconstruction of the morphology, dynamics and thermal characteristics of the Laurentide ice sheet at its maximum. *Arctic and Alpine Research*, 9 (1), 21—47.

    1978: Glacial erosion by the Laurentide ice sheet. *Journal of Glaciology*, 20 (83), 367—91.

    1979: Extremes of a glacial planet. *Geographical Magazine*, 51 (2), 119—28.

Sugden, D. E. and Clapperton, C. M. 1977: The maximum ice extent on island groups in the Scotia Sea, Antarctica. *Quaternary Research*, 7, 268—82.

    1980: West Antarctic ice sheet fluctuations in the Antarctic Peninsula area. *Nature*, 286 (5771), 378—81.

Sugden, D. E. and Hamilton, P. 1971: Scale, systems and regional geography. *Area*, 3 (3), 139—44.

Sugden, D. E. and John, B. S. 1973: The ages of glacier fluctuations in the South Shetland Islands, Antarctica. In Van Zinderen Bakker, E. M. (editor), *Palaeoecology of Africa and of the surrounding islands and Antarctica*, 8, 139—59.

    1976: *Glaciers and landscape.* Edward Arnold, London.

Svarlien, O. 1960: The sector principle in law and practice. *Polar Record*, 10, 248—63.

Swartz, L. G. 1966: Sea cliff birds. In Wilimovsky, N. J. and Wolfe, J. N. (editors), *Environment of the Cape Thompson Region, Alaska.* United States AEC, Division of Technical Information, Springfield, Va.

Swithinbank, C. W. M. 1964: To the valley glaciers that feed the Ross Ice Shelf, *Geographical Journal*, 130 (1), 32—48.

1969: Giant icebergs in the Weddell Sea, 1967—68. *Polar Record*, 14 (91), 477—8.

1972: Arctic pack ice from below. In Karlsson, T. (editor), *Sea ice conference proceedings.* National Research Council, Reykjavik, 246—54.

1977: Glaciological research in the Antarctic Peninsula. *Philosophical Transactions of the Royal Society* (London), B, 279, 161—83.

Swithinbank, C. W. M. and Zumberge, J. H. 1965: The ice shelves. In Hatherton, T. (editor), *Antarctica.* Methuen, London, 199—220.

Sykes, L. R. 1965: The seismicity of the Arctic. *Seismological Society of America Bulletin*, 55, 501—18.

Taaffe, E. J., Morrill, R. L. and Gould P. R. 1963: Transport expansion in underdeveloped countries. *Geographical Review*, 53, 503—29.

Tedrow, J. C. F.,1977: *Soils of the polar landscapes.* Rutgers University Press, New Brunswick.

Tedrow, J. C. F., Drew, J. V., Hill, D. E. and Douglas, L. A. 1958: Major genetic soils of the Arctic Slope of Alaska. *Journal of Soil Science*, 9 (1), 33—45.

Tedrow, J. C. F., and Ugolini, F. C. 1966: Antarctic soils. In Tedrow, J. C. F. (editor), *Antarctic soils and soil forming processes.* American Geophysical Union, Antarctic Research Series, 8, 161—77.

Thalbitzer, W. 1914: The Ammasalik eskimo: contributions to the ethnology of the East Greenland natives. *Meddelelser om Grønland*, 39 (1).

Thom, G. 1981: *Patterned ground in South Georgia, Antarctica.* Unpublished Ph.D. Thesis, University of Aberdeen.

Thomas, D. C. 1969: *Population estimates and distribution of barren-ground caribou in Mackenzie District, N.W.T., Saskatchewan and Alberta — March to May 1977.* Canadian Wildlife Service Report Series, 9.

Timofeyev, V. T. 1963: Interaction of waters from the Arctic Ocean and those from the Atlantic and Pacific. *Okeanologiya*, 3 (4), 569—78, (translation).

Tønnessen, J. N. 1970: Norwegian Antarctic whaling 1905—68: an historical appraisal. *Polar Record*, 15 (96), 283—290.

Tough, G. 1972: Mining in the Canadian north. In Wonders, W. C. (editor), *Studies in Canadian geography: the north.* University of Toronto Press, Toronto, 71—90.

Treshnikov, A. F. and Baranov, G. I. 1973: *Water circulation in the Arctic Basin.* Israel Program for Scientific Translations, Jerusalem.

Treshnikov, A. F., Nikiforov, Ye. G. and Blinov, N. I. 1977: Results of oceanological investigations by the 'North Pole' drifting stations. *Polar Geography*, 1 (1), 22–40.

Vibe, C. 1967: Arctic Animals in relation to climatic fluctuation. *Meddelelser om Grønland*, 170 (5).

Victor, P. E. 1964: *Man and the conquest of the Poles*. Hamish Hamilton, London.

Villiers, A. J. 1925: *Whaling in the frozen south: being the story of the 1923–24 Norwegian Whaling Expedition to the Antarctic*. Hurst & Blackett, London.

Vogt, P. R. and Avery, O. E. 1974: Tectonic history of the Arctic Basins: partial solutions and unsolved mysteries. In Herman, Y. (editor), *Marine geology and oceanography of the Arctic seas*. Springer, Berlin, 83–117.

Vowinckel, E. and Orvig, S. 1970: The climate of the North Polar Basin. In Orvig, S. (editor), *Climate of the polar regions*. Elsevier, Amsterdam, World survey of climatology, vol. 14, 129–225.

Walcott, R. I. 1970: Isostatic response to loading of the crust in Canada. *Canadian Journal of Earth Sciences*, 7, 716–26.

Walker, H. J. 1973: Morphology of the North Slope. In Britton, M. E. (editor), *Alaskan Arctic tundra*. Arctic Institute of North America, Technical Paper 25, 49–92.

Walker, H. J. and Arnborg, L. 1966: Permafrost ice wedge effect on riverbank erosion. In *Proceedings, 1st International Permafrost Conference*. National Academy of Science–National Research Council Publication 1287, 164–71.

Washburn, A. L. 1979: *Geocryology: a survey of periglacial processes and environments*. Edward Arnold, London.

Webber, P. J. 1974: Tundra primary productivity. In Ives, J. D. and Barry, R. G. (editors), *Arctic and alpine environments*. Methuen, London, 445-73.

Weeks, W. F. 1980: Iceberg water: an assessment. *Annals of Glaciology* 1, 5–10.

Weertman, J. 1974: Stability of the junction of an ice sheet and an ice shelf. *Journal of Glaciology*, 13 (67), 3–11.

Weidick, A. 1972: *Holocene shore lines and glacial stages in Greenland — an attempt at correlation*. Grønlands Geologiske Undersøgelse Rapport, 41.

  1975: *Estimates on the mass balance changes of the Inland Ice since Wisconsin-Weichsel*. Grønlands Geologiske Undersøgelse Rapport 68.

  1976: Glaciations of northern Greenland — new evidence. *Polarforschung*, 46 (1), 26–33.

Wilkin, A. 1980: Godthåb: town or city? In Maizels, J. (editor), *Aberdeen University West Greenland Expedition, 1979. Final report*. Department of Geography, University of Aberdeen, 308–17.

Wilson, A. T. 1964: Origin of the Ice Ages: an ice shelf theory for Pleistocene glaciation. *Nature*, 201 (4915), 147–9.

Winsnes, T. S. 1975: Geological background: Svalbard. In Malaurie, J. (editor), *Arctic oil and gas: problems and possibilities*. Mouton, Paris, 56–78.

Wonders, W. C. 1970: Community and regional development in the North. *Arctic,* 23 (4), 281–4.

    1972: The future of northern Canada. In Wonders, W. C. (editor), *Studies in Canadian Geography: the North.* University of Toronto Press, Toronto, 137–46.

Wright, H. E. 1971: Late Quaternary vegetation history of North America. In Turekian, K. (editor), *The Late Cenozoic glacial ages.* Yale University Press, New Haven, 425–64.

Wright, N. 1959: *Quest for Franklin.* Heinemann, London.

Yazykova, V. M. 1977: The Kara Sea: shipping and problems of development. *Polar Geography,* 1 (2), 123–9.

Zeller, E. J., Saunders, D. F. and Angino, E. E. 1973: Putting radioactive wastes on ice – a proposal for an international radionuclide depository in Antarctica. *Science and Public Affairs, Bulletin of the Atomic Scientists,* 24 (4–9), 54–8.

Zeller, E. J., Saunders, D. F. and Angino, E. E. 1976: Antarctica, a potential disposal site for the world's radioactive wastes. *Modern Geology,* 6, 31–6.

Zenkovich, B. A. 1970: Whales and plankton in Antarctic waters. In Holdgate, M. W. (editor), *Antarctic ecology.* Scientific Committee for Antarctic Research, Academic Press, London and New York, 183–90.

Zenkovich, V. P. 1967: *Processes of coastal development.* Oliver & Boyd, Edinburgh.

Ziegler, T. (editor) 1972: *Slamtransportundersøkelser i Norske breelver, 1970.* Norges Vassdrags-og Elektrisitetsvesen Rapport 1/72, Oslo.

Zumberge, J. H. 1974: The remains of Camp Michigan. *Antarctic Journal of the United States,* 9 (3), 84–7.

Zwally, H. J. and Gloersen, P. 1977: Passive microwave images of the Polar Regions and research applications. *Polar Record,* 18 (116), 431–50.

Zwally, H. J., Wilheit, T. T., Gloersen, P. and Mueller, J. L. 1976: Characteristics of Antarctic sea ice as determined by satellite-borne microwave images. In *Proceedings of the symposium on meteorological observations from space: their contribution to the first GARP experiment, 1976.* National Center for Atmospheric Research, Boulder, Colorado, 94–7.

Index

An author index is not included in view of the full bibliography on pages 438–61.